The Compiled Teachings of The Apostle Paul

The accounts of the Apostle Paul's teaching as provided by The Book of Acts and The Letters written by Paul to the churches of Galatia, Corinth, Rome, Thessalonica, Ephesus, Philippi, and Colossae and The Letters written to Timothy, Jude and Philemon.

An Evans Bible Study Companion

Compiled by and copyright Ron A. Evans© 2023
Bible text version: American Standard Version (ASV - 1901)
Copyright for selected NASB Bible text passages, NASB© 1960-1995
First impression March 2023

Also available from Amazon
'The Compiled Gospels of The New Testament' – Paperback: ASIN: B08SCYRWWV – e-Book: ASIN: B08PZ91K25
'The Combined & Compiled Gospels Of The New Testament' – Paperback: ASIN: B09NRDPNXY
'Jesus Of Nazareth' – Single Narrative Of The Life and Ministry Of Jesus Of Nazareth – Paperback & e-Book

Other Bible Study Companion books by Ron Evans

'The Combined & Compiled Gospels of The New Testament'

The Life Story of Jesus of Nazareth as told by Matthew, Mark, Luke, and John, compiled and combined, integrated into a single narrative of the life and the ministry of Jesus, the Christ, Jesus of Nazareth -- with the text of all parallel passages with no redactions, printed together, event-by-event, from all four Gospels printed alongside the narrative of each event.

The language of the ASV (American Standard Version Bible) text has been 'mildly updated' with, for example, 'thee's, thou's, 'ye's and other outdated language words replaced by appropriate alternatives.

'The Combined & Compiled Gospels of The New Testament' is available from Amazon
– Paperback: ASIN: B09NRDPNXY

'The Compiled Gospels of The New Testament'

The compiled Gospels of Matthew, Mark, Luke, and John with the text of all parallel passages with no redactions, printed together, event-by-event, from all four Gospels.

'The Compiled Gospels of The New Testament' is available from Amazon
– Paperback: ASIN: B08SCYRWWV – e-Book: ASIN: B08PZ91K25

'The Compiled Gospels of The New Testament'
is a complementary reference/support source to
'Jesus of Nazareth; A Single Narrative of His Life & Ministry'

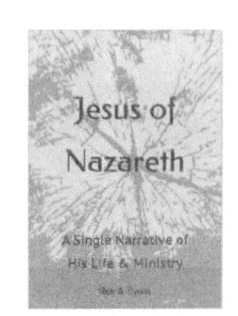

The Compiled Teachings of The Apostle Paul

Introduction *1*

Section 1

A Summarization of The Teachings of Paul The Apostle *3*
Paul's Teaching in the Book of Acts *3*
Paul In Pisidian Antioch *3*
Paul In Jerusalem *4*
Paul In Caesarea *4*

Section 2

Paul's First Missionary Trip *11*
Paul's Second Missionary Trip *17*
Paul's Third Missionary Trip *21*

The Cities and Regions Visited on Paul's Missionary Trips ... *30*

Words of Paul That Define His Ministry *30*

> *The Letters of Paul in this study book are listed in chronological order of writing.*

Section 3

The Letters of The Apostle Paul
Standing of Each of the Pauline Letters (Epistles)
.... ***34***
The Greetings of each of the 'Letters Books' ***34***
The Chronological Order of Paul's Letters *35*

Galatians *42*
1 Corinthians *50*
2 Corinthians *65*
Romans *75*
1 Thessalonians *92*
2 Thessalonians *95*
1 Timothy *97*
Titus *102*
Ephesians *104*
Philippians *110*
Colossians *114*
2 Timothy *118*
Philemon *121*

Section 4

Quick Reference Listing of The Teachings of Paul *122*
An Expanded Summarization of The Teachings of Paul *124*

ADDENDA:

Study On Paul's Teaching On Circumcision **181**
Topic Words List **185**

Full Table of Contents (includes all sub-headings) *186*

The Compiled Teachings of The Apostle Paul, compiled by and copyright Ron A. Evans© 2022, 2023
(April 2022, November 2022, March 2023)
Bible text version: American Standard Version (ASV - 1901)
Copyright for selected NASB Bible text passages, NASB© 1960-1995

Feedback: Feedback is welcomed. Should you discover a missing passage that you feel should have been included, or something that you feel is in any way in error, please email me at revansca@yahoo.com.

Copyright Acknowledgement:
Selected scripture quotations (text and passage titles) taken from the New American Standard Bible® (NASB), Copyright © 1960, 1962, 1963, 1968, 1971, 1972, 1973, 1975, 1977, 1995 by The Lockman Foundation
Used by permission. www.Lockman.org.

The Compiled Teachings of The Apostle Paul

Introduction:

Paul is credited with writing many of the books in the New Testament that follow on after the four Gospels and The Acts of The Apostles, which is credited to Luke as the writer. Paul's writings are not narrative, history recordings like the Gospels or Acts, they are letters, aka epistles, that he wrote to churches that he had founded in areas that are referred to as regions and cities of the Gentiles. In addition to the letters written to churches, the New Testament also includes letters written by Paul to specific individuals; individuals who trained under Paul, spreading the Gospel of Jesus Christ.

The 'Compiled Teachings' book began as a personal project to gain a better insight into what Paul – who was originally known as Saul – taught. What did he teach in each of his letters? Were the same topics taught in each letter, and if so, to what extent were the teachings the same or different, and were the teachings on a specific topic in one letter complementary to teaching on the same topic in another?

In developing my other published books, the 'Combined and Compiled Gospels'; the accounts of Matthew, Mark, Luke and John, I knew there would be many passages, generally referred to as 'parallel accounts', that are an account of a given event that was also written about in more than one gospel, and these provide both corroborating and complementary information, and many which include passages that are a 'repetition' which, in some instances, were near identical, suggesting that Matthew, Mark, and Luke especially, shared or copied from each other's writings.

The concept for this book, The Compiled Teachings of the Apostle Paul, came about after discussion one evening at a men's midweek Bible study session when the question: "What did Paul teach?" was asked, and that made me wonder "could the teachings of Paul that are contained in his letters, be compiled in a manner similar to the way in which I had compiled the teachings of the Gospels?"

The Purpose of This Book

The purpose of this book is to encourage new Christians to come to faith with a solid understanding of why. This book is also written for those who have lived a Christian or Christian-like life but who are seeking a better understanding, a more correct understanding, because they have a desire to make their faith stronger.

In part this is a quick-reference resource and, in part, a "basics about" learning book.

By way of background, I am happy to admit that I have been a Christian all my adult life. My father was a part-time itinerant preacher when I was a young child and, on occasions, I would accompany him on some of the preaching commitments that he had, mostly at small rural chapels in England. Sometimes this would be for a morning service, sometimes an evening service, and occasionally for both morning and evening services. For each of those occasions Dad would be hosted for lunch and tea, and between the services they would also entertain us. When the host was a family with children that were my age or close to, that was generally easy because I could spend the time between the services playing with their children.

When it was an individual or a couple with no children hosting, I would generally have to stay in the same room listening to their conversations although, when I had remembered to, I would have brought a book along with me, one that I could bury myself in; that way I was less of a distraction for the adults.

Although this was many years ago, more than 60, I still recall how some of those families and individuals influenced me. As a young adult, my wife and I raised our two daughters from earlier stages having them attend whatever Church Sunday school program there was at the churches we attended. Their father, me, however, was not an itinerant preacher. But now, from my mid-thirties, today, looking back, would categorize myself today as a Bible student. I never ascribed being an evangelist except in a fairly low-key manner. Maybe that was because I was still searching, seeking confidence.

During the years of 2020 and 2021 when the world was reeling with shutdowns on the lockdowns and breakdowns because of the CoViD-19 pandemic, suddenly I found myself placed on hold. Even though I was retired I had not yet stopped working, but because, my job function as a driving school instructor couldn't be performed given that a 6 ft or 2-meter separation between persons was now required to prevent the disease from being spread, for the first time in a long while I had time on my hands. I woke up earlier than usual one morning well ahead of the alarm clock, and either a voice spoke to me or I spoke to myself, asking, "What are you waiting for? You now have the time. Get on with your project."

That 'project' was one that had been kicking around in the back of my head for at least 5 years, maybe 10 or more, was to compile the four Gospels, identifying every event that is recorded in Matthew, Mark, Luke, and John. I had heard much about, got involved in discussions about, and read some things about the 'synoptic Gospels', or should I say the 'synchronization of the Gospels'. My goal was separate out every event that was recorded in each gospel, identify the parallel passage or passages in the other Gospels where they existed, and place them side-by-side physically. However, that turned out not to be exactly how things could be laid out. So, I ended up compromising with passages side-by-side in two columns, so they were physically parallel, but when there were parallel accounts in three or four gospels, the 3rd and 4th accounts would be below the other two accounts and so be in 'parallel and serial' format with all accounts, a single account, or two, or three, or four accounts all on the same page, or at least on contiguous pages.

The result of my efforts after about 8 or 10 months it was a draft of what I ultimately published as 'The Compiled Gospels of the New Testament', published on Amazon, and available in hard copy printed book form, and a digital version available as an eBook.

As I was preparing to publish the book, one of my reviewers, my wife Chris, made the comment, but I thought you were going to combine them together. So, after launching that first book, I started into a new project, something that was simply an extension of the first; to combine the Gospels into a single narrative of 'The Life and Ministry of Jesus Christ'. So, prior to this book being published, three books had become available on Amazon, 'The Compiled Gospels of the New Testament', 'Jesus of Nazareth; A Single Narrative of the Life and Ministry of Jesus', and the third, a book that combines the two together into one hardback printed book, 'The Combined and Compiled Gospels of the New Testament'.

(As Kindle cannot handle complex formatting, 'The Combined and Compiled Gospels of the New Testament' is not available as an eBook.)

Structure:

There are four main sections to remainder of this book.

- Section 1 is a 'Summarization of The Teachings of The Apostle Paul'.
- Section 2 of this book is the account of Paul provided by Luke in the Acts of The Apostles with commentary notes.
- Section 3 includes all of the Epistles, the Letters, of Paul with notes that in general provide a summary, passage by passage, of each chapter. This covers the teachings of Paul that are documented in Paul's letters, many of which were written to communities that Paul had taken the Gospel to, while others are letters to co-workers.
- Section 4 includes an 'Expanded Summarization of The Teachings of The Apostle Paul' which is organized by topic, and presented in chronological order within each topic.

  Worthy of note is that there is at least one church community that Paul wrote and epistle (letter) to that he had not personally taken the Gospel to, and that is the church in Rome. Also, to help gain an understanding of where and when each letter was written, you'll find a chronological listing of the letters in Section 4 in the 'The Topics of The Letters' section prior to 'The Teaching In The Letters' section.

The Compiled Teachings of The Apostle Paul

Section 1

A Summarization of The Teachings of Paul The Apostle
Paul's Teaching in the Book of Acts 3

Paul In Pisidian Antioch..3
Paul In Jerusalem 4
Paul In Caesarea 4

A Summarization of The Teachings of Paul The Apostle

Summarizing Paul's teachings is something I wanted to tackle when I began thinking about how to approach this project and how best to document his teachings. Paul's teachings begin in the Book of Acts.

This book provides two complementary 'summarization' sections. The first is a narrative style summarization, and the second is a 'topic organized' section. The second summarization, in section 4, is by organized by topic.

Having a Bible – your personal favorite translation, of course – so that you can quickly 'reference, verify and compare' is definitely the best way to take advantage of this book, but large blocks of text, complete chapters in many cases, and later, in Section 3, the complete text of each of Paul's letters are provided so that you can study on the go without having to carry two books.

Paul's Teaching in the Book of Acts

This is a summary account from the Book of Acts of Paul's teaching as he presented his defense at the several hearings and trials that he was brought before:

Paul In Pisidian Antioch

In Acts 13:16-39 Paul addresses the synagogue in Pisidian Antioch, i.e. in the city of Antioch in the region of Pisidia in Asia.

In this sermon, by summarizing the scriptures, Paul lays out very clearly what he believes and why, and concludes by stating *"that through Jesus the forgiveness of sins is proclaimed to you. [39] Through him everyone who believes is set free from every sin."* [Acts 13:39]

...beckoning with the hand (Paul) said, Men of Israel, and you who fear God, hearken (listen): [17] The God of this people Israel chose our fathers, and exalted the people when they sojourned in the land of Egypt, and with a high arm led he them forth out of it. [18] And for about the time of forty years as a nursing-father he endured them in the wilderness. [19] And when he had destroyed seven nations in the land of Canaan, he gave them their land for an inheritance, for about four hundred and fifty years: [20] and after these things he gave them judges until Samuel the prophet. [21] And afterward they asked for a king: and God gave unto them Saul the son of Kish, a man of the tribe of Benjamin, for the space of forty years. [22] And when he had removed him, he raised up David to be their king; to whom also he bare witness and said, I have found David the son of Jesse, a man after my heart, who shall do all my will. [23] Of this man's seed hath God according to promise brought unto Israel a Savior, Jesus; [24] when John had first preached before his coming the baptism of repentance to all the people of Israel. [25] And as John was fulfilling his course, he said, What suppose ye that I am? I am not he. But behold, there comes one after me the shoes of whose feet I am not worthy to unloose.

[26] Brethren, children of the stock of Abraham, and those among you that fear God, to us is the word of this salvation sent forth. [27] For they that dwell in Jerusalem, and their rulers, because they knew him not, nor the voices of the prophets which are read every sabbath, fulfilled them by condemning him. [28] And though they found no cause of death in him, yet asked they of Pilate that he should be slain. [29] And when they had fulfilled all things that were written of him, they took him down from the tree, and laid him in a tomb. [30] But God raised him from the dead: [31] and he was seen for many days of them that came up with him from Galilee to Jerusalem, who are now his witnesses unto the people.

[32] And we bring you good tidings of the promise made to the fathers [33] that God has fulfilled the same unto our children, in that he raised up Jesus; as also it is written in the second psalm, Thou art my Son, this day have I begotten thee. [Ps. 2:7b]

[34] And as concerning that he raised him up from the dead, now no more to return to corruption, he spoke in this way, I will give you the holy and sure blessings of David.

[35] Because he said also in another psalm, You will not give thy Holy One to see corruption. [36] For David, after he had in his own generation served the counsel of God, fell asleep, and was laid unto his fathers, and saw corruption: [37] but he whom God raised up saw no corruption.

[38] Be it known unto you therefore, brethren, that through this man is proclaimed unto you remission of sins: [39] and by him every one that believeth is justified from all things, from which ye could not be justified by the law of Moses.

The Compiled Teachings of The Apostle Paul

This sermon, delivered by Paul, summarizes the scriptural basis for having faith that Jesus of Nazareth who walked this earth was the Christ, and provides a foundation for believing that all who believe that Jesus was the Son of God will be saved. When Paul was challenged by Jews that circumcision was a necessity for forgiveness of sin, Paul's response is found in Acts 15:10:

Acts 15:10 *Now, therefore, why are you putting **God** to the test by placing a yoke on the neck of the disciples that neither our fathers nor we have been able to bear? [11] But we believe that we will be saved through the grace of the Lord Jesus, just as they will."*

Paul In Jerusalem

In Acts 22 Paul attempted to preach to a crowd in Jerusalem that included members of the Jewish leadership by explaining his birth, his upbringing, education and training as a Pharisee (then known as Saul), describing how he persecuted those of the Way - the term used to refer to those who believed and followed Jesus. He then described his encounter with Jesus on the road to Damascus and his recovery from being blinded when Ananias came to visit him in Damascus, and Ananias spoke the words, *"Brother Saul, receive your sight"*, (Paul was still known as Saul at that time), and he was immediately able to see again, and Ananias again spoke and said, *"[14] And he said, The God of our fathers has appointed you to know His will, and to see the Righteous One, and to hear a voice from his mouth. [15] For you shall be a witness for him to all men of what you have seen and heard."* [Acts 22:14]

Paul's preaching, however, angered the Jewish leaders, ending with the Jews wanting to punish Paul [Acts 22:22-23] and seemingly about to cause a riot, so much so that the Commander of the Roman cohort in Jerusalem, to keep the peace, ordered that Paul be taken to the barracks.

Paul was again brought before the Jewish leadership in Jerusalem and defended himself in trial before the Council, aka, the Jewish leadership. [Acts 23:1-9] This hearing also ended with confusion and heated debates that again caused the Commander concern so, again, Paul was taken away from the hearing by force and returned to the barracks. [Acts 22:10-11]

The Jews then conspired and plotted to kill Paul, but the son of Paul's sister (Paul's nephew) learned of the plot and visited Paul and told him of the plans to ambush him, and so Paul requested the Centurion to take his nephew to the Commander who allowed the boy to share his knowledge about the plans for the ambush. That night Paul was moved under heavy escort from Jerusalem to Caesarea and delivered to Felix the Governor of the province. [Acts 23:23-24]

Paul In Caesarea

Paul, now in the custody of Governor Felix in Caesarea, is again scheduled for a hearing before Governor Felix with Ananias the Chief High Priest from Jerusalem (not the same Ananias that Paul encountered in Damascus) and an attorney named Tertullus who was brought in to bring the charges against Paul. The charges that Tertullus brought against Paul were that ' *we have found this man a pestilent fellow, and a mover of insurrections among all the Jews throughout the world, and a ringleader of the sect of the Nazarenes: [6] who moreover assayed to profane the temple: on whom also we laid hold: ... [8] from whom you will be able, by examining him yourself, take knowledge of all these things whereof we accuse him. [9] And the Jews also joined in the charge, affirming that these things were so.'* [Acts 24:5-9]

'[10] When the governor had beckoned to him to speak, Paul answered, 'Forasmuch as I know that you have been of many years a judge to this nation, I cheerfully make my defense: [11] seeing that you can take knowledge that it is no more than twelve days since I went up to worship at Jerusalem: [12] and neither in the temple did they find me disputing with any man or stirring up a crowd, nor in the synagogues, nor in the city. [13] Neither can they prove to you the things which they now accuse me. [14] But this I confess to you, that after the Way which they call a sect, so serve I the God of our fathers, believing all things which are according to the law, and which are written in the prophets; [15] having hope toward God, which these also themselves accept, that there shall be a resurrection both of the just and unjust. [16] Herein I also exercise myself to have a conscience void of offence toward God and men always.' [Acts 24:10-16] and Paul concluded his defense: *'[17] Now after some years I came to bring alms to my nation, and offerings: [18] amidst which they found me purified in the temple, with no crowd, nor yet with tumult: but there were certain Jews from Asia – [19] who should also have been here before you, and to make accusation, if they had anything against me. [20] Or else let these men themselves say what wrong-doing they found when I stood before the council, 21 except it be for this one voice, that I cried (while) standing among them, "For the resurrection of the dead I am on trial before you this day".'* [Acts 24:17-21]

The governor, Felix, then brought the hearing to a close *'[22] But Felix, having more exact knowledge concerning the Way, deferred them, saying, When Lysias the chief captain shall come down, I will determine your matter. [23] And he gave order to the centurion that he should be kept in charge, and should have indulgence; and not to forbid any of his friends to minister to him.'* In other words, while Paul was to be further detained he was permitted to have visitors.

For two years Paul was held in custody until after Felix died and was succeeded by Porcius Festus who, when he visited Jerusalem, was challenged by the Jews to bring Paul from Caesarea back to Jerusalem to stand trial.

Festus responded by inviting the Jews to come to Caesarea where he, Festus, would preside over a trial there.

When Paul was instructed to speak at the trial he said: 'Neither against the law of the Jews, nor against the temple, nor against Caesar, have I sinned at all.'

[Acts 25:8b] to which Festus responded by asking Paul if he would be prepared to go to Jerusalem to stand trial there. Paul responded, *'I am standing before Caesar's judgment-seat, where I ought to be judged: to the Jews have I done no wrong, as you also very well know. ¹¹ If then I am a wrong-doer, and have committed anything worthy of death, I refuse not to die; but if none of those of which I am accused is true, no man can give me up to them. I appeal to Caesar. ¹² Then Festus, when he had conferred with the council, answered, You have appealed to Caesar: to Caesar you shall go.'* [Acts 25:10-12]

However, Paul's departure from Caesarea was delayed because King Agrippa was due to arrive from Jerusalem. Festus discussed Paul's situation with Agrippa explaining all that he knew about Paul, the accusations that the Jews had made against him and the hearing that he had presided over. [Acts 25:13-21] Agrippa asked for a hearing so that he could hear from Paul himself, and Festus agreed and arranged for a hearing to take place the next day. [Acts 25:22-27]

When Paul was brought in and was asked to speak:

Acts 26:1 *'Paul stretched forth his hand, and made his defense: ² I consider myself happy, king Agrippa, that I am to make my defense before you this day addressing all the things of which I am accused by the Jews: ³ especially because you are expert in all customs and questions which are among the Jews: wherefore I beseech you to hear me patiently.*

*⁴ My manner of life from my youth onwards, which was from the beginning among my own nation and in Jerusalem, know all the Jews; ⁵ having knowledge of me from the first, if they are willing to testify, that after the strictest sect of our religion I lived as a Pharisee. ⁶ And now I stand here to be judged for the hope of the promise made of God to our fathers; ⁷ to which promise our twelve tribes, earnestly serving God night and day, hope to attain. And concerning this hope I am accused by the Jews, O king! ⁸ **Why is it judged incredible with you, if God does raise the dead?***

⁹ I thought to myself that I ought to do many things hostile to the name of Jesus of Nazareth. ¹⁰ And this I also did in Jerusalem: and I both shut up many of the saints in prisons, having received authority from the chief priests, and when they were to be put to death I gave my vote against them. ¹¹ And punishing them oftentimes in all the synagogues, I strove to make them blaspheme; and being exceedingly mad against them, I persecuted them even to foreign cities. ¹² Whereupon as I journeyed to Damascus with the authority and commission of the chief priests, ¹³ at midday, O king, I saw on the way a light from heaven, above the brightness of the sun, shining round about me and them that journeyed with me.

*¹⁴ And when we were all fallen to the earth, I heard a voice saying to me in the Hebrew language, Saul, Saul, why are you persecuting me? it is hard for you to kick against the goads. ¹⁵ **And I said, Who are you, Lord? And the Lord said, I am Jesus whom you persecute. ¹⁶ But arise, and stand up on your feet: for to this end have I appeared to you, to appoint you a minister and a witness both of the things wherein you have seen me, and of the things wherein I will appear to you; ¹⁷ delivering you from the people, and from the Gentiles, to whom I am sending you, ¹⁸ to open their eyes, that they may turn from darkness to light and from the power of Satan to God, that they may receive remission of sins and an inheritance among them that are sanctified by faith in me**.*

*¹⁹ Wherefore, O king Agrippa, I was not disobedient to the heavenly vision: ²⁰ but declared both to them in Damascus first, and (then) at Jerusalem, and throughout all the country of Judaea, and also to the Gentiles, that they should repent and turn to God, doing works worthy of repentance. ²¹ For this cause the Jews seized me in the temple, and assayed to kill me. ²² **Having therefore obtained the help that is from God, I stand unto this day testifying both to small and great, saying nothing but what the prophets and Moses did say should come; ²³ how that the Christ must suffer, and how that he first by the resurrection of the dead should proclaim light both to the people and to the Gentiles.***

²⁴ And as he continued to make his defense, Festus said with a loud voice, "Paul, you are mad; your great learning is turning you mad." ²⁵ But Paul said, I am not mad, most excellent Festus; but speak forth words of truth and soberness. ²⁶ For the king knows of these things, and of which I speak freely to you: for I am persuaded that none of these things is hidden from him; for this has not been done in a corner. ²⁷ King Agrippa, do you believe the prophets? I know that you believe. ²⁸ And Agrippa said to Paul, "With but little persuasion thou would fain make me a Christian". ²⁹ And Paul said, I would to God, that whether with little or with much, not you only, but also all that hear me this day, might become such as I am, except these bonds.'

³⁰ And the king rose up, and the governor, and Bernice, and they that sat with them: ³¹ and when they had withdrawn, they spoke one to another, saying, "This man has done nothing worthy of death or of bonds. ³² And Agrippa said to Festus, "This man might have been set at liberty, if he had not appealed to Caesar"

The Compiled Teachings of The Apostle Paul

Section 2

The Apostles Preaching of the Gospel in Jerusalem. *6*
Saul and His Conversion to Paul *9*
Paul's First Missionary Trip.............................. *11*
   How old was Saul, the Saul that became Paul?......................11
   Peter Preaches 12
   Paul Preaches In Antioch of Pisidia 14
   Paul and Barnabas preach again at Antioch in Pisidia 14
   Paul and Barnabas at Iconium 15
   Paul and Barnabas at Lystra..15
   Paul Stoned at Lystra 15
   Paul and Barnabas Return to Antioch in Syria 15
   The Jerusalem Council...16
   The Council's Letter to Gentile Believers...........................17
   Paul and Barnabas Separate 17
Paul's Second Missionary Trip *17*
   Timothy Joins Paul and Silas 17
   The Macedonian Call 17
   The Conversion of Lydia at Phillipi 18
   Paul and Silas in Prison..18
   The Philippian Jailer Converted.....................................18
   Paul Reports That He Is A Roman Citizen........................18
   Paul and Silas in Thessalonica..19
   Paul and Silas in Berea 19
   Paul in Athens..20
   Paul in Corinth 20

   Paul's Third Missionary Trip...21
   Paul Returns to Antioch 21
   Paul Returns to Ephesus..22
   Paul in Macedonia and Greece......................................23
   Luke rejoins Paul on His Mission 23
   Eutychus is Raised from the Dead 23
   Paul Speaks to the Ephesian Elders 23
   Paul Goes to Jerusalem 24
   Paul Visits James 24
   Paul Arrested in the Temple in Jerusalem 24
   Paul Speaks to the People..25
   Paul Shares His Testimony...25
   Paul and the Roman Tribune..25
   Paul Before the Council...25
   A Plot to Kill Paul..26
   Paul Sent to Felix the Governor at Ceasarea 26
   Paul Before Felix 26
   Paul Kept in Custody..26
   Paul Appeals to Caesar 27
   Paul's Defense Before Agrippa......................................27
   Paul Tells of His Conversion...28
   Paul Sails for Rome..28
   The Shipwreck 29

The Cities and Regions Visited on Paul's Missionary Trips....30

Words of Paul That Define His Ministry 30

Paul and The Acts of The Apostles

The person that we know as the Apostle Paul is introduced to us in the Book of Acts as Saul; Saul of Tarsus. The Book of Acts was written by Luke, the writer of The Gospel of Luke.

The Apostles Preaching of the Gospel in Jerusalem

In Acts, Luke records for us the final words spoken by Christ, Jesus of Nazareth and Luke also records the Ascension of Christ.[a] Now Luke was not an eyewitness to Jesus' final words nor the Ascension and so it seems reasonable for us to understand that he must have garnered what he recorded from some of those who were eyewitnesses. Luke, in his Gospel, also recorded for us conversations of Jesus with the Apostles, and others, from the beginning of Jesus's ministry through their gathering in the Upper Room in Jerusalem, the Last Supper, and through the arrest of Jesus, His trial, the crucifixion and events following – Jesus' burial, His resurrection and His Ascension. Among the 'others' who were witnesses were Mary, Jesus' mother, and also Jesus's brothers. There were many others, both men and women, in total about 120,[b] when Peter addressed them. Luke reports that Peter petitioned the others, proposing that Judas, who had betrayed Jesus, should be replaced, and Matthias was chosen.

In chapter 2, Luke records the events of Pentecost when the Holy Spirit fell upon each of the Apostles. From this chapter we do not know for sure if the Holy Spirit anointed Matthias or not, but we can feel sure the Holy Spirit anointed the other eleven apostles.

Luke may have been an eyewitness to some of what he has recorded, but how much we cannot be certain. It seems probable that, for example, he wasn't present prior to verses 37 and 45[c] because Luke uses the term 'they'.

The Compiled Teachings of The Apostle Paul

Had he been an eyewitness, he likely would have used the term 'we'. Later we will see that Luke most likely joined Paul as a companion in Troas on Paul's first missionary journey. [Acts 16:6-13]

Continuing through to Acts chapters 6 & 7, Luke records in significant detail the early events of the preaching of the Gospel in Jerusalem which results in some men, primarily Hellenistic (Greek) Jews, [Acts 6:1] from the Synagogue of The Freedmen becoming angry at Stephen and *"they stirred up the people and the elders and the scribes... and brought him before the Council"*[d] Stephen had to defend himself against the false charge that he, *"incessantly speaks against this holy place and the law; for we have heard him say that this Nazarene, Jesus, will destroy this place and will alter the customs which Moses handed down to us."*[e]

When challenged by the High Priest to respond to the charge, Stephen gave a lengthy and strong defense quoting scripture and prophecy[f] before turning to criticize his accusers and the members of the Council pointing out that their forefathers had persecuted all of the prophets, many of whom were killed[g] and that they themselves had not kept the law.[h] The members of the Council immediately became angry at Stephen's accusations and they drove him out of the city where upon they began stoning him, *"...and the witnesses laid aside their robes at the feet of a young man named Saul."*

Bible references:
[a] Acts 1:3-11; [b] ; [c] Acts 2:14-15; [c] Acts 2:45; [d] Acts 6:12; [e] Acts 6:14; [f] Acts 7:1-50; [g] Acts 7:51-52; [h] Acts 7:53; [i] Acts 7:57-60.
Bible text taken from the American Standard Version (ASV)

So that we have it documented, here is Stephen's sermon which, in the New American Standard Bible (NASB)[1], is referred to as "Stephen's Defense".

Acts 7 [2] *Brethren and fathers, hearken: The God of glory appeared unto our father Abraham, when he was in Mesopotamia, before he dwelt in Haran,* [3] *and said unto him, Get thee out of thy land, and from thy kindred, and come into the land which I shall show thee.* [4] *Then came he out of the land of the Chaldaeans, and dwelt in Haran: and from thence, when his father was dead, God removed him into this land, wherein you now dwell:*[5] *and he gave him no inheritance in it, no, not so much as to set his foot on: and he promised that he would give it to him in possession, and to his seed after him, when as you he had no child.* [6] *And* **God spoke on this wise, that his seed should sojourn in a strange land, and that they should bring them into bondage, and treat them ill, four hundred years.** [7] **And the nation to which they shall be in bondage will I judge, said God: and after that shall they come forth, and serve me in this place**. [8] *And he gave him the covenant of circumcision: and so Abraham begat Isaac, and circumcised him the eighth day; and Isaac begat Jacob, and Jacob the twelve patriarchs.* [9] *And the patriarchs, moved with jealousy against Joseph, sold him into Egypt: and God was with him,* [10] *and delivered him out of all his afflictions, and gave him favor and wisdom before Pharaoh king of Egypt; and he made him governor over Egypt and all his house.* [11] **Now there came a famine over all Egypt and Canaan, and great affliction: and our fathers found no sustenance.** [12] **But when Jacob heard that there was grain in Egypt, he sent forth our fathers the first time.** [13] **And at the second time Joseph was made known to his brethren; and Joseph's race became manifest unto Pharaoh.** [14] **And Joseph sent, and called to him Jacob his father, and all his kindred, threescore and fifteen souls.** [15] **And Jacob went down into Egypt**; *and he died, himself and our fathers;* [16] *and they were carried over unto Shechem, and laid in the tomb that Abraham bought for a price in silver of the sons of Hamor in Shechem.* [17] *But as the time of the promise drew nigh which God vouchsafed unto Abraham, the people grew and multiplied in Egypt,* [18] *till* **there arose another king over Egypt, who knew not Joseph.** [19] **The same dealt craftily with our race, and ill-treated our fathers, that**

---

[1] The dominant translation used throughout is the American Standard Version (ASV) but other translations including the English Standard Version (ESV), the New American Standard Bible (NASB) and the New International Version (NIV) are also used in places, especially to cross reference specific terms.

they should cast out their babes to the end they might not live. ²⁰ *At which season Moses was born, and was exceeding fair; and he was nourished three months in his father's house:* ²¹ *and when he was cast out, Pharaoh's daughter took him up, and nourished him for her own son.* ²² *And Moses was instructed in all the wisdom of the Egyptians; and he was mighty in his words and works.* ²³ *But* **when he was well-nigh forty years old, it came into his heart to visit his brethren the children of Israel.** ²⁴ *And seeing one of them suffer wrong, he defended him, and avenged him that was oppressed, smiting the Egyptian:* ²⁵ *and he supposed that his brethren understood that God by his hand was giving them deliverance; but they understood not.* ²⁶ *And the day following he appeared to them as they strove, and would have set them at one again, saying, Sirs, you are brethren; why do you wrong one to another?* ²⁷ *But he that did his neighbor wrong thrust him away, saying, Who made thee a ruler and a judge over us?* ²⁸ *Would you kill me, as you killed the Egyptian yesterday?* ²⁹ *And* **Moses fled at this saying, and became a sojourner in the land of Midian, where he begat two sons.** ³⁰ *And when forty years were fulfilled, an angel appeared to him in the wilderness of mount Sinai, in a flame of fire in a bush.* ³¹ *And when Moses saw it, he wondered at the sight: and as he drew near to behold, there came a voice of the Lord,* ³² *I am the God of thy fathers, the God of Abraham, and of Isaac, and of Jacob. And Moses trembled, and durst not behold.* ³³ *And the Lord said unto him, Loose the shoes from thy feet: for the place whereon you are standing is holy ground.* ³⁴ *I have surely seen the affliction of my people that is in Egypt, and have heard their groaning, and I am come down to deliver them: and now come, I will send thee into Egypt.* ³⁵ *This Moses whom they refused, saying, Who made thee a ruler and a judge? him has God sent to be both a ruler and a deliverer with the hand of the angel that appeared to him in the bush.* ³⁶ **This man led them forth, having wrought wonders and signs in Egypt, and in the Red sea, and in the wilderness forty years.** ³⁷ **This is that Moses, who said unto the children of Israel, A prophet shall God raise up unto you from among your brethren, like unto me.** ³⁸ *This is he that was in the church in the wilderness with the angel that spoke to him in the mount Sinai, and with our fathers: who received living oracles to give unto us:* ³⁹ *to whom our fathers would not be obedient, but thrust him from them, and turned back in their hearts unto Egypt,* ⁴⁰ *saying unto Aaron, Make us gods that shall go before us: for as for this Moses, who led us forth out of the land of Egypt,* *we know not what is become of him.* ⁴¹ *And they made a calf in those days, and brought a sacrifice unto the idol, and rejoiced in the works of their hands.* ⁴² *But God turned, and gave them up to serve the host of heaven; as it is written in the book of the prophets,*

> *Did you offer up to me slain beasts and sacrifices*
> *Forty years in the wilderness, O house of Israel?*
> ⁴³ *And you took up the tabernacle of Moloch,*
> *And the star of the god Rephan,*
> *The figures which you made to worship them:*
> *And I will carry you away beyond Babylon.*

⁴⁴ *Our fathers had the tabernacle of the testimony in the wilderness, even as he appointed who spoke to Moses, that he should make it according to the figure that he had seen.* ⁴⁵ *Which also our fathers, in their turn, brought in with Joshua when they entered on the possession of the nations, that God thrust out before the face of our fathers, unto the days of David;* ⁴⁶ *who found favor in the sight of God, and asked to find a habitation for the God of Jacob.* ⁴⁷ *But Solomon built him a house.* ⁴⁸ *Howbeit the Most High dwelt not in houses made with hands; as said the prophet,*

⁴⁹ *The heaven is my throne, And the earth the footstool of my feet:*
What manner of house will you build me? saith the Lord:
Or what is the place of my rest? ⁵⁰ *Did not my hand make all these things?*
⁵¹ **You stiff-necked and uncircumcised in heart and ears, you do always resist the Holy Spirit: as your fathers did, so do you.** ⁵² **Which of the prophets did your fathers not persecute? and they killed them that showed before of the coming of the Righteous One; of whom you have now become betrayers and murderers;** ⁵³ **you who received the law as it was ordained by angels, and kept it not.**

⁵⁴ *Now when they (primarily the Hellenistic Jews),* [Acts 6:1] *heard these things, they were cut to the heart, and they gnashed on him with their teeth.* ⁵⁵ *But he, being full of the Holy Spirit, looked up steadfastly into heaven, and saw the glory of God, and Jesus standing on the right hand of God,* ⁵⁶ *and said, Behold, I see the heavens opened, and the Son of man standing on the right hand of God.* ⁵⁷ *But* **they cried out with a loud voice, and stopped their ears, and rushed upon him with one accord;** ⁵⁸ **and they cast him out of the city, and stoned him: and the witnesses laid down their garments at the feet of a young man named Saul** *(who was one of the Hellenistic Jews).* ⁵⁹ **And they stoned Stephen, calling upon the Lord, and saying, Lord Jesus, receive my spirit.** ⁶⁰ *And he kneeled down, and cried with a loud voice, Lord, lay not this sin to their charge. And when he had said this, he fell asleep.*

Thus, Stephen was accused, tried and murdered; making him the first Christian martyr even though the term 'Christian' had not yet been coined.

Acts 8:1 continues, *"Saul was in hearty agreement with putting him [Stephen] to death."* And Acts 8:3 tells us that, *"Saul began ravaging the church entering house after house, dragging off men and women, and he would put them in prison."*

The Compiled Teachings of The Apostle Paul

Acts 9:1 tells us that, *"Saul, still breathing threats and murder against the disciples of the Lord, went to the High Priest, ² and asked for letters from him (the High Priest) to the synagogues at Damascus, so that if he found any belonging to The Way, both men and women, he might bring them bound to Jerusalem."* 'The Way' was the term that had been coined to refer to those who followed the disciples of Jesus.

[A description, by Saul himself, of his upbringing and education is provided in Acts 22:3]   [k] Acts 9:1-2

Saul and His Conversion to Paul

So, Saul, armed with letters of authority, set off for Damascus.

Acts 9:3 And as he journeyed, it came to pass that he drew near to Damascus: and suddenly there shone round about him a light out of heaven: ⁴ and he fell upon the earth, and heard a voice saying unto him, "Saul, Saul, why are you persecuting me?" ⁵ And he said, "Who are you, Lord?" And He said, "I am Jesus whom you persecute: ⁶ but rise, and enter into the city, and it shall be told you what you must do." ⁷ And the men that journeyed with him stood speechless, hearing the voice, but beholding no man. ⁸ And Saul arose from the earth; and when his eyes were opened, he saw nothing; and they led him by the hand, and brought him into (the city of) Damascus. ⁹ And he was three days without sight, and did neither eat nor drink.
¹⁰ Now there was a certain disciple at Damascus, named Ananias; and the Lord said to him in a vision, Ananias. And he said, Behold, I am here, Lord. ¹¹ And the Lord said to him, Arise, and go to the street which is called Straight, and inquire in the house of Judas for one named Saul, a man of Tarsus: for behold, he prayed; ¹² and he had seen a man named Ananias coming in, and laying his hands on him, that he might receive his sight. ¹³ But Ananias answered, "Lord, I have heard from many of this man, how much evil he did to the saints at Jerusalem: ¹⁴ and here he has authority from the chief priests to bind all that call upon your name." ¹⁵ But the Lord said to him, "Go your way: for he is a chosen vessel to me, to bear my name before the Gentiles and kings, and the children of Israel: ¹⁶ for I will show him how many things he must suffer for my name's sake." ¹⁷ And Ananias departed, and entered into the house; and laying his hands on him said, "Brother Saul, the Lord, even Jesus, who appeared to thee in the way which you came, has sent me, that you may receive your sight, and be filled with the Holy Spirit." ¹⁸ And straightway there fell from his eyes as it were scales, and he received his sight; and he arose and was baptized; ¹⁹ and he took food and was strengthened. And he was certain days with the disciples that were at Damascus.

Saul having been converted, began to preach about Jesus proclaiming that Jesus was the Son of God; He is the Christ.

Acts 9 ²⁰ And straightway in the synagogues he proclaimed Jesus, that he is the Son of God. ²¹ And all that heard him were amazed, and said, Is not this he that in Jerusalem made havoc of them that called on this name? and he had come hither for this intent, that he might bring them bound before the chief priests. ²² But Saul increased the more in strength, and confounded the Jews that dwelt at Damascus, proving that this is the Christ.

The Hunter Becomes The Hunted

Saul was now seen by the Jews to be a threat to their teaching, so they plotted to kill him, and he now had to be rescued from the Jews by those who were disciples of the Way.

*Acts 9 ²³ **And when many days were fulfilled, the Jews took counsel together to kill him**: ²⁴ but their plot became known to Saul. And they watched the gates also day and night that they might kill him: ²⁵ but his disciples took him by night, and let him down through the wall, lowering him in a basket.*
*²⁶ And when he was come to Jerusalem, he assayed to join himself to the disciples: and they were all afraid of him, not believing that he was a disciple. ²⁷ But Barnabas took him, and brought him to the apostles, and declared unto them how he had seen the Lord in the way, and that he had spoken to him, and how at Damascus he had preached boldly in the name of Jesus. ²⁸ And **he was with them going in and going out at Jerusalem, ²⁹ preaching boldly in the name of the Lord: and he spoke and disputed against the Grecian Jews; but they were seeking to kill him**. ³⁰ And when the brethren knew it, they brought him down to Caesarea, and sent him forth to Tarsus.*

In this passage we learned that helping Saul escape from Damascus didn't fully solve all of Saul's problems because, when he tried to join the disciples of the Way in Jerusalem he was viewed with suspicion. However, one disciple, Barnabas, a disciple from Damascus, came to Saul's rescue and so Saul was able to preach and when he proclaimed that Jesus of Nazareth was Christ, that only led to some Jews, especially the Grecian Jews, to now seek to kill him. Saul was originally from Tarsus and so the disciples took Saul to Tarsus. Luke writes in Acts 9:31:

Acts 9 ³¹ So the church throughout all Judaea and Galilee and Samaria had peace, being edified; and, walking in the fear of the Lord and in the comfort of the Holy Spirit, was multiplied.

*Acts 11 ¹⁹ They therefore that were scattered abroad upon the tribulation that arose about Stephen travelled as far as Phoenicia, and Cyprus, and Antioch, speaking the word to none save only to Jews. ²⁰ But there were some of them, men of Cyprus and Cyrene, who, when they were come to Antioch, spoke to the Greeks also, preaching the Lord Jesus. ²¹ And the hand of the Lord was with them: and a great number that believed turned unto the Lord. ²² And the report concerning them came to the ears of the church which was in Jerusalem: and **they sent forth Barnabas as far as Antioch: ²³ who, when he was come, and had seen the grace of God, was glad; and he exhorted them all, that with purpose of heart they would cleave to the Lord: ²⁴ for he was a good man, and full of the Holy Spirit and of faith: and many people were added unto the Lord. ²⁵ And he went forth to Tarsus to seek for Saul**; ²⁶ and when he had found him, he brought him unto Antioch. And it came to pass, that even for a whole year they were gathered together with the church, and taught many*

The Compiled Teachings of The Apostle Paul

*people; and that **the disciples were called Christians first in Antioch**. ²⁷ Now in these days there came down prophets from Jerusalem unto Antioch. ²⁸ And there stood up one of them named Agabus, and signified by the Spirit that there should be a great famine over all the world: which came to pass in the days of Claudius. ²⁹ And the disciples, every man according to his ability, determined to send relief unto the brethren that dwelt in Judaea:³⁰ which also they did, sending it to the elders by the hand of Barnabas and Saul.*

And in Acts 12:24-25, Luke writes:
Acts 12 ²⁴ But the word of God grew and multiplied. ²⁵ And Barnabas and Saul returned from Jerusalem, when they had fulfilled their ministration, taking with them John whose surname was Mark.

Ministration: the services of a minister of religion or of a religious institution

*Acts 13 Now there were at Antioch, in the church that was there, prophets and teachers, Barnabas, and Simeon that was called Niger, and Lucius of Cyrene, and Manaen the foster-brother of Herod the tetrarch, and Saul. ² And as they ministered to the Lord, and fasted, **the Holy Spirit said, "Separate [for] me Barnabas and Saul for the work whereunto I have called them**." ³ Then, when they had fasted and prayed and laid their hands on them, they sent them away.*

Paul's First Missionary Trip

*Acts 13 ⁴ So they, **being sent forth by the Holy Spirit, went down to Seleucia; and from thence they sailed to Cyprus**. ⁵ And when they were at Salamis, they proclaimed the word of God in the synagogues of the Jews: and **they had also John as their attendant**. ⁶ And when they had gone through the whole island to Paphos, they found a certain sorcerer, a false prophet, a Jew, whose name was Bar-Jesus; ⁷ who was with the proconsul, Sergius Paulus, a man of understanding. The same called to him Barnabas and Saul, and sought to hear the word of God. ⁸ But Elymas the sorcerer (for so is his name by interpretation) withstood them, seeking to turn aside the proconsul from the faith. But Saul, who is also called **Paul, filled with the Holy Spirit, fastened his eyes on him, ¹⁰ and said, "O full of all guile and all villainy, you son of the devil, you enemy of all righteousness, will you not cease to pervert the right ways of the Lord? ¹¹ And now, behold, the hand of the Lord is upon you, and you shall be blind, not seeing the sun for a season. And immediately there fell upon him a mist and a darkness; and he went about seeking some to lead him by the hand. ¹² Then the proconsul, when he saw what was done, believed, being astonished at the teaching of the Lord.***

Saul has now become also known as Paul, which is the name that we are most familiar with. Paul and Barnabas have travelling with them on this first of three Missionary journeys that are recorded in the Book of Acts, John who is referred to as 'their attendant'. John is a fairly common name and so the question is raised, "Is this John, John The Apostle?" We know from the Gospels that the father of Apostle John was Zebedee, but we are not given his mother's name even though she is referenced when she petitioned Jesus (Matt. 20:20), and they were not from Jerusalem but were from Galilee, and '*and John departed from them and returned to Jerusalem.*' (Acts 13:13). It seems unlikely that the John who had travelled with Paul and Barnabas was the Apostle John.

But there is another John 'who is also known as Mark' referenced in Acts; *"When he realized this, he went to the house of Mary, the mother of John whose other name was Mark,"* (Acts 12:12) and *"Barnabas and Saul returned from Jerusalem when they had completed their service, bringing with them John, whose other name [surname?] was Mark." (Acts 12:25)*. It may well be that this is the John referenced as travelling with Paul and Barnabas. What we do know is that the 'John also known as Mark', did not continue on beyond Perga.

How old was Saul, the Saul that became Paul?

In Acts 7:60 Saul is referred to as a 'young man'. The timeframe from Saul's conversion to his first missionary trip, however, is not clear. It seems likely that it is several years, but how many? If 'young man' at the time of Stephen's death means not yet fully an adult, that could mean less than 20 years old, or even younger. What does seem likely is that by the time Paul embarked on his first missionary journey he may well have still been only in his 20s.

Acts 13 ¹³ Now Paul and his company set sail from Paphos, and came to Perga in Pamphylia: and John departed from them and returned to Jerusalem. ¹⁴ But they, passing through from Perga, came to Antioch of Pisidia; and they went into the synagogue on the sabbath day, and sat down. ¹⁵ And after the reading of the law and the prophets the rulers of the synagogue sent to them, saying, Brethren, if you have any word of exhortation for the people, say on.

Thus far, we have covered the background regarding Saul, who, from this point forward, we will refer to as Paul. The invitation offered up to Barnabas and Paul by the rulers of the synagogue is the first record we have of Paul preaching. Now Paul, while still being known as Saul, quite likely had heard Stephen preach when he was brought before the Council (Acts 7), but almost certainly he would have been listening only with the intention of criticizing. After his conversion Paul quite possibly heard Peter preach because of what he says in Galatians 1:18

The Compiled Teachings of The Apostle Paul

[18] Then after three years I went up to Jerusalem to visit Cephas [Peter], and tarried with him fifteen days.', but it seems unlikely that he would have heard either of the first of the two sermons preached by Peter that are recorded in Acts 2:14-36 and Acts 3:11-26. Paul almost certainly will have heard Barnabas preach. For example, Acts 12:25 and 13:46 reference *'Paul and Barnabas preaching'*. Paul will have heard James, the brother of Jesus (Gal. 1:19) and Gal. 2:1 *Then after the space of fourteen years I went up again to Jerusalem with Barnabas, taking Titus also with me.* It is also possible that Paul may have heard some of the other Apostles preach; but of these sermons we have no record. However, being mindful of the preaching of Peter and Stephen, these earlier sermons will provide us with points of reference that we can compare with the teachings of Paul, identifying commonalities where they exist and also identify traits that exhibit uniqueness. *[Stephen's Sermon before the Council in Jerusalem is printed in pages 7/8.]*

Peter Preaches

In his first sermon, which was delivered before the Council, in Acts 2:16-21 Peter references the prophet Joel, quoting:

> **Acts 2** [16] *And it shall be in the last days, saith God,*
> [17] *I will pour forth of my Spirit upon all flesh:*
> *And your sons and your daughters shall prophesy,*
> *And your young men shall see visions,*
> *And your old men shall dream dreams:*
> [18] *and on my servants and on my handmaidens in those days*
> *Will I pour forth of my Spirit; and they shall prophesy.*

And v21 *And it shall be, that **whosoever shall call on the name of the Lord shall be saved**.*

Peter then continues with:

Acts 2 [22] **Men of Israel, hear these words: Jesus of Nazareth, a man approved of God unto you by mighty works and wonders and signs which God did by him in the midst of you, even as you yourselves know;** [23] *Him, being delivered up by the determinate counsel and foreknowledge of God, you by the hand of lawless men did crucify and slay:* [24] *whom God raised up, having loosed the pangs of death: because it was not possible that he should be holden of it.* [25] *For David said concerning him,*
'I beheld the Lord always before my face;
For he is on my right hand, that I should not be moved:
[26] *Therefore my heart was glad, and my tongue rejoiced;*
Moreover my flesh also shall dwell in hope:
[27] *Because you will not leave my soul to Hades,*
Neither will you give your Holy One to see corruption.
[28] *You made known to me the ways of life; You shall make me full of gladness with thy countenance.'*

[29] *Brethren, I may say unto you freely of the patriarch David, that he both died and was buried, and his tomb is with us to this day.* [30] *Being therefore a prophet, and knowing that God had sworn with an oath to him, that of the fruit of his loins he would set one upon his throne;* [31] **he foreseeing this spoke of the resurrection of the Christ**, *that neither was he left unto Hades, nor did his flesh see corruption.* [32] **This Jesus did God raise up, whereof we all are witnesses.** [33] **Being therefore by the right hand of God exalted, and having received of the Father the promise of the Holy Spirit**, *he has poured forth this, which you see and hear.* [34] *For David did not ascend into the heavens: but he said himself, The Lord said to my Lord, 'sit thou on my right hand,* [35] *Till I make your enemies the footstool for your feet.'*
[36] *Let all the house of Israel therefore know assuredly, that* **God has made him both Lord and Christ**, *this Jesus whom you crucified.*

Included in Peter's preaching are his statement in verse 32 that he and the other Apostles are witnesses, and his direct address to the 'house of Israel', that is the Jews, proclaiming that Jesus is the Christ.
In his second sermon (Acts 3:12-26), Peter, having just healed a man who was lame, said:

Acts 3: [12b] *Men of Israel, why marvel you at this man? or why fasten you your eyes on us, as though by our own power or godliness we had made him to walk?* [13] *The God of Abraham, and of Isaac, and of Jacob, the God of our fathers, has glorified his Servant Jesus; whom you delivered up, and denied before the face of Pilate, when he had determined to release him.* [14] *But you denied the Holy and Righteous One, and asked for a murderer to be granted unto you,* [15] *and killed the Prince of life; whom God raised from the dead; whereof we are witnesses.* [16] *And by faith in his name has his name made this man strong, whom you behold and know: you, the faith which is through him has given him this perfect soundness in the presence of you all.*

[17] *And now, brethren, I know that in ignorance you did it, as did also your rulers.* [18] *But the things which God foreshowed by the mouth of all the prophets, that his Christ should suffer, he thus fulfilled.* [19] **Repent you therefore, and turn again, that your sins may be blotted out**, *that so there may come seasons of refreshing from the presence of the Lord;* [20] *and that he may send the Christ who has been appointed for you, even Jesus:* [21] *whom the heaven must receive until the times of restoration of all things, whereof God spoke by the mouth of his holy prophets that have been from of old.* [22] *Moses indeed said, A prophet shall the Lord God raise up unto you from among your brethren, like unto me; to him shall you hearken in all things whatsoever he shall speak unto you.* [23] *And it shall be, that* **every soul that shall not hearken to that**

The Compiled Teachings of The Apostle Paul

prophet, shall be utterly destroyed from among the people. [24] *You and all the prophets from Samuel and them that followed after, as many as have spoken, they also told of these days.* [25] *You are the sons of the prophets, and of the covenant which God made with your fathers,* *saying unto Abraham, And* **in thy seed shall all the families of the earth be blessed.** [26] *Unto you first God, having raised up his Servant,* **sent him to bless you, in turning away every one of you from your iniquities.**

Note: The primary purpose of printing so extensively the text of The Acts of The Apostles in this section is to allow passages of teaching by Paul and of significance to be highlighted in **bold typeface** and as such provide as a convenient means by which to locate those passages for quick and easy reference.

Where relevant, these passages will be referenced as we move through studying the letters, both those written by Paul and those credited to other authors. One key is to first gain an understanding of which cities Paul visited on each of his three missionary journeys so that we can identify the order in which the letters (epistles) were written.

Peter's exhortation, '*Repent you therefore, and turn again, that your sins may be blotted out,*' [v19] should not have been a surprise to anyone listening who may have known Peter since he had been a disciple of John The Baptist before he became a disciple of Jesus.

Having reminded ourselves of Peter's sermons, let us look at the first reports of Paul preaching.

The first references to Paul teaching are found in Acts 9:

[19b] *For some days he was with the disciples at Damascus.* [20] *And immediately he proclaimed Jesus in the synagogues, saying, "He is the Son of God."* [21] *And all who heard him were amazed and said, "Is not this the man who made havoc in Jerusalem of those who called upon this name? And has he not come here for this purpose, to bring them bound before the chief priests?"* [22] *But Saul increased all the more in strength, and confounded the Jews who lived in Damascus by proving that Jesus was the Christ.*

The next reference to Paul (still known as Saul) is in Acts 11:

[21] *And the hand of the Lord was with them, and a great number who believed turned to the Lord.* [22] *The report of this came to the ears of the church in Jerusalem, and they sent Barnabas to Antioch.* [23] *When he came and saw the grace of God, he was glad, and he exhorted them all to remain faithful to the Lord with steadfast purpose,* [24] *for he was a good man, full of the Holy Spirit and of faith. And a great many people were added to the Lord.* [25] *So Barnabas went to Tarsus to look for Saul,* [26] *and when he had found him, he brought him to Antioch. For a whole year they met with the church and taught a great many people. And in Antioch the disciples were first called Christians.*

Regrettably, we do not have any record of any occasion of preaching by Barnabas prior to him joining Paul on this first missionary journey but recall that Barnabas was among those of 'The Way' in Damascus.

Acts 12 [25] *And Barnabas and Saul returned from Jerusalem when they had completed their service, bringing with them John, whose other name was Mark.*

Barnabas and Saul, who had by now become known as Paul, travelled to Cyprus where first Paul encountered a false prophet named Bar-Jesus:

Acts 13 [6] *And when they had gone through the whole island [of Cyprus] to Paphos, they found a certain sorcerer, a false prophet, a Jew, whose name was Bar-Jesus;* [7] *who was with the proconsul, Sergius Paulus, a man of understanding. The same called to him Barnabas and Saul, and sought to hear the word of God.* [8] *But Elymas the sorcerer (for so is his name by interpretation) withstood them, seeking to turn aside the proconsul from the faith.* [9] **But Saul, who is also called Paul**, *filled with the Holy Spirit, fastened his eyes on him,* [10] *and said, "O full of all guile and all villainy, you son of the devil, you enemy of all righteousness, will you not cease to pervert the right ways of the Lord?* [11] *And now,* **behold, the hand of the Lord is upon you, and you shall be blind, not seeing the sun for a season. And immediately there fell upon him a mist and a darkness**; *and he went about seeking some to lead him by the hand.* [12] *Then the proconsul, when he saw what was done, believed, being astonished at the teaching of the Lord.*

[13] *Now Paul and his company set sail from Paphos, and came to Perga in Pamphylia: and John departed from them and returned to Jerusalem.* [14] *But they, passing through from Perga, came to Antioch of Pisidia; and they went into the synagogue on the sabbath day, and sat down.* [15] *And after the reading of the law and the prophets the rulers of the synagogue sent unto them, saying, Brethren, if ye have any word of exhortation for the people, say on.*

The Compiled Teachings of The Apostle Paul

Paul Preaches In Antioch of Pisidia

Here is the sermon that Paul delivered in the synagogue in Antioch of Pisidia (which is Antioch in Syria and is not to be confused with Antioch which is in modern day Turkey).

Acts 13 [16] *And Paul stood up, and beckoning with the hand said, Men of Israel, and you that fear God, hearken:* [17] *The God of this people Israel chose our fathers, and exalted the people when they sojourned in the land of Egypt, and with a high arm led he them forth out of it.* [18] *And for about the time of forty years as a nursing-father bare he them in the wilderness.* [19] *And when he had destroyed seven nations in the land of Canaan, he gave them their land for an inheritance, for about four hundred and fifty years:* [20] *and after these things he gave them judges until Samuel the prophet.* [21] *And afterward they asked for a king: and God gave unto them Saul the son of Kish, a man of the tribe of Benjamin, for the space of forty years.* [22] *And when he had removed him, he raised up David to be their king; to whom also he bare witness and said, I have found David the son of Jesse, a man after my heart, who shall do all my will.* [23] **Of this man's seed has God according to promise brought unto Israel a Savior, Jesus;** [24] **when John (John The Baptist) had first preached before his coming the baptism of repentance to all the people of Israel.** [25] **And as John was fulfilling his course, he said, What suppose you that I am? I am not he. But behold, there cometh one after me the shoes of whose feet I am not worthy to unloose.** [26] **Brethren, children of the stock of Abraham, and those among you that fear God, to us is the word of this salvation sent forth.** [27] **For they that dwell in Jerusalem, and their rulers, because they knew him not, nor the voices of the prophets which are read every sabbath, fulfilled them by condemning him.** [28] **And though they found no cause of death in him, yet asked they of Pilate that he should be slain.** [29] **And when they had fulfilled all things that were written of him, they took him down from the tree, and laid him in a tomb.** [30] **But God raised him from the dead:** [31] **and he was seen for many days of them that came up with him from Galilee to Jerusalem, who are now his witnesses unto the people.** [32] *And we bring you good tidings of the promise made unto the fathers,* [33] *that God has fulfilled the same unto our children, in that he raised up Jesus; as also it is written in the second psalm, Thou art my Son, this day have I begotten thee.* [34] *And as concerning that he raised him up from the dead, now no more to return to corruption, he has spoken on this wise, I will give you the holy and sure blessings of David.* [35] *Because he said also in another psalm, 'Thou will not give thy Holy One to see corruption.'* [36] *For David, after he had in his own generation served the counsel of God, fell asleep, and was laid unto his fathers, and saw corruption:* [37] *but he whom God raised up saw no corruption.* [38] **Be it known to you therefore, brethren, that through this man is proclaimed unto you remission of sins:** [39] **and by Him every one that believes is justified from all things, from which you could not be justified by the law of Moses.** [40] *Beware therefore, lest that come upon you which is spoken in the prophets: 'For I work a work in your days, A work which you shall in no wise believe, if one declare it to you.'*
[41] *'Behold, you despisers, and wonder, and perish';*
[42] *And as they went out, they besought that these words might be spoken to them the next sabbath.* [43] *Now when the synagogue broke up, many of the Jews and of the devout proselytes followed Paul and Barnabas; who, speaking to them, urged them to continue in the grace of God.*

Comment: This entire sermon delivered by Paul sums up the foundation of all of his teaching, especially the bolded verses of Acts 13:23-31 and 38[b]-39, that Christ was prophesied, was rejected (denied), condemned, put to death but rose from the tomb (resurrected), and then ascended back to the Father in heaven.

Paul and Barnabas preach again in the synagogue at Antioch in Pisidia the next Sabbath

Acts 13: [44] *And the next sabbath almost the whole city was gathered together to hear the word of God.* [45] *But when the Jews saw the multitudes, they were filled with jealousy, and contradicted the things which were spoken by Paul, and blasphemed.* [46] *And Paul and Barnabas spoke out boldly, and said, It was necessary that the word of God should first be spoken to you. Seeing you thrust it from you, and judge yourselves unworthy of eternal life, lo, we turn to the Gentiles.* [47] *For so has the Lord commanded us, saying,* **I have set thee for a light of the Gentiles, that you shouldest be for salvation unto the uttermost part of the earth.** [48] *And as the Gentiles heard this, they were glad, and glorified the word of God: and as many as were ordained to eternal life believed.* [49] *And the word of the Lord was spread abroad throughout all the region.* [50] *But the Jews urged on the devout women of honorable estate, and the chief men of the city, and stirred up a persecution against Paul and Barnabas, and cast them out of their borders.* [51] *But they shook off the dust of their feet against them, and came unto Iconium.* [52] *And the disciples were filled with joy and with the Holy Spirit.*

The Compiled Teachings of The Apostle Paul

Some first observations:
- Both Peter and Paul reference King David.
- Stephen, Peter and Paul reference Moses.
- The Jews (leaders) were inflamed with anger at Stephen and at Paul.
- We have here a reference to both Paul and Barnabas preaching in Antioch in Pisidia;

'Paul and Barnabas spoke out boldly, and said, It was necessary that the word of God should first be spoken to you. Seeing you thrust it from you, and judge yourselves unworthy of eternal life, lo, we turn to the Gentiles.'

'We (or I) have been commanded to take the message of salvation to the Gentiles, everywhere,' is a phrase that Paul most definitely is qualified to use because of the exhortation spoken to Ananias. Recall that in Acts 9, Jesus tells Ananias, "*[15] But the Lord said to him [Ananias], "Go your way: for he is a chosen vessel to me, to bear my name before the Gentiles and kings, and the children of Israel,"* and the 'him' that Jesus is referring to is Saul; the Saul who is known to us as Paul. From Antioch in Pisidia, Paul and Barnabas travelled on to Iconium.

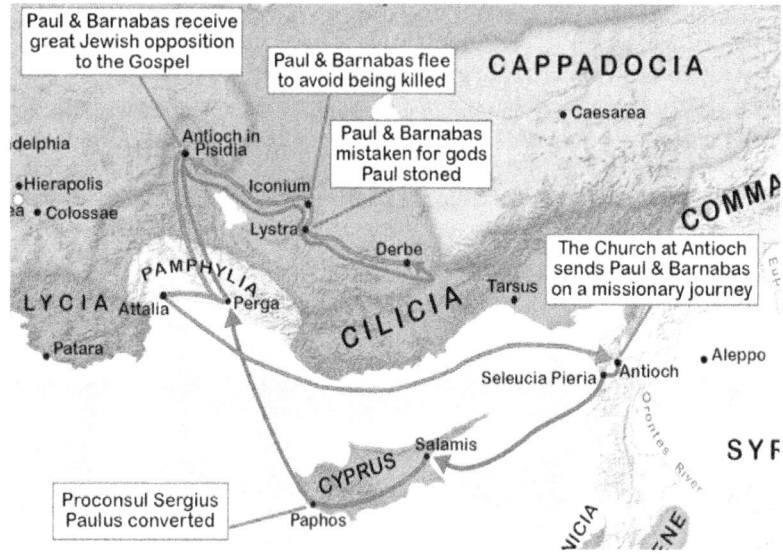

Paul and Barnabas at Iconium

Acts 14 Now at Iconium they entered together into the Jewish synagogue and spoke in such a way that a great number of both Jews and Greeks believed. [2] But the unbelieving Jews stirred up the Gentiles and poisoned their minds against the brothers. [3] So they remained for a long time, speaking boldly for the Lord, who bore witness to the word of his grace, granting signs and wonders to be done by their hands. [4] But the people of the city were divided; some sided with the Jews and some with the apostles. [5] When an attempt was made by both Gentiles and Jews, with their rulers, to mistreat them and to stone them, [6] they learned of it and fled to Lystra and Derbe, cities of Lycaonia, and to the surrounding country, [7] and there they continued to preach the gospel.

Paul and Barnabas at Lystra

14 [8] Now at Lystra there was a man sitting who could not use his feet. He was crippled from birth and had never walked. [9] He listened to Paul speaking. And Paul, looking intently at him and seeing that he had faith to be made well, [10] said in a loud voice, "Stand upright on your feet." And he sprang up and began walking. [11] And when the crowds saw what Paul had done, they lifted up their voices, saying in Lycaonian, "The gods have come down to us in the likeness of men!" [12] Barnabas they called Zeus, and Paul, Hermes, because he was the chief speaker. [13] And the priest of Zeus, whose temple was at the entrance to the city, brought oxen and garlands to the gates and wanted to offer sacrifice with the crowds. [14] But when the apostles Barnabas and Paul heard of it, they tore their garments and rushed out into the crowd, crying out, [15] "Men, why are you doing these things? We also are men, of like nature with you, and we bring you good news, that you should turn from these vain things to a living God, who made the heaven and the earth and the sea and all that is in them. [16] In past generations he allowed all the nations to walk in their own ways. [17] Yet he did not leave himself without witness, for he did good by giving you rains from heaven and fruitful seasons, satisfying your hearts with food and gladness." [18] Even with these words they scarcely restrained the people from offering sacrifice to them.

Paul Stoned at Lystra

14 [19] But Jews came from Antioch and Iconium, and having persuaded the crowds, they stoned Paul and dragged him out of the city, supposing that he was dead. [20] But when the disciples gathered about him, he rose up and entered the city, and on the next day he went on with Barnabas to Derbe. [21] When they had preached the gospel to that city and had made many disciples, they returned to Lystra and to Iconium and to Antioch, [22] strengthening the souls of the disciples, encouraging them to continue in the faith, and saying that through many tribulations we must enter the kingdom of God. [23] And when they had appointed elders for them in every church, with prayer and fasting they committed them to the Lord in whom they had believed.

Paul and Barnabas Return to Antioch in Syria

14 [24] Then they passed through Pisidia and came to Pamphylia. [25] And when they had spoken the word in Perga, they went down to Attalia, [26] and from there they sailed to Antioch, where they had been commended to the grace of God for the work that they had fulfilled. [27] And when they arrived and gathered the church together, they declared all that God had done with them, and how he had opened a door of faith to the Gentiles. [28] And they remained no little time with the disciples.

The Compiled Teachings of The Apostle Paul

As we learned from Acts 14:19-23, in Lystra, Paul triggered a similar reaction to that which Stephen had caused in Jerusalem, on this occasion it was the result of outside influence; jews who had travelled from Antioch and Iconium. Thankfully, although left for dead, Paul was not killed.

After leaving Lystra they travelled through Pisidia to Pamphylia, to Perga and to Attalia, and then returned to Antioch. While in Antioch Paul and Barnabas encountered Jews from Jerusalem who engaged them in argument and debate (the term dissension used in this next passage probably indicates 'strong disagreement'). They and others were 'appointed' to go to Jerusalem to the Apostles to seek council on the matter of circumcision. In Jerusalem they encountered opposition from the Pharisees who maintained that circumcision was necessary for salvation.

The Jerusalem Council

Acts 15 But some men came down from Judea and were teaching the brothers, "Unless you are circumcised according to the custom of Moses, you cannot be saved." ² And after Paul and Barnabas had no small dissension and debate with them, Paul and Barnabas and some of the others were appointed to go up to Jerusalem to the apostles and the elders about this question. ³ So, being sent on their way by the church, they passed through both Phoenicia and Samaria, describing in detail the conversion of the Gentiles, and brought great joy to all the brothers. ⁴ When they came to Jerusalem, they were welcomed by the church and the apostles and the elders, and they declared all that God had done with them. ⁵ But some believers who belonged to the party of the Pharisees rose up and said, "It is necessary to circumcise them and to order them to keep the law of Moses."

Next, we see an occasion in which Paul and Barnabas are in discussion with Peter and Peter (not Paul) who pronounces that he had been chosen to take the gospel to the Gentiles and become believers, and Peter stated, '*and he [God] made no distinction between us and them, having cleansed their hearts by faith." (v9)* and Peter concluded '*we believe that we will be saved through the grace of the Lord Jesus, just as they will." (v11)*

15 ⁶ The apostles and the elders were gathered together to consider this matter. ⁷ And after there had been much debate, Peter stood up and said to them, "Brothers, you know that in the early days God made a choice among you, that by my mouth the Gentiles should hear the word of the gospel and believe. ⁸ And God, who knows the heart, bore witness to them, by giving them the Holy Spirit just as he did to us, ⁹ and he made no distinction between us and them, having cleansed their hearts by faith. ¹⁰ Now, therefore, why are you putting God to the test by placing a yoke on the neck of the disciples that neither our fathers nor we have been able to bear? ¹¹ But we believe that we will be saved through the grace of the Lord Jesus, just as they will."

The discussion might have stopped after verse 11, but it didn't. Barnabas and Paul continued by relating what they had seen accomplished among the Gentiles, no doubt emphasizing how ready the Gentiles were to accept the gospel.

Here, James, picked up the baton, first referencing Simeon and then the prophets ending with '*...that the remnant of mankind may seek the Lord, and all the Gentiles who are called by my name, says the Lord,"* (v17). James endorses what Peter proposed but adding some stipulations: '*abstain from the things polluted by idols, and from sexual immorality, and from what has been strangled, and from blood.* (v20) and finally pointing out that in every city there are already synagogues and therefore worship of God is practiced.

15 ¹² And all the assembly fell silent, and they listened to Barnabas and Paul as they related what signs and wonders God had done through them among the Gentiles.

*¹³ **After they finished speaking, James replied**, "Brothers, listen to me. ¹⁴ Simeon has related (to us) how God first visited the Gentiles, to take from them a people for his name. ¹⁵ And with this the words of the prophets agree, just as it is written,*

¹⁶ "'After this I will return, and I will rebuild the tent of David that has fallen; I will rebuild its ruins, and I will restore it, ¹⁷ that the remnant of mankind may seek the Lord, and all the Gentiles who are called by my name, says the Lord, who makes these things ¹⁸ known from of old.'

¹⁹ Therefore my judgment is that we should not trouble those of the Gentiles who turn to God, ²⁰ but should write to them to abstain from the things polluted by idols, and from sexual immorality, and from what has been strangled, and from blood. ²¹ For from ancient generations Moses has had in every city those who proclaim him, for he is read every Sabbath in the synagogues."

The end result of this debate was that a letter to the Gentiles was drafted.

The Council's Letter to Gentile Believers

15 *²² Then it seemed good to the apostles and the elders, with the whole church, to choose men from among them and send them to Antioch with Paul and Barnabas. They sent Judas called Barsabbas, and Silas, leading men among the brothers, ²³ with the following letter: "The brothers, both the apostles and the elders, to the brothers who are of the Gentiles in Antioch and Syria and Cilicia, greetings. ²⁴ Since we have heard that some persons have gone out from us and troubled you with words, unsettling your minds, although we gave them no instructions, ²⁵ it has seemed good to us, having come to one accord, to choose men and send them to you with our beloved Barnabas and Paul, ²⁶ men who have risked their lives for the name of our Lord Jesus Christ. ²⁷ We have therefore sent Judas and Silas, who themselves will tell you the same things by word of mouth. ²⁸ For it has seemed good to the Holy Spirit and to us to lay on you no greater burden than these requirements: ²⁹ that you abstain from what has been sacrificed to idols, and from blood, and from what has been strangled, and from sexual immorality. If you keep yourselves from these, you will do well. Farewell."*

³⁰ So when they were sent off, they went down to Antioch, and having gathered the congregation together, they delivered the letter. ³¹ And when they had read it, they rejoiced because of its encouragement. ³² And Judas and Silas, who were themselves prophets, encouraged and strengthened the brothers with many words. ³³ And after they had spent some time, they were sent off in peace by the brothers to those who had sent them. ³⁵ But Paul and Barnabas remained in Antioch, teaching and preaching the word of the Lord, with many others also.

So Paul and Barnabas returned to Antioch but it was two others, Jaudas (also called Barsabbas) and Silas, they were sent to deliver the letters to the cities of Syria and Cilicia. As we see in the next passage, after Jaudas and Silas return from delivering the letters, Paul and Barnabas separate and no longer travel together.

Paul and Barnabas Separate

15 *³⁶ And after some days Paul said to Barnabas, "Let us return and visit the brothers in every city where we proclaimed the word of the Lord, and see how they are." ³⁷ **Now Barnabas wanted to take with them John called Mark.** ³⁸ **But Paul thought best not to take with them one who had withdrawn from them in Pamphylia and had not gone with them to the work.** ³⁹ **And there arose a sharp disagreement, so that they separated from each other.** Barnabas took Mark with him and sailed away to Cyprus, ⁴⁰ but Paul chose Silas and departed, having been commended by the brothers to the grace of the Lord. ⁴¹ And he went through Syria and Cilicia, strengthening the churches.*

Paul's Second Missionary Trip

The Book of Acts now follows the missions of Paul.

Timothy Joins Paul and Silas

Acts 16 ¹Paul came also to Derbe and to Lystra. A disciple was there, named Timothy, the son of a Jewish woman who was a believer, but his father was a Greek. ² He was well spoken of by the brothers at Lystra and Iconium. ³ Paul wanted Timothy to accompany him, and he took him and circumcised him because of the Jews who were in those places, for they all knew that his father was a Greek. ⁴ As they went on their way through the cities, they delivered to them for observance the decisions that had been reached by the apostles and elders who were in Jerusalem. ⁵ So the churches were strengthened in the faith, and they increased in numbers daily.

The Macedonian Call

⁶ And they went through the region of Phrygia and Galatia, having been forbidden by the Holy Spirit to speak the word in Asia. ⁷ And when they had come up to Mysia, they attempted to go into Bithynia, but the Spirit of Jesus did not allow them. ⁸ So, passing by Mysia, they went down to Troas. ⁹ And a vision appeared to Paul in the night: a man of Macedonia was standing there, urging him and saying, "Come over to Macedonia and help us." ¹⁰ And when Paul had seen the vision, immediately we sought to go on into Macedonia, concluding that God had called us to preach the gospel to them.

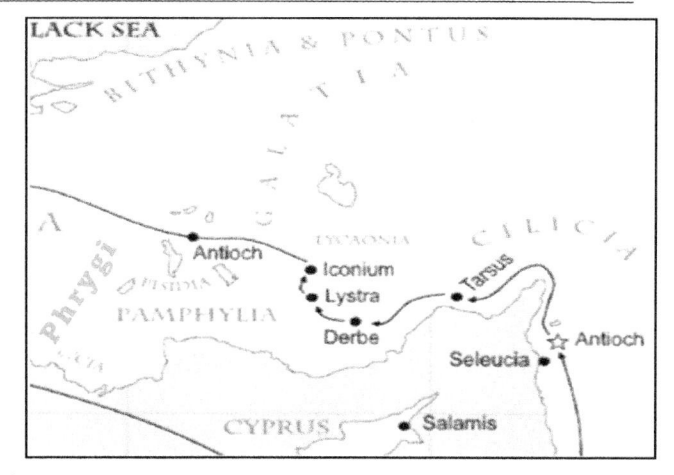

An observation: In Acts 16:7 and 8, Luke writes 'they', whereas in verse 10, Luke writes 'we'. This appears to indicate that it was in Troas that Luke joined Paul and his other companions. It is possible that Luke may have been in Ephesus when Apollos was there and also when Paul arrived in Ephesus, but it was in Troas when Luke was 'invited' to join Paul and his other companions.

The Compiled Teachings of The Apostle Paul

The Conversion of Lydia at Phillipi

16: *¹¹ So, setting sail from Troas, we made a direct voyage to Samothrace, and the following day to Neapolis, ¹² and from there to Philippi, which is a leading city of the district of Macedonia and a Roman colony. We remained in this city some days. ¹³ And on the Sabbath day we went outside the gate to the riverside, where we supposed there was a place of prayer, and we sat down and spoke to the women who had come together. ¹⁴ One who heard us was a woman named Lydia, from the city of Thyatira, a seller of purple goods, who was a worshiper of God. The Lord opened her heart to pay attention to what was said by Paul. ¹⁵ And after she was baptized, and her household as well, she urged us, saying, "If you have judged me to be faithful to the Lord, come to my house and stay." And she prevailed upon us.*

Paul and Silas in Prison

¹⁶ As we were going to the place of prayer, we were met by a slave girl who had a spirit of divination and brought her owners much gain by fortune-telling. ¹⁷ She followed Paul and us, crying out, "These men are servants of the Most High God, who proclaim to you the way of salvation." ¹⁸ And this she kept doing for many days. Paul, having become greatly annoyed, turned and said to the spirit, "I command you in the name of Jesus Christ to come out of her." And it came out that very hour.
¹⁹ But when her owners saw that their hope of gain was gone, they seized Paul and Silas and dragged them into the marketplace before the rulers. ²⁰ And when they had brought them to the magistrates, they said, "These men are Jews, and they are disturbing our city. ²¹ They advocate customs that are not lawful for us as Romans to accept or practice."
²² The crowd joined in attacking them, and the magistrates tore the garments off them and gave orders to beat them with rods. ²³ And when they had inflicted many blows upon them, they threw them into prison, ordering the jailer to keep them safely. ²⁴ Having received this order, he put them into the inner prison and fastened their feet in the stocks.

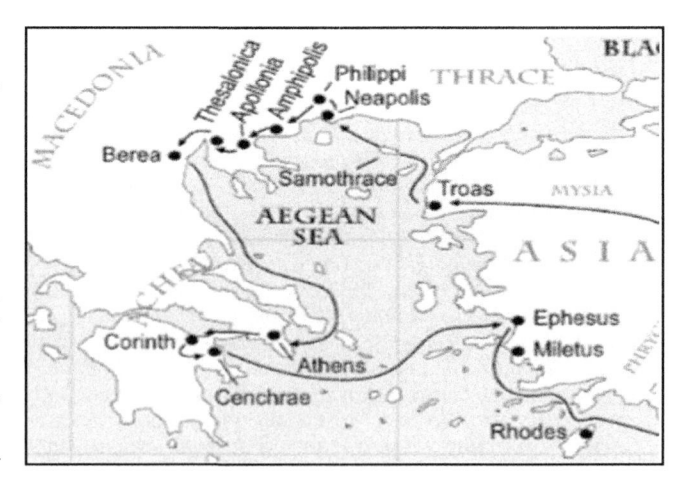

The Philippian Jailer Converted

Acts 16:²⁵ About midnight Paul and Silas were praying and singing hymns to God, and the prisoners were listening to them, ²⁶ and suddenly there was a great earthquake, so that the foundations of the prison were shaken. And immediately all the doors were opened, and everyone's bonds were unfastened. ²⁷ When the jailer woke and saw that the prison doors were open, he drew his sword and was about to kill himself, supposing that the prisoners had escaped. ²⁸ But Paul cried with a loud voice, "Do not harm yourself, for we are all here." ²⁹ And the jailer called for lights and rushed in, and trembling with fear he fell down before Paul and Silas. ³⁰ Then he brought them out and said, "Sirs, what must I do to be saved?" ³¹ And they said, "Believe in the Lord Jesus, and you will be saved, you and your household." ³² And they spoke the word of the Lord to him and to all who were in his house. ³³ And he took them the same hour of the night and washed their wounds; and he was baptized at once, he and all his family. ³⁴ Then he brought them up into his house and set food before them. And he rejoiced along with his entire household that he had believed in God.

** While Paul is in jail in Philippi he writes letters to the churches in Galatia and Corinth.

Paul Reports That He Is A Roman Citizen

³⁵ But when it was day, the magistrates sent the police, saying, "Let those men go." ³⁶ And the jailer reported these words to Paul, saying, "The magistrates have sent to let you go. Therefore come out now and go in peace." ³⁷ But Paul said to them, "They have beaten us publicly, uncondemned, **men who are Roman citizens**, and have thrown us into prison; and do they now throw us out secretly? No! Let them come themselves and take us out." ³⁸ The police reported these words to the magistrates, and they were afraid when they heard that they were Roman citizens. ³⁹ So they came and apologized to them. And they took them out and asked them to leave the city. ⁴⁰ So they went out of the prison and visited Lydia. And when they had seen the brothers, they encouraged them and departed.

The Compiled Teachings of The Apostle Paul

Paul and Silas in Thessalonica

Paul and Silas, travelled through Antioch in Pisidia, to Philippi, Amphipolis and Apollonia to Thessalonica.

Now to get to these four cities, Paul and Silas had to travel via Troas to the north-eastern region of modern-day Greece, east of the region of Macedonia.

On three Sabbath days, meaning that Paul and Silas were in Thessalonica for at least 15 days and being hosted by Jason a resident of Thessalonica, Paul preached and debated in the synagogue. The result was that Jason's home was besieged by an angry mob that had been riled up by the leaders of the Jewish community, and Jason and some of the brothers (believers of the Gospel) were brought before the city authorities; the Jews filing accusations that Paul and Silas were conspiring in some fashion against Caesar, citing that they were claiming there was a king, one who would (or could) oppose Caesar.

> *17 Now when they had passed through Amphipolis and Apollonia, they came to Thessalonica, where there was a synagogue of the Jews. ² And Paul went in, as was his custom, and on three Sabbath days he reasoned with them from the Scriptures, ³ explaining and proving that it was necessary for the Christ to suffer and to rise from the dead, and saying, "This Jesus, whom I proclaim to you, is the Christ." ⁴ And some of them were persuaded and joined Paul and Silas, as did a great many of the devout Greeks and not a few of the leading women. ⁵ But the Jews were jealous, and taking some wicked men of the rabble, they formed a mob, set the city in an uproar, and attacked the house of Jason, seeking to bring them out to the crowd. ⁶ And when they could not find them, they dragged Jason and some of the brothers before the city authorities, shouting, "These men who have turned the world upside down have come here also, ⁷ and Jason has received them, and they are all acting against the decrees of Caesar, saying that there is another king, Jesus." ⁸ And the people and the city authorities were disturbed when they heard these things. ⁹ And when they had taken money as security from Jason and the rest, they let them go.*

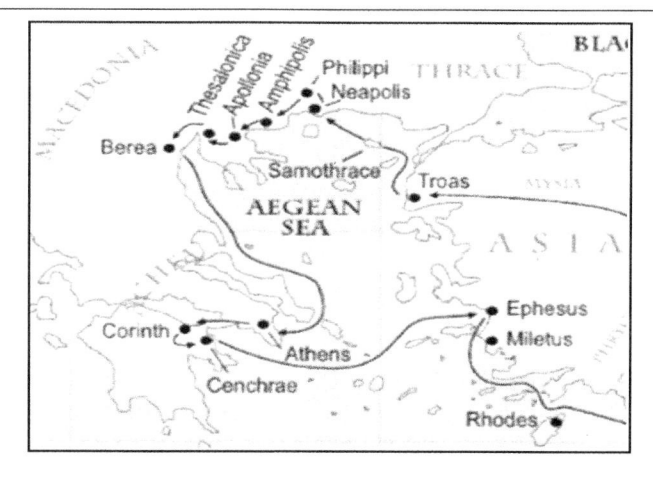

In other words, this was a civil complaint, not an accusation of them acting against their own Jewish community. The result was that security money, i.e. bail, was extracted from Jason and possibly from others too.

On Paul's second missionary journey he travelled via Tarsus through Syria into modern-day Turkey and then sailed across the Aegean Sea to Neapolis, and then to Philippi which Paul and Barnabas had visited on their first journey.[1]

The next reports of teaching in Acts are in chapter 17 where Paul first is in Berea in Macedonia, and then is in Greece, in the city of Athens.

Paul and Silas in Berea

The brothers, Jason and others, helped Paul and Silas leave Thessalonica under the cover of darkness, and Paul and Silas travelled to Berea. The reception that they received in Berea was initially much more positive until Jews came from Thessalonica to agitate 'and stir up the crowds'. Paul then left Berea and sailed to Athens where he waited for Silas and Timothy.

> *Acts 17:¹⁰ The brothers immediately sent Paul and Silas away by night to Berea, and when they arrived they went into the Jewish synagogue. ¹¹ Now these Jews were more noble than those in Thessalonica; they received the word with all eagerness, examining the Scriptures daily to see if these things were so. ¹² Many of them therefore believed, with not a few Greek women of high standing as well as men. ¹³ But when the Jews from Thessalonica learned that the word of God was proclaimed by Paul at Berea also, they came there too, agitating and stirring up the crowds. ¹⁴ Then the brothers immediately sent Paul off on his way to the sea, but Silas and Timothy remained there. ¹⁵ Those who conducted Paul brought him as far as Athens, and after receiving a command for Silas and Timothy to come to him as soon as possible, they departed.*

The Compiled Teachings of The Apostle Paul

Paul in Athens

While waiting in Athens Paul observed that the Athenians worshipped idols, and engaged not only the Jews but also Epicurean and Stoic philosophers in debate.

17 ⁱ⁶ Now while Paul was waiting for them at Athens, his spirit was provoked within him as he saw that the city was full of idols. ¹⁷ So he reasoned in the synagogue with the Jews and the devout persons, and in the marketplace every day with those who happened to be there. ¹⁸ Some of the Epicurean and Stoic philosophers also conversed with him. And some said, "What does this babbler wish to say?" Others said, "He seems to be a preacher of foreign divinities"—because he was preaching Jesus and the resurrection. ¹⁹ And they took him and brought him to the Areopagus, saying, "May we know what this new teaching is that you are presenting? ²⁰ For you bring some strange things to our ears. We wish to know therefore what these things mean."

Acts 17:²¹ Now all the Athenians and the foreigners who lived there would spend their time in nothing except telling or hearing something new. ²² So Paul, standing in the midst of the Areopagus, said: "Men of Athens, I perceive that in every way you are very religious.

²³ For as I passed along and observed the objects of your worship, I found also an altar with this inscription: 'To the unknown god.' What therefore you worship as unknown, this I proclaim to you. ²⁴ The God who made the world and everything in it, being Lord of heaven and earth, does not live in temples made by man, ²⁵ nor is he served by human hands, as though he needed anything, since he himself gives to all mankind life and breath and everything. ²⁶ And he made from one man every nation of mankind to live on all the face of the earth, having determined allotted periods and the boundaries of their dwelling place, ²⁷ that they should seek God, and perhaps feel their way toward him and find him. Yet he is actually not far from each one of us, ²⁸ for "'In him we live and move and have our being'; as even some of your own poets have said, "'For we are indeed his offspring.'

²⁹ Being then God's offspring, we ought not to think that the divine being is like gold or silver or stone, an image formed by the art and imagination of man. ³⁰ The times of ignorance God overlooked, but now he commands all people everywhere to repent, ³¹ because he has fixed a day on which he will judge the world in righteousness by a man whom he has appointed; and of this he has given assurance to all by raising him from the dead."

³² Now when they heard of the resurrection of the dead, some mocked. But others said, "We will hear you again about this." ³³ So Paul went out from their midst. ³⁴ But some men joined him and believed, among whom also were Dionysius the Areopagite and a woman named Damaris and others with them.

Paul in Corinth

Paul did not stay in Athens even though Silas and Timothy had not yet caught up with him.

Paul travelled on to Corinth where he was welcomed by Aquila and Priscilla, a husband and wife from Italy. Aquila and Priscilla had left Italy because the Emperor Claudius had commanded all the Jews to leave Rome. Aquila and Priscilla were tent makers, a trade that Paul had been trained in, and this provided Paul with the opportunity to work as a tent maker to provide for his accommodation. Every Sabbath Paul would attend the synagogue and debate with both Jews and Greeks. When Silas and Timothy caught up with Paul in Corinth, they found Paul in debate *'testifying to the Jews that the Christ was Jesus.'* (v5). In verse 6 we read, *⁶ And when they opposed and reviled him, he shook out his garments and said to them, "Your blood be on your own heads! I am innocent. From now on I will go to the Gentiles."* Paul then went to the home of Titius Justus, *a worshiper of God'* (v7) which was close by the synagogue. And then we read, *'Crispus, the ruler of the synagogue, believed in the Lord, together with his entire household. And many of the Corinthians hearing Paul believed and were baptized.'* (v8)

Acts 18 After this Paul left Athens and went to Corinth. ² And he found a Jew named Aquila, a native of Pontus, recently come from Italy with his wife Priscilla, because Claudius had commanded all the Jews to leave Rome. And he went to see them, ³ and because he was of the same trade he stayed with them and worked, for they were tentmakers by trade. ⁴ And he reasoned in the synagogue every Sabbath, and tried to persuade Jews and Greeks.

⁵ When Silas and Timothy arrived from Macedonia, Paul was occupied with the word, testifying to the Jews that the Christ was Jesus. ⁶ And when they opposed and reviled him, he shook out his garments and said to them, "Your blood be on your own heads! I am innocent. From now on I will go to the Gentiles." ⁷ And he left there and went to the house of a man named Titius Justus, a worshiper of God. His house was next door to the synagogue. ⁸ Crispus, the ruler of the synagogue, believed in the Lord, together with his entire household. And many of the Corinthians hearing Paul believed and were baptized.

This suggests that the home of Titius Justus may have been the first meeting place for believers in Corinth, and that Crispus was a visitor there.

In verse 9 we read, *17:⁹ And the Lord said to Paul one night in a vision, "Do not be afraid, but go on speaking and do not be silent, ¹⁰ for I am with you, and no one will attack you to harm you, for I have many in this city who are my people." ¹¹ And he stayed a year and six months, teaching the word of God among them.*

Acts 18 ¹² *But when Gallio was proconsul of Achaia, the Jews made a united attack on Paul and brought him before the tribunal,* ¹³ *saying, "This man is persuading people to worship God contrary to the law."* ¹⁴ *But when Paul was about to open his mouth, Gallio said to the Jews, "If it were a matter of wrongdoing or vicious crime, O Jews, I would have reason to accept your complaint.* ¹⁵ *But since it is a matter of questions about words and names and your own law, see to it yourselves. I refuse to be a judge of these things."* ¹⁶ *And he drove them from the tribunal.* ¹⁷ *And they all seized Sosthenes, the ruler of the synagogue, and beat him in front of the tribunal. But Gallio paid no attention to any of this.*

So rather than Paul being subjected to trial and judgment, it was Sosthenes, the ruler of the synagogue who was punished.

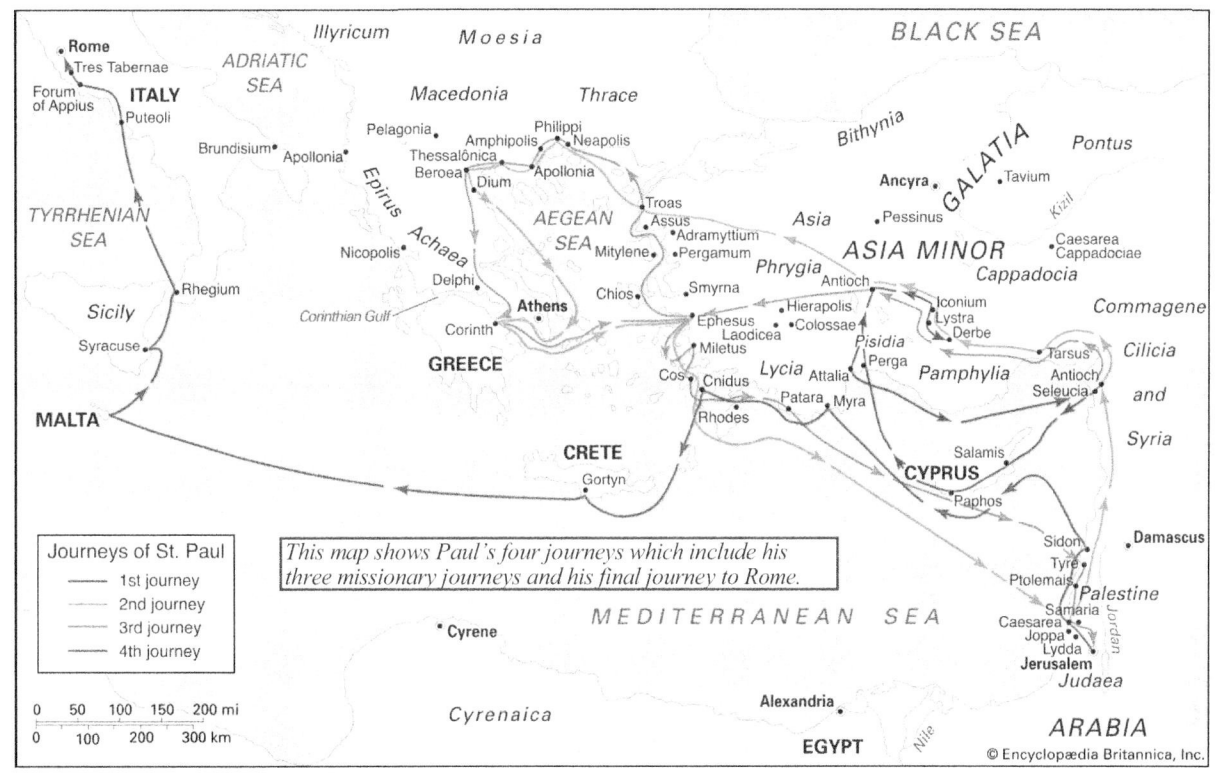

This map shows Paul's four journeys which include his three missionary journeys and his final journey to Rome.

Paul's Third Missionary Trip

Paul Returns to Antioch

18 ¹⁸ *After this, Paul stayed many days longer and then took leave of the brothers and set sail for Syria, and with him Priscilla and Aquila. At Cenchreae he had cut his hair, for he was under a vow.* ¹⁹ *And they came to Ephesus, and he left them there, but he himself went into the synagogue and reasoned with the Jews.* ²⁰ *When they asked him to stay for a longer period, he declined.* ²¹ *But on taking leave of them he said, "I will return to you if God wills," and he set sail from Ephesus.*

²² *When he had landed at Caesarea, he went up and greeted the church, and then went down to Antioch.* ²³ *After spending some time there, he departed and went from one place to the next through the region of Galatia and Phrygia, strengthening all the disciples.*

Apollos Speaks Boldly in Ephesus

²⁴ *Now a Jew named Apollos, a native of Alexandria, came to Ephesus. He was an eloquent man, competent in the Scriptures.* ²⁵ *He had been instructed in the way of the Lord. And being fervent in spirit, he spoke and taught accurately the things concerning Jesus, though he knew only the baptism of John.* ²⁶ *He began to speak boldly in the synagogue, but when Priscilla and Aquila heard him, they took him aside and explained to him the way of God more accurately.* ²⁷ *And when he wished to cross to Achaia, the brothers encouraged him and wrote to the disciples to welcome him. When he arrived, he greatly helped those who through grace had believed,* ²⁸ *for he powerfully refuted the Jews in public, showing by the Scriptures that the Christ was Jesus.*

Paul Returns to Ephesus

Acts 19 And it happened that while Apollos was at Corinth, Paul passed through the inland country and came to Ephesus. **There he found some disciples.** *²* **And he said to them, "Did you receive the Holy Spirit when you believed?" And they said, "No, we have not even heard that there is a Holy Spirit."** *³* **And he said, "Into what then were you baptized?" They said, "Into John's baptism."** *⁴* **And Paul said, "John baptized with the baptism of repentance, telling the people to believe in the one who was to come after him, that is, Jesus."** *⁵* **On hearing this, they were baptized in the name of the Lord Jesus.** *⁶* **And when Paul had laid his hands on them, the Holy Spirit came on them, and they began speaking in tongues and prophesying.** *⁷* **There were about twelve men in all.**

⁸ And he entered the synagogue and for three months spoke boldly, reasoning and persuading them about the kingdom of God. ⁹ But when some became stubborn and continued in unbelief, speaking evil of the Way before the congregation, he withdrew from them and took the disciples with him, reasoning daily in the hall of Tyrannus. ¹⁰ This continued for two years, so that all the residents of Asia heard the word of the Lord, both Jews and Greeks.

Acts 19 ¹¹ And God was doing extraordinary miracles by the hands of Paul, ¹² so that even handkerchiefs or aprons that had touched his skin were carried away to the sick, and their diseases left them and the evil spirits came out of them. ¹³ Then some of the itinerant Jewish exorcists undertook to invoke the name of the Lord Jesus over those who had evil spirits, saying, "I adjure you by the Jesus whom Paul proclaims." ¹⁴ Seven sons of a Jewish high priest named Sceva were doing this. ¹⁵ But the evil spirit answered them, "Jesus I know, and Paul I recognize, but who are you?" ¹⁶ And the man in whom was the evil spirit leaped on them, mastered all of them and overpowered them, so that they fled out of that house naked and wounded. ¹⁷ And this became known to all the residents of Ephesus, both Jews and Greeks. And fear fell upon them all, and the name of the Lord Jesus was extolled. ¹⁸ Also many of those who were now believers came, confessing and divulging their practices. ¹⁹ And a number of those who had practiced magic arts brought their books together and burned them in the sight of all. And they counted the value of them and found it came to fifty thousand pieces of silver. ²⁰ So the word of the Lord continued to increase and prevail mightily.

Acts 19 ²¹ Now after these events Paul resolved in the Spirit to pass through Macedonia and Achaia and go to Jerusalem, saying, "After I have been there, I must also see Rome." ²² And having sent into Macedonia two of his helpers, Timothy and Erastus, he himself stayed in Asia (in Ephesus) for a while.

²³ About that time there arose no little disturbance concerning the Way. ²⁴ For a man named Demetrius, a silversmith, who made silver shrines of Artemis, brought no little business to the craftsmen. ²⁵ These he gathered together, with the workmen in similar trades, and said, **"Men, you know that from this business we have our wealth. ²⁶ And you see and hear that not only in Ephesus but in almost all of Asia this Paul has persuaded and turned away a great many people, saying that gods made with hands are not gods.** *²⁷ And there is danger not only that this trade of ours may come into disrepute but also that the temple of the great goddess Artemis may be counted as nothing, and that she may even be deposed from her magnificence, she whom all Asia and the world worship."*

²⁸ When they heard this they were enraged and were crying out, "Great is Artemis of the Ephesians!" **²⁹ So the city was filled with the confusion, and they rushed together into the theater, dragging with them Gaius and Aristarchus, Macedonians who were Paul's companions in travel. ³⁰ But when Paul wished to go in among the crowd, the disciples would not let him.** *³¹ And even some of the Asiarchs, who were friends of his, sent to him and were urging him not to venture into the theater. ³² Now some cried out one thing, some another, for the assembly was in confusion, and most of them did not know why they had come together. ³³ Some of the crowd prompted Alexander, whom the Jews had put forward. And Alexander, motioning with his hand, wanted to make a defense to the crowd. ³⁴ But when they recognized that he was a Jew, for about two hours they all cried out with one voice, "Great is Artemis of the Ephesians!"*

³⁵ And when the town clerk had quieted the crowd, he said, **"Men of Ephesus, who is there who does not know that the city of the Ephesians is temple keeper of the great Artemis, and of the sacred stone that fell from the sky? ³⁶ Seeing then that these things cannot be denied, you ought to be quiet and do nothing rash.** *³⁷* **For you have brought these men here who are neither sacrilegious nor blasphemers of our goddess. ³⁸ If therefore Demetrius and the craftsmen with him have a complaint against anyone, the courts are open, and there are proconsuls. Let them bring charges against one another. ³⁹ But if you seek anything further it shall be settled in the regular assembly. ⁴⁰ For we really are in danger of being charged with rioting today, since there is no cause that we can give to justify this commotion."** *⁴¹ And when he had said these things, he dismissed the assembly.*

The Compiled Teachings of The Apostle Paul

Paul in Macedonia and Greece

*Acts 20 After the uproar ceased, Paul sent for the disciples, and after encouraging them, he said farewell and departed for Macedonia. ² When he had gone through those regions and had given them much encouragement, he came to Greece. ³ There he spent three months, and when a plot was made against him by the Jews as he was about to set sail for Syria, he decided to return through Macedonia. ⁴ Sopater the Berean, son of Pyrrhus, accompanied him; and of the Thessalonians, Aristarchus and Secundus; and Gaius of Derbe, and Timothy; and the Asians, Tychicus and Trophimus. ⁵ **These went on ahead and were waiting for us at Troas**, ⁶ **but we sailed away** from Philippi after the days of Unleavened Bread, and in five days we came to them at Troas, **where we stayed for seven days**.*

Luke rejoins Paul on His Mission

In Acts 16:7 and 16:8, Luke wrote 'they', whereas in verse 10, Luke wrote 'we', which appears to indicate that it was in Troas that Luke joined Paul and his other companions. Here in Acts 20:5-6, the words 'us' and then 'we' are used suggesting that from Philippi onwards, Luke is again including himself among those travelling with Paul.

Eutychus is Raised from the Dead

Acts 20 ⁷ On the first day of the week, when we were gathered together to break bread, Paul talked with them, intending to depart on the next day, and he prolonged his speech until midnight. ⁸ There were many lamps in the upper room where we were gathered. ⁹ And a young man named Eutychus, sitting at the window, sank into a deep sleep as Paul talked still longer. And being overcome by sleep, he fell down from the third story and was taken up dead. ¹⁰ But Paul went down and bent over him, and taking him in his arms, said, "Do not be alarmed, for his life is in him." ¹¹ And when Paul had gone up and had broken bread and eaten, he conversed with them a long while, until daybreak, and so departed. ¹² And they took the youth away alive, and were not a little comforted.

¹³ But going ahead to the ship, we set sail for Assos, intending to take Paul aboard there, for so he had arranged, intending himself to go by land. ¹⁴ And when he met us at Assos, we took him on board and went to Mitylene. ¹⁵ And sailing from there we came the following day opposite Chios; the next day we touched at Samos; and the day after that we went to Miletus. ¹⁶ For Paul had decided to sail past Ephesus, so that he might not have to spend time in Asia, for he was hastening to be at Jerusalem, if possible, on the day of Pentecost.

Paul Speaks to the Ephesian Elders

Acts 20 ¹⁷ Now from Miletus he sent to Ephesus and called the elders of the church to come to him. ¹⁸ And when they came to him, he said to them:

*"You yourselves know how I lived among you the whole time from the first day that I set foot in Asia, ¹⁹ serving the Lord with all humility and with tears and with trials that happened to me through the plots of the Jews; ²⁰ how **I did not shrink from declaring to you anything that was profitable, and teaching you in public and from house to house,** ²¹ **testifying both to Jews and to Greeks of repentance toward God and of faith in our Lord Jesus Christ.** ²² **And now, behold, I am going to Jerusalem, constrained by the Spirit, not knowing what will happen to me there,** ²³ **except that the Holy Spirit testifies to me in every city that imprisonment and afflictions await me.** ²⁴ **But I do not account my life of any value nor as precious to myself, if only I may finish my course and the ministry that I received from the Lord Jesus, to testify to the gospel of the grace of God.** ²⁵ And now, behold, I know that none of you among whom I have gone about proclaiming the kingdom will see my face again. ²⁶ **Therefore I testify to you this day that I am innocent of the blood of all,** ²⁷ **for I did not shrink from declaring to you the whole counsel of God.** ²⁸ **Pay careful attention to yourselves and to all the flock, in which the Holy Spirit has made you overseers, to care for the church of God, which he obtained with his own blood.** ²⁹ I know that after my departure **fierce wolves will come in among you, not sparing the flock;** ³⁰ **and from among your own selves will arise men speaking twisted things, to draw away the disciples after them.** ³¹ **Therefore be alert, remembering that for three years I did not cease night or day to admonish every one with tears.** ³² **And now I commend you to God and to the word of his grace, which is able to build you up and to give you the inheritance among all those who are sanctified.** ³³ I coveted no one's silver or gold or apparel. ³⁴ You yourselves know that these hands ministered to my necessities and to those who were with me. ³⁵ In all things I have shown you that by working hard in this way **we must help the weak and remember the words of the Lord Jesus, how he himself said, 'It is more blessed to give than to receive.'"***

³⁶ And when he had said these things, he knelt down and prayed with them all. ³⁷ And there was much weeping on the part of all; they embraced Paul and kissed him, ³⁸ being sorrowful most of all because of the word he had spoken, that they would not see his face again. And they accompanied him to the ship.

The Compiled Teachings of The Apostle Paul

Paul Goes to Jerusalem

Acts 21 And when we had parted from them [in Miletus] and set sail, we came by a straight course to Cos [Kos], and the next day to Rhodes, and from there to Patara. [2] And having found a ship crossing to Phoenicia, we went aboard and set sail. [3] When we had come in sight of Cyprus, leaving it on the left we sailed to Syria and landed at Tyre, for there the ship was to unload its cargo. [4] And having sought out the disciples, we stayed there for seven days. And through the Spirit they were telling Paul not to go on to Jerusalem.

[5] When our days there were ended, we departed and went on our journey, and they all, with wives and children, accompanied us until we were outside the city. And kneeling down on the beach, we prayed [6] and said farewell to one another. Then we went on board the ship, and they returned home.

21 *[7] When we had finished the voyage from Tyre, we arrived at Ptolemais, and we greeted the brothers and stayed with them for one day. [8] On the next day we departed and came to Caesarea, and we entered the house of Philip the evangelist, who was one of the seven, and stayed with him. [9] He had four unmarried daughters, who prophesied.* **[10] While we were staying for many days, a prophet named Agabus came down from Judea. [11] And coming to us, he took Paul's belt and bound his own feet and hands and said, "Thus says the Holy Spirit, 'This is how the Jews at Jerusalem will bind the man who owns this belt and deliver him into the hands of the Gentiles.'" [12] When we heard this, we and the people there urged him not to go up to Jerusalem.**

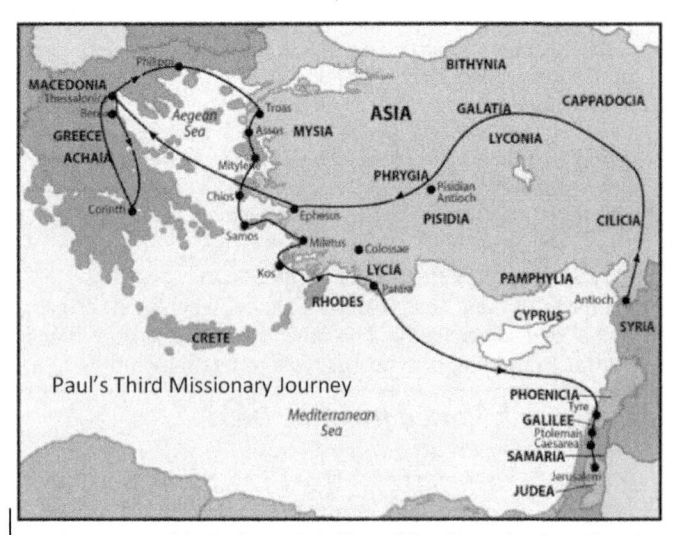

[13] Then Paul answered, "What are you doing, weeping and breaking my heart? For I am ready not only to be imprisoned but even to die in Jerusalem for the name of the Lord Jesus." [14] And since he would not be persuaded, we ceased and said, "Let the will of the Lord be done."

Acts 21 [15] After these days we got ready and went up to Jerusalem. [16] And some of the disciples from Caesarea went with us, bringing us to the house of Mnason of Cyprus, an early disciple, with whom we should lodge.

Paul Visits James

Acts 21 [17] When we had come to Jerusalem, the brothers received us gladly. [18] On the following day Paul went in with us to James, and all the elders were present. [19] After greeting them, he related one by one the things that God had done among the Gentiles through his ministry. [20] And when they heard it, they glorified God. And they said to him, "You see, brother, how many thousands there are among the Jews of those who have believed. They are all zealous for the law, [21] and they have been told about you that you teach all the Jews who are among the Gentiles to forsake Moses, telling them not to circumcise their children or walk according to our customs. [22] What then is to be done? They will certainly hear that you have come. [23] Do therefore what we tell you. We have four men who are under a vow; [24] take these men and purify yourself along with them and pay their expenses, so that they may shave their heads. Thus all will know that there is nothing in what they have been told about you, but that you yourself also live in observance of the law. **[25] But as for the Gentiles who have believed, we have sent a letter with our judgment that they should abstain from what has been sacrificed to idols, and from blood, and from what has been strangled, and from sexual immorality."** *[26] Then Paul took the men, and the next day he purified himself along with them and went into the temple, giving notice when the days of purification would be fulfilled and the offering presented for each one of them.*

Paul Arrested in the Temple in Jerusalem

Acts 21 [27] When the seven days were almost completed, the Jews from Asia, seeing him in the temple, stirred up the whole crowd and laid hands on him, [28] crying out, "Men of Israel, help! **This is the man who is teaching everyone everywhere against the people and the law and this place.** *Moreover, he even brought Greeks into the temple and has defiled this holy place." [29] For they had previously seen Trophimus the Ephesian with him in the city, and they supposed that Paul had brought him into the temple.* **[30] Then all the city was stirred up, and the people ran together. They seized Paul and dragged him out of the temple, and at once the gates were shut. [31] And as they were seeking to kill him, word came to the tribune of the cohort that all Jerusalem was in confusion. [32] He at once took soldiers and centurions and ran down to them. And when they saw the tribune and the soldiers, they stopped beating Paul. [33] Then the tribune came up and arrested him and ordered him to be bound with two chains. He inquired who he was and what he had done. [34] Some in the crowd were shouting one thing, some another. And as he could not learn the facts because of the uproar, he ordered him to be brought into the barracks. [35] And when he came to the steps, he was actually carried by the soldiers because [for fear] of the violence of the crowd, [36] for the mob of the people followed, crying out, "Away with him!"**

The Compiled Teachings of The Apostle Paul

Paul Speaks to the People

Acts 21 ³⁷ As Paul was about to be brought into the barracks, he said to the tribune, "May I say something to you?" And he said, "Do you know Greek? ³⁸ Are you not the Egyptian, then, who recently stirred up a revolt and led the four thousand men of the Assassins out into the wilderness?" ³⁹ Paul replied, "I am a Jew, from Tarsus in Cilicia, a citizen of no obscure city. I beg you, permit me to speak to the people." ⁴⁰ And when he had given him permission, Paul, standing on the steps, motioned with his hand to the people. And when there was a great hush, he addressed them in the Hebrew language, saying:

Acts 22 "Brothers and fathers, hear the defense that I now make before you." ² And when they heard that he was addressing them in the Hebrew language, they became even more quiet. And he said: ³ "I am a Jew, born in Tarsus in Cilicia, but brought up in this city, educated at the feet of Gamaliel according to the strict manner of the law of our fathers, being zealous for God as all of you are this day. ⁴ I persecuted this Way to the death, binding and delivering to prison both men and women, ⁵ as the high priest and the whole council of elders can bear me witness. From them I received letters to the brothers, and I journeyed toward Damascus to take those also who were there and bring them in bonds to Jerusalem to be punished.

Paul Shares His Testimony

⁶ "As I was on my way and drew near to Damascus, about noon a great light from heaven suddenly shone around me. ⁷ And I fell to the ground and heard a voice saying to me, 'Saul, Saul, why are you persecuting me?' ⁸ And I answered, 'Who are you, Lord?' And he said to me, 'I am Jesus of Nazareth, whom you are persecuting.' ⁹ Now those who were with me saw the light but did not understand the voice of the one who was speaking to me. ¹⁰ And I said, 'What shall I do, Lord?' And the Lord said to me, 'Rise, and go into Damascus, and there you will be told all that is appointed for you to do.' ¹¹ And since I could not see because of the brightness of that light, I was led by the hand by those who were with me, and came into Damascus.

¹² "And one Ananias, a devout man according to the law, well spoken of by all the Jews who lived there, ¹³ came to me, and standing by me said to me, 'Brother Saul, receive your sight.' And at that very hour I received my sight and saw him. ¹⁴ And he said, 'The God of our fathers appointed you to know his will, to see the Righteous One and to hear a voice from his mouth; ¹⁵ for you will be a witness for him to everyone of what you have seen and heard. ¹⁶ And now why do you wait? Rise and be baptized and wash away your sins, calling on his name.'

¹⁷ "When I had returned to Jerusalem and was praying in the temple, I fell into a trance ¹⁸ and saw him saying to me, 'Make haste and get out of Jerusalem quickly, because they will not accept your testimony about me.' ¹⁹ And I said, 'Lord, they themselves know that in one synagogue after another I imprisoned and beat those who believed in you. ²⁰ And when the blood of Stephen your witness was being shed, I myself was standing by and approving and watching over the garments of those who killed him.' ²¹ And he said to me, 'Go, for I will send you far away to the Gentiles.'"

Paul and the Roman Tribune

Acts 22 ²² Up to this word they listened to him. Then they raised their voices and said, "Away with such a fellow from the earth! For he should not be allowed to live." ²³ And as they were shouting and throwing off their cloaks and flinging dust into the air, ²⁴ the tribune ordered him to be brought into the barracks, saying that he should be examined by flogging, to find out why they were shouting against him like this. ²⁵ But when they had stretched him out for the whips, Paul said to the centurion who was standing by, "Is it lawful for you to flog a man who is a Roman citizen and uncondemned?" ²⁶ When the centurion heard this, he went to the tribune and said to him, "What are you about to do? For this man is a Roman citizen." ²⁷ So the tribune came and said to him, "Tell me, are you a Roman citizen?" And he said, "Yes." ²⁸ The tribune answered, "I bought this citizenship for a large sum." Paul said, "But I am a citizen by birth." ²⁹ So those who were about to examine him withdrew from him immediately, and the tribune also was afraid, for he realized that Paul was a Roman citizen and that he had bound him.

Paul Before the Council

Acts 22 ³⁰ But on the next day, desiring to know the real reason why he was being accused by the Jews, he unbound him and commanded the chief priests and all the council to meet, and he brought Paul down and set him before them.

Acts 23 And looking intently at the council, Paul said, "Brothers, I have lived my life before God in all good conscience up to this day." ² And the high priest Ananias commanded those who stood by him to strike him on the mouth. ³ Then Paul said to him, "God is going to strike you, you whitewashed wall! Are you sitting to judge me according to the law, and yet contrary to the law you order me to be struck?" ⁴ Those who stood by said, "Would you revile God's high priest?" ⁵ And Paul said, "I did not know, brothers, that he was the high priest, for it is written, 'You shall not speak evil of a ruler of your people.'"

*⁶ **Now when Paul perceived that one part were Sadducees and the other Pharisees, he cried out in the council, "Brothers, I am a Pharisee, a son of Pharisees. It is with respect to the hope and the resurrection of the dead that I am on trial."** ⁷ And when he had said this, a dissension arose between the Pharisees and the Sadducees, and the assembly was divided. ⁸ **For the Sadducees say that there is no resurrection, nor angel, nor spirit, but the Pharisees acknowledge them all.** ⁹ Then a great clamor arose, and some of the scribes of the Pharisees' party stood up and contended sharply, "We find nothing wrong in this man. What if a spirit or an angel spoke to him?" ¹⁰ And when the dissension became violent, the tribune, afraid that Paul would be torn to pieces by them, commanded the soldiers to go down and take him away from among them by force and bring him into the barracks.*

¹¹ The following night the Lord stood by him and said, "Take courage, for as you have testified to the facts about me in Jerusalem, so you must testify also in Rome."

The Compiled Teachings of The Apostle Paul

A Plot to Kill Paul

Acts 23 [12] When it was day, the Jews made a plot and bound themselves by an oath neither to eat nor drink till they had killed Paul. [13] There were more than forty who made this conspiracy. [14] They went to the chief priests and elders and said, "We have strictly bound ourselves by an oath to taste no food till we have killed Paul. [15] Now therefore you, along with the council, give notice to the tribune to bring him down to you, as though you were going to determine his case more exactly. And we are ready to kill him before he comes near."

[16] Now the son of Paul's sister heard of their ambush, so he went and entered the barracks and told Paul. [17] Paul called one of the centurions and said, "Take this young man to the tribune, for he has something to tell him." [18] So he took him and brought him to the tribune and said, "Paul the prisoner called me and asked me to bring this young man to you, as he has something to say to you." [19] The tribune took him by the hand, and going aside asked him privately, "What is it that you have to tell me?" [20] And he said, "The Jews have agreed to ask you to bring Paul down to the council tomorrow, as though they were going to inquire somewhat more closely about him. [21] But do not be persuaded by them, for more than forty of their men are lying in ambush for him, who have bound themselves by an oath neither to eat nor drink till they have killed him. And now they are ready, waiting for your consent." [22] So the tribune dismissed the young man, charging him, "Tell no one that you have informed me of these things."

Paul Sent to Felix the Governor at Ceasarea

Acts 23 [23] Then he called two of the centurions and said, "Get ready two hundred soldiers, with seventy horsemen and two hundred spearmen to go as far as Caesarea at the third hour of the night. [24] Also provide mounts for Paul to ride and bring him safely to Felix the governor." [25] And he wrote a letter to this effect:
[26] "Claudius Lysias, to his Excellency the governor Felix, greetings. [27] This man was seized by the Jews and was about to be killed by them when I came upon them with the soldiers and rescued him, having learned that he was a Roman citizen. [28] And desiring to know the charge for which they were accusing him, I brought him down to their council. [29] I found that he was being accused about questions of their law, but charged with nothing deserving death or imprisonment. [30] And when it was disclosed to me that there would be a plot against the man, I sent him to you at once, ordering his accusers also to state before you what they have against him."

[31] So the soldiers, according to their instructions, took Paul and brought him by night to Antipatris. [32] And on the next day they returned to the barracks, letting the horsemen go on with him. [33] When they had come to Caesarea and delivered the letter to the governor, they presented Paul also before him. [34] On reading the letter, he asked what province he was from. And when he learned that he was from Cilicia, [35] he said, "I will give you a hearing when your accusers arrive." And he commanded him to be guarded in Herod's praetorium.

Paul Before Felix

Acts 24 And after five days the high priest Ananias came down with some elders and a spokesman, one Tertullus. They laid before the governor their case against Paul. [2] And when he had been summoned, Tertullus began to accuse him, saying: "Since through you we enjoy much peace, and since by your foresight, most excellent Felix, reforms are being made for this nation, [3] in every way and everywhere we accept this with all gratitude. [4] But, to detain you no further, I beg you in your kindness to hear us briefly. [5] For we have found this man a plague, one who stirs up riots among all the Jews throughout the world and is a ringleader of the sect of the Nazarenes. [6] He even tried to profane the temple, but we seized him. [8] By examining him yourself you will be able to find out from him about everything of which we accuse him."

[9] The Jews also joined in the charge, affirming that all these things were so. [10] And when the governor had nodded to him to speak, Paul replied: "Knowing that for many years you have been a judge over this nation, I cheerfully make my defense. [11] You can verify that it is not more than twelve days since I went up to worship in Jerusalem, [12] and they did not find me disputing with anyone or stirring up a crowd, either in the temple or in the synagogues or in the city. [13] Neither can they prove to you what they now bring up against me. [14] But this I confess to you, that according to the Way, which they call a sect, I worship the God of our fathers, believing everything laid down by the Law and written in the Prophets, [15] having a hope in God, which these men themselves accept, that there will be a resurrection of both the just and the unjust. [16] So I always take pains to have a clear conscience toward both God and man. [17] Now after several years I came to bring alms to my nation and to present offerings. [18] While I was doing this, they found me purified in the temple, without any crowd or tumult. But some Jews from Asia [19] they ought to be here before you and to make an accusation, should they have anything against me. [20] Or else let these men themselves say what wrongdoing they found when I stood before the council, [21] other than this one thing that I cried out while standing among them: 'It is with respect to the resurrection of the dead that I am on trial before you this day.'"

Paul Kept in Custody

Acts 24 [22] But Felix, having a rather accurate knowledge of the Way, put them off, saying, "When Lysias the tribune comes down, I will decide your case." [23] Then he gave orders to the centurion that he should be kept in custody but have some liberty, and that none of his friends should be prevented from attending to his needs.

[24] After some days Felix came with his wife Drusilla, who was Jewish, and he sent for Paul and heard him speak about faith in Christ Jesus. [25] And as he reasoned about righteousness and self-control and the coming judgment, Felix was alarmed and said, "Go away for the present. When I get an opportunity I will summon you." [26] At the same time he hoped that money would be given him by Paul. So he sent for him often and conversed with him. [27] When two years had elapsed, Felix was succeeded by Porcius Festus. And desiring to do the Jews a favor, Felix [had] left Paul in prison.

The Compiled Teachings of The Apostle Paul

It seems very plausible that some of the letters that Paul wrote to the churches (Rome, Corinth, Thessalonica, Galatia, Ephesus, Philippi, Colossus) and to individuals (Timothy, Titus, Philemon) were written during this 2-year period when Paul was in prison. Researching to identify which letters might have been written during these two years and which most likely were written later, was determined to be beyond the scope of this book.

Paul Appeals to Caesar

Acts 25 Now three days after Festus had arrived in the province, he went up to Jerusalem from Caesarea. ² And the chief priests and the principal men of the Jews laid out their case against Paul, and they urged him, ³ asking as a favor against Paul that he summon him to Jerusalem — **because they were planning an ambush to kill him on the way.** ⁴ Festus replied that Paul was being kept at Caesarea and that he himself intended to go there shortly. ⁵ "So," said he, "let the men of authority among you go down with me, and if there is anything wrong about the man, let them bring charges against him."

⁶ After he stayed among them not more than eight or ten days, he went down to Caesarea. And the next day he took his seat on the tribunal and ordered Paul to be brought. ⁷ When he had arrived, the Jews who had come down from Jerusalem stood around him, bringing many and serious charges against him that they could not prove. ⁸ **Paul argued in his defense, "Neither against the law of the Jews, nor against the temple, nor against Caesar have I committed any offense."** ⁹ **But Festus, wishing to do the Jews a favor, said to Paul, "Do you wish to go up to Jerusalem and there be tried on these charges before me?"** ¹⁰ **But Paul said, "I am standing before Caesar's tribunal, where I ought to be tried. To the Jews I have done no wrong, as you yourself know very well.** ¹¹ **If then I am a wrongdoer and have committed anything for which I deserve to die, I do not seek to escape death. But if there is nothing to their charges against me, no one can give me up to them. I appeal to Caesar."** ¹² Then Festus, when he had conferred with his council, answered, **"To Caesar you have appealed; to Caesar you shall go."**

Paul Before Agrippa and Bernice

Acts 25 ¹³ Now when some days had passed, Agrippa the king and Bernice arrived at Caesarea and greeted Festus. ¹⁴ And as they stayed there many days, **Festus laid Paul's case before the king, saying, "There is a man left prisoner by Felix,** ¹⁵ **and when I was at Jerusalem, the chief priests and the elders of the Jews laid out their case against him, asking for a sentence of condemnation against him.** ¹⁶ **I answered them that it was not the custom of the Romans to give up anyone before the accused met the accusers face to face and had opportunity to make his defense concerning the charge laid against him.** ¹⁷ So when they came together here, I made no delay, but on the next day took my seat on the tribunal and ordered the man to be brought. ¹⁸ **When the accusers stood up, they brought no charge in his case of such evils as I supposed.** ¹⁹ **Rather they had certain points of dispute with him about their own religion and about a certain Jesus, who was dead, but whom Paul asserted to be alive.** ²⁰ Being at a loss how to investigate these questions, I asked whether he wanted to go to Jerusalem and be tried there regarding them. ²¹ But when Paul had appealed to be kept in custody for the decision of the emperor, I ordered him to be held until I could send him to Caesar." ²² Then Agrippa said to Festus, "I would like to hear the man myself." "Tomorrow," said he, "you will hear him."

²³ So on the next day Agrippa and Bernice came with great pomp, and they entered the audience hall with the military tribunes and the prominent men of the city. Then, at the command of Festus, Paul was brought in. ²⁴ And Festus said, "King Agrippa and all who are present with us, you see this man about whom the whole Jewish people petitioned me, both in Jerusalem and here, shouting that he ought not to live any longer.

²⁵ **But I found that he had done nothing deserving death. And as he himself appealed to the emperor, I decided to go ahead and send him.** ²⁶ But I have nothing definite to write to my lord about him. Therefore I have brought him before you all, and especially before you, King Agrippa, so that, after we have examined him, I may have something to write. ²⁷ For it seems to me unreasonable, in sending a prisoner, not to indicate the charges against him."

Paul's Defense Before Agrippa

Acts 26 ¹ So Agrippa said to Paul, "You have permission to speak for yourself." Then Paul stretched out his hand and made his defense:

² "I consider myself fortunate that it is before you, King Agrippa, I am going to make my defense today against all the accusations of the Jews, ³ especially because you are familiar with all the customs and controversies of the Jews. Therefore I beg you to listen to me patiently.

⁴ "My manner of life from my youth, spent from the beginning among my own nation and in Jerusalem, is known by all the Jews. ⁵ They have known for a long time, if they are willing to testify, that according to the strictest party of our religion I have lived as a Pharisee. ⁶ And now I stand here on trial because of my hope in the promise made by God to our fathers, ⁷ to which our twelve tribes hope to attain, as they earnestly worship night and day. And for this hope I am accused by Jews, O king! ⁸ Why is it thought incredible by any of you that God raises the dead?

⁹ "I myself was convinced that I ought to do many things in opposing the name of Jesus of Nazareth. ¹⁰ And I did so in Jerusalem. I not only locked up many of the saints in prison after receiving authority from the chief priests, but when they were put to death I cast my vote against them. ¹¹ And I punished them often in all the synagogues and tried to make them blaspheme, and in raging fury against them I persecuted them even to foreign cities.

Paul Tells of His Conversion

Acts 26 [12] *"In this connection I journeyed to Damascus with the authority and commission of the chief priests.* [13] *At midday, O king, I saw on the way a light from heaven, brighter than the sun, that shone around me and those who journeyed with me.* [14] *And when we had all fallen to the ground, I heard a voice saying to me in the Hebrew language, 'Saul, Saul, why are you persecuting me? It is hard for you to kick against the goads.'* [15] *And I said, 'Who are you, Lord?' And the Lord said, 'I am Jesus whom you are persecuting.* [16] *But rise and stand upon your feet, for I have appeared to you for this purpose, to appoint you as a servant and witness to the things in which you have seen me and to those in which I will appear to you,* [17] *delivering you from your people and from the Gentiles—to whom I am sending you* [18] *to open their eyes, so that they may turn from darkness to light and from the power of Satan to God, that they may receive forgiveness of sins and a place among those who are sanctified by faith in me.'*

(see also Galatians 11:24)

[19] *"Therefore, O King Agrippa, I was not disobedient to the heavenly vision,* [20] *but declared first to those in Damascus, then in Jerusalem and throughout all the region of Judea, and also to the Gentiles, that they should repent and turn to God, performing deeds in keeping with their repentance.* [21] *For this reason the Jews seized me in the temple and tried to kill me.* [22] *To this day I have had the help that comes from God, and so I stand here testifying both to small and great, saying nothing but what the prophets and Moses said would come to pass:* [23] *that the Christ must suffer and that, by being the first to rise from the dead, he would proclaim light both to our people and to the Gentiles."*

[24] *And as he was saying these things in his defense, Festus said with a loud voice, "Paul, you are out of your mind; your great learning is driving you out of your mind."* [25] *But Paul said, "I am not out of my mind, most excellent Festus, but I am speaking true and rational words.* [26] *For the king knows about these things, and to him I speak boldly. For I am persuaded that none of these things has escaped his notice, for this has not been done in a corner.* [27] *King Agrippa, do you believe the prophets? I know that you believe."* [28] *And Agrippa said to Paul, "In a short time would you persuade me to be a Christian?"* [29] *And Paul said, "Whether short or long, I would to God that not only you but also all who hear me this day might become such as I am—except for these chains."*

[30] *Then the king rose, and the governor and Bernice and those who were sitting with them.* [31] *And when they had withdrawn, they said to one another,* **"This man is doing nothing to deserve death or imprisonment."** [32] **And Agrippa said to Festus, "This man could have been set free if he had not appealed to Caesar."**

Paul Sails for Rome

Acts 27 *And when it was decided that we should sail for Italy, they delivered Paul and some other prisoners to a centurion of the Augustan Cohort named Julius.* [2] *And embarking in a ship of Adamitism, which was about to sail to the ports along the coast of Asia, we put to sea, accompanied by Aristarchus, a Macedonian from Thessalonica.* [3] *The next day we put in at Sidon. And Julius treated Paul kindly and gave him leave to go to his friends and be cared for.* [4] *And putting out to sea from there we sailed under the lee of Cyprus, because the winds were against us.* [5] *And when we had sailed across the open sea along the coast of Cilicia and Pamphylia, we came to Myra in Lycia.* [6] *There the centurion found a ship of Alexandria sailing for Italy and put us on board.* [7] *We sailed slowly for a number of days and arrived with difficulty off Cnidus, and as the wind did not allow us to go farther, we sailed under the lee of Crete off Salmone.* [8] *Coasting along it with difficulty, we came to a place called Fair Havens, near which was the city of Lasea.*

[9] *Since much time had passed, and the voyage was now dangerous because even the Fast was already over, Paul advised them,* [10] *saying, "Sirs, I perceive that the voyage will be with injury and much loss, not only of the cargo and the ship, but also of our lives."* [11] *But the centurion paid more attention to the pilot and to the owner of the ship than to what Paul said.* [12] *And because the harbor was not suitable to spend the winter in, the majority decided to put out to sea from there, on the chance that somehow they could reach Phoenix, a harbor of Crete, facing both southwest and northwest, and spend the winter there.*

The Storm at Sea

[13] *Now when the south wind blew gently, supposing that they had obtained their purpose, they weighed anchor and sailed along Crete, close to the shore.* [14] *But soon a tempestuous wind, called the northeaster, struck down from the land.* [15] *And when the ship was caught and could not face the wind, we gave way to it and were driven along.* [16] *Running under the lee of a small island called Cauda, we managed with difficulty to secure the ship's boat.* [17] *After hoisting it up, they used supports to undergird the ship. Then, fearing that they would run aground on the Syrtis, they lowered the gear, and thus they were driven along.* [18] *Since we were violently storm-tossed, they began the next day to jettison the cargo.* [19] *And on the third day they threw the ship's tackle overboard with their own hands.* [20] *When neither sun nor stars appeared for many days, and no small tempest lay on us, all hope of our being saved was at last abandoned.*

[21] **Since they had been without food for a long time, Paul stood up among them and said, "Men, you should have listened to me and not have set sail from Crete and incurred this injury and loss.** [22] **Yet now I urge you to take heart, for there will be no loss of life among you, but only of the ship.** [23] **For this very night there stood before me an angel of the God to whom I belong and whom I worship,** [24] **and he said, 'Do not be afraid, Paul; you must stand before Caesar. And behold, God has granted you all those who sail with you.'** [25] **So take heart, men, for I have faith in God that it will be exactly as I have been told.** [26] **But we must run aground on some island."**

The Compiled Teachings of The Apostle Paul

²⁷ When the fourteenth night had come, as we were being driven across the Adriatic Sea, about midnight the sailors suspected that they were nearing land. ²⁸ So they took a sounding and found twenty fathoms. A little farther on they took a sounding again and found fifteen fathoms. ²⁹ And fearing that we might run on the rocks, they let down four anchors from the stern and prayed for day to come. ³⁰ And as the sailors were seeking to escape from the ship, and had lowered the ship's boat into the sea under pretense of laying out anchors from the bow, ³¹ Paul said to the centurion and the soldiers, "Unless these men stay in the ship, you cannot be saved." ³² Then the soldiers cut away the ropes of the ship's boat and let it go.

³³ As day was about to dawn, Paul urged them all to take some food, saying, "Today is the fourteenth day that you have continued in suspense and without food, having taken nothing. ³⁴ Therefore I urge you to take some food. For it will give you strength, for not a hair is to perish from the head of any of you." ³⁵ And when he had said these things, he took bread, and giving thanks to God in the presence of all he broke it and began to eat. ³⁶ Then they all were encouraged and ate some food themselves. ³⁷ (We were in all 276 persons in the ship.) ³⁸ And when they had eaten enough, they lightened the ship, throwing out the wheat into the sea.

The Shipwreck

Acts 27 ³⁹ Now when it was day, they did not recognize the land, but they noticed a bay with a beach, on which they planned if possible to run the ship ashore. ⁴⁰ So they cast off the anchors and left them in the sea, at the same time loosening the ropes that tied the rudders. Then hoisting the foresail to the wind they made for the beach. ⁴¹ But striking a reef, they ran the vessel aground. The bow stuck and remained immovable, and the stern was being broken up by the surf. ⁴² The soldiers' plan was to kill the prisoners, lest any should swim away and escape. ⁴³ But the centurion, wishing to save Paul, kept them from carrying out their plan. He ordered those who could swim to jump overboard first and make for the land, ⁴⁴ and the rest on planks or on pieces of the ship. And so it was that all were brought safely to land.

Acts 28 After we were brought safely through, we then learned that the island was called Malta. ² The native people showed us unusual kindness, for they kindled a fire and welcomed us all, because it had begun to rain and was cold. ³ **When Paul had gathered a bundle of sticks and put them on the fire, a viper came out because of the heat and fastened on his hand.** ⁴ **When the native people saw the creature hanging from his hand, they said to one another, "No doubt this man is a murderer. Though he has escaped from the sea, Justice has not allowed him to live."** ⁵ **He, however, shook off the creature into the fire and suffered no harm.** ⁶ **They were waiting for him to swell up or suddenly fall down dead. But when they had waited a long time and saw no misfortune come to him, they changed their minds and said that he was a god.**

⁷ Now in the neighborhood of that place were lands belonging to the chief man of the island, named Publius, who received us and entertained us hospitably for three days. ⁸ It happened that the father of Publius lay sick with fever and dysentery. And Paul visited him and prayed, and putting his hands on him, healed him. ⁹ And when this had taken place, the rest of the people on the island who had diseases also came and were cured. ¹⁰ They also honored us greatly, and when we were about to sail, they put on board whatever we needed.

Acts 28 ¹¹ After three months we set sail in a ship that had wintered in the island, a ship of Alexandria, with the twin gods as a figurehead. ¹² Putting in at Syracuse, we stayed there for three days. ¹³ And from there we made a circuit and arrived at Rhegium. And after one day a south wind sprang up, and on the second day we came to Puteoli. ¹⁴ There we found brothers and were invited to stay with them for seven days. And so we came to Rome. ¹⁵ And the brothers there, when they heard about us, came as far as the Forum of Appius and Three Taverns to meet us. On seeing them, Paul thanked God and took courage. ¹⁶ And when we came into Rome, Paul was allowed to stay by himself, with the soldier who guarded him.

Acts 28 ¹⁷ **After three days he called together the local leaders of the Jews, and when they had gathered, he said to them, "Brothers, though I had done nothing against our people or the customs of our fathers, yet I was delivered as a prisoner from Jerusalem into the hands of the Romans.** ¹⁸ **When they had examined me, they wished to set me at liberty, because there was no reason for the death penalty in my case.** ¹⁹ **But because the Jews objected, I was compelled to appeal to Caesar – though I had no charge to bring against my nation.** ²⁰ **For this reason, therefore, I have asked to see you and speak with you, since it is because of the hope of Israel that I am wearing this chain."** ²¹ And they said to him, "We have received no letters from Judea about you, and none of the brothers coming here has reported or spoken any evil about you. ²² But we desire to hear from you what your views are, for with regard to this sect we know that everywhere it is spoken against."

²³ When they had appointed a day for him, they came to him at his lodging in greater numbers. **From morning till evening he expounded to them, testifying to the kingdom of God and trying to convince them about Jesus both from the Law of Moses and from the Prophets.** ²⁴ And some were convinced by what he said, but others disbelieved. ²⁵ And disagreeing among themselves, they departed after Paul had made one statement: "The Holy Spirit was right in saying to your fathers through Isaiah the prophet:
²⁶ "'Go to this people, and say, "You will indeed hear but never understand, and you will indeed see but never perceive."
²⁷ For this people's heart has grown dull, and with their ears they can barely hear, and their eyes they have closed; lest they should see with their eyes and hear with their ears and understand with their heart and turn, and I would heal them.'
²⁸ **Therefore let it be known to you that this salvation of God has been sent to the Gentiles; they will listen."**

³⁰ He lived there two whole years at his own expense, and welcomed all who came to him, ³¹ proclaiming the kingdom of God and teaching about the Lord Jesus Christ with all boldness and without hindrance.

The Compiled Teachings of The Apostle Paul

Note: The primary purpose of printing so extensively the text of The Acts of The Apostles in this section is to allow passages of teaching by Paul to be highlighted in **bold typeface** and as such provide as a convenient means by which to locate those passages for quick and easy reference.

Where relevant, these passages will be referenced as we move through studying the letters, both those written by Paul and those credited to other authors. One key is to gain an understanding first of which cities Paul visited on each of his three missionary journeys so that we can identify the order in which they were written.

The Cities and Regions Visited on Paul's Missionary Trips

First Missionary Trip		Second Missionary Trip		Third Missionary Trip	
Antioch in Syria	13:1; 14:26	Antioch in Syria	15:30	Antioch in Syria	18:22
Seleucia	13:4	CYPRUS	15:39	Ephesus	18:19; 19:1
CYPRUS	13:4	Derbe	16:1	Greece	20:2
Salamis	13:5	Lystra	16:1	Assos	20:13
Paphos	13:6	Iconium	16:2	Mitylene	20:14
Perga	13:13; 14:25	PHRYGIA	16:6; 18:23	Chios	20:15
PAMPHYLIA	13:13; 14:24	GALATIA	16:6; 18:23	Samos	20:15
PISIDIA	13:14; 14:24	ASIA	16:6; 19:10; 19:22	Miletus	20:15
Pisidian Antioch	13:14; 14:21	Mysia	16:7, 8	Cos	21:1
Iconium	13:51; 14:1, 21	Bithnia	16:7	Rhodes	21:1
Lycaonia	14:6	Troas	16:8, 11; 20:6	Patara	21:1
Lystra	14:6, 8, 21	Samothrace	16:11	PHOENICIA	21:2
Derbe	14:6, 20	Neapolis	16:11	Tyre	21:3
Attalia	14:25	Philippi	16:12; 20:6	SYRIA	21:3
		MACEDONIA	16:12; 19:21; 20:1, 20:2	Ptolemais	21:7
		Amphipolis	17:1	Ceasarea	21:8
		Apollonia	17:1	Jerusalem	21:1
		Thessalonica	17:1		
		Berea	17:10		
		Athens	17:15		
		Corinth	18:1		
		Nicopolis (Titus 3:12)			
		ACHAIA	18:12; 19:21		
		Cenchrea	18:18		

- Cities are in normal text
- Regions are in UPPER CASE text
- Multiple verse entries indicate return visits

Words of Paul That Define His Ministry

Before Paul set off on any of his missionary trips he had become familiar with many of the other Apostles in Jerusalem. On visiting Ephesus his third missionary trip and then returning to Jerusalem, Luke records these passages that help us see how Paul viewed himself:

Acts 20:24 *[Paul is in Ephesus]*
[24]But I do not account my life of any value nor as precious to myself, if only I may finish my course and the ministry that I received from the Lord Jesus, to testify to the gospel of the grace of God. [25] And now, behold, I know that none of you among whom I have gone about proclaiming the kingdom will see my face again.

> ***Acts 21:18*** *[Paul has returned to Jerusalem]*
> *[18]On the following day Paul went in with us to James, and all the elders were present. [19] After greeting them, he related one by one the things that God had done among the Gentiles through his ministry. [20] And when they heard it, they glorified God.*

The Compiled Teachings of The Apostle Paul

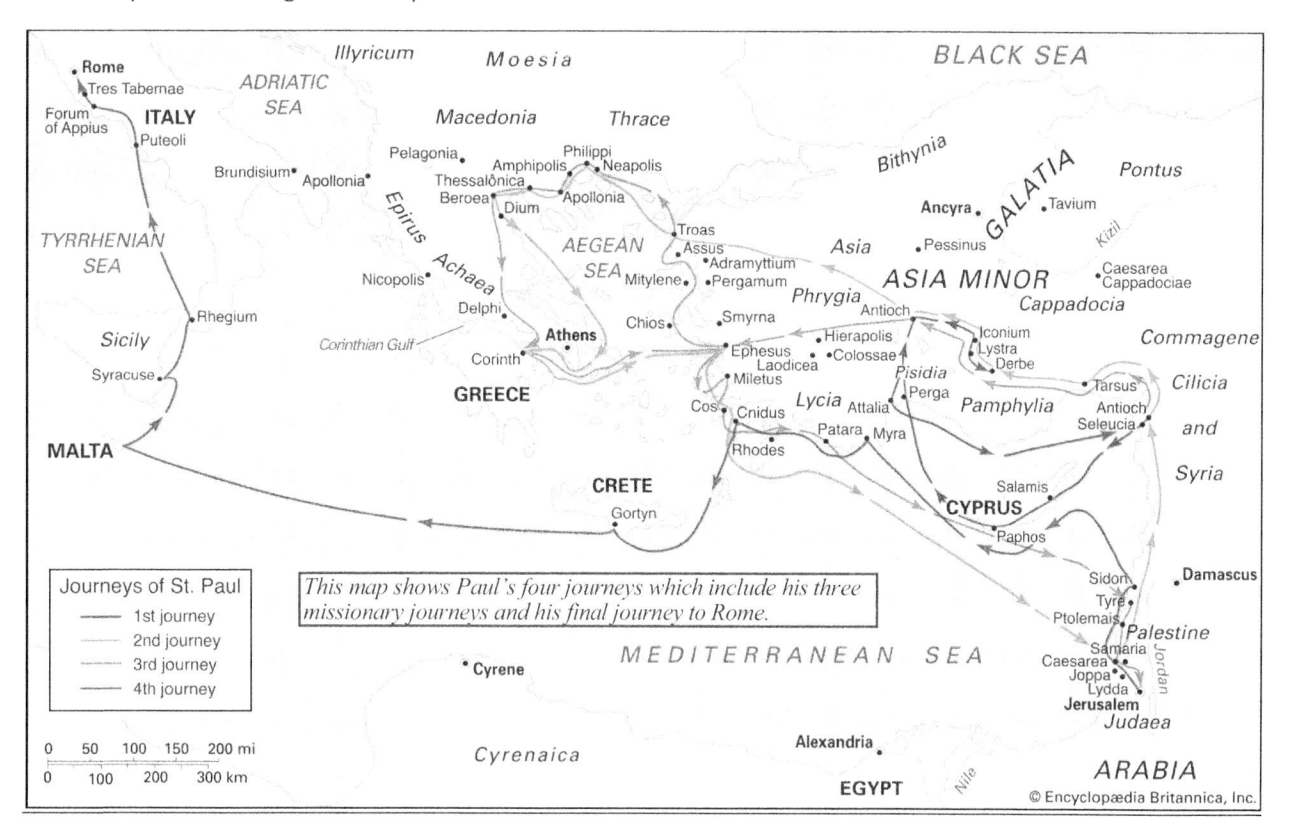

Section 3

The Letters of The Apostle Paul

Standing of Each of the Pauline Letters (Epistles) 34

The Greetings of each of the 'Letters Books' 34

   The Chronological Order of Paul's Letters 35

The Teachings In The Letters 37

Transition Passages 40

Galatians 44

   The Council At Jerusalem 44
   Paul Opposes Cephas (Peter) 45
   Faith Brings Righteousness 45
   Intent Of The Law 46
   Sonship In Christ 46
   Paul's Concern for the Galatians 47
   Hagar and Sarah 47
   Walk by the Spirit 48
   Life by the Spirit 48
   Bear One Another's Burdens 49
   Not Circumcision but the New Creation 49

1 Corinthians 50

   Proclaiming Christ Crucified 50
   Wisdom from the Spirit 50
   Divisions in the Church 51
   The Ministry of Apostles 51
   Sexual Immorality Defiles the Church 52
   Lawsuits Against Believers 52
   Flee Sexual Immorality 53
   Principles for Marriage 53
   Live as You Are Called 54
   The Unmarried and the Widowed 54
   Food Offered to Idols 55
   Paul Surrenders His Rights 55
   Living Off The Gospel 56
   Warning Against Idolatry 56
   Flee From Idolatry 57
   Do All to the Glory of God 57
   Be Imitators of Me, As I Am of Christ 57
   The Lord's Supper 58
   Spiritual Gifts 58
   One Body with Many Members 59
   The Way of Love 59
   Speaking In Tongues 60
   Orderly Worship 60
   The Resurrection of Christ 61
   The Resurrection of the Dead 61
   The Resurrection Body 62
   Mystery and Victory 63

The Collection for the Saints 63
Plans for Travel 63
Final Instructions 63
Salutations 64

2 Corinthians 65
Paul's Change of Plans 65
Reaffirm Your Love 65
Ministers of a New Covenant 66
Paul's Apostolic Ministry 67
The Temporal and Eternal 67
Paul Commends Their Ministry 68
Paul Reveals His Heart 69
Great Generosity 70
God Gives Most 71
Paul Describes Himself 71
Paul Defends His Apostleship 72
Paul's Vision 73
All Things Beloved Are For Your Edifying 74
Examine Yourselves 74

Romans 75
The Righteous Shall Live by FaithRomans 1:16-32 76
God's Wrath on Unrighteousness 76
The Righteous Judgment of God 76
Judgment and the Law 77
Righteousness 77
Righteousness Through Faith 78
Justification Through Faith 78
God's Promise To Abraham 79
Faith and Grace 79
Promise Realized Through Faith 79
Faith Brings Peace 79
Through The Gift of Righteousness Comes Justification 80
Being Dead to Sin is to be Alive to God 80
Slaves to Righteousness and Sanctification 80
Released from the Law 81
The Law and Sin 81
Life in the Spirit 82
Heirs with Christ 82
Our Victory In Christ: Redemption 82
All Things Work Together For Good 83
God's Everlasting Love 83
God's Sovereign Choice; Solicitude For Israel 83
Israel's Unbelief 84
The Message of Salvation to All 84
Denial By Israel 85
The Remnant of Israel: Israel Is Not Cast Away ... 85
Salvation Comes To The Gentiles (Who Are Grafted In) 85
The Mystery of Israel's Salvation 86
Dedicated Service: A Living Sacrifice 86
Gifts of Grace: Abhor What Is Evil 87
Marks of the True Christian 87
Submission to Government Authorities 87
Fulfilling the Law Through Love 88
Put On The Armor Of Light 88
Do Not Pass Judgment on One Another 88
Do Not Cause Another to Stumble 89
Self-denial: The Example of Christ 89
Christ is the God of Hope of Jews and Gentiles .. 89
Paul the Minister to the Gentiles 90
Paul's Plan to Visit Rome 90
Personal Greetings 90
Final Instructions and Greetings 91
Doxology 91
Observations: 91

1 Thessalonians 92
Thanksgiving For These Believers 92
Paul's Ministry 92
Encouragement of Timothy's Visit 93
Sanctification and Love 93
Those Who Died in Christ 94
The Day of The Lord 94

2 Thessalonians 95
Thanksgiving For These Believers 95
Man of Sin 95
Exhortation 96

1 Timothy 97
Misleading Teaching In Doctrine and Living 97
A Call To Prayer 98
Overseers and Deacons 98
Apostasy and A Good Minister's Discipline 99
Treat Others With Respect 99
Concerning Elders 100
Instructions to Those Who Minister 100

Titus 102
Qualifications of Elders 102
Duties of the Older and the Younger 102
Godly Living 103
Personal Concerns 103

Ephesians 104
The Blessings of Redemption 104
Gratitude and Prayers 104
Made Alive In Christ 105
Paul's Stewardship 106
Unity of the Spirit 106
The Christian's Walk 107
Be Imitators of God 107
Marriage Like Christ and the Church 108
Children and Parents 108
Slaves and Masters 109
The Armor of God 109

Philippians 110
Thanksgiving 110
The Gospel is preached 110
To Live Is Christ 111
Be Like Christ 111

The Compiled Teachings of The Apostle Paul

Timothy and Epaphroditus	*112*	*Speak With Grace*	*117*
Warnings and Reminders	*112*	***2 Timothy***	***118***
The Goal of Life	*113*	*Timothy Charged to Guard His Trust*	*118*
Stand Fast In The Lord Philippians 4:1-9	*113*	*Be Strong*	*118*
God's Provisions	*113*	*Difficult Times Will Come*	*119*
Colossians	***114***	*Preach the Word*	*120*
Thankfulness for Spiritual Attainments	*114*	***Philemon***	***121***
You Are Built Up in Christ	*115*	*Philemon's Love and Faith*	*121*
Put On the New Self	*116*	*Plea for Onesimus, a Free Man*	*121*
Family Relations	*117*		

To begin with, in this section we will review the essential teachings of Paul from his letters as they are listed in our Bibles:

- Romans
- 1 Corinthians
- 2 Corinthians
- Galatians
- Ephesians *(Deutero-Pauline epistle)*
- Philippians
- Colossians *(Deutero-Pauline epistle)*
- 1 Thessalonians
- 2 Thessalonians *(Deutero-Pauline epistle)*
- 1 Timothy *(Considered as possibly not written by Paul)*
- 2 Timothy *(Considered as possibly not written by Paul)*
- Titus *(Considered as probably not written by Paul)*
- Philemon

Standing of Each of the Pauline Letters (Epistles)
Undisputed Pauline epistles: Romans, 1 Corinthians, 2 Corinthians, Galatians, Philippians, 1 Thessalonians, Philemon
Deutero-Pauline epistles; considered authentic: Ephesians*, Colossians*, 2 Thessalonians*,
Pastoral epistles; probably not authentic Pauline: Timothy**, 2 Timothy**, Titus**

The Greetings of each of the 'Letters Books':
In these initial greeting lines or paragraphs, we see the following:

1. Paul consistently references himself as being an apostle, but more than that he references that he was called by God to be an apostle: *'called to be an apostle, set apart for the gospel of God' (Rom. 1.1); 'called by the will of God' (1 Cor. 1:1); 'an apostle of Christ Jesus by the will of God' (Gal. 1:1, Eph. 1:1, Col. 1:1)); 'by command of God our Savior and of Christ Jesus' (1 Tim. 1:1, 2 Tim. 1:1).*
2. Paul identifies that he is writing on behalf of himself and a second person in four of these letters: Sothenes in the letter to 1 Corinthians, and Timothy in the letters to 2 Corinthians, Philippians and Colossians, and Timothy is also referenced in the letter to Philemon.
3. Paul formally mentions the recipient's name in many of the letters: the letter to the Ephesians, the two letters to the church in Corinth and the two letters to the church in Thessalonica. A less formal reference – 'To all those in Rome…' – is made in the letter to the Romans.
4. The most consistent 'hallmark' of the greetings of the 'Letters books' is the inclusion of "Grace and peace", either in the form of 'to you' or in the form of 'from God', in which 'to you' is implied.

Romans	*Paul, a servant of Christ Jesus, called to be an apostle, set apart for the gospel of God*
1 Corinthians	*Paul, called by the will of God to be an apostle of Christ Jesus, and our brother Sosthenes,*
2 Corinthians	*Paul, an apostle of Christ Jesus by the will of God, and Timothy our brother,*
Galatians	*Paul, an apostle – not from men nor through man, but through Jesus Christ and God the Father, who raised him from the dead*
Ephesians	*Paul, an apostle of Christ Jesus by the will of God,*
Philippians	*Paul and Timothy, servants of Christ Jesus,*
Colossians	*Paul, an apostle of Christ Jesus by the will of God, and Timothy our brother,*
1 Thessalonians	*Paul, and Silvanus, and Timothy, To the church of the Thessalonians in God the Father and the Lord Jesus Christ: Grace to you and peace.*
2 Thessalonians	*Paul, and Silvanus, and Timothy, To the church of the Thessalonians in God the Father and the Lord Jesus Christ: Grace to you and peace from God our Father and the Lord Jesus Christ.*

The Compiled Teachings of The Apostle Paul

1 Timothy *Paul, an apostle of Christ Jesus by command of God our Savior and of Christ Jesus our hope,*
2 Timothy *Paul, an apostle of Christ Jesus by the will of God according to the promise of the life that is in Christ Jesus,*
Titus *Paul, a servant of God and an apostle of Jesus Christ, for the sake of the faith of God's elect and their knowledge of the truth, which accords with godliness,*
Philemon *Paul, a prisoner for Christ Jesus, and Timothy our brother, To Philemon our beloved fellow worker*

Paul's letters consistently begin with a greeting, but the greetings of the two letters to the church in Thessalonica – stand out as being distinctly different from the other eleven. Because the greetings of these two books are so different in style, the letters are considered suspect as regards to who the writer of Thessalonians was, however, they have been included in this study for academic reasons. The book of Hebrews has not been included.

The letters to the Philippians and Philemon also have greetings that exhibit a notable difference; these greetings do not reference Paul as being an Apostle. As both letters are addressed as being from Paul and Timothy, is it possible that they were written by Timothy based on dictation by Paul? An example of a 'Pauline Letter' being written or scribed by someone on behalf of Paul is The Letter to The Romans which was, at least in part, written or scribed by Tertius [Rom. 16:22].

<u>Note</u>: *It is important to be cognizant that the order in which the 'letters books' of The New Testament is not chronological per the order in which they were written; they are listed from longest text to shortest.*

The Chronological Order of Paul's Letters

The Letters (epistles) of Paul are listed in our Bible in the order of longest first to shortest last. However, this is not the order in which they were written.

1. Galatians, 1 Corinthians and 2 Corinthians were both written while Paul was in Ephesus on his 3rd mission journey.
2. Romans, 1 Thessalonians and 2 Thessalonians were written while Paul was in Corinth.
3. 1 Timothy and Titus were both written while Paul was in Nicopolis. *[Nicopolis is mentioned in Paul's letter to Titus (Titus 3:12) suggesting that he is at Nicopolis at the time of writing, but that is not fully conclusive. Paul may not have been in Nicopolis but rather may have been in Corinth but planning with the winter coming to go to Nicopolis.]*
4. Ephesians, Philippians, Colossians, 2 Timothy, and Philemon were all written while Paul was in Rome.

Paul's letters were written to the leaders of the some of the churches in the major cities that he had visited during the course of his three missionary journeys.

This reference map, courtesy of www.conformingtojesus.com, shows the locations that Paul wrote each of his letters from (as well as identifying where the authors of other books of the New Testament were when they written).

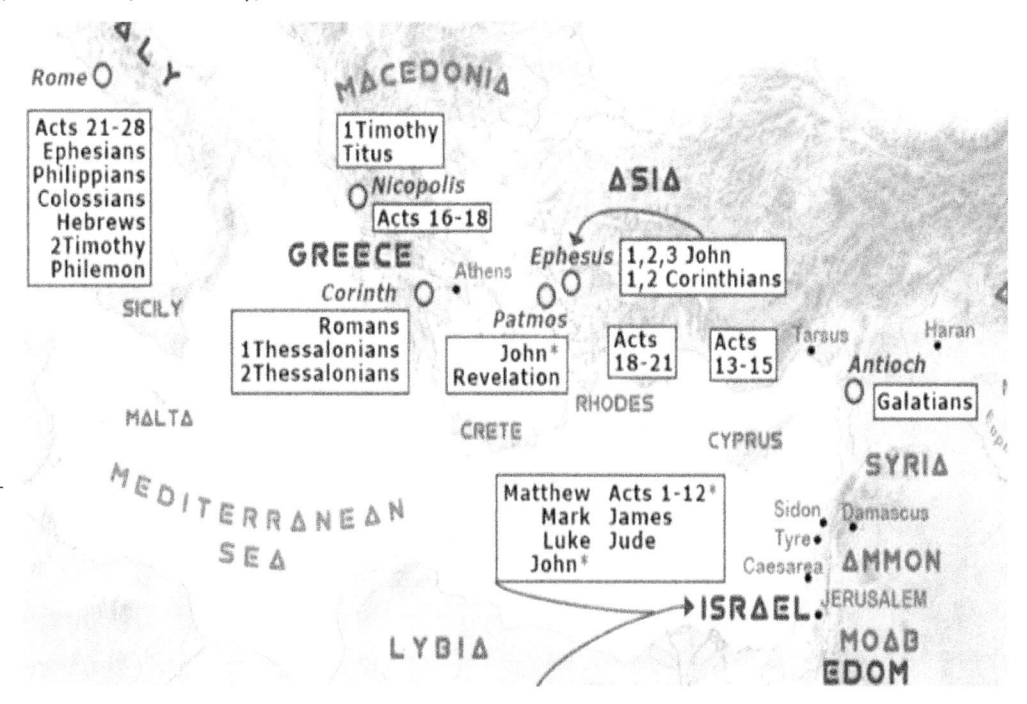

The Compiled Teachings of The Apostle Paul

Note: *The above map highlights include also books written by Matthew, Mark, and John ,in addition to the books written by Luke (The Gospel of Luke and The Acts of The Apostles) and the epistles written by Paul.*

The Compiled Teachings of The Apostle Paul

From this point forward we will be viewing the Letters of Paul in the chronological order in which they were written.

The Teachings In The Letters

In this section we begin to compile the teachings of Paul, although some parts of the greetings and opening paragraphs of each letter have already been separated out and listed earlier, for easy reference they are duplicated in this section. **In this section the epistles are listed in chronological order determined by where they written from** rather than being listed in the order in which they are printed in standard Bibles:

> The Letters of Paul in chronological order, in the order in which they were written.

Galatians
1 *Paul, an apostle—not from men nor through man, but through Jesus Christ and God the Father, who raised him from the dead –* ² *and all the brothers who are with me,*
To the churches of Galatia:
³ *Grace to you and peace from God our Father and the Lord Jesus Christ,* ⁴ **who gave himself for our sins to deliver us from the present evil age, according to the will of our God and Father,** ⁵ *to whom be the glory forever and ever.*

1 Corinthians
1 *Paul,* **called by the will of God to be an apostle of Christ Jesus**, *and our brother Sosthenes,*
² To the church of God that is in Corinth, *to those sanctified in Christ Jesus, called to be saints together with all those who in every place call upon the name of our Lord Jesus Christ, both their Lord and ours:*
³ **Grace to you and peace from God our Father and the Lord Jesus Christ.**

2 Corinthians
1 *Paul,* **an apostle of Christ Jesus by the will of God**, *and Timothy our brother,*
To the church of God that is at Corinth, *with all the saints who are in the whole of Achaia:*
² **Grace to you and peace from God our Father and the Lord Jesus Christ.**

Romans
1 *Paul, a servant of Christ Jesus, called to be an apostle, set apart for the gospel of God,* ² *which he promised beforehand through his prophets in the holy Scriptures,* ³ *concerning his Son, who was descended from David according to the flesh* ⁴ *and was declared to be the Son of God in power according to the Spirit of holiness by his resurrection from the dead, Jesus Christ our Lord,* ⁵ *through whom we have received grace and apostleship to bring about the obedience of faith for the sake of his name among all the nations,* ⁶ *including you who are called to belong to Jesus Christ,* ⁷ To all those in Rome *who are loved by God and called to be saints:*
Grace to you and peace from God our Father and the Lord Jesus Christ.

1 Thessalonians
1 *Paul, and Silvanus, and Timothy,* to the church of the Thessalonians *in God the Father and the Lord Jesus Christ:* Grace to you and peace.

2 Thessalonians
1 *Paul, and Silvanus, and Timothy,* to the church of the Thessalonians *in God our Father and the Lord Jesus Christ;* ² Grace to you and peace from God the Father *and the Lord Jesus Christ.*

1 Timothy
1 *Paul,* **an apostle** *of Christ Jesus by command of God our Savior and of Christ Jesus our hope;* Grace, mercy, and peace from God the Father and Christ Jesus our Lord.

Titus
1 *Paul, a servant of God and* **an apostle** *of Jesus Christ, for the sake of the faith of God's elect and their knowledge of the truth, which accords with godliness,* ² *in hope of eternal life, which God, who never lies, promised before the ages began* ³ *and at the proper time manifested in his word through the preaching with which I have been entrusted by the command of God our Savior;*
⁴ *To Titus, my true child in a common faith:*
Grace and peace from God the Father and Christ Jesus our Savior.

Ephesians 1:11-14
1 ¹¹ *In him we have obtained an inheritance, having been predestined according to the purpose of him who works all things according to the counsel of his will,* ¹² *so that we who were the first to hope in Christ might be to the praise of his glory.* ¹³ *In him you also, when you heard the word of truth, the gospel of your salvation, and believed in him, were sealed with the promised Holy Spirit,* ¹⁴ *who is the guarantee of our inheritance until we acquire possession of it, to the praise of his glory.*

Philippians
1 *Paul and Timothy, servants of Christ Jesus,* To all the saints in Christ Jesus who are at Philippi, *with the overseers and deacons:* ² **Grace to you and peace from God our Father and the Lord Jesus Christ.**

The Compiled Teachings of The Apostle Paul

Colossians	**2 Timothy**	**Philemon**
1 *Paul, **an apostle** of Christ Jesus by the will of God, and Timothy our brother,* ² <u>To the saints and faithful brothers in Christ at Colossae</u>: *Grace to you and peace from God.*	**1** *Paul, **an apostle** of Christ Jesus by the will of God according to the promise of the life that is in Christ Jesus,* ² *To Timothy, my beloved child:* **Grace, mercy, and peace from God the Father and Christ Jesus our Lord.**	**1** *Paul, a prisoner for Christ Jesus, and Timothy our brother, To Philemon our beloved fellow worker* ² *and Apphia our sister and Archippus our fellow soldier, and the church in your house:*

Next we continue with the verses each of the letters that follow the opening 'greeting lines':

Galatians 1:6-10
⁶ *I am astonished that you are so quickly deserting him who called you in the grace of Christ and are turning to a different gospel –* ⁷ *not that there is another one, but there are some who trouble you and want to distort the gospel of Christ.* ⁸ *But even if we or an angel from heaven should preach to you a gospel contrary to the one we preached to you, let him be accursed.* ⁹ *As we have said before, so now I say again: If anyone is preaching to you a gospel contrary to the one you received, let him be accursed.*
¹⁰ *For am I now seeking the approval of man, or of God? Or am I trying to please man? If I were still trying to please man, I would not be a servant of Christ.*

1 Corinthians 1:4-9
⁴ ***I give thanks*** *to my God always for you because of the grace of God that was given you in Christ Jesus,* ⁵ *that in every way you were enriched in him in all speech and all knowledge –* ⁶ *even as the testimony about Christ was confirmed among you –* ⁷ *so that you are not lacking in any gift, as you wait for the revealing of our Lord Jesus Christ,* ⁸ *who will sustain you to the end, guiltless in the day of our Lord Jesus Christ.* ⁹ *God is faithful, by whom you were called into the fellowship of his Son, Jesus Christ our Lord.*

2 Corinthians 1:3-7
³ **Blessed be the God and Father of our Lord Jesus Christ, the Father of mercies and God of all comfort**, ⁴ *who comforts us in all our affliction, so that we may be able to comfort those who are in any affliction, with the comfort with which we ourselves are comforted by God.* ⁵ *For as we share abundantly in Christ's sufferings, so through Christ we share abundantly in comfort too.* ⁶ *If we are afflicted, it is for your comfort and salvation; and if we are comforted, it is for your comfort, which you experience when you patiently endure the same sufferings that we suffer.* ⁷ *Our hope for you is unshaken, for we know that as you share in our sufferings, you will also share in our comfort.*

Romans 1:8-10
⁸ *First,* ***I thank*** *my God through Jesus Christ for all of you, because your faith is proclaimed in all the world.* ⁹ *For God is my witness, whom I serve with my spirit in the gospel of his Son, that without ceasing I mention you* ¹⁰ *always in my prayers, asking that somehow by God's will, I may now at last succeed in coming to you.*

1 Thessalonians 1:2-7
² ***We give thanks*** *to God always for all of you, constantly mentioning you in our prayers,* ³ *remembering before our God and Father your work of faith and labor of love and steadfastness of hope in our Lord Jesus Christ.* ⁴ *For we know, brothers loved by God, that he has chosen you,* ⁵ *because our gospel came to you not only in word, but also in power and in the Holy Spirit and with full conviction. You know what kind of men we proved to be among you for your sake.* ⁶ *And you became imitators of us and of the Lord, for you received the word in much affliction, with the joy of the Holy Spirit,* ⁷ *so that you became an example to all the believers in Macedonia and in Achaia.*

2 Thessalonians 1:3-4
³ ***We ought always to give thanks*** *to God for you, brothers, as is right, because your faith is growing abundantly, and the love of every one of you for one another is increasing.* ⁴ *Therefore we ourselves boast about you in the churches of God for your steadfastness and faith in all your persecutions and in the afflictions that you are enduring.*

1 Timothy 1:3-7
³ *As **I urged you** when I was going to Macedonia, remain at Ephesus* **so that you may charge certain persons not to teach any different doctrine**, ⁴ *nor to devote themselves to myths and endless genealogies, which promote speculations rather than the stewardship from God that is by faith.* ⁵ *The aim of our charge is love that issues from a pure heart and a good conscience and a sincere faith.* ⁶ **Certain persons, by swerving from these, have wandered away into vain discussion,** ⁷ **desiring to be teachers of the law, without understanding either what they are saying or the things about which they make confident assertions.**

The Compiled Teachings of The Apostle Paul

Titus 1:5-9
⁵ This is why I left you in Crete, so that you might put what remained into order, and appoint elders in every town as I directed you – ⁶ if anyone is above reproach, the husband of one wife, and his children are believers and not open to the charge of debauchery or insubordination. ⁷ For an overseer, as God's steward, must be above reproach. He must not be arrogant or quick-tempered or a drunkard or violent or greedy for gain, ⁸ but hospitable, a lover of good, self-controlled, upright, holy, and disciplined. ⁹ He must hold firm to the trustworthy word as taught, so that he may be able to give instruction in sound doctrine and also to rebuke those who contradict it.

Ephesians 1:3-10
³ Blessed be the God and Father of our Lord Jesus Christ, who has blessed us in Christ with every spiritual blessing in the heavenly places, ⁴ even as he chose us in him before the foundation of the world, that we should be holy and blameless before him. In love ⁵ he predestined us for adoption to himself as sons through Jesus Christ, according to the purpose of his will, ⁶ to the praise of his glorious grace, with which he has blessed us in the Beloved. ⁷ In him we have redemption through his blood, the forgiveness of our trespasses, according to the riches of his grace, ⁸ which he lavished upon us, in all wisdom and insight ⁹ making known to us the mystery of his will, according to his purpose, which he set forth in Christ ¹⁰ as a plan for the fullness of time, to unite all things in him, things in heaven and things on earth.

Philippians 1:3-11
*³ **I thank my God** in all my remembrance of you, ⁴ always in every prayer of mine for you all making my prayer with joy, ⁵ because of your partnership in the gospel from the first day until now. ⁶ And I am sure of this, that he who began a good work in you will bring it to completion at the day of Jesus Christ. ⁷ It is right for me to feel this way about you all, because I hold you in my heart, for you are all partakers with me of grace, both in my imprisonment and in the defense and confirmation of the gospel. ⁸ For God is my witness, how I yearn for you all with the affection of Christ Jesus. ⁹ And it is my prayer that your love may abound more and more, with knowledge and all discernment, ¹⁰ so that you may approve what is excellent, and so be pure and blameless for the day of Christ, ¹¹ filled with the fruit of righteousness that comes through Jesus Christ, to the glory and praise of God.*

Colossians 1:3-8
*³ **We always thank God**, the father of our Lord Jesus Christ, when we pray for you, ⁴ since we heard of your faith in Christ Jesus and of the love that you have for all the saints, ⁵ because of the hope laid up for you in heaven. Of this you have heard before in the word of the truth, the gospel, ⁶ which has come to you, as indeed in the whole world it is bearing fruit and increasing – as it also does among you, since the day you heard it and understood the grace of God in truth, ⁷ just as you learned it from Epaphras our beloved fellow servant. He is a faithful minister of Christ on your behalf ⁸ and has made known to us your love in the Spirit.*

2 Timothy 1:3-7
*³ **I thank God whom I serve**, as did my ancestors, with a clear conscience, as I remember you constantly in my prayers night and day. ⁴ As I remember your tears, I long to see you, that I may be filled with joy. ⁵ I am reminded of your sincere faith, a faith that dwelt first in your grandmother Lois and your mother Eunice and now, I am sure, dwells in you as well. ⁶ For this reason I remind you to fan into flame the gift of God, which is in you through the laying on of my hands, ⁷ for God gave us a spirit not of fear but of power and love and self-control.*

Philemon 4-7
*⁴ **I thank my God** always when I remember you in my prayers, ⁵ because I hear of your love and of the faith that you have toward the Lord Jesus and for all the saints, ⁶ and I pray that the sharing of your faith may become effective for the full knowledge of every good thing that is in us for the sake of Christ. ⁷ For I have derived much joy and comfort from your love, my brother, because the hearts of the saints have been refreshed through you.*

Observations:
- In reviewing each of these opening sections (paragraphs) we see a common theme in that Paul expressing thanks in Romans, 1 Corinthians, Galatians, Ephesians, Philippians, Colossians, 1 Thessalonians, 2 Thessalonians and 2 Timothy, but in 2 Corinthians and Philemon there are no expressions of thanks,
- In 2 Corinthians and Ephesians we see '*Blessed be the God and Father* of our Lord Jesus Christ' being used, and it is only in these two epistles that it is used.
- In the remaining books of 1 Timothy, Titus, and Hebrews we see a significant departure with Paul speaking very directly to both Timothy and Titus in a manner explaining an action that he had taken.
- The text of the book of Hebrews is substantially different from all of the other books, lending credence to the opinion of many scholars that it is not a book written or orally authored by Paul.

However, we have yet to reach any passages of teaching per se, and before we get to passages of teaching we have verses in all of the letters that I have labelled these verses 'Transition Passages':

The Compiled Teachings of The Apostle Paul

Transition Passages
Each of these passages I view as being a 'buffer' between the greeting and the main writings in the letters.

To begin with, here is a compilation of these transition passages of the Letters - which are in chronological order - following which the next section provides the same passages but with commentary.

Even without commentary, reading through these transition passages provides an overview of how Paul's ministry became defined and how his preaching and teaching evolved.

In writing to the Galatians which, chronologically, is the first of the letters written by Paul, and in which he defends his ministry.

<u>Note</u>: *Bible text printed in the left column is an intentional duplication of the same text on previous pages.*

Gal. 1 *[ESV]* *11 For I would have you know, brothers, that the gospel that I preached is not man's gospel. 12 For neither did I receive it from man, nor was I taught it, but it came to me through revelation of Jesus Christ. 13 For you have heard of my manner of life in time past in the Jews' religion, how that beyond measure I persecuted the church of God, and made havoc of it: 14 and I advanced in the Jews' religion beyond many of mine own age among my countrymen, being more exceedingly zealous for the traditions of my fathers. 15 But when it was the good pleasure of God, who separated me, even from my mother's womb, and called me through his grace, 16 to reveal his Son in me, that I might preach him among the Gentiles; straightway I conferred not with flesh and blood: 17 neither went I up to Jerusalem to them that were apostles before me: but I went away into Arabia; and again I returned to Damascus.*
18 Then after three years I went up to Jerusalem to visit Cephas [Peter], and tarried with him fifteen days. 19 But other of the apostles saw I none, save James the Lord's brother. 20 Now touching the things which I write to you, behold, before God, I lie not. 21 Then I came into the regions of Syria and Cilicia. 22 And I was still unknown by face to the churches of Judaea which were in Christ: 23 but they only heard say, He that once persecuted us now preach the faith of which he once made havoc; 24 and they glorified God in me.

Galatians 1:11-24
It is clear from the first verse in this passage that Paul has been challenged as to the authority of his teaching. Whether that challenge was particularly evident from the Church in Galatia or whether this had become a general defense that Paul had adopted is not clear, however, it was important enough to Paul to address the topic. Without giving any real details, Paul references his conversion. It was the incident that took place on the road to Damascus in which Saul 'met Jesus'. ²Paul's personal and direct encounter with Jesus is what Paul is referring to when he states, *'12 For neither did I receive it from man, nor was I taught it, but it came to me through revelation of Jesus Christ.'* Paul describes his prior life and specifically his involvement in persecuting those of 'The Way', the term used at that time to refer to believers, and references his 'religious education' under the tutelage of Gamaliel[2]. Paul then states very clearly that he believes he was chosen, even before he was born to be an Apostle to preach to the Gentiles. Paul states that he did not immediately go to Jerusalem to meet with the other Apostles but went away to Arabia. It was three years later when he returned to Damascus which would be where we learn from Acts 9:26-30 that Paul first came to Jerusalem *"trying to associate with the disciples. and they were all afraid of him, not believing that he was a disciple."* Paul describes that other than 15 days that he spent with Peter (Cephas) it was only James the brother of Jesus that he spent time with and mentions that throughout the churches of Judea he was referred to as, *'He that once persecuted us now preach(es) the faith of which he once made havoc.'*

In writing his first letter to the believers in Corinth, Paul indicates the reason for his letter is to address quarreling and division.

1 Corinthians 1:10-16
10 I appeal to you, brothers, by the name of our Lord Jesus Christ, that all of you agree, and that there be no divisions among you, but that you be united in the same mind and the same judgment. 11 For it has been reported to me by Chloe's people that there is quarreling among you, my brothers. 12 What I mean is that each one of you says, "I follow Paul," or "I follow Apollos," or "I follow Cephas," or "I follow Christ." 13 Is Christ divided? Was Paul crucified for you? Or were you baptized in the name of Paul? 14 I thank God that I baptized none of you except Crispus and Gaius, 15 so that no one may say that you were baptized in my name. 16 (I did baptize also the household of Stephanas. Beyond that, I do not know whether I baptized anyone else.) 17 For Christ did not send me to baptize but to preach the gospel, and not with words of eloquent wisdom, lest the cross of Christ be emptied of its power.

---

[2] Acts 22:3

The Compiled Teachings of The Apostle Paul

The next passage in the second letter to the Thessalonians, immediately follows the report of success that the Gospel is being accepted and that the church in Thessalonica is recognized and talked about as an example of successful ministry (verses 3-5) – is an exhortation that appears to be a response to news of persecution and are the first words recorded of threats of what is to come for those who have rejected the Gospel; writing that contributes to the dispute over the authorship.

2 Thessalonians 1:5-12

[5] This is evidence of the righteous judgment of God, that you may be considered worthy of the kingdom of God, for which you are also suffering – [6] since indeed God considers it just to repay with affliction those who afflict you, [7] and to grant relief to you who are afflicted as well as to us, when the Lord Jesus is revealed from heaven with his mighty angels [8] in flaming fire, inflicting vengeance on those who do not know God and on those who do not obey the gospel of our Lord Jesus. [9] They will suffer the punishment of eternal destruction, away from the presence of the Lord and from the glory of his might, [10] when he comes on that day to be glorified in his saints, and to be marveled at among all who have believed, because our testimony to you was believed. [11] To this end we always pray for you, that our God may make you worthy of his calling and may fulfill every resolve for good and every work of faith by his power, [12] so that the name of our Lord Jesus may be glorified in you, and you in him, according to the grace of our God and the Lord Jesus Christ.

The verses in 1 Timothy that precede this next passage, vs 3-8, exhort Timothy to challenge those who were teaching against the Gospel and correct those who were teaching a misleading version of the Gospel. Paul states; *'The aim of our charge is love that issues from a pure heart and a good conscience and a sincere faith'* and he expands in some detail on why the law is necessary. Paul then explains why he believes he was chosen, was forgiven, and was then charged with preaching the Gospel.

1 Timothy 1:8-16

[8] Now we know that the law is good, if one uses it lawfully, [9] understanding this, that the law is not laid down for the just but for the lawless and disobedient, for the ungodly and sinners, for the unholy and profane, for those who strike their fathers and mothers, for murderers, [10] the sexually immoral, men who practice homosexuality, enslavers, liars, perjurers, and whatever else is contrary to sound doctrine, [11] in accordance with the gospel of the glory of the blessed God with which I have been entrusted. [12] I thank him who has given me strength, Christ Jesus our Lord, because he judged me faithful, appointing me to his service, [13] though formerly I was a blasphemer, persecutor, and insolent opponent. But I received mercy because I had acted ignorantly in unbelief, [14] and the grace of our Lord overflowed for me with the faith and love that are in Christ Jesus. [15] The saying is trustworthy and deserving of full acceptance, that Christ Jesus came into the world to save sinners, of whom I am the foremost. [16] But I received mercy for this reason, that in me, as the foremost, Jesus Christ might display his perfect patience as an example to those who were to believe in him for eternal life.

The second passage in Ephesians might be considered a statement of faith and also an explanation of how Paul sees his ministry. First, referring to himself primarily but using the inclusive term 'we', Paul states that his ministry was predestined, and by God he was preordained to be the first to preach the Gospel of Jesus Christ as we know it. The writer (Paul?) explains that his purpose is to be approved by God for sharing the message of the Holy Spirit which offers those who accept the Gospel, the truth that Jesus of Nazareth is Christ the living Son of God, a "guarantee of being inherited"; adopted as children of God.

Ephesians 1:11-14

[11] In him we have obtained an inheritance, having been predestined according to the purpose of him who works all things according to the counsel of his will, [12] so that we who were the first to hope in Christ might be to the praise of his glory. [13] In him you also, when you heard the word of truth, the gospel of your salvation, and believed in him, were sealed with the promised Holy Spirit, [14] who is the guarantee of our inheritance until we acquire possession of it, to the praise of his glory.

In Philippians Paul continues from his words of encouragement (Phil. 1:3-11) into a report on what he sees as having been accomplished by his ministry and recognizes others (brothers) for also becoming confident in their preaching. He then references some of the wrong reasons for preaching while explaining what the only proper motivation is.

Philippians 1:12-18

[12] I want you to know, brothers, that what has happened to me has really served to advance the gospel, [13] so that it has become known throughout the whole imperial guard and to all the rest that my imprisonment is for Christ. [14] And most of the brothers, having become confident in the Lord by my imprisonment, are much more bold to speak the word without fear. [15] Some indeed preach Christ from envy and rivalry, but others from good will. [16] The latter do it out of love, knowing that I am put here for the defense of the gospel. [17] The former proclaim Christ out of selfish ambition, not sincerely but thinking to afflict me in my imprisonment. [18] What then? Only that in every way, whether in pretense or in truth, Christ is proclaimed, and in that I rejoice.

The next verses in Colossians, following on from Col. 1:3-8 (in which Paul made mention by name of Epaphras who is ministering in Colossus), Paul references how he and his companions have been continually praying for those in Colossus. Paul finishes these verses with the statement of what the goal of preaching the Gospel is, and that is to *'deliver us from the domain of darkness and transfer us to the kingdom of his beloved Son, [14] in whom we have redemption, the forgiveness of sins.'* (vs13-14).

Colossians 1:9-14

[9] And so, from the day we heard, we have not ceased to pray for you, asking that you may be filled with the knowledge of his will in all spiritual wisdom and understanding, [10] so as to walk in a manner worthy of the Lord, fully pleasing to him: bearing fruit in every good work and increasing in the knowledge of God; [11] being strengthened with all power, according to his glorious might, for all endurance and patience with joy; [12] giving thanks to the Father, who has qualified you to share in the inheritance of the saints in light. [13] **He has delivered us from the domain of darkness and transferred us to the kingdom of his beloved Son, [14] in whom we have redemption, the forgiveness of sins.**

Paul continues and concludes his second letter to Timothy after having commended and encouraged him with exhortation, referencing his own conversion and appointment as *'a preacher and apostle and teacher'*.

Encouraging Timothy to continue to follow in his own footsteps teaching *'the faith and love that are in Christ Jesus'*, Paul concludes by naming some that failed him and some from whom he received support and encouragement, referencing both Rome and Ephesus.

2 Timothy 1:8-18

[8] Therefore do not be ashamed of the testimony about our Lord, nor of me his prisoner, but share in suffering for the gospel by the power of God, [9] who saved us and called us to a holy calling, not because of our works but because of his own purpose and grace, which he gave us in Christ Jesus before the ages began, [10] and which now has been manifested through the appearing of our Savior Christ Jesus, who abolished death and brought life and immortality to light through the gospel, [11] for which I was appointed a preacher and apostle and teacher, [12] which is why I suffer as I do. But I am not ashamed, for I know whom I have believed, and I am convinced that he is able to guard until that day what has been entrusted to me. [13] Follow the pattern of the sound words that you have heard from me, in the faith and love that are in Christ Jesus. [14] By the Holy Spirit who dwells within us, guard the good deposit entrusted to you. [15] You are aware that all who are in Asia turned away from me, among whom are Phygelus and Hermogenes. [16] May the Lord grant mercy to the household of Onesiphorus, for he often refreshed me and was not ashamed of my chains, [17] but when he arrived in Rome he searched for me earnestly and found me – [18] may the Lord grant him to find mercy from the Lord on that day! – and you well know all the service he rendered at Ephesus.

Titus 1:10-16

[10] For there are many who are insubordinate, empty talkers and deceivers, especially those of the circumcision party. [11] They must be silenced, since they are upsetting whole families by teaching for shameful gain what they ought not to teach. [12] One of the Cretans, a prophet of their own, said, "Cretans are always liars, evil beasts, lazy gluttons. [13] This testimony is true. Therefore rebuke them sharply, that they may be sound in the faith, [14] not devoting themselves to Jewish myths and the commands of people who turn away from the truth. [15] To the pure, all things are pure, but to the defiled and unbelieving, nothing is pure; but both their minds and their consciences are defiled. [16] They profess to know God, but they deny him by their works. They are detestable, disobedient, unfit for any good work.

In this letter to Titus, in verses 5-9, the writer (Paul?) has set guidelines for selecting Elders making this letter somewhat different in focus to all of the other letters. These next verses detail negative behaviors, even quoting a prophet of Crete who describes the typical characteristics of Cretans and with those words he concludes the letter. By any standards this seems to be a very different Paul who is writing.

The Compiled Teachings of The Apostle Paul

Previously in Acts 20:5-6 we noted that Luke had begun travelling with Paul and Barnabas, Here, in Paul's letter to Philemon, we see that Luke is confirmed as still travelling with Paul, be it that they are in prison together.

In this letter to Philemon, Paul acknowledges his age and he also states in the letter, '*I, Paul, write this with my own hand*', and makes an appeal to Philemon to give Onesimus who had been a bonded servant (slave) to Philemon was a fellow coworker who hosted a church in his house, asking Philemon to give Onesimus a second chance; '*he is indeed (now) useful to you and to me… that he might serve me on your behalf during my imprisonment for the gospel*' (vs 11-13). It is clear from how Paul ends the letter that he believes he will be released from prison and will be able to reunite with Philemon.

Philemon 4-7

⁸ Accordingly, though I am bold enough in Christ to command you to do what is required, ⁹ yet for love's sake I prefer to appeal to you – I, Paul, an old man and now a prisoner also for Christ Jesus – ¹⁰ I appeal to you for my child, Onesimus, whose father I became in my imprisonment. ¹¹ (Formerly he was useless to you, but now he is indeed useful to you and to me.) ¹² I am sending him back to you, sending my very heart. ¹³ I would have been glad to keep him with me, in order that he might serve me on your behalf during my imprisonment for the gospel, ¹⁴ but I preferred to do nothing without your consent in order that your goodness might not be by compulsion but of your own accord. ¹⁵ For this perhaps is why he was parted from you for a while, that you might have him back forever, ¹⁶ no longer as a bondservant but more than a bondservant, as a beloved brother – especially to me, but how much more to you, both in the flesh and in the Lord.

¹⁷ So if you consider me your partner, receive him as you would receive me. ¹⁸ If he has wronged you at all, or owes you anything, charge that to my account. ¹⁹ I, Paul, write this with my own hand: I will repay it – to say nothing of your owing me even your own self. ²⁰ Yes, brother, I want some benefit from you in the Lord. Refresh my heart in Christ.

²¹ Confident of your obedience, I write to you, knowing that you will do even more than I say. ²² At the same time, prepare a guest room for me, for I am hoping that through your prayers I will be graciously given to you.

Paul concludes his letter to Philemon naming those who are prison with him:

²³ Epaphras, my fellow prisoner in Christ Jesus, sends greetings to you, ²⁴ and so do Mark, Aristarchus, Demas, and Luke, my fellow workers.

In the following pages we will work through the remaining verses and chapters of each of the Letters of Paul, **Letter-by-Letter in chronological order of when they were written.**

The Compiled Teachings of The Apostle Paul

Galatians

The Council At Jerusalem 44	Hagar and Sarah 47
Paul Opposes Cephas (Peter) 45	Walk by the Spirit 48
Faith Brings Righteousness 45	Life by the Spirit 48
Intent Of The Law 46	Bear One Another's Burdens 49
Sonship In Christ 46	Not Circumcision but the New Creation 49
Paul's Concern for the Galatians 47	

Paul's Letter To The Churches In Galatia written by Paul at Ephesus

For notes on Gal. 1:1-10, see 'The Greetings of each of the 'Letters Books' and 'Transition Passages' on pages 29-34.

Important to understanding The Letter To The Galatians is understanding where Galatia is: Acts 18 tells us *'18 22 When he had landed at Caesarea, he went up and greeted the church, and then went down to Antioch. 23 After spending some time there, he departed and went from one place to the next through the region of Galatia and Phrygia, strengthening all the disciples.'* From this and from referring to maps of the Asia Minor region we can see that Paul travelled down through Galatia and also Phrygia to Pisidian Antioch (Antioch in Pisidia).

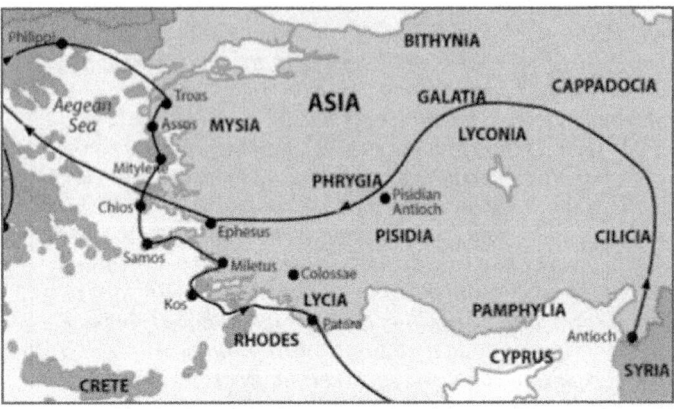

For the location of Caesarea, see the maps on page 30 or 32

The Council At Jerusalem
Gal. 2:1-10

2. Then after the space of fourteen years I went up again to Jerusalem with Barnabas, taking Titus also with me. ² And I went up by revelation; and I laid before them the gospel which I preach among the Gentiles but privately before them who were of repute, lest by any means I should be running, or had run, in vain. ³ But not even Titus who was with me, being a Greek, was compelled to be circumcised: ⁴ and that because of the false brethren privately brought in, who came in privately to spy out our liberty which we have in Christ Jesus, that they might bring us into bondage: ⁵ to whom we gave place in the way of subjection, no, not for an hour; that the truth of the gospel might continue with you. ⁶ But from those who were reputed to be somewhat whatsoever they were, it makes no matter to me: God accepts not man's person – they, I say, who were of repute imparted nothing to me: ⁷ but contrariwise, when they saw that I had been entrusted with the gospel of the uncircumcision, even as Peter with the gospel of the circumcision ⁸ (for he who was at work for Peter to the apostleship of the circumcision was at work for me also to the Gentiles)^NASB ⁹ and when they perceived the grace that was given to me, James and Cephas (Peter) and John, they who were reputed to be pillars, gave to me and Barnabas the right hands of fellowship, that we should go to the Gentiles, and they to the circumcised; ¹⁰ only they would that we should remember the poor; which very thing I was also zealous to do.

Paul provides us with a timeframe reference as well as identifying who accompanied him; 14 years had passed since he last visited Jerusalem; 17 years since his conversion, and his missionary companions included Barnabas and Titus, meaning that if as Saul at the stoning of Stephen was only 17. His age would now be in his mid 30s. Paul preached to the Apostles including *⁹ᵇ James and Cephas (Peter) and John.* Paul tells us, that Titus, who was a Greek, *'³ᵇ was compelled to be circumcised'* – we presume to make him acceptable to go into the temple. The topic of being circumcised was clearly a major issue with Paul who insisted that circumcision was not essential except for those who chose to be circumcised. Paul insisted that *'⁵ᵇ that the truth of the gospel might continue... '* and he reports that he was successful in convincing *'James and Cephas (Peter) and John'* that while they should preach circumcision to the Jews, he and Barnabas, and their companions, should preach to the Gentiles with no demand for circumcision.

This next passage begins with a somewhat surprising transition. In verse 10, Paul has reported that he received support from James, John and Peter to pursue with Barnabas the mission of taking the Gospel to the Gentiles. But, here in verse 11, Paul writes in this letter to the Galatians that he confronted Peter when Peter visited Antioch in Pisidia.

The Compiled Teachings of The Apostle Paul

Paul Opposes Cephas (Peter) — Gal. 2:11-21

> *[11] But when Cephas (Peter) came to Antioch, I resisted him to the face, because he stood condemned. [12] For before that certain men came from James, he ate with the Gentiles; but when they came, he drew back and separated himself, fearing them that were of the circumcision. [13] And the rest of the Jews dissembled likewise with him; insomuch that even Barnabas was carried away with their dissimulation. [14] But when I saw that they walked not uprightly according to the truth of the gospel, I said to Cephas before them all, If you, being a Jew, lives as do the Gentiles, and not as do the Jews, how compelled you the Gentiles to live as do the Jews? [15] We being Jews by nature, and not sinners of the Gentiles, [16] yet knowing that a man is not justified by the works of the law but through faith in Jesus Christ, even we believed on Christ Jesus, that we might be justified by faith in Christ, and not by the works of the law: because by the works of the law shall no flesh be justified. [17] But if, while we sought to be justified in Christ, we ourselves also were found sinners, is Christ a minister of sin? God forbid. [18] For if I build up again those things which I destroyed, I prove myself a transgressor. [19] For I through the law died unto the law, that I might live unto God. [20] I have been crucified with Christ; and it is no longer I that live, but Christ lives in me: and that life which I now live in the flesh I live in faith, the faith which is in the Son of God, who loved me, and gave himself up for me. [21] I do not make void the grace of God: for if righteousness is through the law, then Christ died for no purpose.*

Paul writes about confronting Peter over the issues of eating with the Gentiles and the need to be circumcised and he is writing and explaining what the issue of disagreement was: *'[12]When he first arrived, he ate with the Gentile Christians, who were not circumcised. But afterward, when some friends of James came, Peter wouldn't eat with the Gentiles anymore. He was afraid of criticism from these people who insisted on the necessity of circumcision.[NLT]*
Paul writes that *'[13b] even Barnabas was carried away [led astray] with their dissimulation. [hypocrisy]'* And *'that they did not walk uprightly'*, in effect accusing Peter and others of being hypocrites, Paul challenged Peter on the grounds that what Jesus taught was *'[16b] that a man is not justified by the works of the law but through faith in Jesus Christ'*. Paul suggested that if those preaching the Gospel are found to be sinners, then that would make *'Christ a minister of sin'*, and he argued that justification was not through the law but his faith was founded in *'the grace of God: for if righteousness is through the law, then Christ [had] died for no purpose.'*

Faith Brings Righteousness — Gal. 3:1-14

> *3. O foolish Galatians, who did bewitch you, before whose eyes Jesus Christ was openly set forth crucified? [2] This only would I learn from you, Did you receive the Spirit by the works of the law, or by the hearing of faith? [3] Are you so foolish? having begun in the Spirit, are you now perfected in the flesh? [4] Did you suffer so many things in vain? if it be indeed in vain. [5] He therefore that supplies to you the Spirit, and works miracles among you, does he do so by the works of the law, or by the hearing of faith? [6] Even as Abraham believed God, and it was reckoned to him for righteousness. [7] Know therefore that they that are of faith, the same are sons of Abraham. [8] And the scripture, foreseeing that God would justify the Gentiles by faith, preached the gospel beforehand to Abraham, saying, In thee shall all the nations be blessed. [9] So then they that are of faith are blessed with the faithful Abraham. [10] For as many as are of the works of the law are under a curse: for it is written, Cursed is everyone who continues not in all things that are written in the book of the law, to do them. [11] Now that no man is justified by the law before God, is evident: for, The righteous shall live by faith; [12] and the law is not of faith; but, He that does, they shall live in them. [13] Christ redeemed us from the curse of the law, having become a curse for us; for it is written, Cursed is every one that hangs on a tree:[14] that upon the Gentiles might come the blessing of Abraham in Christ Jesus; that we might receive the promise of the Spirit through faith.*

In this passage, Paul is explaining how faith supersedes the law. Paul writes that Abraham believed God. That was faith. *'[6] Even as Abraham believed God, and it was reckoned to him for righteousness.'* [Gen. 15:6] Paul explains, that as Abraham was justified, so shall all of his descendants be justified; justified by faith. *'[8b] In you shall all the nations be blessed.* [Gen. 12:3b] *[9] So then they that are of faith are blessed with the faithful Abraham.'*
Regarding the law, Paul writes *'[10b] for it is written, Cursed is everyone who continues not in all things that are written in the book of the law, to do them. [11] Now that no man is justified by the law before God, is evident: for, The righteous shall live by faith'* and Paul concludes by quoting two prophesies: *'[13b] Cursed is man that hangs on a tree:* [Deut. 21:23] and *[14] that upon the Gentiles might come the blessing of Abraham in Christ Jesus;* [Hab. 2:4] *that we might receive the promise of the Spirit through faith.'*

Intent Of The Law
Gal. 3:15-29

3 ¹⁵ Brethren, I speak after the manner of men: Though it be but a man's covenant, yet when it has been confirmed, no one makes it void, or added thereto. ¹⁶ Now to Abraham [to whom] were the promises spoken, and to his seed. He said not, And to seeds, as of many; but as of one, And to thy seed, which is Christ. ¹⁷ Now this I say: the law, which came four hundred and thirty years afterward, does not annul a covenant previously ratified by God, [ESV] so as to nullify the promise.[NASB] ¹⁸ For if the inheritance is of the law, it is no more of promise: but God has granted it to Abraham by promise. ¹⁹ What then is the law? It was added because of transgressions, till the seed should come to whom the promise has been made; and it was ordained through angels by the hand of a mediator. ²⁰ Now a mediator is not a mediator of one; but God is one. ²¹ Is the law then against the promises of God? God forbid: for if there had been a law given which could make alive, verily righteousness would have been of the law. ²² But the scripture shut up all things under sin, that the promise by faith in Jesus Christ might be given to them that believe.
²³ But before faith came, we were kept in ward under the law, shut up unto the faith which should afterwards be revealed. ²⁴ So that the law is become our tutor to bring us to Christ, that we might be justified by faith. ²⁵ But now that faith is come, we are no longer under a tutor. ²⁶ For you are all sons of God, through faith, in Christ Jesus. ²⁷ For as many of you as were baptized into Christ did put on Christ. ²⁸ There can be neither Jew nor Greek, there can be neither bond nor free, there can be no male and female; for you all are one man in Christ Jesus. ²⁹ And if you are Christ's, then you are Abraham's seed, heirs according to promise.

To make the intent of the law clear Paul writes, 'This is what I mean: *the law, which came 430 years afterward, does not annul a covenant previously ratified by God, so as to make the promise void.*' [ESV] and he adds emphasis by stating, '¹⁸ᵇ *God has granted it to Abraham by promise.*' Paul spells out that the law, which was given to Moses, was ᵈ¹⁹ᵇ *added because of transgressions, till the seed should come to whom the promise has been made;*' and adds, '²²ᵇ *that the promise by faith in Jesus Christ might be given to them that believe.*' Using a phrase that appears to be the same or similar to one that Peter used in his first sermon, which was delivered before the Council in Jerusalem, Paul is explaining that the promise was that righteousness would be through belief in the Messiah meaning those who believe will receive God's Spirit in a powerful way after believing in Jesus, but before doing any works of the law.
Second, scripture shows God's blessing coming by faith, and His curse coming by the law. Christ has paid the price of that curse on the cross.
Third, God's covenant with Abraham is like a legal document, and it cannot be revoked.
Acts 2:³² This Jesus did God raise up, whereof we all are witnesses. ³³ *Being therefore by the right hand of God exalted, and having received of the Father the promise of the Holy Spirit, he has poured forth this, which you see and hear.*

Sonship In Christ
Gal. 4:1-7

4 What I am saying is that as long as an heir is underage, he is no different from a slave, although he owns the whole estate. ² The heir is subject to guardians and trustees until the time set by his father. ³ So also, when we were underage, we were in slavery under the elemental spiritual forces of the world. ⁴ But when the set time had fully come, God sent his Son, born of a woman, born under the law, ⁵ to redeem those under the law, that we might receive adoption to sonship. ⁶ Because you are his sons, God sent the Spirit of his Son into our hearts, the Spirit who calls out, "Abba, Father." ⁷ So you are no longer a slave, but God's child; and since you are his child, God has made you also an heir.

In this passage Paul is specifically speaking to the Jews; those who are under the law. He tells them that those who are the descendants of Abraham are heirs but until each becomes of age, he has no standing above that of a slave, that is to say the heir is owned even though there is an inheritance awaiting them. Paul explains that until the heir is freed from that slavery, that is redeemed, they are slaves of '³ *the elemental spiritual forces of the world.*'. God set the timeframe for them as a people to be redeemed, and that was when '*God sent his Son, born of a woman, born under the law,*'ᵃ '⁵*to redeem those under the law, that we might receive adoption to sonship.*'ᵇ '⁶ *God sent the Spirit of his Son into our hearts, the Spirit who calls out, "Abba, Father"*.'ᶜ

Paul has referenced Antioch in Pisidia, in this letter to the Galatians, so to which church was this letter delivered to? Was it delivered to a church in Galatia that we don't have a precise identity for, or was it delivered to the church in Pisidian Antioch and from there passed to and around the churches in Galatia?

a. *Luke 2:11* b. *Isaiah* c. *Mark 14:36*

Paul's Concern for the Galatians   Gal. 4:8-20

4 *⁸ Formerly, when you did not know God, you were slaves to those who by nature are not gods. ⁹ But now that you know God – or rather are known by God – how is it that you are turning back to those weak and miserable forces? Do you wish to be enslaved by them all over again? ¹⁰ You are observing special days and months and seasons and years! ¹¹ I fear for you, that somehow I have wasted my efforts on you. ¹² I plead with you, brothers and sisters, become like me, for I became like you. You did me no wrong. ¹³ As you know, it was because of an illness that I first preached the gospel to you, ¹⁴ and even though my illness was a trial to you, you did not treat me with contempt or scorn. Instead, you welcomed me as if I were an angel of God, as if I were Christ Jesus himself. ¹⁵ Where, then, is your blessing of me now? I can testify that, if you could have done so, you would have torn out your eyes and given them to me. ¹⁶ Have I now become your enemy by telling you the truth?*

¹⁷ Those people are zealous to win you over, but for no good. What they want is to alienate you from us, so that you may have zeal for them. ¹⁸ It is fine to be zealous, provided the purpose is good, and to be so always, not just when I am with you. ¹⁹ My dear children, for whom I am again in the pains of childbirth until Christ is formed in you, ²⁰ how I wish I could be with you now and change my tone, because I am perplexed about you!

Paul is still primarily addressing the Jews in Galatia and it would seem that many are abandoning Jesus Christ and are returning to worshipping idols. Paul expresses concern and exasperation to the extent he questions, *"Did I waste my efforts on you?"* Paul then mentions an illness, *'¹³ As you know, it was because of an illness that I first preached the gospel to you'*. Paul continues and he refers to "Those People" – *'¹⁷ Those people are zealous to win you over, but for no good. What they want is to alienate you from us, so that you may have zeal for them.'* And Paul concedes that he has to begin all over again because they are not, and perhaps never were, mature in Christ, *'¹⁹ My dear children, for whom I am again in the pains of childbirth until Christ is formed in you'*

Hagar and Sarah   Gal. 4:21-31

4 *²¹ Tell me, you who want to be under the law, are you not aware of what the law says? ²² For it is written that Abraham had two sons, one by the slave woman and the other by the free woman. ²³ His son by the slave woman was born according to the flesh, but his son by the free woman was born as the result of a divine promise.*
²⁴ These things are being taken figuratively: The women represent two covenants. One covenant is from Mount Sinai and bears children who are to be slaves: This is Hagar. ²⁵ Now Hagar stands for Mount Sinai in Arabia and corresponds to the present city of Jerusalem, because she is in slavery with her children. ²⁶ But the Jerusalem that is above is free, and she is our mother. ²⁷ For it is written: "Be glad, barren woman, you who never bore a child; shout for joy and cry aloud, you who were never in labor; because more are the children of the desolate woman than of her who has a husband."
²⁸ Now you, brothers and sisters, like Isaac, are children of promise. ²⁹ At that time the son born according to the flesh persecuted the son born by the power of the Spirit. It is the same now. ³⁰ But what does Scripture say? "Get rid of the slave woman and her son, for the slave woman's son will never share in the inheritance with the free woman's son." [Gen. 21:10-13] ³¹ Therefore, brothers and sisters, we are not children of the slave woman, but of the free woman.

In this passage Paul is referencing Hagar to whom Ishmael was born and Sarah to who Isaac was born. Paul likens Hagar to the Jerusalem on earth, and likens Sarah to the Jerusalem in heaven: [Is. 54:1] *'²⁶ …the Jerusalem that is above'*.
This passage in Isaiah 54 continues:
² "Enlarge the place of your tent; Stretch out the curtains of your dwellings, do not spare them;… ³ For you will spread out to the right and to the left. And your descendants will possess nations and will resettle the desolate cities.
⁴ "Fear not, for you will not be put to shame; and do not feel humiliated, for you will not be disgraced; but you will forget the shame of your youth, and no longer remember the disgrace of your widowhood. ⁵ For your husband is your Maker, whose name is the LORD of armies; and your Redeemer is the Holy One of Israel, who is called the God of all the earth. ⁶ For the LORD has called you, like a wife forsaken and grieved in spirit, even like a wife of one's youth when she is rejected," Says your God.
⁷ "For a brief moment I abandoned you, but with great compassion I will gather you. ⁸ In an outburst of anger I hid My face from you for a moment, but with everlasting favor I will have compassion on you," Says the LORD your Redeemer. [NASB]

Paul concludes this passage that explains the separation of the chosen people from all others by firmly stating that those who are Jews are descendants of Abraham born of Sarah.

Walk by the Spirit
Gal. 5:1-12

5. It is for freedom that Christ has set us free. Stand firm, then, and do not let yourselves be burdened again by a yoke of slavery. ² Mark my words! I, Paul, tell you that if you let yourselves be circumcised, Christ will be of no value to you at all. ³ Again I declare to every man who lets himself be circumcised that he is obligated to obey the whole law. ⁴ You who are trying to be justified by the law have been alienated from Christ; you have fallen away from grace. ⁵ For through the Spirit we eagerly await by faith the righteousness for which we hope. ⁶ For in Christ Jesus neither circumcision nor uncircumcision has any value. The only thing that counts is faith expressing itself through love.

⁷ You were running a good race. Who cut in on you to keep you from obeying the truth? ⁸ That kind of persuasion does not come from the one who calls you. ⁹ "A little yeast works through the whole batch of dough. ¹⁰ I am confident in the Lord that you will take no other view. The one who is throwing you into confusion, whoever that may be, will have to pay the penalty. ¹¹ Brothers and sisters, if I am still preaching circumcision, why am I still being persecuted? In that case the offense of the cross has been abolished. ¹² As for those agitators, I wish they would go the whole way and emasculate themselves!

Continuing with the themes of slavery and freedom, first Paul speaks to the Jews stating that it is Christ who has set us free from the *'yoke of slavery'*. Then, speaking to the Gentiles he writes that *'²ᵇ…if you let yourselves be circumcised, Christ will be of no value to you at all.'* for which he gives the reason: *'³Again I declare to every man who lets himself be circumcised that he is obligated to obey the whole law. …⁶ For in Christ Jesus neither circumcision nor uncircumcision has any value. The only thing that counts is faith expressing itself through love.'* Paul now references *'running a race'* rhetorically asking, *'who cut in on you from obeying the truth?'* and Paul then references just how effective a small amount of yeast is when it is added to a batch of dough, and Paul then suggests that those who are not preaching the truth should emasculate themselves. Now, emasculate can mean simply to *'lessen or weaken'*, but it can also mean *'deprive (a man) of his male role or identity'*, and Paul wrote, *'go the whole way'*.

>**Acts 26** ²⁹ And Paul said, "Whether short or long, I would to God that not only you but also all who hear me this day might become such as I am—except for these chains."

Life by the Spirit
Gal. 5:13-26

5 ¹³ You, my brothers and sisters, were called to be free. But do not use your freedom to indulge the flesh; rather, serve one another humbly in love. ¹⁴ For the entire law is fulfilled in keeping this one command: "Love your neighbor as yourself." ¹⁵ If you bite and devour each other, watch out or you will be destroyed by each other.

¹⁶ So I say, walk by the Spirit, and you will not gratify the desires of the flesh. ¹⁷ For the flesh desires what is contrary to the Spirit, and the Spirit what is contrary to the flesh. They are in conflict with each other, so that you are not to do whatever you want. ¹⁸ But if you are led by the Spirit, you are not under the law.

¹⁹ The acts of the flesh are obvious: sexual immorality, impurity and debauchery; ²⁰ idolatry and witchcraft; hatred, discord, jealousy, fits of rage, selfish ambition, dissensions, factions ²¹ and envy; drunkenness, orgies, and the like. I warn you, as I did before, that those who live like this will not inherit the kingdom of God. ²² But the fruit of the Spirit is love, joy, peace, forbearance, kindness, goodness, faithfulness, ²³ gentleness and self-control. Against such things there is no law. ²⁴ Those who belong to Christ Jesus have crucified the flesh with its passions and desires. ²⁵ Since we live by the Spirit, let us keep in step with the Spirit. ²⁶ Let us not become conceited, provoking and envying each other.

Here Paul returns to the theme of love, warning that the freedom that one gains through believing does not include *'¹³ᵇfreedom to indulge the flesh'*. Instead, Paul implores them to *'¹³ᶜserve one another humbly in love.'* Paul then quotes what Jesus said when asked which is the greatest commandment, *'¹⁴ For the entire law is fulfilled in keeping this one command: "Love your neighbor as yourself.'* [Matt. 23:39; Mark 12:31] and Paul then adds a warning about criticizing and attacking each other which causes division and leads to destruction; self-destruction.

Paul next explains that if you don't walk by the spirit you will always be giving in to the temptations of the flesh, and that living by the spirit and giving in to the temptations of the flesh are in direct conflict and giving in to the temptations of the flesh leads to one not being saved. Paul lists out what is bad and should be avoided and also what is good and should be embraced, and finally (again) points a finger at the apparent issue of back-biting: *'²⁵ Since we live by the Spirit, let us keep in step with the Spirit. ²⁶ Let us not become conceited, provoking and envying each other.'*

Bear One Another's Burdens

Gal. 6:1-10

6. Brothers and sisters, if someone is caught in a sin, you who live by the Spirit should restore that person gently. But watch yourselves, or you also may be tempted. ² Carry each other's burdens, and in this way you will fulfill the law of Christ. ³ If anyone thinks they are something when they are not, they deceive themselves. ⁴ Each one should test their own actions. Then they can take pride in themselves alone, without comparing themselves to someone else, ⁵ for each one should carry their own load. ⁶ Nevertheless, the one who receives instruction in the word should share all good things with their instructor.
⁷ Do not be deceived: God cannot be mocked. A man reaps what he sows. ⁸ Whoever sows to please their flesh, from the flesh will reap destruction; whoever sows to please the Spirit, from the Spirit will reap eternal life. ⁹ Let us not become weary in doing good, for at the proper time we will reap a harvest if we do not give up. ¹⁰ Therefore, as we have opportunity, let us do good to all people, especially to those who belong to the family of believers.

In first 10 verses of this chapter of the Letter To The Galatians, Paul sets out guidelines for all to adopt and adhere to. His approach is direct but cautious, and gentle but also firm.

Not Circumcision but the New Creation

Gal. 6:11-18

6 ¹¹ See what large letters I use as I write to you with my own hand! ¹² Those who want to impress people by means of the flesh are trying to compel you to be circumcised. The only reason they do this is to avoid being persecuted for the cross of Christ. ¹³ Not even those who are circumcised keep the law, yet they want you to be circumcised that they may boast about your circumcision in the flesh. ¹⁴ May I never boast except in the cross of our Lord Jesus Christ, through which the world has been crucified to me, and I to the world. ¹⁵ Neither circumcision nor uncircumcision means anything; what counts is the new creation. ¹⁶ Peace and mercy to all who follow this rule – to the Israel of God.
¹⁷ From now on, let no one cause me trouble, for I bear on my body the marks of Jesus.
¹⁸ The grace of our Lord Jesus Christ be with your spirit, brothers and sisters. Amen.

Paul states that he is the one writing and emphasizes that he is intentionally writing large letters. He follows this statement with a criticism of *'¹² Those who want to impress people by means of the flesh are trying to compel you to be circumcised.'* and he then adds that the only reason for them to persuade all to become circumcised is so that they can boast about how much influence they carry and he contrasts that to him choosing to only boast about Jesus Christ and not about himself and he references that he bears on his body *'¹⁷ᵇ the marks of Jesus'*. Paul is not referring to marks put on his body by Jesus directly, but marks that Paul received when he was persecuted because he preached about Jesus (2 Cor. 11:24–25). He now wore the marks as signs of Jesus' ownership of him.[3]

2 Cor. 11:2⁴ *Of the Jews five times received I forty stripes save one. ²⁵ Thrice was I beaten with rods, once was I stoned, thrice I suffered shipwreck, a night and a day have I been in the deep.*

---

[3] https://www.bibleref.com/

The Compiled Teachings of The Apostle Paul

1 Corinthians

Proclaiming Christ Crucified 50	*Be Imitators of Me, As I Am of Christ* 57
Wisdom from the Spirit 50	*The Lord's Supper* 58
Divisions in the Church 51	*Spiritual Gifts* 58
The Ministry of Apostles 51	*One Body with Many Members* 59
Sexual Immorality Defiles the Church 52	*The Way of Love* 59
Lawsuits Against Believers 52	*Speaking In Tongues* 60
Flee Sexual Immorality 53	*Orderly Worship* 60
Principles for Marriage 53	*The Resurrection of Christ* 61
Live as You Are Called 54	*The Resurrection of the Dead* 61
The Unmarried and the Widowed 54	*The Resurrection Body* 62
Food Offered to Idols 55	*Mystery and Victory* 63
Paul Surrenders His Rights 55	*The Collection for the Saints* 63
Living Off The Gospel 56	*Plans for Travel* 63
Warning Against Idolatry 56	*Final Instructions* 63
Flee From Idolatry 57	*Salutations* 64
Do All to the Glory of God 57	

Paul's First Letter To The Church In Corinth written by Paul at Ephesus

See 'The Letters of Paul' or your own copy of The Holy Bible for the full text.

For notes on 1 Cor. 1, see 'The Greetings of each of the 'Letters Books' and 'Transition Passages' on pages 31- 34.

Proclaiming Christ Crucified

1 Corinthians 2:1-5

> *2: And I, brethren, when I came to you, came not with excellency of speech or of wisdom, proclaiming to you the testimony of God. ² For I determined not to know anything among you, save Jesus Christ, and him crucified. ³ And I was with you in weakness, and in fear, and in much trembling. ⁴ And my speech and my preaching were not in persuasive words of wisdom, but in demonstration of the Spirit and of power: ⁵ that your faith should not stand in the wisdom of men, but in the power of God.*

Paul begins this passage, even though it is not the opening sentence of his letter, by referring to his past visit to Corinth and explains what his purpose for that visit was, emphasizing that it was because of the Holy Spirit and the power of God that he came *'proclaiming to you the testimony of God.'*

Wisdom from the Spirit

1 Corinthians 2:6-16

> *⁶ We speak wisdom, however, among them that are full-grown: yet a wisdom not of this world, nor of the rulers of this world, who are coming to nought: ⁷ but we speak God's wisdom in a mystery, even the wisdom that has been hidden, which God foreordained before the worlds to our glory: ⁸ which none of the rulers of this world has known: for had they known it, they would not have crucified the Lord of glory: ⁹ but as it is written,*
>   *'Things which eye saw not, and ear heard not,*
>   *And which entered not into the heart of man,* [Is. 64:4; 65:17]
>   *Whatsoever things God prepared for them that love him.'*
>
> *¹⁰ But to us God revealed them through the Spirit: for the Spirit searches all things, yea, the deep things of God. ¹¹ For who among men knows the things of a man, save the spirit of the man, which is in him? even so the things of God none knows, save the Spirit of God. ¹² But we did not receive the spirit of the world, but the spirit which is from God; that we might know the things that were freely given to us of God. ¹³ Which things also we speak, not in words which man's wisdom teaches, but which the Spirit teaches; combining spiritual things with spiritual words. ¹⁴ Now the natural man receives not the things of the Spirit of God: for they are foolishness to him; and he cannot know them, because they are spiritually judged. ¹⁵ But he that is spiritual judges all*

Paul introduces the term 'full-grown' (grown up) in this passage as he teaches about wisdom. He also introduces the term 'this world', a term that Jesus used on several occasions: *Matt. 12:32; Luke 16:8; Luke 20:34; John 8:23; John 9:39; John 11:9; John 12:25; John 12:31; John 13:1; John 16:11; John 18:36.*

John points to the 'rulers of this world', referring to the Romans as not having wisdom for if they had they would not have crucified Jesus. We might look at this and react by saying that it was the leaders of the Jews who insisted that Jesus be crucified, but Paul is writing here to both Jews and Gentiles who have accepted Christ and are in leadership positions in the church in Corinth.

Paul then explains that it is by the Spirit which is from God, and that is the source of the wisdom that he teaches, finally pointing out that *'¹⁶ᵇ we have the mind of Christ'*.

things, and he himself is judged of no man. ¹⁶ For who has known the mind of the Lord, that he should instruct him? But we have the mind of Christ.

Divisions in the Church

1 Corinthians 3:1-23

3: And I, brethren, could not speak to you as to spiritual, but as to carnal, as to babes in Christ. ² I fed you with milk, not with meat; for you were not yet able to bear it: nay, not even now are you able; ³ for you are yet carnal: for whereas there is among you jealousy and strife, are you not carnal, and do you not walk after the manner of men? ⁴ For when one says, I am of Paul; and another, I am of Apollos; are you not men? ⁵ What then is Apollos? and what is Paul? Ministers through whom you believed; and each as the Lord gave to him. ⁶ I planted, Apollos watered; but God gave the increase. ⁷ So then neither is he that plants anything, neither he that waters; but God that gives the increase. ⁸ Now he that plants and he that waters are one: but each shall receive his own reward according to his own labor. ⁹ For we are God's fellow-workers: you are God's husbandry, God's building.

¹⁰ According to the grace of God which was given to me, as a wise master-builder I laid a foundation; and another builds thereon. But let each man take heed how he builds thereon. ¹¹ For other foundation can no man lay than that which is laid, which is Jesus Christ. ¹² But if any man builds on the foundation gold, silver, costly stones, wood, hay, stubble; ¹³ each man's work shall be made manifest: for the day shall declare it, because it is revealed in fire; and the fire itself shall prove each man's work of what sort it is. ¹⁴ If any man's work shall abide which he built thereon, he shall receive a reward. ¹⁵ If any man's work shall be burned, he shall suffer loss: but he himself shall be saved; yet so as through fire.

¹⁶ Do you not know that you are God's temple and that God's Spirit dwells in you? ¹⁷ If anyone destroys God's temple, God will destroy him. For God's temple is holy, and you are that temple. [ESV].

¹⁸ Let no man deceive himself. If any man thinks that he is wise among you in this world, let him become a fool, that he may become wise. ¹⁹ For the wisdom of this world is foolishness with God. For it is written, He that takes the wise in their craftiness: ²⁰ and again, The Lord knows the reasonings of the wise, that they are vain. ²¹ Wherefore let no one glory in men. For all things are yours; ²² whether Paul, or Apollos, or Cephas, or the world, or life, or death, or things present, or things to come; all are yours; ²³ and ye are Christ's; and Christ is God's.

In this passage Paul refers to his preaching while he was in Corinth telling them that they were not yet 'full-grown', and so he had to teach them according to their maturity, ²ᵇ *you were not yet able to bear it: nay,* adding *not even now are you able; ³ for you are [still] carnal.* Paul then explains that they are still carnal because they have chosen to identify themselves with himself, Paul, or with Apollos, or Cephas (Peter), or with another, and Paul challenges them with the question, ⁴ᶜ *are you not men?* (Are you not yet man enough to stand on your own feet; stand by your own convictions?) Paul does not discredit Apollos or any other minister but rather he explains that he sowed and laid a foundation upon which Apollos and others have built. *1 Cor. 3:10-11*

Paul then issues a warning that how one builds on a foundation that has already been put in place will become clear or obvious to the eye or mind, first in terms of the materials that are chosen, some of which are expensive but are durable and lasting but others being less expensive not so durable and can be easily destroyed. If your faith in Christ is solid, it will save you but if your faith in Christ is weak you will perish. Paul emphasizes that with God's spirit dwelling in you, you are God's temple and thus you are holy.

Again, without throwing criticism at Apollos, Cephas (Peter), or any other who has ministered to them, Paul cautions to not be fooled by unwise teaching, that is 'wisdom of the world', and we should discern carefully so as to be sure to only choose that which is consistent with '*the spirit which is from God*'. [1 Cor. 3:12]

Finally, Paul points out that if you are Christ's, then you are God's because Christ is God's.

The Ministry of Apostles

1 Corinthians 4:1-21

4: Let a man so account of us, as of ministers of Christ, and stewards of the mysteries of God. ² Here, moreover, it is required in stewards, that a man be found faithful. ³ But with me it is a very small thing that I should be judged of you, or of man's judgment: yea, I judge not my own self. ⁴ For I know nothing against myself; yet am I not hereby justified: but he that judges me is the Lord. ⁵ Wherefore judge nothing before the time, until the Lord come, who will both bring to light the hidden things of darkness, and make manifest the counsels of the hearts; and then shall each man have his praise from God.

⁶ Now these things, brethren, I have in a figure transferred to myself and Apollos for your sakes; that in us you might learn not to go beyond the things which are written; that no one of you be puffed up for the one against the other. ⁷ For who causes you to differ? and what have you that you did not receive? but if you did receive it, why do you glory as if you have not received it? ⁸ Already are

Paul now focuses on those who are, or are candidates to be ministers of God, who he ascribes the responsibility of stewards to. By referring to himself, Paul points out that it is only God that is qualified to judge us; ⁴ᵇ *he that judges me is the Lord.*

Paul then makes reference to who he believes the apostles to be; that they are *'set forth'* to be *⁹...last of all, as men doomed to death: for we are made a*

you filled, already you have become rich, you have come to reign without us: yea and I would that you did reign, that we also might reign with you. ⁹ For, I think, God has set forth us the apostles last of all, as men doomed to death: for we are made a spectacle to the world, both to angels and men. ¹⁰ We are fools for Christ's sake, but you are wise in Christ; we are weak, but you are strong; you have glory, but we have dishonor. ¹¹ Even unto this present hour we both hunger, and thirst, and are naked, and are buffeted, and have no certain dwelling-place; ¹² and we toil, working with our own hands: being reviled, we bless; being persecuted, we endure; ¹³ being defamed, we entreat: we are made as the filth of the world, the offscouring of all things, even until now.

¹⁴ I write not these things to shame you, but to admonish you as my beloved children. ¹⁵ For though you have ten thousand tutors in Christ, yet have you not many fathers; for in Christ Jesus I begat you through the gospel. ¹⁶ I beseech you therefore, be imitators of me. ¹⁷ For this cause have I sent to you Timothy, who is my beloved and faithful child in the Lord, who shall put you in remembrance of my ways which are in Christ, even as I teach everywhere in every church. ¹⁸ Now some are puffed up, as though I were not coming to you. ¹⁹ But I will come to you shortly, if the Lord will; and I will know, not the word of them that are puffed up, but the power. ²⁰ For the kingdom of God is not in word, but in power. ²¹ What will ye? shall I come to you with a rod, or [come] in love and a spirit of gentleness?

spectacle to the world, both to angels and men.' and Paul continues describing the apostles status ending with ¹³ᵇ*'we are made as the filth of the world, the offscouring of all things, even until now.*

Paul concludes this passage by explaining that his purpose was to admonish and correct, but not to shame anyone. Paul encourages them to each become as he is; *'be imitators of me.'*.

Paul then introduces Timothy to them, and describes him as being his *'beloved and faithful child in the Lord'* and Paul explains that Timothy will teach them as he, Paul, does.

Sexual Immorality Defiles the Church

1 Corinthians 5:1-13

5: It is actually reported that there is fornication among you, and such fornication as is not even among the Gentiles, that one of you has his father's wife. ² And you are puffed up, and did not rather mourn, that he that had done this deed might be taken away from among you. ³ For I verily, being absent in body but present in spirit, have already as though I were present judged him that has so wrought this thing, ⁴ in the name of our Lord Jesus, you being gathered together, and my spirit, with the power of our Lord Jesus, ⁵ to deliver such a one to Satan for the destruction of the flesh, that the spirit may be saved in the day of the Lord Jesus. ⁶ Your glorying is not good. Know you not that a little leaven leavens the whole lump? ⁷ Purge out the old leaven, that you may be a new lump, even as you are unleavened. For our Passover also has been sacrificed, even Christ: ⁸ wherefore let us keep the feast, not with old leaven, neither with the leaven of malice and wickedness, but with the unleavened bread of sincerity and truth.

⁹ I wrote to you in my epistle to have no company with fornicators; ¹⁰ not at all meaning with the fornicators of this world, or with the covetous and extortioners, or with idolaters; for then must you needs go out of the world: ¹¹ but as it is, I wrote to you not to keep company, if any man that is named a brother be a fornicator, or covetous, or an idolater, or a reviler, or a drunkard, or an extortioner; with such a one no, not to eat. ¹² For what have I to do with judging them that are without? Do you not judge them that are within? ¹³ But them that are without God judges. Put away the wicked man from among yourselves.

Now Paul, who concluded the last passage by asking, What would you prefer, that I come with a rod to discipline you or come with *'love and a spirit of gentleness?'* directly tackles a matter of disapproval, that of sexual conduct, and he makes it clear that the behavior that has been reported to him is not even common practice among gentiles and he references that someone, a male and one who presumably is an elder of the church, upon the death of his father took his father's wife to be his own wife. At best this would mean that his father had remarried (so the son had not married his mother), or at worst this person had taken his own mother to be his wife. Paul then acknowledges that he received this information second or third hand and not first-hand, in-person, and is guilty of already having judged and so had prayed that this person might be condemned and delivered to Satan. Paul then uses the analogy of how leaven (yeast) causes the 'whole lump', meaning the entire body, to rise, and so giving understanding to the phrase *'you are puffed up'* [v2] and he insists that they must clean out the old leaven entirely and replace it with ⁸ᵇ*the unleavened bread of sincerity and truth.*

Paul then concludes this passage by explaining that they should concern themselves only with judging those inside the church, and writes: *'¹²For what have I to do with judging them that are without?'… '¹³…them that are without God judges.'*

Lawsuits Against Believers

1 Corinthians 6:1-11

6: Dare any of you, having a matter against his neighbor, go to law before the unrighteous, and not before the saints? ²Or know you not that the saints shall judge the world? and if the world is judged by you, are you unworthy to judge the smallest matters? ³Know you not that we shall judge angels? how much

Paul now turns to a different issue; that of handling disputes. Should Christian brothers bring legal action against each other for when you do, you are seeking judgment be made by an unrighteous person against the Christian brother you bring before the court? Paul points

more, things that pertain to this life? ⁴If then you have to judge things pertaining to this life, do you set them before a judge who is of no account in the church? ⁵I say this to move you to shame.

What, cannot there be found among you one wise man who shall be able to decide between his brethren, ⁶but brother goes to law with brother, and that before unbelievers? ⁷No, already it is altogether a defect in you, that you have lawsuits one with another. Why not rather take wrong? why not rather be defrauded? ⁸No, but you yourselves do wrong, and defraud, and [at] that your brethren. ⁹ Or know you not that the unrighteous shall not inherit the kingdom of God? Be not deceived: neither fornicators, nor idolaters, nor adulterers, nor effeminate, nor abusers of themselves with men, ¹⁰ nor thieves, nor covetous, nor drunkards, nor revilers, nor extortioners, shall inherit the kingdom of God. ¹¹And such were some of you: but you were washed, but you were sanctified, but you were justified in the name of the Lord Jesus Christ, and in the Spirit of our God.

out that is we – who Paul references as saints – that should be judging the world rather than us seeking to have the world judge us. ²ᵇ...*are you unworthy to judge the smallest matters?* Paul asks. ⁴*If then you have to judge things pertaining to this life, do you set them before a judge who is of no account in the church?* ⁵ᵇ...*cannot there be found among you one wise man who shall be able to decide between his brethren?* Paul ends his argument by pointing out that the righteous are not going to inherit the kingdom of God and he lists categories of those who are unrighteous and whose behavior is offensive to God, pointing out some of those in the church were practicing such behaviors, but they have been justified into the Spirit of God by believing in and accepting Jesus as their savior.

Flee Sexual Immorality

1 Corinthians 6:12-20

¹²All things are lawful for me; but not all things are expedient. All things are lawful for me; but I will not be brought under the power of any. ¹³Meats for the belly, and the belly for meats: but God shall bring to naught both it and them. But the body is not for fornication, but for the Lord; and the Lord for the body: ¹⁴and God both raised the Lord, and will raise up us through his power.

¹⁵Know you not that your bodies are members of Christ? shall I then take away the members of Christ, and make them members of a harlot? God forbid.¹⁶Or know you not that he that is joined to a harlot is one body? for, The twain, said he, shall become one flesh. ¹⁷But he that is joined unto the Lord is one spirit. ¹⁸Flee fornication. Every sin that a man does is without the body; but he that commits fornication sins against his own body. ¹⁹Or know you not that your body is a temple of the Holy Spirit which is in you, which you have from God? and you are not your own; ²⁰for you were bought with a price: glorify God therefore in your body.

In this passage Paul is referring to food and to dietary restrictions. Although he is a Jew he states that all things (foods) are lawful for him meaning that he can eat whatever he chooses, but some foods are less beneficial than others. What we choose to eat is one way by which we take of our bodies. Our bodies are a temple [1 Cor. 3:16] ¹³ᵇ*But the body is not for fornication.* In fact, Paul writes, '¹⁵*Know you not that your bodies are members of Christ?* and then Paul points out that fornication joins two bodies together (¹⁶ᵇ*he that is joined to a harlot is one body*). Fornication is a sin against one's own body and the act of fornication thus separates you from the Spirit of God. *[You cannot be both contaminated and pure at the same time.]*

Fornication is, of course, sexual intercourse between a male and a female who are not married to each other. *[In many countries, even countries that are secular, there are laws forbidding adultery and fornication.]*

Principles for Marriage

1 Corinthians 7:1-17

7: Now concerning the things whereof you wrote: It is good for a man not to touch a woman. ²But, because of fornications, let each man have his own wife, and let each woman have her own husband. ³Let the husband render to the wife her due: and like-wise also the wife to the husband. ⁴The wife has not power over her own body, but the husband: and like-wise also the husband has not power over his own body, but the wife. ⁵Do not defraud one the other, except it be by consent for a season, that you may give yourselves up to prayer, and may be together again, that Satan not tempt you because of your lack of self restraint. ⁶ But this I say by way of concession, not of commandment. ⁷Yet I would that all men were even as I myself. Howbeit each man has his own gift from God, one after this manner, and another after that. ⁸But I say to the unmarried and to widows, it is good for them if they abide even as I. ⁹But if they have not continency, let them marry: for it is better to marry than to burn. ¹⁰But to the married I give charge, yea not I, but the Lord, That the wife depart not from her husband ¹¹(but should she depart, let her remain unmarried, or else be reconciled to her husband); and that the husband leave not his wife. ¹²But to the rest say I, not the Lord: If any brother has an unbelieving

Paul builds on the previous passage by explaining what is acceptable. Becoming married is the solution to growing families and to satisfying the carnal nature of man Paul advocates:

² because of fornications, let each man have his own wife, and let each woman have her own husband.

This statement promotes the practice of monogamy. *[Jesus said, 'I say to you, that every one that puts away his wife, except for the cause of fornication, makes her an adulteress: and whosoever that might marry her when she is put away also commits adultery.'* [Matt. 5:32] *and 'John said to Herod, It is not lawful for thee to have thy brother's wife.'* [Mark 6:18]*]*

wife, and she is content to dwell with him, let him not leave her. [13] *And the woman that has an unbelieving husband, and he is content to dwell with her, let her not leave her husband.* [14] *For the unbelieving husband is sanctified in the wife, and the unbelieving wife is sanctified in the brother [her husband]: else were your children unclean; but now are they holy.* [15] *Yet if the unbelieving departs, let them depart: the brother or the sister is not under bondage in such cases: but God has called us in peace.* [16] *For how knows you, O wife, whether you shall save your husband? or how do you know, O husband, whether you shall save thy wife?* [17] *Only, as the Lord has distributed to each man, as God has called each, so let him walk. And so I ordain in all the churches.*

Paul teaches to those who are married and are both believers and also teaches to those who are married to a partner (husband or wife) who is not a believer. Paul refers to the believers as brothers and sisters meaning they are brothers and sisters in Christ.

Paul addresses the situation regarding children of marriages that are between a believer and a non-believer explaining that the children are sanctified by their believing parent: [14b] *else were your children unclean; but now are they holy.*

Live as You Are Called

1 Corinthians 7:18-24

[18] *Was any man called being circumcised? let him not become uncircumcised. Has any been called in uncircumcision? let him not be circumcised.* [19] *Circumcision is nothing, and uncircumcision is nothing; but the keeping of the commandments of God.* [20] *Let each man abide in that calling wherein he was called.* [21] *Were you called being a bondservant? care not for it: no, even if you cannot become free, use it rather.* [22] *For he that was called in the Lord being a bondservant, is the Lord's freedman: likewise he that was called being free, is Christ's bondservant.* [23] *You were bought with a price; become not bond-servants of men.* [24] *Brethren, let each man, wherein he was called, therein abide with God.*

The two passages in this pericope have one thing in common; both are status at the time of calling. When God called on Abraham he was uncircumcised, but Abraham did not remain uncircumcised. Being called to circumcision is generally regarded as something for Jews and not for others, and Paul makes it clear that a Gentile does not need to become circumcised.

In the second part Paul discusses being a bondservant. Many were born into being bondservants and becoming free is something that was often not even a remote possibility. Having showed understanding for those in servitude and assuring them that they can be free in the Lord, he transitions to the choice of being a bondservant to Christ, which Paul encourages all to choose, and at the same time warns against becoming a bondservant of men: [23] *You were bought with a price; become not bondservants of men.*

The Unmarried and the Widowed

1 Corinthians 7:25-40

[25] *Now concerning virgins I have not (received a) commandment of the Lord: but I give my judgment, as one that has obtained mercy of the Lord to be trustworthy.* [26] *I think therefore that this is good by reason of the distress that is upon us, namely, that it is good for a man to be as he is.* [27] *Are you bound to a wife? seek not to be freed. Are you freed from a wife? seek not a wife.* [28] *But should you marry, you have not sinned; and if a virgin marry, she has not sinned. Yet such shall have tribulation in the flesh: and I would spare you.* [29] *But this I say, brethren, the time is shortened, that henceforth both those that have wives may be as though they had none;* [30] *and those that weep, as though they wept not; and those that rejoice, as though they rejoiced not; and those that buy, as though they possessed not;* [31] *and those that use the world, as not using it to the full: for the fashion of this world pass away.* [32] *But I would have you to be free from cares. He that is unmarried is careful for the things of the Lord, how he may please the Lord:* [33] *but he that is married is careful for the things of the world, how he may please his wife,* [34] *and is divided. So also the woman that is unmarried and the virgin is careful for the things of the Lord, that she may be holy both in body and in spirit: but she that is married is careful for the things of the world, how she may please her husband.* [35] *And this I say for your own*

Continuing with the link of wanting to be free, Paul returns to discussing marriage, but here the focus is on young adults and even youth. Starting form the perspectives of someone who is married and someone who was married, Paul asks, '[27] *Are you bound to a wife? seek not to be freed. Are you freed from a wife? seek not a wife.*' Paul then transitions directly into the topic of getting married: '[28] *But should you marry, you have not sinned;*' and in this same sentence Paul raises the topic of virginity: [28b] *if a virgin marry, she has not sinned.* and from that statement Paul moves into prophecy, first by predicting tribulation: '[28c] *such shall have tribulation in the flesh*', and then '*the time is shortened, that henceforth both those that have wives may be as though they had none;* [30] *and those that weep, as though they wept not; and those that rejoice, as though they rejoiced not; and those that buy, as though they possessed not;* [31] *and those that use the world, as not using it to the full: for the fashion(s) of this world pass away.*'

The next statement that Paul makes is '[33] *...he that is married is careful for the things of the world, how he may please his wife,* [34] *and is divided.*' This is a statement that rings true of Jesus' teaching that a man cannot serve two masters. [Luke 16:13] *No servant can serve two masters: for either he will hate the one, and love the other; or else he will hold to one, and despise the other. You cannot serve God and mammon.*]

In verse 36 Paul takes on what one might consider a challenging issue, 'Is it acceptable for a father to marry his daughter?' Was this one of the practices that had been reported to him? One might assume it must be. At face value in modern terms, it seems that when Paul says, 'Let them marry' he is giving approval to incest and possibly also to bigamy. However, how likely might it have been that a daughter

The Compiled Teachings of The Apostle Paul

profit; not that I may cast a snare upon you, but for that which is seemly, and that you may attend upon the Lord without distraction. ³⁶ But if any man thinketh that he behaves himself unseemly toward his virgin daughter, if she be past the flower of her age, and if need so requires, let him do what he will; he sins not; let them marry. ³⁷ But he that stands steadfast in his heart, having no necessity, but has power as touching his own will, and has determined this in his own heart, to keep his own virgin daughter, shall do well. ³⁸ So then both he that giveth his own virgin daughter in marriage does well; and he that giveth her not in marriage shall do better. ³⁹ A wife is bound for so long time as her husband lives; but if the husband be dead, she is free to be married to whom she will; only in the Lord. ⁴⁰ But she is happier if she abides as she is, after my judgment: and I think that I also have the Spirit of God.

would be prepared to marry her father if her mother was still alive? Not likely, but perhaps what was quite likely is that the elder daughter has become a surrogate for her deceased mother; quite likely a mother who died in childbirth or from some other cause. The older daughter would in almost all cases step up and take care of her siblings including a new born. Paul began by stating, *³⁶But if any man thinketh that he behaves himself unseemly toward his virgin daughter, if she be past the flower of her age, and if need so requires, let him do what he will; he sins not; let them marry*. In other words, the father is finding his own daughter as attractive to him as he found her mother and she has in some shown her love for him, and so Paul says *'let them marry'*. Then Paul continues to explain that there should be no expectation of either the father or the daughter to marry, and that the father who gives up his daughter to marrying another man does equally well, but the father that does not give his daughter in marriage *'shall do better'*. Paul then adds a complementary explanation regarding a wife whose husband dies, *³⁹ᵃ if the husband be dead, she is free to be married to whom she will; only in the Lord. ⁴⁰But she is happier if she abides as she is,…* and Paul ends with stating *'and I think that I also have the Spirit of God.'* – meaning that he believes his counsel has the approval of God.

Food Offered to Idols

8: Now concerning things sacrificed to idols: We know that we all have knowledge. Knowledge puffed up, but love edifies. ² If any man thinks that he knows anything, he knows not yet as he ought to know; ³ but if any man loves God, the same is known by him.
⁴ Concerning therefore the eating of things sacrificed to idols, we know that no idol is anything in the world, and that there is no God but one. ⁵ For though there be that are called gods, whether in heaven or on earth; as there are gods many, and lords many; ⁶ yet to us there is one God, the Father, of whom are all things, and we to him; and one Lord, Jesus Christ, through whom are all things, and we through him. ⁷ Howbeit there is not in all men that knowledge: but some, being used until now to the idol, eat as of a thing sacrificed to an idol; and their conscience being weak is defiled. ⁸ But food will not commend us to God: neither, if we eat not, are we the worse; nor, if we eat, are we the better. ⁹ But take heed lest by any means this liberty of yours become a stumbling block to the weak. ¹⁰ For if a man sees you who has knowledge sitting at meat in an idol's temple, will not his conscience, if he is weak, be emboldened to eat things sacrificed to idols? ¹¹ For through your knowledge he that is weak perishes, the brother for whose sake Christ died. ¹² And thus, sinning against the brethren, and wounding their conscience when it is weak, you sin against Christ. ¹³ Wherefore, if meat causes my brother to stumble, I will eat no flesh for evermore, that I cause not my brother to stumble.

1 Corinthians 8:1-13

Paul explains in this passage that there is only one true God; all other gods are merely idols, and it is because of lack of knowledge that not everyone understands this: *'⁶to us there is one God, the Father, of whom are all things… ⁷Howbeit there is not in all men that knowledge'*. Paul explains that we understand that eating sacrificial food *'⁸will not commend us to God: neither, if we eat not, are we the worse; nor, if we eat, are we the better.'*
Paul refers to those who don't know Jesus as being weak, and if someone who is weak sees you eating in an idol's temple – eating food that has been sacrificed to that idol – then they too will choose to do likewise. If you are eating sacrificed food in an idol's temple then you are sinning against the brethren, and so you are sinning against Christ. Moreover, you are causing the weak to stumble, and Paul says, *¹³ Wherefore, if meat causes my brother to stumble, I will eat no flesh for evermore, that I cause not my brother to stumble.*

Paul Surrenders His Rights

9. Am I not free? am I not an apostle? have I not seen Jesus our Lord? are not you my work in the Lord? ² If to others I am not an apostle, yet at least I am to you; for the seal of my apostleship are you in the Lord. ³ My defense to them that examine me is this. ⁴ Have we no right to eat and to drink? ⁵ Have we no right to lead about a wife that is a believer, even as the rest of the apostles, and the brethren of the Lord, and Cephas (Peter)? ⁶ Or I only and Barnabas, have we not a right to forbear working? ⁷ What soldier ever serves at his own charges? who plants a vineyard, and eats not the fruit

1 Corinthians 9:1-12

In this passage Paul presents an argument attacking those who claim that he is not an apostle. He points out that he has seen Jesus, referring to what happened on the road to Damascus. Paul points out that he has the right to eat and drink, and also the right to have a wife (although he doesn't have a wife) and points to Peter as having a wife and to Barnabas and himself as not having wives. (one should note that Barnabas was not one of the twelve apostles chosen by Jesus, and Barnabas did not, as far as we know, have a direct encounter with Jesus as did Paul.) Paul argues that one who in service as a soldier doesn't eat at his own cost, and one who has a vineyard surely eats grapes from the vines, and a goatherd surely drinks milk from the goats. Paul

The Compiled Teachings of The Apostle Paul

thereof? or who feeds a flock, and eats not of the milk of the flock?
⁸ Do I speak these things after the manner of men? or does not the law say also the same? ⁹ For it is written in the law of Moses, You shall not muzzle the ox when he treads out the corn.

Is it for the oxen that God cares, ¹⁰ or did he say it assuredly for our sake? Yes, for our sake it was written: because he that plows ought to plow in hope, and he that threshes, to thresh in hope of partaking. ¹¹ If we sowed to you spiritual things, is it a great matter if we shall reap your carnal things? ¹² If others partake of this right over you, do not we yet more? Nevertheless, we did not use this right; but we bear all things, that we may cause no hindrance to the gospel of Christ.

then references that an ox that is treading corn shall not be muzzled, thus it is not prevented from eating the corn, and asks, 'why did God command this? Was it for the ox's benefit or was it for man's benefit?' His response to these two questions is that it was for man's benefit because man had plowed the field and had sown the seed from which the corn grew, but not only should one reap what one sows but also he that threshes should also partake, which is for the ox's benefit.

Paul then continues to identify himself as one who sowed spiritually and argues that because he (and Barnabas) sowed spiritual things, they should also be allowed to share in carnal things, but they chose not to because they believed that would be a hindrance to them sharing the Gospel of Christ (which, of course, is the spiritual seed that they sowed).

Living Off The Gospel

1 Corinthians 9:13-26

¹³ Do you not know that they that minister about sacred things eat of the things of the temple, and they that wait upon the altar have their portion with the altar? ¹⁴ Even so did the Lord ordain that they that proclaim the gospel should live of the gospel. ¹⁵ But I have used none of these things: and I write not these things that it may be so done in my case; for it were good for me rather to die, than that any man should make my glorying void. ¹⁶ For if I preach the gospel, I have nothing to glory of; for necessity is laid upon me; for woe is to me if I preach not the gospel. ¹⁷ For if I do this of mine own will, I have a reward: but if not of mine own will, I have a stewardship entrusted to me. ¹⁸ What then is my reward? That, when I preach the gospel, I may make the gospel without charge, so as not to use to the full my right in the gospel. ¹⁹ For though I was free from all men, I brought myself under bondage to all, that I might gain the more. ²⁰ And to the Jews I became as a Jew, that I might gain Jews; to them that are under the law, as under the law, not being myself under the law, that I might gain them that are under the law; ²¹ to them that are without law, as without law, not being without law to God, but under law to Christ, that I might gain them that are without law. ²² To the weak I became weak, that I might gain the weak: I am become all things to all men, that I may by all means save some. ²³ And I do all things for the gospel's sake, that I may be a joint partaker thereof. ²⁴ Know you not that they that run in a race all run, but one receives the prize? Even so run; that you may attain. ²⁵ And every man that strives in the games, exercises self-control in all things. Now they do it to receive a corruptible crown; but we an incorruptible [recognition]. ²⁶ I therefore so run, as not uncertainly; so I fight, as not beating the air: ²⁷ but I buffet my body, and bring it into bondage: lest by any means, after that I have preached to others, I myself should be rejected.

In this passage Paul points out that *"they that wait upon the altar have their portion with the altar* and finally finishes up the justification for why he and others in ministry should benefit from their works. Paul is referring to shelter, food and drink. He then transitions to explain why he has chosen to minister. He references that he *'²⁰became as a Jew, that I might gain Jews'* and *'²¹ to them that are without [outside/not under] law, as without law, not being without law to God, but under law to Christ, that I might gain them that are without law.' ²²ᵇ I am become all things to all men, that I may by all means save some.'* Paul ends explaining that he prepares himself for rejection: *'²⁷ but I buffet my body, and bring it into bondage: lest by any means, after that I have preached to others, I myself should be rejected'*.

Warning Against Idolatry

1 Corinthians 10:1-13

10. For I would not, brethren, have you ignorant, that our fathers were all under the cloud, and all passed through the sea; ² and were all baptized to Moses in the cloud and in the sea; ³ and did all eat the same spiritual food; ⁴ and did all drink the same spiritual drink: for they drank of a spiritual rock that followed them: and the rock was Christ. ⁵ Howbeit with most of them God was not well pleased: for they were overthrown in the wilderness. ⁶ Now these things were our examples, to the intent we should not lust after evil things, as they also lusted. ⁷ Neither be idolaters, as were some of them; as it is written, The people sat down to eat and drink, and rose up to play. ⁸ Neither let us commit fornication, as some of them committed, and fell in one day three and twenty thousand. ⁹ Neither let us make trial of the Lord, as some of them made trial, and perished by the serpents. ¹⁰ Neither murmur, as some of them murmured, and perished by the destroyer. ¹¹ Now these things happened to them by way of example; and they were written for our admonition, upon who the ends of the ages are come. ¹² Wherefore let him that thinks he stands take heed

Speaking specifically to Jews, Paul reminds them that their fathers [ancestors] followed and lived with Moses in the wilderness, and although their ancestors did not know Jesus, Christ was their spiritual rock. Paul points out that they displeased God and were punished for it. Some died because they committed sins of fornication, some tested the Lord and were killed by serpents [snakes]. Some complained and were killed by the destroyer, which The NLT translates as 'the angel of death'. [NLT – New Living Translation]

These things of the past, Paul writes were written down so that they (Paul and everyone living) would have the benefit of knowing these things: *¹¹they were written for our admonition [guidance].* Paul

lest he fall. ¹³ *No temptation has taken you but such as man can bear: but God is faithful, who will not suffer you to be tempted above that you are able; but will with the temptation make also the way of escape, that you may be able to endure it.*

writes that you will not be tempted beyond that you are able to bear: '¹³*God is faithful, who will not suffer you to be tempted above that you are able.'*

Flee From Idolatry

1 Corinthians 10:14-22

¹⁴ *Wherefore, my beloved, flee from idolatry.* ¹⁵ *I speak as to wise men; judge what I say.* ¹⁶ *The cup of blessing which we bless, is it not a communion of the blood of Christ? The bread which we break, is it not a communion of the body of Christ?* ¹⁷ *seeing that we, who are many, are one bread, one body: for we all partake of the one bread.* ¹⁸ *Behold Israel after the flesh: have not they that eat the sacrifices communion with the altar?* ¹⁹ *What say I then? that a thing sacrificed to idols is anything, or that an idol is anything?* ²⁰ *But I say, that the things which the Gentiles sacrifice, they sacrifice to demons, and not to God: and I would not that you should have communion with demons.* ²¹ *You cannot drink the cup of the Lord, and [also] the cup of demons: you cannot partake of the table of the Lord, and [also] of the table of demons.* ²² *Or do we provoke the Lord to jealousy? are we stronger than he?*

Paul now turns to address the topic of idolatry beginning with the simple statement, '^{14b} *flee from idolatry*' and then proceeds to summarize how Christians worship and remember Christ: '^{17b}*[we] are one bread, one body: for we all partake of the one bread.'*. Paul acknowledges that Jews (Israel) do make religious sacrifices:1⁸ *Look at the people of Israel; are those who eat the sacrifices not partners in the altar?* [NASB] But Paul then expresses the view that Gentiles, who the NIV refers to as pagans, make sacrifices to demons and not sacrifices to God. [After all, other than Christ on the Cross, there is no image of God, but the 'gods' of the Gentiles all had recognizable images. Again, Paul echoes Jesus teaching that you cannot serve two masters.

Do All to the Glory of God

1 Corinthians 10:23-33

²³ *All things are lawful; but not all things are expedient. All things are lawful; but not all things edify.* ²⁴ *Let no man seek his own, but each his neighbor's good.* ²⁵ *Whatsoever is sold in the market, eat, asking no question for conscience' sake;* ²⁶ *for the earth is the Lord's, and the fulness thereof.* ²⁷ *If one of them that believes not bids you to a feast, and you are disposed to go; whatsoever is set before you, eat, asking no question for conscience' sake.* ²⁸ *But if any man say to you, This has been offered in sacrifice, eat not, for his sake that showed it, and for conscience' sake;* ²⁹ *conscience, I say, not your own, but the other's; for why is my liberty judged by another conscience?* ³⁰ *If I partake with thankfulness, why is evil spoken of me for that for which I give thanks?* ³¹ *Whether therefore you eat, or drink, or whatsoever you do, do all to the glory of God.* ³² *Give no occasion of stumbling, either to Jews, or to Greeks, or to the church of God:* ³³ *even as I also please all men in all things, not seeking mine own profit, but the profit of the many, that they may be saved.*

Does Paul really mean all things are permitted (lawful)? Surely Leviticus 11:1-47 and Deuteronomy 12:1-7 detail restrictions on what may be eaten by Jews, laws that surely Paul does not have the authority to overrule. In this passage Paul acknowledges the environment in which the people of Corinth live. The markets are not kosher and so he comments: '²⁶*the earth is the Lord's, and the fulness thereof.'* Paul also advises that if a Gentile invites you to a feast, accept the invitation and eat '^{27b}*whatsoever is set before you*', but then Paul spells out the exception: do not eat anything that you know has been offered in sacrifice to any idol – '²⁸ *But if any man say to you, This has been offered in sacrifice, eat not*'… '³¹ *Whether therefore you eat, or drink, or whatsoever you do, do all to the glory of God.* ³² *Give no occasion of stumbling, either to Jews, or to Greeks, or to the church of God*'.

Paul's final statement in verse 33 essentially says, 'I choose to make myself acceptable to others so that I can reach them.'

Be Imitators of Me, As I Am of Christ

1 Corinthians 11:1-16

11. Become imitators of me, even as I also am of Christ. ² *Now I praise you that you remember me in all things, and hold fast the traditions, even as I delivered them to you.* ³ *But I would have you know, that the head of every man is Christ; and the head of the woman is the man; and the head of Christ is God.* ⁴ *Every man praying or prophesying, having his head covered, dishonors his head.* ⁵ *But every woman praying or prophesying with her head unveiled dishonors her head; for it is one and the same thing as if she were shaven.* ⁶ *For if a woman is not veiled, let her also be shorn: but if it is a shame to a woman to be shorn or shaven, let her be veiled.* ⁷ *For a man indeed ought not to have his head veiled, forasmuch as he is the image and glory of God: but the woman is the glory of the man.* ⁸ *For the man is not of the woman; but the woman of the man;* ⁹ *for neither was the man created for the woman; but the woman for the man:* ¹⁰ *for this cause ought the woman to have a sign of authority on her head, because of the angels.* ¹¹ *Nevertheless, neither is the woman without the man, nor the man without the woman, in the Lord.* ¹² *For as the woman is of the man, so is the man also by the woman; but*

Paul begins this passage with an instruction, '*Become imitators of me*', and then, Paul introduces the topic of traditions. '^{3b} *know, that the head of every man is Christ; and the head of the woman is the man; and the head of Christ is God.* ⁴ *Every man praying or prophesying, having his head covered, dishonors his head.* ⁵ *But every woman praying or prophesying with her head unveiled dishonors her head,'* and Paul continues to explain why it is right for a woman to have long hair while '^{14b} *if a man has long hair, it is a dishonor to him.'* Paul then concludes with, '¹⁶ *But if*

all things are of God. ¹³ *Judge yourselves: is it seemly that a woman pray to God unveiled?* ¹⁴ *Does not even nature itself teach you, that, if a man has long hair, it is a dishonor to him?* ¹⁵ *But if a woman has long hair, it is a glory to her: for her hair is given her for a covering.* ¹⁶ *But if any man seems to be contentious, we have no such custom, neither the churches of God.*

any man seems to be contentious, we have no such custom, neither [do] the churches of God', as if advising, 'this is not a topic for discussion or debate'.

The Lord's Supper

¹⁷ *But in giving you this charge, I praise you not, that you come together not for the better but for the worse.* ¹⁸ *For first of all, when you come together in the church, I hear that divisions exist among you; and I partly believe it.* ¹⁹ *For there must be also factions among you, that they that are approved may be made manifest among you.* ²⁰ *When therefore assemble yourselves together, it is not possible to eat the Lord's supper:* ²¹ *for in your eating each one takes before others his own supper; and one is hungry, and another is drunken.* ²² *What, have you not houses to eat and to drink in? or do you despise the church of God, and put them to shame that have not? What shall I say to you? shall I praise you? In this I praise you not.* ²³ *For I received of the Lord that which also I delivered to you, that the Lord Jesus in the night in which he was betrayed took bread;* ²⁴ *and when he had given thanks, he broke it, and said, This is my body, which is for you: this do in remembrance of me.* ²⁵ *In like manner also the cup, after supper, saying, This cup is the new covenant in my blood: this do, as often as you drink it, in remembrance of me.* ²⁶ *For as often as you eat this bread, and drink the cup, you proclaim the Lord's death till he comes.* ²⁷ *Wherefore whosoever shall eat the bread or drink the cup of the Lord in an unworthy manner, shall be guilty of the body and the blood of the Lord.* ²⁸ *But let a man prove himself, and so let him eat of the bread, and drink of the cup.* ²⁹ *For he that eats and drinks, eats and drinks judgment upon himself, if he discerns not the body.* ³⁰ *For this cause many among you are weak and sickly, and not a few sleep.* ³¹ *But if we discerned ourselves, we should not be judged.* ³² *But when we are judged, we are chastened of the Lord, that we may not be condemned with the world.* ³³ *Wherefore, my brethren, when you come together to eat, wait one for another.* ³⁴ *If any man is hungry, let him eat at home; that your coming together be not to judgment. And the rest will I set in order whensoever I come.*

1 Corinthians 11:17-34

Paul references 'hearing about divisions' within the church, which was the topic of 1 Cor. 3. He points out that they, as a church, cannot come together to eat the Lord's supper: '²⁰ *When therefore assemble yourselves together, it is not possible to eat the Lord's supper'*.

The description that Paul gives leads one to feel that there is some degree of greediness and drunkenness in how they are eating together. Paul rebukes them: '^{22b}*What shall I say to you? shall I praise you? In this I praise you not'*, and then he reminds them of how he had shared the tradition of the Lord's supper *(1 Cor. 11:23-28)*. Verse 29, '²⁹ *For he that eats and drinks, eats and drinks judgment upon himself, if he discerns not the body'* needs to be understood as referencing the body of Christ; the Lord's body, rather than each of our own bodies. Whenever we eat, we should be conscious of what we eat and drink and how much we eat and drink so that we take care of our physical needs correctly, healthily and in balance, but the Lord's supper is to be for remembrance not for meeting our physical daily needs: '³⁴ *If any man is hungry, let him eat at home.*

Spiritual Gifts

12. Now concerning spiritual gifts, brethren, I would not have you ignorant. ² *You know that when you were Gentiles you were led away to those dumb idols, howsoever you might be led.* ³ *Wherefore I make known to you, that no man speaking in the Spirit of God said, Jesus is anathema; and no man can say, Jesus is Lord, except in the Holy Spirit.* [anathema – disliked, loathed]
⁴ *Now there are diversities of gifts, but the same Spirit.*
⁵ *And there are diversities of ministrations, and the same Lord.* ⁶ *And there are diversities of workings, but the same God, who works all things in all.* ⁷ *But to each one is given the manifestation of the Spirit to profit likewise.* ⁸ *For to one is given through the Spirit the word of wisdom; and to another the word of knowledge, according to the same Spirit:* ⁹ *to another faith, in the same Spirit; and to another gifts of healings, in the one Spirit;* ¹⁰ *and to another workings of miracles; and to another prophecy; and to another discerning of spirits: to another diverse kinds of tongues; and to another*

1 Corinthians 12:1-11

Paul now focuses on spiritual gifts. He says he does not want them to be ignorant about spiritual gifts. When you were Gentiles, Paul says, 'you were led to idols, and taught to worship them, and to make sacrifices to them'. Paul also says, 'no man speaking in the spirit of God can claim that Jesus is an anathema; and no man can say, 'Jesus Lord', except in the Holy Spirit'. Paul explains there is one God from whom there is one spirit, but different spiritual gifts are given to different individuals. each is given a different spiritual gift, or gifts, for different purposes, and each serves that purpose or purposes:

⁸ *For to one is given through the Spirit the word of wisdom; and to another the word of knowledge, according to the same Spirit:* ⁹ *to another faith, in the same Spirit; and to another gifts of healings, in the one Spirit;* ¹⁰ *and to another workings of miracles; and to another prophecy; and to another discerning of spirits: to another diverse kinds of tongues; and to another the interpretation of tongues.*

One Body with Many Members

1 Corinthians 12:12-31

12 For as the body is one, and has many members, and all the members of the body, being many, are one body; so also is Christ. 13 For in one Spirit were we all baptized into one body, whether Jews or Greeks, whether bond or free; and were all made to drink of one Spirit. 14 For the body is not one member, but many. 15 If the foot shall say, Because I am not the hand, I am not of the body; it is not therefore not of the body. 16 And if the ear shall say, Because I am not the eye, I am not of the body; it is not therefore not of the body. 17 If the whole body were an eye, where were the hearing? If the whole were hearing, where were the smelling? 18 But now God has set the members each one of them in the body, even as it pleased him. 19 And if they were all one member, where were the body? 20 But now they are many members, but one body. 21 And the eye cannot say to the hand, I have no need of thee: or again the head to the feet, I have no need of you. 22 Nay, much rather, those members of the body which seem to be more feeble are necessary: 23 and those parts of the body, which we think to be less honorable, upon these we bestow more abundant honor; and our uncomely parts have more abundant comeliness; 24 whereas our comely parts have no need: but God tempered the body together, giving more abundant honor to that part which lacked; 25 that there should be no schism in the body; but that the members should have the same care one for another. 26 And whether one member suffers, all the members suffer with it; or one member is honored, all the members rejoice with it. 27 Now you are the body of Christ, and severally members thereof. 28 And God hath set some in the church, first apostles, secondly prophets, thirdly teachers, then miracles, then gifts of healings, helps, governments, diverse kinds of tongues. 29 Are all apostles? are all prophets? are all teachers? are all workers of miracles? 30 have all gifts of healings? do all speak with tongues? do all interpret? 31 But desire earnestly the greater gifts. And moreover a most excellent way show I to you.

Together we are the body of Christ, and just as the human body is made up of many members – *18 God has set the members each one of them in the body, even as it pleased him.* So is the body of Christ, into which we have all been baptized, made up of many members. Paul explains how all parts of our bodies are necessary and all are dependent on other parts; none are independent and *25b '...that the members should have the same care one for another.'*

While all members (parts) are important, are all parts equal? Paul writes, *'28 And God hath set some in the church, first apostles, secondly prophets, thirdly teachers, then miracle [workers], then [those with] gifts of healings, helps, governments, diverse kinds of tongues. 29 Are all apostles? are all prophets? 30 have all gifts of healings? do all speak are all teachers? are all workers of miracles? with tongues? do all interpret? 31 But desire earnestly the greater gifts.'*

Paul is encouraging all to desire those gifts that are considered more Spiritual than the others, and he suggests he can teach them in the best possible – *a most excellent* – way.

The Way of Love

1 Corinthians 13:1-13; 14:1-5

13. If I speak with the tongues of men and of angels, but have not love, I am become sounding brass, or a clanging cymbal. 2 And if I have the gift of prophecy, and know all mysteries and all knowledge; and if I have all faith, so as to remove mountains, but have not love, I am nothing. 3 And if I bestow all my goods to feed the poor, and if I give my body to be burned, but have not love, it profits me nothing. 4 Love suffers long, and is kind; love envies not; love vaunts not itself, is not puffed up, 5 does not behave itself unseemly, seeks not its own, is not provoked, takes not account of evil; 6 rejoices not in unrighteousness, but rejoices with the truth; 7 bears all things, believes all things, hopes all things, endures all things. 8 Love never fails: but whether there be prophecies, they shall be done away; whether there be tongues, they shall cease; whether there be knowledge, it shall be done away. 9 For we know in part, and we prophesy in part; 10 but when that which is perfect is come, that which is in part shall be done away.
11 When I was a child, I spoke as a child, I felt as a child, I thought as a child: now that I am become a man, I have put away childish things. 12 For now we see in a mirror, darkly; but then face to face: now I know in part; but then shall I know fully even as also I was fully known. 13 But now abides faith, hope, love, these three; and the greatest of these is love.

14. Follow after love; yet desire earnestly spiritual gifts, but rather that you may prophesy. 2 For he that speaks in a tongue speaks not to men, but to God; for no man understands; but in the spirit he speaks mysteries. 3 But

The 'most excellent way' that Paul referenced in the last passage is the 'excellent way of love'. Paul now references gifts and talents – prophecy, knowledge and faith – but, *'2c have not love, I am nothing.' 3 And if I bestow all my goods to feed the poor, and if I give my body to be burned, but have not love, it profits me nothing.'* This chapter of the first letter to the Corinthians is often referred to as the 'love chapter'. In the next ten verses – 4 through 13 – Paul lists the many virtues of love closing the chapter with *'13But now abides faith, hope, love, these three; and the greatest of these is love.'*

Paul's teaching of this passage continues with *'Follow after love; yet desire earnestly spiritual gifts, but rather that you may prophesy'*, and in the next four verses –

The Compiled Teachings of The Apostle Paul

he that prophesies speaks to men edification, and exhortation, and consolation. ⁴ He that speaks in a tongue edifies himself; but he that prophesies edifies the church. ⁵ Now I would have you all speak with tongues, but rather that you should prophesy: and greater is he that prophesies than he that speaks with tongues, except he interprets, that the church may receive edifying.

verses 2 through 5 – Paul lists the virtues of prophesying and, implicitly, Paul introduces the topics of speaking in tongues and interpreting.

Speaking In Tongues

⁶ But now, brethren, if I come to you speaking with tongues, what shall I profit you, unless I speak to you either by way of revelation, or of knowledge, or of prophesying, or of teaching. ⁷ Even things without life, giving a voice, whether pipe or harp, if they give not a distinction in the sounds, how shall it be known what is piped or harped? ⁸ For if the trumpet give an uncertain voice, who shall prepare himself for war? ⁹ So also you, unless you utter by the tongue speech easy to be understood, how shall it be known what is spoken? for you will be speaking into the air. ¹⁰ There are, it may be, so many kinds of voices in the world, and no kind is without significance. ¹¹ If then I know not the meaning of the voice, I shall be to him that speaks [as] a barbarian, and he that speaks will be [as] a barbarian to me. ¹² So also you, since you are zealous of spiritual gifts, seek that you may abound to the edifying of the church. ¹³ Wherefore let him that speaks in a tongue pray that he may interpret. ¹⁴ For if I pray in a tongue, my spirit prays, but my understanding is unfruitful. ¹⁵ What is it then? I will pray with the spirit, and I will pray with the understanding also: I will sing with the spirit, and I will sing with the understanding also. ¹⁶ Else if you bless with the spirit, how shall he that fills the place of the unlearned say the Amen at your giving of thanks, seeing he knows not what you say? ¹⁷ For you verily give thanks well, but the other is not edified. ¹⁸ I thank God, I speak with tongues more than you all: ¹⁹ howbeit in the church I had rather speak five words with my understanding, that I might instruct others also, than ten thousand words in a tongue. ²⁰ Brethren, be not children in mind: yet in malice be babes, but in mind be men. ²¹ In the law it is written, By men of strange tongues and by the lips of strangers will I speak to this people; and not even thus will they hear me, says the Lord. ²² Wherefore tongues are for a sign, not to them that believe, but to the unbelieving: but prophesying is for a sign, not to the unbelieving, but to them that believe. ²³ If therefore the whole church be assembled together and all speak with tongues, and there come in men unlearned or unbelieving, will they not say that ye are mad? ²⁴ But if all prophesy, and there come in one unbelieving or unlearned, he is reproved by all, he is judged by all; ²⁵ the secrets of his heart are made manifest; and so he will fall down on his face and worship God, declaring that God is among you indeed.

1 Corinthians 14:6-25

Paul explains in this passage that the gift of tongues is a desirable spiritual gift, but unless there is someone who can interpret what is being spoken in tongues, no one can benefit from that gift – *⁹ So also you, unless you utter by the tongue speech easy to be understood, how shall it be known what is spoken?* In referencing *¹⁰ There are, it may be, so many kinds of voices in the world, and no kind is without significance. ¹¹ If then I know not the meaning of the voice, I shall be to him that speaks [as] a barbarian, and he that speaks will be [as] a barbarian to me.'* Paul is referring to there being many different languages spoken, and so the gift of interpreter is even more prized – *¹³ Wherefore let him that speaks in a tongue pray that he may interpret.* Interpretation enables ¹⁶ᵇ *'the unlearned say the Amen at your giving of thanks'*. Only then with interpretation are others edified. Paul admits (or even boasts) that he speaks in tongues but adds *¹⁹ᵇ in the church I had rather speak five words with my understanding, that I might instruct others also, than ten thousand words in a tongue.'*. Paul does not state clearly whether he is able to interpret or not, but as he acknowledges he must speak not in tongues for others to understand, he probably does not interpret.

Paul now references children and babes: *'be not children in mind: yet in malice be babes, but in mind be men.'*. The word 'malice' means evil intent or desire to do harm and so Paul is telling the church in Corinth to have no intentional desire to cause harm. Paul then quotes Isaiah 28:11 *¹¹ Nay, but by men of strange lips and with another tongue will he speak to this people;* which could simply mean speaking in another language (tongue), or it might mean speaking in tongues. Paul points out that those who are unlearned (about Christ) and are unbelieving might, should they experience a congregation speaking in tongues consider what they are hearing madness, but if there is one person who is able to interpret, then the unbelieving or unlearned will understand and will *'fall down on his face and worship God, declaring that God is among you indeed.'*.

Orderly Worship

²⁶ What is it then, brethren? When you come together, each one has a psalm, has a teaching, has a revelation, has a tongue, has an interpretation. Let all things be done to edify. ²⁷ If any man speaks in a tongue, let it be by two, or at the most three, and that in turn; and let one interpret: ²⁸ but if there be no interpreter, let him keep silent in the church; and let him speak to himself, and to God. ²⁹ And let the prophets speak by two or three, and let the others discern. ³⁰ But if a revelation be made to another sitting by, let the first keep silence. ³¹ For you all can prophesy one by one, that all may learn, and all may be

1 Corinthians 14:26-40

Paul now turns his focus on establishing and maintaining orderly worship and in doing so establishes an 'order of service' that all meetings can follow: Reading a psalm, a teaching, a revelation, a prophesy, and speaking in tongues with interpretation. Prophets and those with revelations should speak one at a time, with two or three at most speaking, one after the other.

The Compiled Teachings of The Apostle Paul

exhorted; ^{32} *and the spirits of the prophets are subject to the prophets;* ^{33} *for God is not a God of confusion, but of peace. As in all the churches of the saints,* ^{34} *let the women keep silent in the churches: for it is not permitted to them to speak; but let them be in subjection, as also says the law.* ^{35} *And if they would learn anything, let them ask their own husbands at home: for it is shameful for a woman to speak in the church.* ^{36} *What? was it from you that the word of God went forth? or came it to you alone?* ^{37} *If any man thinks himself to be a prophet, or spiritual, let him take knowledge of the things which I write to you, that they are the commandment of the Lord.* ^{38} *But if any man is ignorant, let him be ignorant.* ^{39} *Wherefore, my brethren, desire earnestly to prophesy, and forbid not to speak with tongues.* ^{40} *But let all things be done decently and in order.*

Women in the church should remain silent, '*it is not permitted for them to speak*' Paul advises (verse 34) referencing the law, and he continues: ^{35} *And if they would learn anything, let them ask their own husbands at home: for it is shameful for a woman to speak in the church.*' Paul then writes specifically regarding those that might feel they are spiritual or even a prophet, admonishing them to take note of all he (Paul) is writing, or choose to be ignorant.

The Resurrection of Christ
1 Corinthians 15:1-11

15. Now I make known to you brethren, the gospel which I preached to you, which also you received, wherein also you stand, ^{2} *by which also you are saved, if you hold fast the word which I preached to you, except you believed in vain.* ^{3} *For I delivered to you first of all that which also I received: that Christ died for our sins according to the scriptures;* ^{4} *and that he was buried; and that he was raised on the third day according to the scriptures;* ^{5} *and that he appeared to Cephas [Peter]; then to the twelve;* ^{6} *then he appeared to more than five hundred brethren at once, of whom the greater part remain until now, but some are fallen asleep;* ^{7} *then he appeared to James; then to all the apostles;* ^{8} *and last of all, as to the child untimely born, he appeared to me also.* ^{9} *For I am the least of the apostles, that am not fit to be called an apostle, because I persecuted the church of God.* ^{10} *But by the grace of God I am what I am: and his grace which was bestowed upon me was not found vain; but I labored more abundantly than they all: yet not I, but the grace of God which was with me.* ^{11} *Whether then it be I or they, so we preach, and so you believed.*

In verses 1-8 Paul provides a summary "statement of faith" but in verse 2: '^{2} *by which also you are saved, if you hold fast the word which I preached to you, except you believed in vain.*'. The phrase '*except you believed in vain*' appears to negate the value of being a believer; and these words are how many Bible translations read. "We have believed in vain? How so?" Perhaps a more correct translation would be, '*or otherwise you have believed in vain.*' In other words '*we believe that we are saved, but if this is not true, then we have held to this belief in vain*'. Then Paul describes himself as being the least of the Apostles, and he gives a reason for considering himself to be the least: ^{9} *For I am the least of the apostles, that am not fit to be called an apostle, because I persecuted the church of God*. Here Paul is referring to when he was Saul and is recorded by Luke in the Book of Acts as, '*Saul, still breathing threats and murder against the disciples of the Lord, went to the High Priest, and asked for letters from him (the High Priest) to the synagogues at Damascus, so that if he found any belonging to The Way, both men and women, he might bring them bound to Jerusalem.*' (Acts 9:1)

Paul now completes his statement of faith by stating that it is by the grace of God that he is what he is; a preacher of the gospel.

An alternative understanding of what Paul might have been addressing the phrase 'except you believed in vain' in verse 1 is that the Corinthians could have been believing the gospel in vain if they did not and were not believing the gospel as he had preached it to them. In other words, if anyone was believing a false version of the gospel of Jesus, that person should not think that they have any standing before God. An example of a false version of the Gospel is one in which, while there is faith in believing Christ's death, there is not faith and belief in His resurrection. [4] Those who were teaching that there is no resurrection were teaching a false Gospel.

In verse 5, Paul writes that Jesus appeared before the twelve disciples, and in verse 6 adds, '*then he appeared to more than five hundred brethren at once, of whom the greater part remain until now, but some are fallen asleep*'. There is no corroboration in any of the four gospels or in the Book of Acts, but it might possibly be that Paul learned this from James (Gal. 1:19; Gal. 2:9), who Paul has also mentioned in verse 7 [1 cor. 15:7] as a witness to the resurrection of Christ.

The next passage, 1 Cor. 15, is teaching by Paul regarding the second coming of Christ and the periods of tribulation, rapture and Armageddon that Jesus warned His disciples of [Matt. 24:15-28; Luke 17:22-37], which shows that not only was Paul well studied in the Scriptures (of the Old Testament) which he learned as a pharisee, but he had learned well about Christ from 'studying' with the Apostles and other disciples. – See also 1 Thess. 4:14-18.

The Resurrection of the Dead
1 Corinthians 15:12-34

^{12} *Now if Christ is preached that he has been raised from the dead, how say some among you that there is no resurrection of the dead?* ^{13} *But if there is no resurrection of the dead, neither has Christ been raised:* ^{14} *and if Christ has not been raised, then*

Regarding Paul's question, '^{12b} *how say some among you that there is no resurrection of the dead?*', Paul would be referring to the Sadducees and possibly others who believe there is no resurrection, and Paul presents the

---

[4] Commentary credit: https://www.bibleref.com/

is our preaching vain, your faith also is vain. ¹⁵ *Yea, and we are found false witnesses of God; because we witnessed of God that he raised up Christ: whom he raised not up, if so be that the dead are not raised.* ¹⁶ *For if the dead are not raised, neither has Christ been raised:* ¹⁷ *and if Christ has not been raised, your faith is vain; you are yet in your sins.*

argument that if there is no resurrection, then Christ could not have been raised up from death: ¹³ *But if there is no resurrection of the dead, neither has Christ been raised*. Paul completes a chain of logical thinking to point out that if Christ didn't rise (wasn't raised) from death, then '*we are of all men most pitiable*' (v18). Paul, of course, rejects that as a reality because the evidence of eyewitnesses, the Apostles and others, assures us that Christ was resurrected.

¹⁸ *Then they also that are fallen asleep in Christ have perished.* ¹⁹ *If we have only hoped in Christ in this life, we are of all men most pitiable.*

²⁰ *But now has Christ been raised from the dead, the first-fruits of them that are asleep.* ²¹ *For since by man came death, by man came also the resurrection of the dead.* ²² *For as in Adam all die, so also in Christ shall all be made alive.* ²³ *But each in his own order: Christ the first-fruits; then they that are Christ's, at his coming* ²⁴ *Then comes the end, when he will deliver up the kingdom to God, even the Father; when he shall have abolished all rule and all authority and power.* ²⁵ *For he must reign, till he has put all his enemies under his feet.* ²⁶ *The last enemy that shall be abolished is death.* ²⁷ *For, He put all things in subjection under his feet. But when he said, All things are put in subjection, it is evident that he is excepted who did subject all things to him.* ²⁸ *And when all things have been subjected to him, then shall the Son also himself be subjected to him that did subject all things to him, that God may be all in all.*

Paul explains that Christ's death was the start and that was followed by Christ's resurrection. Just as Adam died because he sinned, all of mankind will also die because of sin, but that is just the death of our physical bodies. Because Christ died and was raised from the dead and then ascended into heaven we can be confident that those who believe will also be resurrected, not physically, but spiritually. In Christ we shall all be made alive.*

All things are put in subjection [to Jesus] but '²⁷ᵇ *it is evident that he is excepted who did subject all things to him.*' meaning that God is not subjected to Jesus, but Jesus is subjected to God.

The next verses, 29 & 30 raise two questions: The first is: 'If individuals are responsible to God for their own sin and their own personal faith in Christ for the forgiveness of that sin, why would any person be baptized on behalf of another person, especially one who is dead?' Since being '*baptized for the dead*' is not a Christian practice, it may have been a practice of a group that were followers of a leader who preached against resurrection. If this was so it would make logical sense for Paul to ask what the point of baptism for the dead if they did not believe in the resurrection of the dead.

²⁹ *Else what shall they do that are baptized for the dead? If the dead are not raised at all, why then are they baptized for them?* ³⁰ *why do we also stand in jeopardy every hour?* ³¹ *I protest by that glorying in you, brethren, which I have in Christ Jesus our Lord, I die daily.* ³² *If after the manner of men I fought with beasts at Ephesus, what does it profit me? If the dead are not raised, let us eat and drink, for tomorrow we die.* ³³ *Be not deceived: Evil companionships corrupt good morals.* ³⁴ *Awake to soberness righteously, and sin not; for some have no knowledge of God: I say this to move you to shame.*

The second question is 'what is meant by '*stand in jeopardy every hour*'? Here Paul is asking why do he and his fellow preachers of the gospel of Jesus live in constant danger if there is no resurrection from the dead? Which leads us to speculate on what danger. Paul and his companions preach the Gospel knowing that they are in danger of being abused, beaten or even imprisoned, or were other dangers that were being suggested; danger from those who were dead?

*Natural death is not the end of life for Christians; it is the last step before receiving a glorified, resurrected body like that of the risen Christ. That "spiritual" body will be as different from our current bodies as a star is from a fish. In that moment, for all who have believed in Christ, living and dead, death will be defeated for good. ⁴

⁴ *Commentary credit: https://www.bibleref.com*

The Resurrection Body

1 Corinthians 15:35-50

³⁵ *But someone will say, How are the dead raised? and with what manner of body do they come?* ³⁶ *You foolish one, that which you yourself sows is not quickened except it dies:* ³⁷ *and that which you sow, you sow not the body that shall be, but a bare grain, it may chance of wheat, or of some other kind;* ³⁸ *but God gives it a body even as it pleased him, and to each seed a body of its own.*

³⁹ *All flesh is not the same flesh: but there is one flesh of men, and another flesh of beasts, and another flesh of birds, and another of fishes.* ⁴⁰ *There are also celestial bodies, and bodies terrestrial: but the glory of the celestial is one, and the glory of the terrestrial is another.* ⁴¹ *There is one glory of the sun, and another glory of the moon, and another glory of the stars; for one star differs from another star in glory.* ⁴² *So also is the resurrection of the dead. It is sown in corruption; it is raised in incorruption [purity]:* ⁴³ *it is sown in dishonor; it is raised in glory: it is sown in weakness; it is raised in power:* ⁴⁴ *it is sown a natural body; it is raised a spiritual body. If there is a natural body, there is also a spiritual body.* ⁴⁵ *So also it is written, The first man Adam became a living soul. The last Adam became a life-giving spirit.*

Paul presents an argument that there are two bodies, our natural, earthly body and our spiritual body: "⁴⁴ *it [the seed] is sown a natural body; it is raised a spiritual body.*' In verse 40 Paul refers to terrestrial bodies and celestial bodies, and in verse 42 Paul tells us that our terrestrial body is sown in corruption and our celestial body is sown in incorruption; in purity. In verse 45 Paul writes, "⁴⁵ *So also it is written, The first man, Adam, became a living soul. The last Adam became a life-giving spirit.*' The last Adam is Christ.

As explained in Genesis 2:7, the first Adam became a living earthly being after God formed him from the dust of the ground. The last Adam, who is Christ, became a "life-giving spirit" after being resurrected from death to life by God. Jesus was raised as a life-giving spirit in the sense that through

The Compiled Teachings of The Apostle Paul

⁴⁶ Howbeit that is not first which is spiritual, but that which is natural; then that which is spiritual. ⁴⁷ The first man is of the earth, earthly: the second man is of heaven. ⁴⁸ As is the earthly, such are they also that are earthly: and as is the heavenly, such are they also that are heavenly. ⁴⁹ And as we have borne the image of the earthly, we shall also bear the image of the heavenly.
⁵⁰ Now this I say, brethren, that flesh and blood cannot inherit the kingdom of God; neither does corruption inherit incorruption.

Him, and Him alone, those who are born again can look forward to being resurrected as He was. Paul concludes this passage by pointing out *'⁵⁰ that flesh and blood cannot inherit the kingdom of God; neither does corruption inherit incorruption.'*

Mystery and Victory

*⁵¹ Behold, I tell you a mystery: We all shall not sleep, but we shall all be changed, ⁵² in a moment, in the twinkling of an eye, at the last trump: for the trumpet shall sound, and the dead shall be raised incorruptible, and we shall be changed. ⁵³ For this corruptible must put on incorruption, and this mortal must put on immortality. ⁵⁴ But when this corruptible shall have put on incorruption, and this mortal shall have put on immortality, then shall come to pass the saying that is written, **Death is swallowed up in victory. ⁵⁵ O death, where is thy victory? O death, where is thy sting? ⁵⁶ The sting of death is sin; and the power of sin is the law: ⁵⁷ but thanks be to God, who gives us the victory through our Lord Jesus Christ.***
⁵⁸ Wherefore, my beloved brethren, be steadfast, unmovable, always abounding in the work of the Lord, forasmuch as you know that your labor is not vain in the Lord.

1 Corinthians 15:51-58

Paul now extends his explanation of our celestial future. *'We all shall not sleep, but we shall all be changed ⁵² in a moment, in the twinkling of an eye'... '⁵³ For this mortal must put on immortality.'* Paul explains that we will be raised incorruptible and immortal and he next references what may have been a known saying of the time (predating William Shakespeare) *'Death is swallowed up in victory. ⁵⁵ O death, where is thy victory? O death, where is thy sting? ⁵⁶ The sting of death is sin; and the power of sin is the law.'*

Paul concludes this passage with the single-sentence benediction: *'⁵⁷ but thanks be to God, who gives us the victory through our Lord Jesus Christ.'* followed by final words of encouragement.

The Collection for the Saints

16. Now concerning the collection for the saints, as I gave order to the churches of Galatia, so also do you. ² Upon the first day of the week let each one of you lay by him in store, as he may prosper, that no collections be made when I come. ³ And when I arrive, whomsoever you shall approve, them will I send with letters to carry your bounty to Jerusalem: ⁴ and if it be meet [appropriate] for me to go also, they shall go with me.

1 Corinthians 16:1-4

Paul begins this passage referencing collections asking the church to make collections that should be set aside for the church in Jerusalem. Paul references that he has made a similar request of the churches in Galatia (to whom the Letter to the Galatians was written and has already been delivered). Paul explains that when he arrives in Corinth, he will provide letters to the church in Jerusalem to take with what has been collected and entrust it to those who they (those in Corinth) approve to take it to Jerusalem.

Plans for Travel

⁵ But I will come to you, when I shall have passed through Macedonia; for I pass through Macedonia; ⁶ but with you it may be that I shall abide, or even winter, that you may set me forward on my journey whithersoever I go. ⁷ For I do not wish to see you now by the way; for I hope to tarry a while with you, if the Lord permits. ⁸ But I will tarry at Ephesus until Pentecost; ⁹ for a great door and effectual is opened to me, and there are many adversaries.
¹⁰ Now if Timothy comes, see that he is with you without fear; for he works the work of the Lord, as I also do: ¹¹ let no man therefore despise him. But set him forward on his journey in peace, that he may come to me: for I expect him with the brethren.

1 Corinthians 16:5-11

Before coming to Corinth, however, Paul indicates that he will be coming via Macedonia and he suggests that he may be staying in Corinth for some time: *'⁶ but with you it may be that I shall abide, or even winter, that you may set me forward on my journey whithersoever I go.'* While he has already suggested he could go to Jerusalem (*⁴ and if it be appropriate for me to go also, they shall go with me.*) after leaving Corinth, there is nothing set in concrete: *'⁶ᵇ that you may set me forward on my journey whithersoever I go.'*. The next statement confirms that Paul is in Ephesus while writing this letter: *'⁸ But I will tarry at Ephesus until Pentecost'* where he has found much to do and many challenges.

Clearly Timothy is not with Paul in Ephesus, but Paul at least considers it a possibility that Timothy might visit Corinth.

Final Instructions

¹² But as touching Apollos the brother, I besought him much to come to you with the brethren: and it was not at all his will to come now; but he will come when he shall have opportunity.
¹³ Watch, stand fast in the faith, act like men, be strong. ¹⁴ Let all that you do be done in love.

1 Corinthians 16:12-18

Paul now references Apollos and shares with the Corinthians that he had asked him to visit Corinth, but Apollos was not willing to go immediately but has indicated he will go to Corinth when he has the opportunity.

> *¹⁵ Now I beseech you, brethren (you know the house of Stephanas, that it is the first-fruits of Achaia, and that they have set themselves to minister to the saints), ¹⁶ that you also be in subjection to such, and to everyone that helps in the work and labors. ¹⁷ And I rejoice at the coming of Stephanas and Fortunatus and Achaicus: for that which was lacking on your part they supplied. ¹⁸ For they refreshed my spirit and yours: acknowledge them therefore those that are such.*

V13 and 14 clearly are words of encouragement that might be viewed as being tied into the news Paul shared about Apollos, or they could be intended as an introduction to the next verses in which Paul mentions Stephanas, Fortunatus, and Achaicus expressing gratitude for what they did: *'¹⁸ For they refreshed my spirit and yours'*.

Salutations

1 Corinthians 16:19-24

> *¹⁹ The churches of Asia salute you. Aquila and Prisca salute you much in the Lord, with the church that is in their house. ²⁰ All the brethren salute you. Salute one another with a holy kiss.*
> *²¹ The salutation of me Paul with my own hand. ²² If any man loves not the Lord, let him be anathema. Maranatha. ²³ The grace of the Lord Jesus Christ be with you.*
> *²⁴ My love be with you all in Christ Jesus. Amen.*

Paul then mentions *'the churches of Asia',* and Aquila and Prisca, passing on salutations., and finally adds his own salutation mentioning that he is writing this letter himself: *'²¹ The salutation of me Paul with my own hand.'*

Following this salutation, prior to Paul's benediction is a single sentence denouncement of those who don't believe, *'²² If any man loves not the Lord, let him be anathema. Maranatha.'*

Anathema means 'disliked, detested or loathed', and Maranatha means "the Lord is coming" or "come, O Lord".

The Compiled Teachings of The Apostle Paul

2 Corinthians

Paul's Change of Plans...65	Great Generosity...70
Reaffirm Your Love 65	God Gives Most...71
Ministers of a New Covenant.................................66	Paul Describes Himself...71
Paul's Apostolic Ministry..67	Paul Defends His Apostleship.................................72
The Temporal and Eternal.....................................67	Paul's Vision 73
Paul Commends Their Ministry..............................68	All Things Beloved Are For Your Edifying...............74
Paul Reveals His Heart...69	Examine Yourselves..74

Paul's Second Letter To The Church In Corinth written by Paul at Ephesus

For notes on 2 Cor. 1:1-11, see 'The Greetings of each of the 'Letters Books' and 'Transition Passages' on pages 31- 34.

Paul's Change of Plans

1. ¹² For our glorying is this, the testimony of our conscience, that in holiness and sincerity of God, not in fleshly wisdom but in the grace of God, we behaved ourselves in the world, and more abundantly toward you. ¹³ For we write no other things to you, than what you read or even acknowledge, and I hope you will acknowledge to the end: ¹⁴ as also you did acknowledge us in part, that we are your glorying, even as you also are ours, in the day of our Lord Jesus.

¹⁵ And in this confidence I was minded to come first to you, that you might have a second benefit; ¹⁶ and by you to pass into Macedonia, and again from Macedonia to come to you, and of you to be set forward on my journey to Judaea.

¹⁷ When I therefore was reminded, did I show fickleness? or the things that I purpose, do I purpose according to the flesh, that with me there should be the yea, yea and the nay nay? ¹⁸ But as God is faithful, our word toward you is not yea and nay. ¹⁹ For the Son of God, Jesus Christ, who was preached among you by us, even by me and Silvanus and Timothy, was not yea and nay, but in Him is yea. ²⁰ For how ever many are the promises of God, in Him is the yea: wherefore also through Him is the Amen, to the glory of God through us. ²¹ Now He that established us with you in Christ, and anointed us, is God; ²² who also sealed us, and gave us the earnest of the Spirit in our hearts.

²³ But I call God for a witness upon my soul, that to spare you I refrained to come to Corinth. ²⁴ Not that we have lordship over your faith, but are helpers of your joy: for in faith you stand fast.

2 Corinthians 1:12-24

The NASB translation uses the phrase 'proud confidence' instead of the single word 'glorying' in this passage, and the ESV (English Standard Version) uses the word 'boast'. The modern-day term 'brag' might an appropriate alternative. So, Paul is bragging – that is, proclaiming – that his actions and those of his companions are guided by their desire to be holy and their enthusiasm to share the Gospel.

Paul then acknowledges that his initial plan was to visit (travel to) Corinth first and from there go on to other cities in the neighboring region of Macedonia, and then to return to Corinth before returning to Judaea.

Paul had previously visited Corinth, which is when he (presumably) made the commitment to return, and now was explaining why he and his companions Timothy and Silvanus had not returned. In verse 21, Paul points out that it was God that appointed him to preach about Jesus, the son of God, and the promise of eternal life through coming to believe in the resurrection of Jesus Christ, and Paul concludes his apology by pointing out that he and his companions are simply helpers, '*helpers of your joy*' and he proclaims that they stand firm in their faith, '*for in faith you stand fast*'.

Reaffirm Your Love

2. But I determined this for myself, that I would not come again to you with sorrow. ² For if I make you sorry, who then is he that makes me glad but he that is made sorry by me? ³ And I wrote this very thing, lest, when I came, I should have sorrow from them of whom I ought to rejoice; having confidence in you all, that my joy is the joy of you all. ⁴ For out of much affliction and anguish of heart I wrote to you with many tears; not that you should be made sorry, but that you might know the love which I have more abundantly toward you.

⁵ But if any has caused sorrow, he has caused sorrow, not to me, but in part (that I press not too heavily) to you all. ⁶ Sufficient to such a one is this punishment which was inflicted by the many; ⁷ so that you should rather forgive him otherwise and comfort him, lest by any means such a one should be swallowed up with his

2 Corinthians 2:1-17

In this passage Paul is writing first about sorrow and then about forgiveness and he repeatedly references his concern that his actions – his change of plans – have caused sorrow among them.

Paul expresses that he has confidence in them which is something that gives him joy and makes him have the need to express his love for them.

Paul references that someone other than himself has caused sorrow among them and immediately begins to defend who ever that person (or persons) might

overmuch sorrow. ⁸ *Wherefore I ask you to confirm your love toward him.* ⁹ *For to this end also did I write, that I might know the proof of you, whether you are obedient in all things.* ¹⁰ *But to whom you forgive anything, I forgive also: for what I also have forgiven, if I have forgiven anything, for your sakes have I forgiven it in the presence of Christ;* ¹¹ *that no advantage may be gained over us by Satan: for we are not ignorant of his devices.*

¹² *Now when I came to Troas for the gospel of Christ, and when a door was opened to me in the Lord,* ¹³ *I had no relief for my spirit, because I found not Titus my brother: but taking my leave of them, I went forth into Macedonia.*

¹⁴ *But thanks be unto God, who always leads us in triumph in Christ, and makes manifest through us the savor of his knowledge in every place.* ¹⁵ *For we are a sweet savor of Christ to God, in them that are saved, and in them that perish;* ¹⁶ *to the one a savor from death unto death; to the other a savor from life unto life. And who is sufficient for these things?* ¹⁷ *For we are not as the many, corrupting the word of God: but as of sincerity, but as of God, in the sight of God, speak we in Christ.*

be, and he pleads on their behalf for forgiveness, concluding with '*But to whom you forgive anything, I forgive also... for your sakes have I forgiven it in the presence of Christ*'.
Paul then explains what happened when he arrived in Troas. He had expected to be met by Titus, but as Titus wasn't there he decided to continue on into the region of Macedonia on his own where, he reports, he was able to share the gospel.

In the past Paul had enjoyed a close relationship with the Corinthians. He had founded the church in Corinth and led many of them to faith in Christ. Their deep respect for him had diminished, though, over time. Some had pledged their allegiance to other apostles and teachers over him, some who are referred to as 'false apostles'.[5] Paul had rebuked others involved in various sins and foolish practices. More recently, Corinthians had stood with Paul defending him against those who challenged his authority. The teaching in this chapter addresses this issue.

Ministers of a New Covenant

2 Corinthians 3:1-18

3. Are we beginning again to commend ourselves? or do we need, as do some, epistles of commendation to you or from you? ² *You are our epistle, written in our hearts, known and read of all men;* ³ *being made manifest that you are an epistle of Christ, ministered by us, written not with ink, but with the Spirit of the living God; not in tablets of stone, but in tablets that are hearts of flesh.* ⁴ *And such confidence have we through Christ to God-ward:* ⁵ *not that we are sufficient of ourselves, to account anything as from ourselves; but our sufficiency is from God;* ⁶ *who also made us sufficient as ministers of a new covenant; not of the letter, but of the spirit: for the letter kills, but the spirit gives life.* ⁷ *But if the ministration of death, written, and engraved on stones, came with glory, so that the children of Israel could not look steadfastly upon the face of Moses for the glory of his face; which glory was passing away:* ⁸ *how shall not rather the ministration of the spirit be with glory?* ⁹ *For if the ministration of condemnation has glory, much rather does the ministration of righteousness exceed in glory.* ¹⁰ *For verily that which has been made glorious has not been made glorious in this respect, by reason of the glory that surpasses.* ¹¹ *For if that which passes away was with glory, much more that which remains is in glory.*

¹² *Having therefore such a hope, we use great boldness of speech,* ¹³ *and are not as Moses, who put a veil upon his face, that the children of Israel should not look steadfastly on the end of that which was passing away:* ¹⁴ *but their minds were hardened: for until this very day at the reading of the old covenant the same veil remains, it not being revealed to them that it is done away in Christ.* ¹⁵ *But to this day, whenever Moses is read, a veil lies upon their heart.* ¹⁶ *But whenever it shall turn to the Lord, the veil is taken away.* ¹⁷ *Now the Lord is the Spirit: and where the Spirit of the Lord is, there is liberty.* ¹⁸ *But we all, with unveiled face beholding as in a mirror the glory of the Lord, are transformed into the same image from glory to glory, even as from the Lord the Spirit.*

Paul asks, "*do we need to provide written letters of commendation as others* (who are new and unknown to you) *carry?*" Paul insists that Christ's presence in their hearts should be all the evidence they need that his ministry is true. Paul compares the limited glory revealed by the Old Covenant between God and Israel with the far greater glory revealed by Christ to all who come to Him by faith. That glory is revealed only when the veil of unbelief is removed through Christ by the Holy Spirit's power. '⁵ *but our sufficiency is from God;* ⁵ *who also made us sufficient as ministers of a new covenant; not of the letter, but of the spirit: for the letter kills, but the spirit gives life.*' Those who see God's glory in Christ begin to be changed to become like Him.[5]

¹²ᵇ *we use great boldness of speech, [in sharing the Gospel]* ¹³ *and are not as Moses, who put a veil upon his face, that the children of Israel should not look steadfastly on the end of that which was passing away...*
¹⁵ *But to this day, whensoever Moses is read, a veil lies upon their heart.* ¹⁶ *But whensoever it shall turn to the Lord, the veil is taken away...*
¹⁸ *But we all, with unveiled face [looking as in a mirror] behold the glory of the Lord, are transformed into the same image from glory to glory, even as from the Lord the Spirit.*

---

[5] Commentary credit: https://www.bibleref.com/

Paul's Apostolic Ministry

4. *Therefore seeing we have this ministry, even as we obtained mercy, we faint not:* ² *but we have renounced the hidden things of shame, not walking in craftiness, nor handling the word of God deceitfully; but by the manifestation of the truth commending ourselves to every man's conscience in the sight of God.* ³ *And even if our gospel is veiled, it is veiled in them that perish:* ⁴ *in whom the god of this world has blinded the minds of the unbelieving, that the light of the gospel of the glory of Christ, who is the image of God, should not dawn upon them.* ⁵ *For we preach not ourselves, but Christ Jesus as Lord, and ourselves as your servants for Jesus' sake.* ⁶ *Seeing it is God, that said, Light shall shine out of darkness* [Is. 59:15b-21; 60:1-3], *who shined in our hearts, to give the light of the knowledge of the glory of God in the face of Jesus Christ.*

⁷ *But we have this treasure in earthen vessels, that the exceeding greatness of the power may be of God, and not from ourselves;* ⁸ *we are pressed on every side, yet not straitened; perplexed, yet not to despair;* ⁹ *pursued, yet not forsaken; smitten down, yet not destroyed;* ¹⁰ *always bearing about in the body the dying of Jesus, that the life also of Jesus may be manifested in our body.* ¹¹ *For we who live are always delivered to death for Jesus' sake, that the life also of Jesus may be manifested in our mortal flesh.* ¹² *So then death works in us, but life in you.* ¹³ *But having the same spirit of faith, according to that which is written, I believed, and therefore did I speak; we also believe, and therefore also we speak;* ¹⁴ *knowing that He that raised up the Lord Jesus shall raise up us also with Jesus, and shall present us with you.* ¹⁵ *For all things are for your sakes, that the grace, being multiplied through the many, may cause the thanksgiving to abound to the glory of God.*

¹⁶ *Wherefore we faint not; but though our outward man is decaying, yet our inward man is renewed day by day.* ¹⁷ *For our light affliction, which is for the moment, works for us more and more exceedingly an eternal weight of glory;* ¹⁸ *while we look not at the things which are seen, but at the things which are not seen: for the things which are seen are temporal; but the things which are not seen are eternal.*

2 Corinthians 4:1-18

In this passage, with absolute honesty and openness, Paul details the foundation on which his ministry is based, referencing prophesy from the book of Isaiah, and expressing in his own words that he works for the Gospel and the Gospel works for everyone who will believe, and, in verses 14-18, he describes his great confidence in God's ability to sustain him and his great hope in the life to come.[a]

¹⁸ **while we look not at the things which are seen, but at the things which are not seen: for the things which are seen are temporal; but the things which are not seen are eternal.**

Paul's teaching of his ministry reminds us also of the prophesy in Isaiah 53:

¹*Who has believed our message? and to whom the arm of Jehovah has been revealed.* ² *For he grew up before him as a tender plant, and as a root out of a dry ground: he has no form nor comeliness; and when we see him, there is no beauty that we should desire him.* ³ *He was despised, and rejected of men; a man of sorrows, and acquainted with grief: and as one from whom men hide their face he was despised; and we esteemed him not.*

⁴ *Surely he has borne our griefs, and carried our sorrows; yet we did esteem him stricken, smitten of God, and afflicted.*

⁵ *But he was wounded for our transgressions, he was bruised for our iniquities; the chastisement of our peace was upon him; and with his stripes we are healed.*

⁶ *All we like sheep have gone astray; we have turned everyone to his own way; and Jehovah has laid on him the iniquity of us all.*

[a] Commentary credit: https://www.bibleref.com

The Temporal and Eternal

5. *For we know that if the earthly house of our tabernacle be dissolved, we have a building from God, a house not made with hands, eternal, in the heavens.* ² *For verily in this we groan, longing to be clothed with our habitation which is from heaven:* ³ *if so be that being clothed we shall not be found naked.* ⁴ *For indeed we that are in this tabernacle do groan, being burdened; not for that we would be unclothed, but that we would be clothed upon, that what is mortal may be swallowed up of life.* ⁵ *Now He that wrought us for this very thing is God, who gave to us the earnest of the Spirit.* ⁶ *Being therefore always of good courage, and knowing that, whilst we are at home in the body, we are absent from the Lord* ⁷ *(for we walk by faith, not by sight);* ⁸ *we are of good courage, I say, and are willing rather to be absent from the body, and to be at home with the Lord.* ⁹ *Wherefore also we make it our aim, whether at home or absent, to be well-pleasing to him.* ¹⁰ *For we must all be made manifest before the judgment-seat of Christ; that each one may receive the things done in the body, according to what he has done, whether it be good or bad.*

¹¹ *Knowing therefore the fear of the Lord, we persuade men, but we are made manifest unto God; and I hope that we are made manifest also in your consciences.*

2 Corinthians 5:1-21

Paul describes life on this side of eternity, in a sin-ravaged world, as only a temporary dwelling place which he calls a tabernacle but some translations use the word 'tent'. Waiting for him in eternity is a dwelling place made by Christ. By groaning, Paul means yearning or longing. When we face death, which is inevitable, Paul writes, ⁸ *we are of good courage, I say, and are willing rather to be absent from the body, and to be at home with the Lord.* Paul references *'the judgment seat of Christ'* that we must all come before; ¹⁰ᵇ *that each one*

The Compiled Teachings of The Apostle Paul

¹² We are not again commending ourselves to you, but speak as giving you occasion of glorying on our behalf, that you may have wherewith to answer them that glory in appearance, and not in heart. ¹³ For whether we are beside ourselves, it is to God; or whether we are of sober mind, it is to you. ¹⁴ For the love of Christ constrains us; because we thus judge, that one died for all, therefore all died; ¹⁵ and He died for all, that they that live should no longer live to themselves, but to him who for their sakes died and rose again. ¹⁶ Wherefore we henceforth know no man after the flesh: even though we have known Christ after the flesh, yet now we know him so no more. ¹⁷ Wherefore if any man is in Christ, he is a new creature: the old things are passed away; behold, they are become new. ¹⁸ But all things are of God, who reconciled us to himself through Christ, and gave to us the ministry of reconciliation; ¹⁹ to wit, that God was in Christ reconciling the world to himself, not reckoning to them their trespasses, and having committed to us the word of reconciliation.
²⁰ We are ambassadors therefore on behalf of Christ, as though God were entreating by us: we beseech you on behalf of Christ, be reconciled to God. ²¹ Him who knew no sin he made to be sin on our behalf; that we might become the righteousness of God in him.

may receive [for] the things done in the body, according to what he has done, whether it be good or bad.
Paul explains that Jesus ¹⁵ *died for all, that they that live should no longer live to themselves, but to him who for their sakes died and rose again;* and ¹⁷ *if any man is in Christ, he is a new creature: the old things are passed away; behold, they are become new.* ¹⁸ *...all things are of God, who reconciled us to himself through Christ.*

In verse 16, Paul is explaining that we have all lived according to what the world teaches, but we must now live according to what God teaches: ¹⁶ *Wherefore we henceforth know no man after the flesh: even though we have known Christ after the flesh, yet now we know Him (in this way) no more.* And we can only do that by rejecting our past worldly view.

Regarding 2 Corinthians 5:18-20...
Paul Describes His Ministry As A Ministry of Reconciliation To The Church In Corinth
- God, who reconciled us to himself through Christ, gave us the ministry of reconciliation
- God was in Christ reconciling the world to Himself, not counting their wrongdoings against them, and He has committed to us the word of reconciliation.
- all who trust in Christ's death in their place, for their sin, will be given a gift of God's grace: credit for Jesus' righteous life. Being "in Christ" in this way will cause the old separation between themselves and God to be removed. They will be reconciled to Him.
- God reconciled Paul and his co-workers to Himself in Christ in this way and then immediately gave them the ministry of telling others about it. For Paul, this happened when Christ called his name while he was on the road to Damascus (Acts 9).
- sins once stood between every person and God as an obstacle that could not be moved (Romans 3:23). Christ removed the obstacle by paying the price for each believer's sin with His death.
- Now all who trust in Christ can be reconciled to God. Paul understood his mission in life to be delivering this message to everyone he could.
- we (Paul and his coworkers, and all who share and help spread the Gospel) are ambassadors for Christ, as though God were making an appeal through us; we beg you on behalf of Christ, be reconciled to God.

Paul Commends Their Ministry

2 Corinthians 6:1-18

6. And working together with him we entreat also that you do not receive the grace of God in vain ² (for he said, AT AN ACCEPTABLE TIME I HEARKENED UNTO THEE, AND IN A DAY OF SALVATION DID I SUCCOR THEE: [Is. 49:8] behold, now is the acceptable time; behold, now is the day of salvation) ³ giving no occasion of stumbling in anything, that our ministration be not blamed; ⁴ but in everything commending ourselves, as ministers of God, in much patience, in afflictions, in necessities, in distresses, ⁵ in stripes (beatings), in imprisonments, in tumults, in labors, in watchings, in fastings; ⁶ in pureness, in knowledge, in longsuffering, in kindness, in the Holy Spirit, in love unfeigned, ⁷ in the word of truth, in the power of God; by the armor of righteousness on the right hand and on the left, ⁸ by glory and dishonor, by evil report and good report; as deceivers, and yet true; ⁹ as unknown, and yet well known; as dying, and behold, we live; as chastened, and not killed; ¹⁰ as sorrowful, yet always rejoicing; as poor, yet making many rich; as having nothing, and yet possessing all things.

Paul begins this passage offering reassurance that he and his co-workers are pursuing only one goal; that they will receive the grace of God, and now, today, is the day of salvation that was prophesied in Is. 49:8 and Paul lists out all of the possible circumstances that he and his co-workers might encounter, finishing but by assuring the Corinthians that he has a big heart for them. ¹¹ *Our mouth is open to you, O Corinthians, our heart is enlarged.*
In verse 12, Paul tells the Corinthians that he has not lost any of his affection for them; ¹²ᵃ *You are not straitened in us,* however, Paul shares concern that the same might not be true of their feelings

The Compiled Teachings of The Apostle Paul

¹¹ Our mouth is open to you, O Corinthians, our heart is enlarged. ¹² You are not straitened in us, but you are straitened in your own affections. ¹³ Now for a recompense in like kind (I speak as to my children), be you also enlarged. ¹⁴ Be not unequally yoked with unbelievers: for what fellowship have righteousness and iniquity? or what communion has light with darkness? ¹⁵ And what concord has Christ with Belial? or what portion has a believer with an unbeliever? ¹⁶ And what agreement has a temple of God with idols? for we are a temple of the living God; even as God said, I WILL DWELL IN THEM, AND WALK IN THEM; AND I WILL BE THEIR GOD, AND THEY SHALL BE MY PEOPLE. [Jer. 24:7] ¹⁷ Wherefore COME OUT FROM AMONG THEM, AND BE SEPARATE, says the Lord,
AND TOUCH NO UNCLEAN THING; [Ez. 11:2; Ez. 44:23]
AND I WILL RECEIVE YOU,
¹⁸ AND WILL BE TO YOU A FATHER,
AND YOU SHALL BE SONS AND DAUGHTERS TO ME, [Jer. 31:1]
says the Lord Almighty.

for him and his co-workers for Christ: *¹²ᵇ but you are straitened in your own affections.*

In verses 14-17 Paul references Christ and Balial, pointing out that believers should not be unequally yoked and there should be no idols in the homes of believers nor in their meeting places. Paul emphasizes that every believer is a temple of the living God: *'¹⁶ᵇ for we are a temple of the living God'.*

Paul brings this passage to closure by quoting from God's covenant with David (2 Sam. 12-16; 1 Chron. 17:11-14) with a reference to sons and daughters prophesied in Jeremiah 31:1.

Paul Reveals His Heart

2 Corinthians 7:1-16

7. Having therefore these promises, beloved, let us cleanse ourselves from all defilement of flesh and spirit, perfecting holiness in the fear of God. ² Open your hearts to us: we wronged no man, we corrupted no man, we took advantage of no man. ³ I say it not to condemn you: for I have said before, that you are in our hearts to die together and live together.
⁴ Great is my boldness of speech toward you, great is my glorying on your behalf: I am filled with comfort, I overflow with joy in all our affliction. ⁵ For even when we came into Macedonia our flesh had no relief, but we were afflicted on every side; without were conflicts, within were fears. ⁶ Nevertheless he that comforts the lowly, even God, comforted us by the coming of Titus; ⁷ and not by his coming only, but also by the comfort wherewith he was comforted in you, while he told us your longing, your mourning, your zeal for me; so that I rejoiced yet more. ⁸ For though I made you sorry with my epistle, I do not regret it: though I did regret it (for I see that that epistle made you sorry, though but for a season), ⁹ I now rejoice, not that you were made sorry, but that you were made sorry to repentance; for you were made sorry after a godly sort, that you might suffer loss by us in nothing. ¹⁰ For godly sorrow works repentance to salvation, a repentance which brings no regret: but the sorrow of the world works death. ¹¹ For behold, this selfsame thing, that you were made sorry after a godly sort, what earnest care it wrought in you, yea what clearing of yourselves, yea what indignation, yea what fear, yea what longing, yea what zeal, yea what avenging! In everything you approved yourselves to be pure in the matter. ¹² So although I wrote to you, I wrote not for his cause that did the wrong, nor for His cause that suffered the wrong, but that your earnest care for us might be made manifest to you in the sight of God. ¹³ Therefore we have been comforted: and in our comfort we rejoiced the more exceedingly for the joy of Titus, because his spirit had been refreshed by you all. ¹⁴ For if in anything I have gloried to him on your behalf, I was not put to shame; but as we spoke all things to you in truth, so our glorying also which I made before Titus was found to be truth. ¹⁵ And his affection is more abundantly toward you, while he remembered the obedience of you all; how with fear and trembling you received him. ¹⁶ I rejoice that in everything I am of good courage concerning you.

Following on from pointing out that believers should not be unequally yoked and there should be no idols in the homes of believers nor in their meeting places, Paul references holiness. *'⁷:¹beloved, let us cleanse ourselves from all defilement of flesh and spirit, perfecting holiness in the fear of God.'*

Paul then pleads that they should open their hearts to him and his co-workers, offering a defense which seems to imply that accusations had been made against them; possibly regarding their intentions and possibly their practices: *'² Open your hearts to us: we wronged no man, we corrupted no man, we took advantage of no man.'*

Paul then relates the past challenges encountered in Macedonia mentioning Titus and how much comfort he brought. In verse 12, Paul writes, *'I wrote not for his cause that did the wrong, nor for His cause that suffered the wrong,'* confirming that someone was wronged, but who was wronged or in what matter, and who committed the wrong are not detailed in any way, but it seems that Titus was in some way involved in helping resolve the matter as Paul continues to lavish praise upon Titus.

Great Generosity

2 Corinthians 8:1-24

8. *Moreover, brethren, we make known to you the grace of God which has been given in the churches of Macedonia;* ² *how that in much proof of affliction the abundance of their joy and their deep poverty abounded to the riches of their liberality.* ³ *For according to their power, I bear witness, yea and beyond their power, they gave of their own accord,* ⁴ *beseeching us with much entreaty in regard of this grace and the fellowship in the ministering to the saints:* ⁵ *and this, not as we had hoped, but first they gave their own selves to the Lord, and to us through the will of God.* ⁶ *Insomuch that we exhorted Titus, that as he had made a beginning before, so he would also complete in you this grace also.* ⁷ *But as you abound in everything, in faith, and utterance, and knowledge, and in all earnestness, and in your love to us, see that you abound in this grace also.* ⁸ *I speak not by way of commandment, but as proving through the earnestness of others the sincerity also of your love.* ⁹ *For you know the grace of our Lord Jesus Christ, that, though he was rich, yet for your sakes he became poor, that you through his poverty might become rich.* ¹⁰ *And herein I give my judgment: for this is expedient for you, who were the first to make a beginning a year ago, not only to do, but also to will.* ¹¹ *But now complete the doing also; that as there was the readiness to will, so there may be the completion also out of your ability.* ¹² *For if the readiness is there, it is acceptable according as a man has, not according as he has not.* ¹³ *For I say not this that others may be eased and you distressed;* ¹⁴ *but by equality: your abundance being a supply at this present time for their want, that their abundance also may become a supply for your want; that there may be equality:* ¹⁵ *as it is written,*

HE THAT GATHERED MUCH HAD NOTHING IN EXCESS; AND HE THAT GATHERED LITTLE HAD NO LACK. [Ex. 16:18]

¹⁶ *But thanks be to God, who puts the same earnest care for you into the heart of Titus.* ¹⁷ *For he accepted indeed our exhortation; but being himself very earnest, he went forth to you of his own accord.* ¹⁸ *And we have sent together with him the brother whose praise in the gospel is spread through all the churches;* ¹⁹ *and not only so, but who was also appointed by the churches to travel with us in the matter of this grace, which is ministered by us to the glory of the Lord, and to show our readiness:* ²⁰ *avoiding this, that any man should blame us in the matter of this bounty which is ministered by us:* ²¹ *for we take thought for things honorable, not only in the sight of the Lord, but also in the sight of men.* ²² *And we have sent with them our brother, whom we have many times proved earnest in many things, but now much more earnest, by reason of the great confidence which he has in you.* ²³ *Whether any inquire about Titus, he is my partner and my fellow-worker among you; our brethren, they are the messengers of the churches, they are the glory of Christ.* ²⁴ *Show therefore to them, before the churches, the proof of your love, and of our glorying on your behalf.*

Paul continues the letter recognizing the generosity of the churches in Macedonia and thanks them and shares encouragement that they would continue to give support to Titus, himself and his co-workers.

Paul exhorts the church in Corinth to continue their generosity and states that he is not commanding them but rather is pleading: '⁸ *I speak not by way of commandment, but as proving through the earnestness of others the sincerity also of your love.*' Paul references that Jesus '⁹ᵇ*...yet for your sakes became poor, that you through his poverty might become rich*' and Paul emphasizes '¹¹ᵇ *readiness to will, so there may be the completion also out of your ability.* ¹² *For if the readiness is there, it is acceptable according as a man has, not according as he has not.*' and he concludes with pointing out, '¹⁴ᵇ *your abundance being a supply at this present time for their want, that their abundance also may become a supply for your want; that there may be equality*'.

Paul describes the background to Titus being selected to be sent to Corinth together with a brother who is not named but is described as '¹⁸ᵇ *the brother whose praise in the gospel is spread through all the churches*'. Paul adds that this brother '*was also appointed by the churches to travel with us in the matter of this grace*', a phrase that suggests this brother was not a choice of Paul himself. (This brother most likely was one of the Apostles and may have been Peter or John.)

Paul then references, and again does not name, a third person who is travelling with Titus and the other brother: '²² *And we have sent with them our brother, whom we have many times proved earnest in many things, but now much more earnest, by reason of the great confidence which he has in you.*'.

Finally, Paul again references Titus and he finishes by again repeating his request for the churches of Corinth to be generous as '*the proof of your love*'.

The Compiled Teachings of The Apostle Paul

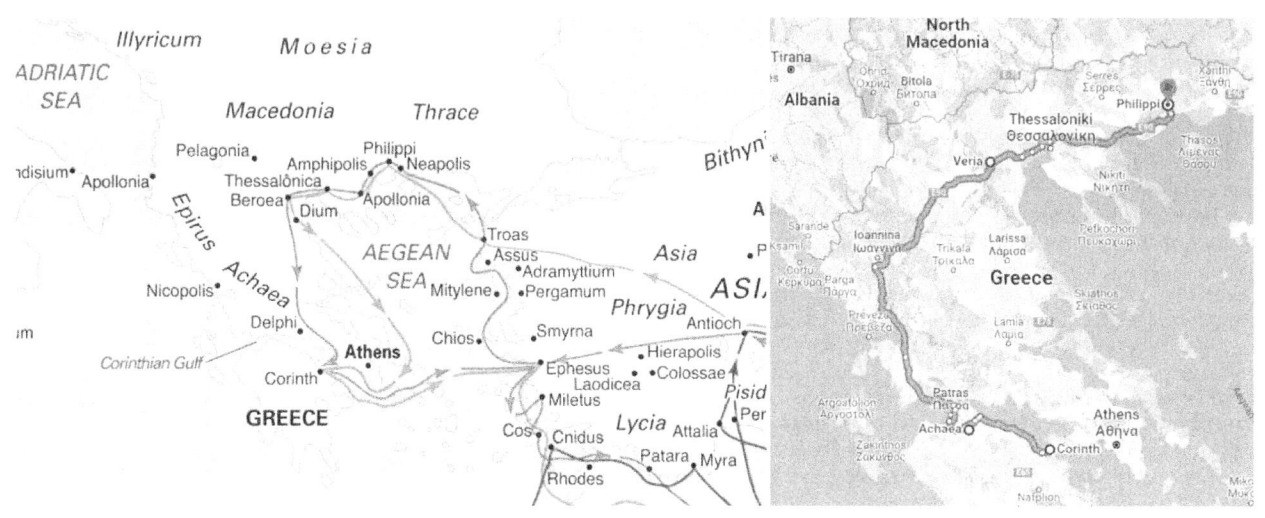

While Paul is writing to the church in Corinth, travelling to visit the churches in Macedonia is mentioned frequently. Beroea (today called Veria in English), Thessalonica, and Philippi are cities that we recognize from the Book of Acts and letters of Paul. The journey from Corinth to Philippi is approximately 450 miles/ 700 Kilometers.

God Gives Most

2 Corinthians 9:1-15

9. For as touching the ministering to the saints, it is superfluous for me to write to you: ² for I know your readiness, of which I glory on your behalf to them of Macedonia, that Achaia has been prepared for a year past; and your zeal hath stirred up very many of them. ³ But I have sent the brethren, that our glorying on your behalf may not be made void in this respect; that, even as I said, you may be prepared:4 lest by any means, if there come with me any of Macedonia and find you unprepared, we (that we say not, you) should be put to shame in this confidence. ⁵ I thought it necessary therefore to entreat the brethren, that they would go before to you, and make up beforehand your previously promised bounty, that the same might be ready as a matter of bounty, and not of extortion.

⁶ But this I say, He that sows sparingly shall reap also sparingly; and he that sows bountifully shall reap also bountifully. ⁷ Let each man do according as he has purposed in his heart: not grudgingly, or of necessity: for God loves a cheerful giver. ⁸ And God is able to make all grace abound to you; that you, having always all sufficiency in everything, may abound to every good work: ⁹ as it is written, HE HAS SCATTERED ABROAD, HE HAS GIVEN TO THE POOR; HIS RIGHTEOUSNESS ABIDES FOREVER. ¹⁰ And He that supplies seed to the sower and bread for food, shall supply and multiply your seed for sowing, and increase the fruits of your righteousness: ¹¹ you being enriched in everything to all liberality, which through us produces thanksgiving to God. ¹² For the ministration of this service not only fills up the measure of the wants of the saints, but abounds also through many thanks-givings to God; ¹³ seeing that through the proving of you by this ministration they glorify God for the obedience of your confession unto the gospel of Christ, and for the liberality of your contribution unto them and unto all; ¹⁴ while they themselves also, with supplication on your behalf, long after you by reason of the exceeding grace of God in you. ¹⁵ Thanks be to God for his unspeakable gift.

Here Paul is preparing the way for taking up a collection of financial support for the church in Jerusalem. He is very direct in his approach making it clear that he expects to collect what he refers to in v5 as *'previously promised bounty'*.

Paul exhorts the churches in Corinth and in Macedonia to *'sow bountifully'* in order that they might *'reap bountifully'* with the promise that *'God loves a cheerful giver'*. Paul adds that their giving will *'increase the fruits of your righteousness:¹¹ you being enriched in everything to all liberality, which through us produces thanksgiving to God.'* reminding them that it is on their behalf that Paul and his co-workers share the Gospel.

Paul Describes Himself

2 Corinthians 10:1-18

10. Now I Paul myself entreat you by the meekness and gentleness of Christ, I who in your presence am lowly among you, but being absent am of good courage toward you: ² yea, I beseech you, that I may not when present show courage with the confidence wherewith I count to be bold against some, who count of us as if we walked according to the flesh. ³ For though we walk in the flesh, we do not war according to the flesh ⁴ (for the weapons of our warfare are not of the flesh, but mighty before God to the casting down of strongholds); ⁵ casting down imaginations, and

In this passage Paul addresses hearsay and rumors about his writings: *'¹⁰ His letters, they say, are weighty and strong; but his bodily presence is weak, and his speech of no account.'* Paul begins by acknowledging that, *'in your presence [I] am lowly among you, but being absent am of good courage toward you: ² yea, I beseech you, that I may not when present show courage with the confidence with which I count to be bold against*

- 71 -

every high thing that is exalted against the knowledge of God, and bringing every thought into captivity to the obedience of Christ; ⁶ and being in readiness to avenge all disobedience, when your obedience shall be made full. ⁷ You look at the things that are before your face. If any man trusts in himself that he is Christ's, let him consider this again with himself, that, even as he is Christ's, so also are we. ⁸ For though I should glory somewhat abundantly concerning our authority (which the Lord gave for building you up, and not for casting you down), I shall not be put to shame: ⁹ that I may not seem as if I would terrify you by my letters. ¹⁰ For, His letters, they say, are weighty and strong; but his bodily presence is weak, and his speech of no account. ¹¹ Let such a one reckon this, that, what we are in word by letters when we are absent, such are we also in deed when we are present.
¹² For we are not bold to number or compare ourselves with certain of them that commend themselves: but they themselves, measuring themselves by themselves, and comparing themselves with themselves, are without understanding. ¹³ But we will not glory beyond our measure, but according to the measure of the province which God apportioned to us as a measure, to reach even to you. ¹⁴ For we stretch not ourselves overmuch, as though we reached not to you: for we came even as far as to you in the gospel of Christ: ¹⁵ not glorying beyond our measure, that is, in other men's labors; but having hope that, as your faith grows, we shall be magnified in you according to our province to further abundance, ¹⁶ so as to preach the gospel even to the parts beyond you, and not to glory in another's province in regard of things ready to our hand. ¹⁷ But he that glories, let him glory in the Lord. ¹⁸ For not he that commends himself is approved, but whom the Lord commends.

some, who count of us as if we walked according to the flesh.' Paul adds, '³ For though we walk in the flesh, we do not war according to the flesh' meaning we are not going to respond to physical threats with a physical response, and Paul adds, '¹² For we are not bold to number or compare ourselves with certain of them that commend themselves: but they themselves, measuring themselves by themselves, and comparing themselves with themselves, [they] are without understanding.' Paul's bottom line is this:
⁷ᵇ 'If any man trusts in himself that he is Christ's, let him consider this again with himself, that, even as he is Christ's, so also are we. ⁸ For though I should glory somewhat abundantly concerning our authority,... I shall not be put to shame: ⁹ that I may not seem as if I would terrify you by my letters.' ¹⁰ For, His letters, they say, are weighty and strong; but his bodily presence is weak, and his speech of no account. Paul concludes by saying that much is accomplished by himself and his coworkers, but much more is accomplished with their help:
¹⁵ not glorying beyond our measure, that is, in other men's labors; but having hope that, as your faith grows, we shall be magnified in you according to our province to further abundance, ¹⁶ so as to preach the gospel even unto the parts beyond you...

Paul Defends His Apostleship

2 Corinthians 11:1-33

11. Would that you could bear with me in a little foolishness: but indeed you do bear with me. ² For I am jealous over you with a godly jealousy: for I espoused you to one husband, that I might present you as a pure virgin to Christ. ³ But I fear, lest by any means, as the serpent beguiled Eve in his craftiness, your minds should be corrupted from the simplicity and the purity that is toward Christ. ⁴ For if he that comes preaches another Jesus, whom we did not preach, or if you receive a different spirit, which you did not receive, or a different gospel, which you did not accept, you do well to bear with him. ⁵ For I reckon that I am not a whit behind the very chief-most (most eminent of) the) apostles. ⁶ But though I be rude in speech, yet am I not in knowledge; no, in every way have we made this manifest to you in all things.
⁷ Or did I commit a sin in abasing myself that you might be exalted, because I preached to you the gospel of God for nought? ⁸ I robbed other churches, taking wages of them that I might minister to you; ⁹ and when I was present with you and was in want, I was not a burden on any man; for the brethren, when they came from Macedonia, supplied the measure of my want; and in everything I kept myself from being a burden to you, and so will I keep myself. ¹⁰ As the truth of Christ is in me, no man shall stop me of this glorying in the regions of Achaia.
¹¹ Wherefore? because I love you not? God knows. ¹² But what I do, that I will do, that I may cut off occasion from them that desire an occasion; that wherein they glory, they may be found even as we. ¹³ For such men are false apostles, deceitful workers, fashioning themselves into apostles of Christ. ¹⁴ And no marvel; for even Satan fashions himself into an angel of light. ¹⁵ It is no great thing therefore if his ministers also fashion themselves as ministers of righteousness; whose end shall be according to their works.

Paul makes a passing reference to the other apostles in this passage: '⁵ For I reckon that I am not a whit behind the very chief-most (most eminent of the) apostles.' but, more significantly, there is a connection between this passage and that of chapter 9 which addressed the need to raise and collect funds to provide financial support for the church in Jerusalem. In this passage Paul explains that he preached the gospel in Corinth without support on his previous visit, '⁷...did I commit a sin in abasing myself that you might be exalted, because I preached to you the gospel of God for nought?'
Paul then justifies this by writing, '⁸ I robbed other churches, taking wages of them that I might minister to you; ⁹ and when I was present with you and was in want, I was not a burden on any man; for the brethren, when they came from Macedonia, supplied the measure of my want; and in everything I kept myself from being a burden to you, and so will I keep myself.' In making this claim Paul has also reminded the Corinthians that what he is asking of them, he is also asking of other churches, and the sin that he referred to was that he robbed other churches by taking advantage of funds that were intended for Jerusalem.

> [16] I say again, Let no man think me foolish; but if you do, yet as foolish receive me, that I also may glory a little. [17] That which I speak, I speak not after the Lord, but as in foolishness, in this confidence of glorying. [18] Seeing that many glory after the flesh, I will glory also. [19] For you bear with the foolish gladly, being wise yourselves. [20] For you bear with a man, if he brings you into bondage, if he devours you, if he takes you captive, if he exalts himself, if he smites you on the face. [21] I speak by way of disparagement, as though we had been weak. Yet whereinsoever any is bold (I speak in foolishness), I am bold also. [22] Are they Hebrews? so am I. Are they Israelites? so am I. Are they the seed of Abraham? so am I. [23] Are they ministers of Christ? (I speak as one beside himself) I more; in labors more abundantly, in prisons more abundantly, in stripes above measure, in deaths oft. [24] Of the Jews five times received I forty stripes save one. [25] Thrice was I beaten with rods, once was I stoned, thrice I suffered shipwreck, a night and a day have I been in the deep; [26] in journeyings often, in perils of rivers, in perils of robbers, in perils from my countrymen, in perils from the Gentiles, in perils in the city, in perils in the wilderness, in perils in the sea, in perils among false brethren; [27] in labor and travail, in watchings often, in hunger and thirst, in fastings often, in cold and nakedness. [28] Besides those things that are without, there is that which presses upon me daily, anxiety for all the churches. [29] Who is weak, and I am not weak? who is caused to stumble, and I burn not? [30] If I must needs glory, I will glory of the things that concern my weakness. [31] The God and Father of the Lord Jesus, He who is blessed for evermore know that I lie not. [32] In Damascus the governor under Aretas the king guarded the city of the Damascenes in order to take me: [33] and through a window was I let down in a basket by the wall, and escaped his hands.

In addition to referencing financial support, Paul makes reference of others who might come (or have come) to preached another Gospel. Paul does not directly question the teachings of these others, but he does question their authority and the truthfulness of the gospel that they might be preaching, '[13] For such men are false apostles, deceitful workers, fashioning themselves into apostles of Christ.' and he lists out the many challengers and sufferings that he has endured, inviting comparison. Paul also questions the backgrounds of those that the Corinthians might have chosen to listen to: [22] Are they Hebrews? so am I. Are they Israelites? so am I. Are they the seed of Abraham? so am I. [23] Are they ministers of Christ? (I speak as one beside himself) I more; in labors more abundantly, in prisons more abundantly, in stripes above measure, in deaths oft. [24] Of the Jews five times received I forty stripes save one. [25] Thrice was I beaten with rods, once was I stoned,

Paul's Vision

> [12.] I must needs glory, though it is not expedient; but I will come to visions and revelations of the Lord. [2] I know a man in Christ, fourteen years ago (whether in the body, I know not; or whether out of the body, I know not; God knows), such a one caught up even to the third heaven. [3] And I know such a man (whether in the body, or apart from the body, I know not; God knows), [4] how that he was caught up into Paradise, and heard unspeakable words, which it is not lawful for a man to utter. [5] On behalf of such a one will I glory: but on mine own behalf I will not glory, save in my weaknesses. [6] For if I should desire to glory, I shall not be foolish; for I shall speak the truth: but I forbear, lest any man should account of me above that which he sees me to be, or hears from me. [7] And by reason of the exceeding greatness of the revelations, that I should not be exalted overmuch, there was given to me a thorn in the flesh, a messenger of Satan to buffet me, that I should not be exalted overmuch. [8] Concerning this thing I besought the Lord three times, that it might depart from me. [9] And He has said to me, 'My grace is sufficient for you: for my power is made perfect in weakness'. Most gladly therefore will I rather glory in my weaknesses, that the power of Christ may rest upon me. [10] Wherefore I take pleasure in weaknesses, in injuries, in necessities, in persecutions, in distresses, for Christ's sake: for when I am weak, then am I strong.
>
> [11] I am become foolish: you compelled me; for I ought to have been commended of you: for in nothing was I behind the very most chief apostles, though I am nothing. [12] Truly the signs of an apostle were shown among you in all patience, by signs and wonders and mighty works. [13] For what is there wherein you were made inferior to the rest of the churches, except it be that I myself was not a burden to you? forgive me this wrong.

2 Corinthians 12:1-14

The first verse here in the NASB is translated as, *'Boasting is necessary, though it is not beneficial; but I will go on to visions and revelations of the Lord.'* Paul has chosen to share an unverifiable story of an event of 14 years ago. His account raises the questions of whether he had an out-of-body experience, whether or not he was 'transported' into a different realm, the third heaven, which he also refers to as paradise; or perhaps it was all just a vision. Paul reports he *'heard unspeakable words'*, things he was forbidden to reveal to anyone else. *John was given a similar command to keep certain details silent when being given his revelation. (Revelation 10:4)*

In this passage Paul again draws comparison between himself and the other apostles: *'[11] I am become foolish: you compelled me; for I ought to have been commended of you: for in nothing was I behind the very most chief apostles, though I am nothing. [12] Truly the signs of an apostle were wrought among you in all patience, by signs and wonders and mighty works.'* (see also 2 Cor. 11:5).

In regard to 2 Cor. 12:2, Paul mentions 'the third heaven'. In the Old Testament, the third heaven is often referred to as the highest heaven, a place created by God where He lives and where angels praise Him (1 Kings 8:27; Nehemiah 9:6; Psalm 148:4). Most commentators understand the first heaven—or first heavens—to be the sky above the earth. The second would be the realm of the sun, moon, and stars: what we would now refer to as outer space. Paul emphasizes that only God knows whether he physically travelled to the third heaven in his body or whether it was an out-of-body experience. Paul wrote that this happened 14 years before the time of his writing the Second Letter to the church in Corinth. That would put the experience sometime around AD 42–44; prior to his first missionary journey. [Credit: www.bibleref.com]

All Things Beloved Are For Your Edifying

14 Behold, this is the third time I am ready to come to you; and I will not be a burden to you: for I seek not yours, but you: for the children ought not to lay up for the parents, but the parents for the children. 15 And I will most gladly spend and be spent for your souls. If I love you more abundantly, am I loved the less? 16 But be it so, I did not myself burden you; but, being crafty, I caught you with guile. 17 Did I take advantage of you by any one of them whom I have sent to you? 18 I exhorted Titus, and I sent the brother with him. Did Titus take any advantage of you? walked we not in the same spirit? walked we not in the same steps?

19 You think all this time that we are excusing ourselves to you. In the sight of God speak we in Christ. But all things, beloved, are for your edifying. 20 For I fear, lest by any means, when I come, I should find you not such as I would, and should myself be found of you such as you would not; lest by any means there should be strife, jealousy, wraths, factions, backbitings, whisperings, swellings, tumults; 21 lest again when I come my God should humble me before you, and I should mourn for many of them that have sinned heretofore, and repented not of the uncleanness and fornication and lasciviousness which they committed.

2 Corinthians 12:1-14

Returning to the theme of support for his ministry, Paul confirms that he will be coming to Corinth and promises not to be a burden. Paul asks, *'17 Did I take advantage of you by any one of them whom I have sent to you? 18 I exhorted Titus, and I sent the brother with him. Did Titus take any advantage of you?'*

Paul finishes up this passage listing things which Christians should avoid being caught up with, in, or doing.

Examine Yourselves

13. This is the third time I am coming to you. At the mouth of two witnesses or three shall every word be established. 2 I have said beforehand, and I do say beforehand, as when I was present the second time, so now, being absent, to them that have sinned heretofore, and to all the rest, that, if I come again, I will not spare; 3 seeing that you seek a proof of Christ that speaks in me; who is not weak toward you, but is powerful in you: 4 for He was crucified through weakness, yet he lives through the power of God. For we also are weak in him, but we shall live with him through the power of God toward you. 5 Try your own selves, whether you are in the faith; prove your own selves. Or know you not as to your own selves, that Jesus Christ is in you? unless indeed you fail the test. 6 But I hope that you shall know that we do not fail the test. 7 Now we pray to God that you do no evil; not that we may appear approved, but that you may do that which is honorable, though we may appear unapproved. 8 For we can do nothing against the truth, but for the truth. 9 For we rejoice, when we are weak, and you are strong: this we also pray for, even your perfecting. 10 For this cause I write these things while absent, that I may not when present deal sharply, according to the authority which the Lord gave me for building up, and not for casting down.

11 Finally, brethren, farewell. Be perfected; be comforted; be of the same mind; live in peace: and the God of love and peace shall be with you. 12 Salute one another with a holy kiss.
13 All the saints salute you.
14 The grace of the Lord Jesus Christ, and the love of God, and the communion of the Holy Spirit, be with you all.

1 Corinthians 13:1-14

Paul writes a stern warning to those *2b ...that have sinned heretofore, and to all the rest,'* warning them that, *'if I come again, I will not spare.'*

Paul states clearly that he understands what they are demanding of him, *'3... proof of Christ that speaks in me; who is not weak toward you, but is powerful in you:'*

In verse 4 Paul explains that we are weak, but God's power is what supports those who believe, and in verse 5 Paul challenges them to each examine and test themselves, even asking them if they know themselves or not, directing them to repent of past actions and to restoration, both individually and as a church body.

Paul adds a comment regarding *'10b ...the authority which the Lord gave me'* which he states is *'for building up, and not for casting down.'*

Paul then closes this letter with a farewell paragraph of reassurance and then a blessing which, when compared to the blessings that close out his other letters, is the only blessing that articulates the Trinity.

Romans

The Righteous Shall Live by Faith Romans 1:16-32	76
God's Wrath on Unrighteousness	76
The Righteous Judgment of God	76
Judgment and the Law	77
Righteousness	77
Righteousness Through Faith	78
Justification Through Faith	78
God's Promise To Abraham	79
Faith and Grace	79
Promise Realized Through Faith	79
Faith Brings Peace	79
Through The Gift of Righteousness Comes Justification	80
Being Dead to Sin is to be Alive to God	80
Slaves to Righteousness and Sanctification	80
Released from the Law	80
The Law and Sin	81
Life in the Spirit	82
Heirs with Christ	82
Our Victory In Christ: Redemption	82
All Things Work Together For Good	83
God's Everlasting Love	83
God's Sovereign Choice; Solicitude For Israel	83
Israel's Unbelief	84
The Message of Salvation to All	84
Denial By Israel	85
The Remnant of Israel: Israel Is Not Cast Away	85
Salvation Comes To The Gentiles (Who Are Grafted In)	85
The Mystery of Israel's Salvation	86
Dedicated Service: A Living Sacrifice	86
Gifts of Grace: Abhor What Is Evil	87
Marks of the True Christian	87
Submission to Government Authorities	87
Fulfilling the Law Through Love	88
Put On The Armor Of Light	88
Do Not Pass Judgment on One Another	88
Do Not Cause Another to Stumble	89
Self-denial: The Example of Christ	89
Christ is the God of Hope of Jews and Gentiles	89
Paul the Minister to the Gentiles	90
Paul's Plan to Visit Rome	90
Personal Greetings	90
Final Instructions and Greetings	91
Doxology	91
Observations:	91

Paul's Letter To The Church In Rome written by Paul at Corinth

In writing this Letter to The Romans, Paul is writing to a church that he did not personally establish as he had never visited Rome. Paul references Timothy in the final chapter of this Letter and we know that Timothy preached alongside Paul in Corinth. *(It may be that Timothy had travelled to Rome but there is no written account of that in The Book of Acts.)*

Romans 1:1-7
***Paul, a servant of Christ Jesus, called to be an apostle**, set apart for the gospel of God, [2] which he promised beforehand through his prophets in the holy Scriptures, [3] concerning his Son, who was descended from David according to the flesh [4] and was declared to be the Son of God in power according to the Spirit of holiness by his resurrection from the dead, Jesus Christ our Lord, [5] through whom we have received grace and apostleship to bring about the obedience of faith for the sake of his name among all the nations, [6] including you who are called to belong to Jesus Christ, [7] <u>To all those in Rome</u> who are loved by God and called to be saints:*
Grace to you and peace from God our Father and the Lord Jesus Christ.

Romans 1:8-10
*[8] First, **I thank** my God through Jesus Christ for all of you, because your faith is proclaimed in all the world. [9] For God is my witness, whom I serve with my spirit in the gospel of his Son, that without ceasing I mention you [10] always in my prayers, asking that somehow by God's will, I may now at last succeed in coming to you.*

Romans 1:11-15
The next verses in Romans (Romans 1:11-15) might be considered to be a statement of purpose being expressed by Paul in that he details his desire and reasons for wanting to visit and he sets both expectations and boundaries.

In the Letter to the Romans, Paul was writing to the leaders of the church in Rome; a church that he didn't personally plant and a church that he had never visited. Acts 2:7-11 tells us that on the day of Pentecost there were '... strangers from Rome ...' *(NKJV)* or '... and visitors from Rome ...' *(NASB)* suggesting that the Church in Rome was planted by those from Rome, just visiting or living in, who were in Jerusalem on the Day of Pentecost and were witnesses to the outpouring of the Holy Spirit upon the apostles and those who were gathered with them. It may

The Compiled Teachings of The Apostle Paul

also be that the church in Rome was planted or strengthened by Roman citizens who had heard Paul preaching in other countries – Asia, Macedonia or Greece – and had become converts to (believers of) the gospel.

In the following passages Paul shows that he has been made aware of practices of the church in Rome that are in conflict with the teachings of Jesus, and so is explaining to them that such practices will result in their condemnation, not in their salvation.	1 ¹¹ *For I long to see you, that I may impart to you some spiritual gift to strengthen you –* ¹² *that is, that we may be mutually encouraged by each other's faith, both yours and mine.* ¹³ *I do not want you to be unaware, brothers, that I have often intended to come to you (but thus far have been prevented), in order that I may reap some harvest among you as well as among the rest of the Gentiles.* ¹⁴ *I am under obligation both to Greeks and to barbarians, both to the wise and to the foolish.* ¹⁵ *So I am eager to preach the gospel to you also who are in Rome.*

The Righteous Shall Live by Faith   Romans 1:16-32

Paul began this passage with a strong statement regarding his mission to Jews and Gentiles, being specific to focus on the Greek, which, given that The Epistle To The Church In Rome is in Italy and not in Greece, might seem slightly odd, but he knows that the church in Rome was established by 'Greeks from Rome'. The second of these two passages (Rom. 1:18-32) is nothing short of a condemnation of what has been communicated to him and it sets the stage for his teaching that follows:	1 ¹⁶ *For I am not ashamed of the gospel, for it is the power of God for salvation to everyone who believes, to the Jew first and also to the Greek.* ¹⁷ *For in it the righteousness of God is revealed from faith for faith, as it is written, "The righteous shall live by faith."* ***God's Wrath on Unrighteousness*** ¹⁸ *For the wrath of God is revealed from heaven against all ungodliness and unrighteousness of men, who by their unrighteousness suppress the truth.* ¹⁹ *For what can be known about God is plain to them, because God has shown it to them.* ²⁰ *For his invisible attributes, namely, his eternal power and divine nature, have been clearly perceived, ever since the creation of the world, in the things that have been made. So they are without excuse.* ²¹ *For although they knew God, they did not honor him as God or give thanks to him, but they became futile in their thinking, and their foolish hearts were darkened.* ²² *Claiming to be wise, they became fools,* ²³ *and exchanged the glory of the immortal God for images resembling mortal man and birds and animals and creeping things.* ²⁴ *Therefore God gave them up in the lusts of their hearts to impurity, to the dishonoring of their bodies among themselves,* ²⁵ *because they exchanged the truth about God for a lie and worshiped and served the creature rather than the Creator, who is blessed forever! Amen.*

²⁶ *For this reason God gave them up to dishonorable passions. For their women exchanged natural relations for those that are contrary to nature;* ²⁷ *and the men likewise gave up natural relations with women and were consumed with passion for one another, men committing shameless acts with men and receiving in themselves the due penalty for their error.*
²⁸ *And since they did not see fit to acknowledge God, God gave them up to a debased mind to do what ought not to be done.* ²⁹ *They were filled with all manner of unrighteousness, evil, covetousness, malice. They are full of envy, murder, strife, deceit, maliciousness. They are gossips,* ³⁰ *slanderers, haters of God, insolent, haughty, boastful, inventors of evil, disobedient to parents,* ³¹ *foolish, faithless, heartless, ruthless.* ³² *Though they know God's righteous decree that those who practice such things deserve to die, they not only do them but [they] give approval to those who practice them.*

The Righteous Judgment of God   Rom. 2:1-11

2. Wherefore you are without excuse, O man, whosoever you are that judges: for in whatever you judge another, you condemn yourself; for you that judge practice the same things. ² *And we know that the judgment of God is according to truth against those that practice such things.* ³ *And reckon this, O man, who judges those that practice such things, and does the same, that will you escape the judgment of God?* ⁴ *Or do you despise the riches of his goodness and forbearance and longsuffering, not knowing that the goodness of God leads you to repentance?* ⁵ *but after your hardness and impenitent heart treasures up for*	Paul begins his teaching by pointing out that you can't judge a person on a specific matter if you yourself are practicing the same thing, and certainly seems logical. Paul then poses the question, *'who judges those that practice such things while doing the same thing will escape the judgment of God?'* and, of course, the answer is a logical, 'no one'. Paul then points out it is the desires of the heart that *'treasures up for yourself wrath'*, and he lists out those desires summing up the

- 76 -

yourself wrath in the day of wrath and revelation of the righteous judgment of God; ⁶ who will render to every man according to his works: ⁷ to those that by patience in well-doing seek for glory and honor and incorruption, eternal life: ⁸ but to those that are factious, and do not obey the truth, but obey unrighteousness, shall be wrath and indignation, ⁹ tribulation and anguish, upon every soul of man that works evil, of the Jew first, and also of the Greek; ¹⁰ but glory and honor and peace to every man that works good, to the Jew first, and also to the Greek: ¹¹ for there is no respect of persons with God.

situation by writing that God "⁶***will render to every man according to his works: ⁷ to those that by patience in well-doing seek for glory and honor and incorruption, eternal life: ⁸ but to those that are factious, and do not obey the truth, but obey unrighteousness, shall be wrath and indignation, ⁹ tribulation and anguish, upon every soul of man that works evil'*** ... ¹⁰ '*glory and honor and peace to every man that works good'*. Finally, Paul points out that none are excluded.

Judgment and the Law

Rom. 2:12-29

2 ¹² For as many as have sinned without the law shall also perish without the law: and as many as have sinned under the law shall be judged by the law; ¹³ for not the hearers of the law are just before God, but the doers of the law shall be justified; ¹⁴ (for when Gentiles that do not have the law do by nature the things of the law, these, not having the law, are the law unto themselves; ¹⁵ in that they show the work of the law written in their hearts, their conscience bearing witness therewith, and their thoughts one with another accusing or else excusing them); ¹⁶ in the day when God shall judge the secrets of men, according to my gospel, by Jesus Christ.
¹⁷ But if you bear the name of a Jew, and rest upon the law, and glory in God, ¹⁸ and know his will, and approve the things that are excellent, being instructed out of the law, ¹⁹ and are confident that you yourself are a guide of the blind, a light of them that are in darkness, ²⁰ a corrector of the foolish, a teacher of babes, having in the law the form of knowledge and of the truth; ²¹ You therefore that teach another, (do you not) teach yourself? You that preaches a man should not steal, do you steal? ²² You that says a man should not commit adultery, do you commit adultery? You that abhors idols, do you rob temples? ²³ You who glories in the law, (but who) through your transgression of the law, (do you not) dishonor God? ²⁴ For the name of God is blasphemed among the Gentiles because of you, even as it is written. ²⁵ For circumcision indeed profits, if you are a doer of the law: but if you are a transgressor of the law, your circumcision is become uncircumcision. ²⁶ If therefore the uncircumcision keep the ordinances of the law, shall not their uncircumcision be reckoned for circumcision? ²⁷ and shall not the uncircumcision which is by nature, if it fulfil the law, judge you, who with the letter and circumcision are a transgressor of the law? ²⁸ For he is not a Jew who is one outwardly; neither is that circumcision which is outward in the flesh: ²⁹ but he is a Jew who is one inwardly; and circumcision is that of the heart, in the spirit not in the letter; whose praise is not of men, but of God.

Two verses that are key in this passage are:
¹³ᵇ *Doers of the law will be justified.*
²⁶ *If therefore the uncircumcision keep the ordinances of the law, shall not their uncircumcision be reckoned for circumcision?*

While the bottom-line focus of this passage is that both Jews and Gentiles can be justified, Paul has to convince those who have strong Jewish heritage that circumcision is not a necessity. In verses 17-25 Paul presents logic- and Bible-based arguments that support the justification of the uncircumcised.

Righteousness

Rom. 3:1-20

3. What advantage then hath the Jew? or what is the profit of circumcision? ² Much every way: first of all, that they were entrusted with the oracles of God. ³ For what if some were without faith? shall their want of faith make of none effect the faithfulness of God? ⁴ God forbid: yea, let God be found true, but every man a liar; as it is written, That you might be justified in your words, and might prevail when you come into judgment.
⁵ But if our unrighteousness commends the righteousness of God, what shall we say? Is God unrighteous who visits with wrath? (I speak after the manner of men.) ⁶ God forbid: for then how shall God judge the world? ⁷ But if the truth of God through my lie abounded unto his glory, why am I also still judged as a sinner? ⁸ and why not (as we are slanderously reported, and as some affirm that we say), Let us do evil, that good may come? whose condemnation is just.

Paul poses the question that if he is not being truthful about God but brings people to know God, why would he be judged to be sinful, and he points out that some are accusing him of proposing that people should do evil so that they can receive forgiveness: ⁷ *But if the truth of God through my lie abounds to his glory, why am I also still judged as a sinner?* ⁸ᵇ ...*Let us do evil, that good may come*, and Paul points out that those who do evil should justly be condemned: ⁸ᶜ *whose condemnation is just..*

The Compiled Teachings of The Apostle Paul

*⁹ What then? are we better than they? No, in no way: **for we before laid to the charge both of Jews and Greeks, that they are all under sin**; ¹⁰ as it is written,*
"THERE IS NONE RIGHTEOUS, NO, NOT ONE; ¹¹ THERE IS NONE THAT UNDERSTANDS, THERE IS NONE THAT SEEKS AFTER GOD; ¹² THEY HAVE ALL TURNED ASIDE, THEY HAVE TOGETHER BECOME UNPROFITABLE; THERE IS NONE THAT DOES GOOD, NO, NOT SO MUCH AS ONE: ¹³ THEIR THROAT IS AN OPEN SEPULCHER; WITH THEIR TONGUES THEY HAVE USED DECEIT: THE POISON OF ASPS IS UNDER THEIR LIPS: ¹⁴ WHOSE MOUTH IS FULL OF CURSING AND BITTERNESS: ¹⁵ THEIR FEET ARE SWIFT TO SHED BLOOD; ¹⁶ DESTRUCTION AND MISERY ARE IN THEIR WAYS; ¹⁷ AND THE WAY OF PEACE HAVE THEY NOT KNOWN: ¹⁸ THERE IS NO FEAR OF GOD BEFORE THEIR EYES."
¹⁹ Now we know that what things soever the law says, it speaks to those that are under the law; that every mouth may be stopped, and all the world may be brought under the judgment of God: ²⁰ because by the works of the law shall no flesh be justified in his sight; for through the law comes the knowledge of sin.

Paul then makes the case that Jews are not better than Gentiles, and Gentiles are not better than Jews. *⁹ᵇ for we before laid to the charge both of Jews and Greeks, that they are all under sin:*

And Paul concludes his argument with:
¹⁹ᵇ that every mouth may be stopped, and all the world may be brought under the judgment of God: ²⁰ because by the works of the law shall no flesh be justified in his sight; for through the law comes the knowledge of sin.

Righteousness Through Faith   Rom. 3:21-31

3 ²¹ But now apart from the law a righteousness of God has been manifested, being witnessed by the law and the prophets; ²² even the righteousness of God through faith in Jesus Christ to all them that believe; for there is no distinction; ²³ for all have sinned, and fall short of the glory of God; ²⁴ being justified freely by his grace through the redemption that is in Christ Jesus: ²⁵ whom God set forth to be a propitiation, through faith, in his blood, to show his righteousness because of the passing over of the sins done aforetime, in the forbearance of God; ²⁶ for the showing, I say, of his righteousness at this present season: that he might himself be just, and the justifier of him that has faith in Jesus. ²⁷ Where then is the glorying? It is excluded. By what manner of law? of works? Nay: but by a law of faith. ²⁸ We reckon therefore that a man is justified by faith apart from the works of the law. ²⁹ Or is God the God of Jews only? is he not the God of Gentiles also? Yea, of Gentiles also: ³⁰ if so be that God is one, and he shall justify the circumcision by faith, and the uncircumcision through faith. ³¹ Do we then make the law of none effect through faith? God forbid: nay, we establish the law.

Paul now begins to focus his arguments on the resurrection of Jesus which Paul points out sets Jews free (set apart) from the law.
Paul re-iterates that for Jews and gentiles *²²ᵇ there is no distinction; ²³ for all have sinned, and fall short of the glory of God;* and he further states that those who believe and have faith that Jesus was the Son of God through believing in the resurrection will be justified because of their faith, *²⁴ being justified freely by his grace through the redemption that is in Christ Jesus:* to which Paul adds, *²⁵...God set forth [Jesus] to be a propitiation, through faith, in his blood, to show his righteousness because of the passing over of the sins done aforetime, in the forbearance of God;*
And Paul concludes by stating: *²⁸ We reckon therefore that a man is justified by faith apart from the works of the law. ³⁰ ... that God is one, and he shall justify [both] the circumcised by faith, and the uncircumcised through faith.*

Justification Through Faith   Rom. 4:1-8

*4. What then shall we say that Abraham, our forefather, has found according to the flesh? ² For if Abraham was justified by works, he has whereof to glory; but not toward God. ³ For what does the scripture say? And **Abraham believed God, and it was reckoned unto him for righteousness.** ⁴ Now to him that works, the reward is not reckoned as of grace, but as of debt. ⁵ But to him that works not, but believes in him that justifies the ungodly, his faith is reckoned for righteousness. ⁶ Even as David also pronounced blessing upon the man, to whom God reckoned righteousness apart from works, ⁷ saying, "Blessed are they whose iniquities are forgiven, And whose sins are covered. ⁸ Blessed is the man to whom the Lord will not reckon sin."*

In this passage Paul is explaining that whoever believes in the resurrection (that Jesus was raised by God from the dead and ascended into heaven) will be justified; it is faith that leads to righteousness, and Paul references Psalm 32 in which King David wrote, *"Blessed are they whose iniquities are forgiven, and whose sins are covered. ⁸ Blessed is the man to whom the Lord will not reckon sin."*
Abraham's faith and trust in God was tested when He told Abraham that he was to take his son Isaac with him to the mountain to make a sacrifice (Gen. 22).

The Compiled Teachings of The Apostle Paul

God's Promise To Abraham
Rom. 4:9-12

4 ⁹ Is this blessing then pronounced upon the circumcision, or upon the uncircumcision also? for we say, "To Abraham his faith was reckoned for righteousness." ¹⁰ How then was it reckoned? when he was in circumcision, or [when he was] in uncircumcision? Not in circumcision, but in uncircumcision: ¹¹ and he received the sign of circumcision, a seal of the righteousness of the faith which he had while he was in uncircumcision: that he might be the father of all them that believe, though they be in uncircumcision, that righteousness might be reckoned to them; ¹² and the father of circumcision to them who not only are of the circumcision, but who also walk in the steps of that faith of our father Abraham which he had in uncircumcision.

Paul explains (reminds us) that Abraham had not been circumcised when God tested him, and that the promise *¹¹ ...was to make Abraham the father of all who believe without being circumcised, so that righteousness would be counted to them as well.* [NASB]

With this explanation, Paul is endeavoring to ensure that there is no discrimination between Jew and Gentile, and that justification is dependent on faith and faith alone.

Faith and Grace
Rom. 4:9-13-20

*4 ¹³ For not through the law was the promise to Abraham or to his seed that he should be heir of the world, but through the righteousness of faith. ¹⁴ For if those that are of the law are heirs, faith is made void, and the promise is made of no effect: ¹⁵ for the law worketh wrath; but where there is no law, neither is there transgression. ¹⁶ **For this cause it is of faith, that it may be according to grace**; to the end that the promise may be sure to all the seed; not to that only which is of the law, but to that also which is of the faith of Abraham, who is the father of us all ¹⁷ (as it is written, A father of many nations have I made thee) before him whom he believed, even God, who gives life to the dead, and calls the things that are not, as though they were. ¹⁸ Who in hope believed against hope, to the end that he might become a father of many nations, according to that which had been spoken, 'So shall thy seed be'. ¹⁹ And without being weakened in faith he considered his own body now as good as dead (he being about a hundred years old), and the deadness of Sarah's womb; ²⁰ yet, looking to the promise of God, he wavered not through unbelief, but waxed strong through faith, giving glory to God.*

Paul continues with his explanation of how faith works, and turns his focus on the law, referring to the books of The Torah pointing out that if there is a dependency on the law, then faith is nullified, and he states, *'¹⁶ For this cause it is of faith, that it may be according to grace'*.

For the benefit of those that might not fully understand the story of Abraham (since Paul knew he was writing to people that he had not personally met), Paul relates many of the significant details regarding Abraham and Sarah to ensure that his audience had these critical facts.

Promise Realized Through Faith
Rom. 4:21-25

*4 ²¹ and being fully assured that what he had promised, he was able also to perform. ²² Wherefore also it was reckoned to him for righteousness. ²³ Now it was not written for his sake alone, that it was reckoned to him; ²⁴ but for our sake also, **to whom it shall be reckoned, who believe in him that raised Jesus our Lord from the dead,** ²⁵ **who was delivered up for our trespasses, and was raised for our justification.***

Paul finishes up this chapter by restating that 'whoever by faith believes in the resurrection will be justified', which is making essentially the same statement as we are familiar with in John 3:16: *'For God so loved the world, that he gave his only begotten Son, that whosoever believes in him should not perish, but have eternal life.'*

Faith Brings Peace
Rom. 5:1-11

5. Being therefore justified by faith, we have peace with God through our Lord Jesus Christ; ² through whom also we have had our access by faith into this grace wherein we stand; and we rejoice in hope of the glory of God. ³ And not only so, but we also rejoice in our tribulations: knowing that tribulation works steadfastness; ⁴ and steadfastness [works] approval; and approval [builds] hope: ⁵ and hope puts not to shame; because the love of God has been shared abroad in our hearts through the Holy Spirit which was given to us. ⁶ For while we were yet weak, in due season Christ died for the ungodly. ⁷ For scarcely for a righteous man will one die: for perhaps for the good man someone would even dare to die. ⁸ But God commends his own love toward us, in that, while we were yet sinners, Christ died for us. ⁹ Much more then, being now justified by his blood, shall we be saved from the wrath of God through him. ¹⁰ For if, while we were enemies, we were reconciled to God through the death of his Son, much more, being reconciled, shall we be saved by his life; ¹¹ and not only so, but we also rejoice in God through our Lord Jesus Christ, through whom we have now received the reconciliation.

Jesus, Paul tells us, *6ᵇ 'Christ died for the ungodly'* and that it is belief in the resurrection that has given us *²ᵇ 'access by faith into this grace'*, and Paul adds *⁸ᵇ'Christ died for us.* ⁹ *Much more then, being now justified by his blood, shall we be saved from the wrath of God through him.'* and Paul explains that because Jesus died we have been reconciled to God: *'¹⁰ᵇwe were reconciled to God through the death of his Son.'*

The Compiled Teachings of The Apostle Paul

Through The Gift of Righteousness Comes Justification   Rom. 5:12-21

5 ¹² Therefore, as through one man sin entered into the world, and death through sin; and so death passed to all men, for that all sinned: ¹³ for until the law sin was in the world; but sin is not imputed when there is no law. ¹⁴ Nevertheless death reigned from Adam until Moses, even over them that had not sinned after the likeness of Adam's transgression, who is a figure of him that was to come. ¹⁵ But not as the trespass, so also is the free gift. For if by the trespass of the one the many died, much more did the grace of God, and the gift by the grace of the one man, Jesus Christ, abound to the many. ¹⁶ And not as through one that sinned, so is the gift: for the judgment came of one to condemnation, but the free gift came of many trespasses to justification. ¹⁷ For if, by the trespass of the one, death reigned through the one; much more shall they that receive the abundance of grace and of the gift of righteousness reign in life through the one, even Jesus Christ. ¹⁸ So then as through one trespass the judgment came unto all men to condemnation; even so through one act of righteousness the free gift came to all men to justification of life. ¹⁹ For as through the one man's disobedience the many were made sinners, even so through the obedience of the one shall the many be made righteous. ²⁰ And the law came in besides, that the trespass might abound; but where sin abounded, grace did abound more exceedingly: ²¹ that, as sin reigned in death, even so might grace reign through righteousness unto eternal life through Jesus Christ our Lord.

Paul continues to explain grace, judgment, righteousness and justification:

^{15b}'*the gift by the grace of the one man, Jesus Christ, abound to the many*'

^{16b}'*for the judgment came of one to condemnation, but the free gift came of many trespasses to justification.*'

^{17b}'*much more shall they that receive the abundance of grace and of the gift of righteousness reign in life through the one, even Jesus Christ*'

^{18b}'*through one act of righteousness the free gift came to all men to justification of life.*

^{19b}'*even so through the obedience of the one shall the many be made righteous*'

^{20b}' *but where sin abounded, grace did abound more exceedingly*'

^{21b}'*even so might grace reign through righteousness unto eternal life through Jesus Christ our Lord.*

Being Dead to Sin is to be Alive to God   Rom. 6:1-14

6. What shall we say then? Shall we continue in sin, that grace may abound? ² God forbid. We who died to sin, how shall we any longer live therein? ³ Or are you ignorant that all (of us) who were baptized into Christ Jesus were baptized into his death. ⁴ We were buried therefore with him through baptism into death: that just as Christ was raised from the dead through the glory of the Father, so we also might walk in newness of life. ⁵ For if we have become united with him in the likeness of his death, we shall be also in the likeness of his resurrection; ⁶ knowing this, that our former self was crucified with him, that the body of sin might be done away, that so we should no longer be in bondage to sin; ⁷ for he that has died is justified from sin. ⁸ But if we died with Christ, we believe that we shall also live with him; ⁹ knowing that Christ being raised from the dead die no more; death no more has dominion over him. ¹⁰ For the death that he died, he died to sin once: but the life that he lives, he lives to God. ¹¹ Even so consider yourselves to be dead to sin, but alive to God in Christ Jesus.

¹² Let not sin therefore reign in your mortal body, that you should obey the lusts thereof: ¹³ neither present your members to sin as instruments of unrighteousness; but present yourselves to God, as alive from the dead, and your members as instruments of righteousness to God. ¹⁴ For sin shall not have dominion over you: for you are not under law, but under grace.

Paul presents the rhetorical question, "should we sin more so as to gain more grace?" to which he immediately responds, "No, of course not. If we have died to sin, Paul argues, how can we go back to living in sin? Don't you understand that when we are baptized, we have committed to bury (change from) our former self in order that we will be justified from sin?" Paul explains that ⁸ *...if we died with Christ, we believe that we shall also live with him... ¹¹ Even so consider yourselves to be dead to sin, but alive to God in Christ Jesus.*

The challenge Paul points out, that as humans we are all tempted (¹² *Let not sin therefore reign in your mortal body, that you should obey the lusts thereof*) and he encourages that we should: ^{13b} *present (y)ourselves to God, as alive from the dead, and (y)our members as instruments of righteousness to God.*

Finally, in this passage, Paul reminds us that we are not under the law, but we are under grace.

Slaves to Righteousness and Sanctification   Rom. 6:15-23

6 ¹⁵ What then? shall we sin, because we are not under law, but under grace? God forbid. ¹⁶ Do you not understand that to whom you present yourselves as servants to obedience, his servants you are whom you obey; whether of sin to death, or of obedience to righteousness? ¹⁷ But thanks be to God, that, whereas you were servants of sin, you became obedient from the heart to that form of teaching whereunto you were delivered; ¹⁸ and being made free from sin, you became servants of righteousness. ¹⁹ I speak after the manner of men because of the infirmity of your flesh: for as you presented your members

This passage appears to begin much the same as the prior passage, asking almost the same rhetorical question. But it is a different question. This question references the law, which as non-Jews, we do not come under (unless one has chosen to). What Paul is saying here is that by choosing to be baptized, you have chosen to become obedient to God: ^{16b} *...obedient from the heart to that form of teaching whereunto you were delivered.* To which, Paul adds: ¹⁸ *and being made free from sin, you became servants of righteousness.*

as servants to uncleanness and to iniquity unto iniquity, even so now present your members as servants to righteousness to sanctification. ²⁰ For when you were servants of sin, you were free in regard of righteousness. ²¹ What fruit then did you have at that time in the things of which you are now ashamed? for the end of those things is death. ²² But now being made free from sin and become servants to God, you have your fruit unto sanctification, and the end eternal life. ²³ For the wages of sin is death; but the free gift of God is eternal life in Christ Jesus our Lord.

Paul then hits hard at the heart of the problem which is a practice of the church in Rome that includes temple prostitutes.
¹⁹ I speak after the manner of men because of the infirmity of your flesh: for as you presented your members as servants to uncleanness and to iniquity unto iniquity,
Paul continues his explanation and finishes by pointing out: *²³ For the wages of sin is death; but the free gift of God is eternal life in Christ Jesus our Lord.*

Released from the Law   Rom. 7:1-13

7. Or are you ignorant, brethren (for I speak to men who know the law), that the law has had dominion over a man for as long as he lives? ² For the woman that has a husband is bound by law to the husband while he lives; but if the husband dies, she is discharged from the law of the husband. ³ So then if, while the husband lives and she is joined to another man, she shall be called an adulteress: but if the husband dies, she is free from the law, so that she is not an adulteress and [even though] she may be joined to another man. ⁴ Wherefore, my brethren, you also were made dead to the law through the body of Christ; [so] that you should be joined to another, even to him who was raised from the dead, that we might bring forth fruit unto God. ⁵ For when we were in the flesh, the sinful passions, which were through the law, wrought in our members to bring forth fruit unto death. ⁶ But now we have been discharged from the law, having died to that wherein we were held; so that we serve in newness of the spirit, and not in oldness of the letter.
⁷ What shall we say then? Is the law sin? God forbid. Howbeit, I had not known sin, except through the law: for I had not known coveting, except the law had said, You shall not covet: ⁸ but sin, finding occasion, wrought in me through the commandment all manner of coveting: for apart from the law sin is dead. ⁹ And I was alive apart from the law once: but when the commandment came, sin revived, and I died; ¹⁰ and the commandment, which was to life, this I found to be to death: ¹¹ for sin, finding occasion, through the commandment beguiled me, and through it slew me. ¹² So that the law is holy, and the commandment holy, and righteous, and good. ¹³ Did then that which is good become death to me? God forbid. But sin, that it might be shown to be sin, by working death to me through that which is good; – that through the commandment sin might become exceeding sinful.

Paul uses the direct analogy of a man being joined to a woman who becomes his wife which is to the glory of God for procreation by a man and his wife is blessed. When a wife loses her husband by cause of death, Paul explains, the wife is free to remarry. However, if the woman while married has sexual relations with a man other than her husband she is deemed guilty of adultery.

When one – man or woman – is baptized then you have in effect become married to God, and those passions which cause us to be sinful, meaning engaging in sexual relations outside of a marriage relationship, are not acceptable even though they were considered acceptable under the law, which is implying, if not stating, that a man who is married should not – like the wife – engage in sexual relations outside of the marriage relationship. With references to fruit brought forth (born), Paul is stating that children born outside of a true marriage partnership are not 'brought forth unto God but are brought forth to death.'

Posing yet a third rhetorical question, Paul asks, 'Is the law sin?' and immediately states, 'No, that cannot be' (my interpretation of the term "God forbid' used by Paul). Paul then admits that he did not have the worldly-experience that he knew his audience had; *"I had not known sin, except through the law: for I had not known coveting, except the law had said, You shall not covet: 8 but sin, finding occasion, wrought in me through the commandment all manner of coveting: for apart from the law sin is dead."* Paul continues to explain that at one time he was *⁹...alive apart from the law once* – meaning that he at one time was practicing what he believed based on the law to be right, but when had his personal encounter with Jesus he realized that much of what he had been doing was wrong. Paul states that *¹²… the law is holy, and the commandment holy, and righteous, and good* and he acknowledges that because of the commandment, sin - meaning any sin - could be fatal.

The Law and Sin   Rom. 7:14-25

7 ¹⁴ For we know that the law is spiritual: but I am carnal, sold under sin. ¹⁵ For that which I do I know not: for not what I would, that do I practice; but what I hate, that I do. ¹⁶ But if what I would not, that I do, I consent unto the law that it is good. ¹⁷ So now it is no more I that do it, but sin which dwelleth in me. ¹⁸ For I know that in me, that is, in my flesh, dwelleth no good thing: for to will is present with me, but to do that which is good is not. ¹⁹ For the good which I would I do not: but the evil which I would not, that I practice.

In this passage we see Paul struggling. First he shares about his struggles now that he recognizes his sinful carnal nature. He speaks very frankly about his 'members' which have him captive to the law of sin: *²³ᵇ...bringing me into captivity under the law of sin which is in my members. ²⁴ Wretched man that I am! who shall deliver me out of the body of this death?*

The Compiled Teachings of The Apostle Paul

²⁰ But if what I would not, that I do, it is no more I that do it, but sin which dwelleth in me. ²¹ I find then the law, that, to me who would do good, evil is present. ²² For I delight in the law of God after the inward man: ²³ but I see a different law in my members, warring against the law of my mind, and bringing me into captivity under the law of sin which is in my members. ²⁴ Wretched man that I am! who shall deliver me out of the body of this death? ²⁵ I thank God through Jesus Christ our Lord. So then I of myself with the mind, indeed, serve the law of God; but with the flesh the law of sin.

Paul finishes this passage by stating that while God has his mind, sin still has his carnal self. Was Paul, perhaps, writing intentionally to show that he is not without temptation? Recall verses 7-8: *⁷ᵇHowbeit, I had not known sin, except through the law: for I had not known coveting, except the law had said, You shall not covet:⁸ but sin, finding occasion, wrought in me through the commandment all manner of coveting: for apart from the law sin is dead.*

Life in the Spirit   Rom. 8:1-11

8. There is therefore now no condemnation to them that are in Christ Jesus. ² For the law of the Spirit of life in Christ Jesus made me free from the law of sin and of death. ³ For what the law could not do, in that it was weak through the flesh, God, sending his own Son in the likeness of sinful flesh and for sin, condemned sin in the flesh: ⁴ that the ordinance of the law might be fulfilled in us, who walk not after the flesh, but after the Spirit. ⁵ For they that are after the flesh mind the things of the flesh; but they that are after the Spirit (mind) the things of the Spirit. ⁶ For the mind of the flesh is death; but the mind of the Spirit is life and peace: ⁷ because the mind of the flesh is enmity against God; for it is not subject to the law of God, neither indeed can it be: ⁸ and they that are in the flesh cannot please God. ⁹ But you are not in the flesh but in the Spirit, if so be that the Spirit of God dwells in you. But if any man does not have the Spirit of Christ, he is none of his. ¹⁰ And if Christ is in you, the body is dead because of sin; but the spirit is life because of righteousness. ¹¹ But if the Spirit of him that raised up Jesus from the dead dwells in you, he that raised up Christ Jesus from the dead shall give life also to your mortal bodies through his Spirit that dwells in you.

Because those who believe in the resurrection *Rom. 5:¹⁷ᵇ receive the abundance of grace and of the gift of righteousness reign in life through the one, even Jesus Christ', Rom. 8:¹ There is therefore now no condemnation to those who are in Christ Jesus.* This is because, although man is weak, *Rom. 8:³ᵇ God, sending his own Son in the likeness of sinful flesh and for sin, condemned sin in the flesh.* *Rom. 8: ⁵ For they that are after the flesh mind the things of the flesh;* - meaning they care only about - *but they that are after the Spirit* - care about - *the things of the Spirit. ⁶ For the mind of the flesh is death; but the mind of the Spirit is life and peace: ⁷ because the mind of the flesh is enmity against God; for it is not subject to the law of God, neither indeed can it be: ⁸ and they that are in the flesh cannot please God.*

In verses 10 and 11, Paul brings the explanation to a conclusion that the spirit is life because of righteousness, and that God, through the spirit of Jesus – *¹¹ᵇ...his Spirit that dwells in you* – gives life to the body.

Heirs with Christ   Rom. 8:12-17

*8 ¹² So then, brethren, we are debtors, not to the flesh, to live after the flesh: ¹³ for if you live after the flesh, you must die; but if by the Spirit you put to death the deeds of the body, you shall live. ¹⁴ For as many as are led by the Spirit of God, these are sons of God. ¹⁵ For you received not the spirit of bondage again unto fear; but you received the spirit of adoption, whereby we cry, Abba, Father. ¹⁶ **The Spirit himself bears witness with our spirit, that we are children of God**: ¹⁷ and if children, then heirs; heirs of God, and joint-heirs with Christ; if so be that we suffer with him, that we may be also glorified with him.*

¹⁵ ... if you live by the Spirit you put to death the deeds of the body, you will live.
¹⁶ The Spirit himself bears witness with our spirit that we are children of God,
¹⁷ – heirs of God and fellow heirs with Christ, provided we suffer with him in order that we may also be glorified with him.

Our Victory In Christ: Redemption   Rom. 8:18-30

8 ¹⁸ For I reckon that the sufferings of this present time are not worthy to be compared with the glory which shall be revealed to us-ward. ¹⁹ For the earnest expectation of the creation waits for the revealing of the sons of God. ²⁰ For the creation was subjected to vanity, not of its own will, but by reason of him who subjected it, in hope ²¹ that the creation itself also shall be delivered from the bondage of corruption into the liberty of the glory of the children of God. ²² For we know that the whole creation groans and travails in pain together until now. ²³ And not only so, but ourselves also, who have the first-fruits of the Spirit, even we ourselves groan within ourselves, waiting for our adoption, to wit, the redemption of our body. ²⁴ For in hope we were saved: but hope that is seen is not hope: for who hopes for that which he sees? ²⁵ But if we hope for that which we cannot see, then it is with patience that we wait for it.

Paul acknowledges that there are sacrifices and struggles but shares his vision of what the future reward is: *¹⁹ For the earnest expectation of the creation waits for the revealing of the sons of God.* Paul states that *²¹ the creation itself also shall be delivered from the bondage of corruption into the liberty of the glory of the children of God.* And Paul refers to himself and others *²³ᵇ who have the first-fruits of the Spirit, even we ourselves groan within ourselves, waiting for our adoption – the redemption of our body.*

In verses 24 and 25 Paul points out that hope that we can see surely is not hope; but if we hope for that which we cannot see, we must wait patiently.

The Compiled Teachings of The Apostle Paul

All Things Work Together For Good — Rom. 8:26-30

8 26 And in like manner the Spirit also helps our infirmity: for we know not how to pray as we should; but the Spirit himself makes intercession for us with groanings which cannot be uttered; 27 and he that searches the hearts knows what is the mind of the Spirit, because he makes intercession for the saints according to the will of God. 28 And we know that to them that love God all things work together for good, even to them that are called according to his purpose. 29 For whom he foreknew, he also foreordained to be conformed to the image of his Son, that he might be the firstborn among many brethren: 30 and whom he foreordained, them he also called: and whom he called, them he also justified: and whom he justified, them he also glorified.

Paul tells us that the Spirit is our helper and an intercessor on our behalf: *27 he that searches the hearts knows what is the mind of the Spirit, because he makes intercession for the saints according to the will of God.*
In this passage Paul gives us one of the best-known Bible verses, *28 And we know that to them that love God all things work together for good, even to them that are called according to his purpose.* A passage that is often quoted in reference to God having a plan for each of us, and in verse *29* Paul references the apostles who were chosen by Jesus: *30 and whom he foreordained, them he also called: and whom he called, them he also justified: and whom he justified, them he also glorified.*

God's Everlasting Love — Rom. 8:31-39

8 31 What then shall we say to these things? **If God is for us, who is against us?** *32* **He that spared not his own Son, but delivered him up for us all, how shall he not also with him freely give us all things?** *33 Who shall lay anything to the charge of God's elect? It is God that justifies; 34 who is he that condemned? It is Christ Jesus that died, yea rather, that was raised from the dead, who is at the right hand of God, who also makes intercession for us. 35 Who shall separate us from the love of Christ? shall tribulation, or anguish, or persecution, or famine, or nakedness, or peril, or sword? 36 Even as it is written, 'For thy sake we are killed all the day long; We were accounted as sheep for the slaughter.' 37 Nay, in all these things we are more than conquerors through him that loved us. 38 For* **I am persuaded, that neither death, nor life, nor angels, nor principalities, nor things present, nor things to come, nor powers,** *39* **nor height, nor depth, nor any other creature, shall be able to separate us from the love of God, which is in Christ Jesus our Lord.**

Paul makes the case that God sacrificed His own son, and , yes, Jesus was raised from the dead and he ascended into heaven, and so Paul poses the question;
'35 Who shall separate us from the love of Christ?' and ends this passage by stating his firm belief that nothing is able to *39b separate us from the love of God, which is in Christ Jesus our Lord.*

God's Sovereign Choice; Solicitude For Israel — Rom. 9:1-21

*9 I say the truth in Christ, I lie not, my conscience bearing witness with me in the Holy Spirit, 2 that I have great sorrow and unceasing pain in my heart. 3 For I could wish that I myself were anathema from Christ for my brethren's sake, my kinsmen according to the flesh: 4 who are Israelites; whose is the adoption, and the glory, and the covenants, and the giving of the law, and the service of God, and the promises; 5 whose are the fathers, and of whom is Christ as concerning the flesh, who is over all, God blessed for ever. Amen.
6 But it is not as though the word of God has come to nothing. For they are not all Israel, that are of Israel: 7 neither, because they are Abraham's seed, are they all children: but, in Isaac shall thy seed be called. 8 That is, it is not the children of the flesh that are children of God; but the children of the promise are reckoned for a seed. 9 For this is a word of promise, According to this season will I come, and Sarah shall have a son. 10 And not only so; but Rebecca also having conceived by one, even by our father Isaac — 11 for the children being not yet born, neither having done anything good or bad, that the purpose of God according to election might stand, not of works, but of him that calls, 12 it was said to her, The elder shall serve the younger. 13 Even as it is written, Jacob I loved, but Esau I hated.
14 What shall we say then? Is there unrighteousness with God? God forbid. 15 For he said to Moses, I will have mercy on whom I have mercy, and I will have compassion on whom I have compassion. 16 So then it is not of him that wills, nor of him that runs, but of God that has mercy. 17 For the scripture said to Pharaoh, For this very purpose did I raise you up, that I might show in you my power, and that my name might be published abroad in all the earth. 18* **So then he has mercy on whom he will, and whom he will he harden.**

Paul makes the statement that he wishes that he were rejected and shunned by Christ (anathema) because he is concerned for the Jews who are Israelites because they have rejected Jesus, and Paul recounts the history of Abraham and Sarah, and of Isaac and Rebecca who gave birth to Jacob and Esau and of whom God told Rebecca while she was still carrying her unborn children, *12 The elder shall serve the younger. 13 Even as it is written, Jacob I loved, but Esau I hated.*
Paul then references Pharoah (the Pharoah of Moses' time) whose heart God hardened:
Ex. 9 *16 but in very deed for this cause have I made thee to stand, to show thee my power, and that my name may be declared throughout all the earth.*
God, Paul is telling us, makes choices. *18 So then he has mercy on whom he will, and whom he will he harden.* Paul then references a potter who works with clay and asks the question, *20b Shall the thing formed say to him that formed it, Why did you*

19 You will say then to me, Why does he still find fault? For who [is able to] withstand his will? 20 Nay but, O man, who are you that replies against God? Shall the thing formed say to him that formed it, Why did you make me like this? 21 Or has not the potter a right over the clay, from the same lump to make one part a vessel to honor, and another to dishonor?

make me like this? 21 Or has not the potter a right over the clay, from the same lump to make one part a vessel to honor, and another to dishonor?

Israel's Unbelief

Rom. 9:22-29

9 22 What if God, willing to show his wrath, and to make His power known, endured with much longsuffering vessels of wrath prepared for destruction: 23 and that he might make known the riches of his glory upon vessels of mercy, which he before prepared to glory, 24 even us, whom he also called, not from the Jews only, but also from the Gentiles?
25 As he said also in Hosea:
I will call that my people, which was not my people; And her beloved, that was not beloved. (Hos. 2:23)
26 And it shall be, that in the place where it was said to them, 'You were not my people,' [I will say] 'You are my people!' And they will say, 'You are my God!'
27 And Isaiah cried concerning Israel, If the number of the children of Israel be as the sand of the sea, it is the remnant that shall be saved: 28 for the Lord will execute His word upon the earth, finishing it and cutting it short [thoroughly and quickly]. (Is. 10:22-23)
29 And, as Isaiah has said before,
Except the Lord of Sabaoth had left us a seed, [Is. 1:9]
We had become as Sodom, and become like Gomorrah.
30 What shall we say then? That the Gentiles, who followed not after righteousness, attained to righteousness, even the righteousness which is of faith: 31 but Israel, following after a law of righteousness, did not arrive at that law.
32 Why? Because they sought it not by faith, but as it were by works. They stumbled at the stone of stumbling; 33 even as it is written, Behold, I lay in Zion a stone of stumbling and a rock of offence: And he that believeth in Him shall not be put to shame. [Is. 28:16]

In this passage Paul quotes Old Testament prophecy from Hosea and Isaiah. First from Hosea in which Hosea prophesies that God will turn to the Gentiles (those who were not His people) and say, 'You are My people' [Hosea 2:23] which makes all people God's people. Paul's reference to Isaiah is a direct indictment on the Church in Rome that they have become like Sodom and Gomorrah. Paul then turns his attention onto the people of Israel pointing out that they did not have the correct motivation. The Jews had their focus on becoming pious and pretentious in their ways, not putting their faith in God and trusting Him as they should and Paul references Isaiah's prophecy that God would place a stumbling block in the path of the people of Israel, that stumbling block being referenced as a stumbling stone that would also be the cornerstone and a 'rock of offence': *"Behold, I am laying a stone in Zion, a tested stone, A precious cornerstone for the foundation, firmly placed. The one who believes in it will not be disturbed.* [Is. 28:16 NASB] That 'rock' is, of course, Jesus Christ; [Rom. 4:24] *but for our sake also, to whom it shall be reckoned, who believe in him that raised Jesus our Lord from the dead, 25 who was delivered up for our trespasses, and was raised for our justification.*

The Message of Salvation to All

Rom. 10:1-15

*10 Brethren, my heart's desire and my supplication to God is for them, that they may be saved. 2 For I bear them witness that they have a zeal for God, but not according to knowledge. 3 For being ignorant of God's righteousness, and seeking to establish their own, they did not subject themselves to the righteousness of God. 4 For Christ is the end of the law to righteousness to everyone that believes. 5 For Moses wrote that the man that does the righteousness which is of the law shall live thereby. 6 But the righteousness which is of faith says thus, Say not in your heart, Who shall ascend into heaven? (that is, to bring Christ down:) 7 or, Who shall descend into the abyss? (that is, to bring Christ up from the dead.) 8 But what does it say? The word is in you, in your mouth, and in your heart: this is, the word of faith [that] which we preach: 9 because **if you confess with your mouth Jesus as Lord, and believe in your heart that God raised Him from the dead, you will be saved: 10 for with the heart man believes unto righteousness; and with the mouth confession is made into salvation.** 11 For the scripture says, Whosoever believes in Him shall not be put to shame. 12 **For there is no distinction between Jew and Greek: for the same Lord is Lord of all, and is rich unto all that call upon Him: 13 for, whosoever shall call upon the name of the Lord shall be saved.** 14 How then shall they call on Him in someone they have not believed? and how shall they believe in Him whom they have not heard?*

Paul, having been trained up by Gamaliel, *'strictly according to the law of our fathers, being zealous for God'* (Acts 22:3b) writes in support of living under the Law – *2 I bear them witness that they have a zeal for God.* But he then adds, *'but not according to knowledge. 3 For being ignorant of God's righteousness, and seeking to establish their own, they did not subject themselves to the righteousness of God',* adding *4 For Christ is the end of the law to righteousness to everyone that believes.* and he then references Moses who wrote, *5 ... that the man that does the righteousness which is of the law shall live thereby. [Ye shall therefore keep my statutes, and mine ordinances; which if a man do, he shall live in them: I am Jehovah* Lev.18:5 ASV*]* adding *6 But the righteousness which is of faith says thus, Say not in your heart, Who shall ascend into heaven? 7 or, Who shall descend into the abyss?*

This passage is a reference to Deuteronomy 30:11-14 which reads:
12 It is not in heaven, that thou shouldest say, Who shall go up for us to heaven, and bring it unto us, and make us to hear it, that we may do it? 13 Neither is it beyond the sea, that thou shouldest say, Who shall go over the sea for us, and bring it unto us, and make us to hear it, that we

The Compiled Teachings of The Apostle Paul

and how shall they hear without a preacher? ¹⁵ and how shall they preach, except they be sent? even as it is written, How beautiful are the feet of them that bring glad tidings of good things!

may do it? ¹⁴ But the word is very nigh unto thee, in thy mouth, and in thy heart, that thou mayest do it. Deut. 30:11-14 ASV
Notice the similarity to words that Jesus taught: *'for out of the abundance of the heart the mouth speaks.'* [Matt. 12:34ᵇ]

Even though Paul is writing to Gentiles, he uses this reference back to instructions given to the Jews to make the statement, *'⁹ if you confess with your mouth Jesus as Lord, and believe in your heart that God raised Him from the dead, you will be saved: ¹⁰ for with the heart man believes unto righteousness; and with the mouth confession is made into salvation.'* Getting the people of Rome understanding this was for Paul absolutely key. He emphasizes this by stating ¹² *For there is no distinction between Jew and Greek: for the same Lord is Lord of all, and is rich unto all that call upon Him: ¹³ for, whosoever shall call upon the name of the Lord shall be saved.* Paul ends by delivering a message of justification for his ministry.

Denial By Israel   Rom. 10:16-21

10 ¹⁶ But they did not all hearken to the glad tidings. **For Isaiah said, Lord, who has believed our report? ¹⁷ So belief comes of hearing, and hearing by the word of Christ.** *¹⁸ But I say, Did they not hear? Yea, verily, Their sound went out into all the earth, And their words to the ends of the world.*
¹⁹ But I say [ask], Did Israel not know? First Moses said, I will provoke you to jealousy with that which is no nation; With a nation void of understanding will I anger you.
²⁰ And Isaiah is very bold, and said, I was found of them that sought me not; I became manifest to them that asked not of me. ²¹ But as to Israel he said, All the day long did I spread out my hands to a disobedient people who were in denial.

Paul references Isaiah 53:1, *Who has believed our message? and to whom the arm of Jehovah has been revealed?* Again, Paul references Moses who hinted at Israel becoming humiliated by another nation, a nation that did not know God, and then he references Isaiah to make the point that Israel remained stubborn and refused to listen, even to outright disobey.

The Remnant of Israel: Israel Is Not Cast Away   Rom. 11:1-10

11 I say then, Did God cast off his people? God forbid. For I also am an Israelite, of the seed of Abraham, of the tribe of Benjamin. ² God did not cast off his people which he foreknew. Or do you not know what the scripture says of Elijah? how he pleaded with God against Israel: ³ Lord, they have killed your prophets, they have dug down thine altars; and I am left alone, and they seek my life. ⁴ But what was the answer of God to him? "I have left for myself seven thousand men, who have not bowed the knee to Baal."
*⁵ **Even so then at this present time also there is a remnant according to the election of grace. ⁶ But if it is by grace, it is no more of works: otherwise grace is no more grace.** ⁷ What then? That which Israel seeks for, that he obtained not; but the election obtained it, and the rest were hardened: ⁸ according as it is written, 'God gave them a spirit of stupor, eyes that they should not see, and ears that they should not hear, to this very day'. ⁹ And David said:*
  Let their table be made a snare, and a trap, and a stumbling block, and a recompense to them:
¹⁰ Let their eyes be darkened, that they may not see, and bow thou down their back always. [bend their backs continually ᴺᴬˢᴮ]

Paul begins this passage by identifying that he belongs to the tribe of Benjamin and Paul references Elijah and how Elijah went before God on behalf of the people of Israel. God responded to Elijah by telling him that He would set aside a remnant, 7,000 who would not bow down to Baal, and, of course, worshipping various idols was very much part of the culture of Rome at that time. Paul pivots back to referencing being saved by grace and not of works. *⁵ Even so then at this present time also there is a remnant according to the election of grace. ⁶ But if it is by grace, it is no more of works: otherwise grace is no more grace.*

For those (Israelites) who chose to worship Baal, Paul points out even David asked that they be cursed.

Salvation Comes To The Gentiles (Who Are Grafted In)   Rom. 11:11-24

*11 ¹¹ I say then, Did they stumble that they might fall? God forbid: but by their fall salvation is come to the Gentiles, to provoke them to jealousy. ¹² Now if their fall is the riches of the world, and their loss the riches of the Gentiles; how much more their fulness? ¹³ But I speak to you that are Gentiles. Inasmuch then as I am an apostle of Gentiles, I glorify my ministry; ¹⁴ if by any means I may provoke to jealousy them that are my flesh, and may save some of them. ¹⁵ For if the casting away of them is the reconciling of the world, what shall the receiving of them be, but life from the dead? ¹⁶ And **if the first-fruit [the first piece of dough] is holy, so is the lump: and if the root is holy, so are the branches.** ¹⁷ But if some of the branches were broken off, and you, being a wild olive, was grafted in among them, and became a partaker with them of the*

Paul explains that it was because the people of Israel stumbled that the door for the Gentiles to gain salvation was opened, and Paul uses the phrase *'¹² the riches of the world'* – meaning that all Jews and all non-Jews – are now invited to become saved. Paul then explains that he is an apostle to the Gentiles and, as such, it is his duty to God to:
¹⁴ provoke to jealousy them that are my [his] flesh and the purpose of such a mission was to *¹⁴ᵇ save some of them.* Paul then describes the event of the Jews being cast away from God as the path to reconciling the world, which he describes as bringing *¹⁵ but life from the dead.*

The Compiled Teachings of The Apostle Paul

> *root of the fatness of the olive tree;* [18] *glory not over the branches: but if you glory, it is not you that bears the root, but the root [bears] you.* [19] *Thou wilt say then, Branches were broken off, that I might be grafted in.* [20] *Well; by their unbelief they were broken off, and you stood by your faith. Be not high-minded, but fear:* [21] *for if God spared not the natural branches, neither will he spare you.* [22] *Behold then the goodness and severity of God: toward them that fell, severity; but toward you, God's goodness, if you continue in his goodness: otherwise you also shall be cut off.* [23] *And they also, if they continue not in unbelief, shall be grafted in: for God is able to graft them in again.* [24] *For if you were cut out of that which is by nature a wild olive tree, and was grafted contrary to nature into a good olive tree; how much more shall these, which are the natural branches, be grafted into their own olive tree?*

Using the analogy of a gardener who tends olive trees Paul explains that all is dependent upon the root. What we see of the tree are the trunk, the branches, the leaves, and the fruit, but all of which are dependent upon the [health of] the root. A gardener cuts and removes any branches that not healthy, and in a similar manner God will cut off those that do not [22] *continue in his goodness;* but if they return to God, like a gardener who is able to graft a branch onto a healthy tree, God will restore them: [23b] *for God is able to graft them in again.*

Those that Paul was referring to as becoming saved are described by Paul as branches that are [24] *cut out of that which is by nature a wild olive tree.*

...if the root is holy, so are the branches.

The Mystery of Israel's Salvation
Rom. 11:25-36

> 11 [25] *For I would not, brethren, have you ignorant of this mystery, lest you be wise in your own conceits, that a hardening in part has befallen Israel, until the fulness of the Gentiles has come in;* [26] *and so all Israel shall be saved: even as it is written,*
> *There shall come out of Zion the Deliverer;*
> *He shall turn away ungodliness from Jacob:*
> [27] *And this is my covenant to them,*
> *When I shall take away their sins.*
> [28] *As touching the gospel, they are enemies for your sake: but as touching the election, they are beloved for the fathers' sake.* [29] *For the gifts and the calling of God are not repented of.* [30] *For as you in time past were disobedient to God, but now have obtained mercy by their disobedience,* [31] *even so have these also now been disobedient, that by the mercy shown to you they also may now obtain mercy.* [32] *For God has shut up all to disobedience, that he might have mercy upon all.* [33] *O the depth of the riches both of the wisdom and the knowledge of God! how unsearchable are his judgments, and his ways past tracing out!* [34] *For who has known the mind of the Lord? or who has been his counsellor?* [35] *or who has first given to him, and it shall be recompensed to him again?* [36] *For of him, and through him, and to him, are all things. To him be the glory forever. Amen.*

Paul writes that he [25] *'...would not have you ignorant of this mystery'*. When we read Paul quoting Isaiah 59:20, Paul is referencing the prophecy that Jews had long understood to be prophecy of the coming of the Messiah; the Deliverer being, of course, Jesus Christ.

Next Paul uses the phrase *'As touching the gospel'*. Other Bible translations use word 'concerning' or 'regarding', or the phrases *'according to'* and *'from the standpoint of'*, or *'from the viewpoint of'*, in place of the word touching. Then there is the similar phrase that Paul writes, *'but as touching the election'*, and testing each of the alternative words and phrases, *'from the viewpoint of'*, seems to me to be the best translation although my own personal way of saying what I understand Paul is saying is, *'As far as the Gospel goes they are enemies'* and, *'As far as the elected go they are beloved (for sake of Abraham and Isaac)'*.

Next Paul reiterates that it is because of the Jews falling from grace that has granted the Gentiles the opportunity of grace, but now mercy is being afforded to all, both Jew and Gentile.

Verses 33-36 of Romans 10 appear to reflect passages taken from the book of Psalms:
Psalm 92:5 [ESV] [5] *How great are your works, O Lord! Your thoughts are very deep!*
Psalm 145:3-4 [ESV] [3] *Great is the Lord, and greatly to be praised, and his greatness is unsearchable.*
and Paul also writes a passage with a similar message to the Corinthians; 1 Cor. 2:10 [ESV]:
[10] *these things God has revealed to us through the Spirit. For the Spirit searches everything, even the depths of God.*

Dedicated Service: A Living Sacrifice
Rom. 12:1-2

> 12. *Therefore, I urge you, brothers and sisters, by the mercies of God, to **present your bodies as a living and holy sacrifice, acceptable to God, which is your spiritual service of worship**.* [2] *And do not be conformed to this world, but be transformed by the renewing of your mind, so that you may prove what the will of God is, that which is good and acceptable and perfect.*

These verses exhorting the Christians in the church in Rome throw down a huge challenge to them to change their ways. Paul tells them to consider their bodies as holy because Paul has learned of their practices which include sexual permissiveness that Paul references as [2] *'do not be conformed to this world'*, but instead to replace those practices with [2c] *'that which is good and acceptable and perfect.'*

We know that Paul is writing from a position of authority because from reading The Book of Acts we have learned about Paul. It is because Paul had a direct encounter with Jesus that caused him to be blind and was given back his sight. It is this knowledge that allows us to understand while Paul refers to himself as an apostle even though he was not part of those who were chosen, taught and ministered to by Jesus. In this next passage, Paul begins by referring to grace that was given to him by Jesus and

The Compiled Teachings of The Apostle Paul

makes the comment that each person should *'not to think more highly of himself than he ought to think; but to think so as to have sound judgment, as God has allotted to each a measure of faith.'* The church leaders in Rome didn't have The Book of Acts to teach them, but they had been taught by those who founded the church about the resurrection, and the promise of being saved by grace. Some of those who founded the church may have been in Jerusalem on the day of Pentecost when the Holy Spirit descended upon the apostles, and had learned sufficient to understand that something beyond a simple confession of faith was required. In this passage Paul suggests that how much faith a person has may depend on how much faith God has allotted to them: [3c] *'...**as God has allotted to each a measure of faith.**'*

Gifts of Grace: Abhor What Is Evil — Rom. 12:3-8

> 12 [3] *For I say, through the grace that was given me, to every man that is among you, not to think of himself more highly than he ought to think; but so to think as to think soberly, according as God hath dealt to each man a measure of faith.* [4] *For even as* **we have many members in one body, and all the members have not the same office:** [5] **so we, who are many, are one body in Christ**, *and severally members one of another.* [6] *And* **having gifts differing according to the grace that was given to us**, *whether prophecy, let us prophesy according to the proportion of our faith;* [7] *or ministry, let us give ourselves to our ministry; or he that teaches, to his teaching;* [8] *or he that exhorts, to his exhorting: he that gives, let him do it with liberality; he that rules, with diligence; he that shows mercy, with cheerfulness.*

Paul then continues to explain that we are not all given the same gifts; we are one body that is made up of parts with different functions and different abilities [5] ***so we, who are many, are one body in Christ, and individually parts of one another.*** Paul may have been aware of Jesus' teachings (e.g. Matt. 13: [16] *But blessed are your eyes, for they see; and your ears, for they hear, and Matt. 6:* [22] *The lamp of the body is the eye*) and Paul lists abilities that are gifts: serving, teaching, exhorting (encouraging), giving, leading, and caring (mercy).

Marks of the True Christian — Rom. 12:9-21

> 12 [9] *Let love be without hypocrisy. Abhor that which is evil; cleave to that which is good.* [10] *In love of the brethren be tenderly affectioned [committed] one to another; in honor preferring one another;* [11] *in diligence not slothful; fervent in spirit; serving the Lord;* [12] *rejoicing in hope; patient in tribulation; continuing steadfastly in prayer;* [13] *communicating to the necessities of the saints; given to hospitality.*
> [14] *Bless them that persecute you; bless, and curse not.* [15] *Rejoice with them that rejoice; weep with them that weep.*
> [16] *Be of the same mind one toward another. Set not your mind on high things, but condescend to things that are lowly. Be not wise in your own conceits.*
> [17] *Render to no man evil for evil. Take thought for things honorable in the sight of all men.* [18] *If it is possible, as much as in you lies, be at peace with all men.*
> [19] *Avenge not yourselves, beloved, but give place to the wrath of God: for it is written, Vengeance belongs to me**; I will recompense, says the Lord.* [20] *But if your enemy hungers, feed him; if he thirsts, give him drink: for in so doing you will heap coals of fire upon his head.* [21] *Be not overcome of evil, but overcome evil with good.*

Paul continues to list first virtues, pointing out that we must be free of hypocrisy and must focus on what is good and reject that which is not good. Paul exhorts those in the church to be fully committed to each other, showing brotherly love and giving preference to spending time with one another in serving the Lord. Rejoice in hope and remain patient during difficult times (tribulation), always in prayer lifting up the needs of others; welcoming and caring for others.

In verses 14-21 Paul focuses on challenges and behavior sharing teaching in a style that is almost reminiscent of Proverbs and most certainly reminds one of Jesus' teaching in the Sermon on the Mount.

* *Jer. 46:10*   [Matt. 5:1-12; Luke 6:17-38]

Submission to Government Authorities — Rom. 13:1-7

> 13. *Let every soul be in subjection to the higher powers: for* **there is no power but of God; and the powers that be are ordained of God.** [2] **Therefore he that resists the power, withstands the ordinance of God: and they that withstand shall receive to themselves judgment.** [3] *For rulers are not a terror to the good work, but to the evil. And would you have no fear of the power? do that which is good, and you shall have praise from the same:* [4] *for he is a minister of God to you for good. But if you do that which is evil, be afraid; for he bears not the sword in vain: for he is a minister of God, an avenger for wrath to him that does evil.* [5] *Wherefore you must needs be in subjection, not only because of the wrath, but also for conscience' sake.*

[1b] *...there is no authority except from God, and those that exist have been instituted by God.* [2] *Therefore whoever resists the authorities resists what God has appointed, and those who resist will incur judgment.* [NASB]

Paul's warning in these verses reminds one of Jesus' teaching in which he said, *Render therefore to Caesar the things that are Caesar's; and to God the things that are God's,* (Matt. 22:15-22; Mark 12:13-17; Luke 20:19-26) however, Paul adds a warning that choosing to resist and refusing to subject oneself to *'the powers that be'* has consequences pointing out that [3] *...rulers are not a terror to the good work, but to the evil.* Again, as if referencing Jesus teaching, Paul adds: [6] *For for this cause you pay tribute also; for they are ministers of God's service, attending continually upon this very thing.* [7] *Render to all their dues: tribute to whom tribute is due.*

The Compiled Teachings of The Apostle Paul

> *⁶ For this cause you pay tribute also; for they are ministers of God's service, attending continually upon this very thing. ⁷ Render to all their dues: tribute to whom tribute is due; custom to whom custom; fear to whom fear; honor to whom honor.*

Paul continues with more teaching that reminds us of Jesus' teaching:
'*Render therefore to Caesar the things that are Caesar's; and unto God the things that are God's.*' (Matt. 22:21.

Fulfilling the Law Through Love

Rom. 13:8-10

> *13 ⁸ Owe no man anything, save to love one another: for he that loves his neighbor has fulfilled the law. ⁹ For this, You shall not commit adultery, You shall not kill, You shall not steal, You shall not covet, and if there be any other commandment, it is summed up in this word, namely, You shall love thy neighbor as thyself. ¹⁰ Love works no ill to his neighbor: love therefore is the fulfilment of the law.*

In this passage Paul with a focus on explaining 'love thy neighbor', quotes the same commandments (Ex. 20:12-17) as Jesus quoted to the 'rich, young ruler' (Matt. 19:16-26, Mark 10:17-27 Luke 18:18-30) finishing with the conclusion that love is the fulfilment of the law.

Put On The Armor Of Light

Rom. 13:11-14

> *13 ¹¹ And this, knowing the season, that already it is time for you to wake out of sleep: for now is salvation nearer to us than when we first believed. ¹² The night is far spent, and the day is at hand: let us therefore cast off the works of darkness, and let us put on the armor of light. ¹³ Let us walk becomingly, as in the day; not in reveling and drunkenness, not in chambering and wantonness, not in strife and jealousy. ¹⁴ But put on the Lord Jesus Christ, and do not make provision for the flesh, to fulfil the lusts thereof.*

The final verses in Romans 13 sound like a battle rally cry with Paul referencing armor – *the armor of light.* Paul encourages the people of Rome to ¹²ᵇ'*cast off the works of darkness...* and to ¹³ '*walk becomingly, as in the day; not in reveling and drunkenness,*' and then, finally, ¹⁴ '*put on the Lord Jesus Christ, and do not make provision for the flesh, to fulfil the lusts thereof.*'

Jesus told the disciples '*...look on the fields, that they are already white to harvest. ³⁶ He that reaps receives wages, and gathers fruit to life eternal; [so] that he that sows and he that reaps may rejoice together*' (John 4:35b-36) and Jesus also said, '*The harvest indeed is plenteous, but the laborers are few.*' (Matt. 9:37)

Do Not Pass Judgment on One Another

Rom. 14:1-12

> *14 But him that is weak in faith receives you, yet not for decision of scruples. ² One man has faith to eat all things: but he that is weak [in faith] eats herbs. ³ Let not him that eats sit with him that eats not; and let not him that eats not judge him that eats: for God has received him. ⁴ Who are you that judges the servant of another? to his own lord he stands or falls. Yea, he shall be made to stand; for the Lord has power to make him stand. ⁵ One man esteems one day over another: another esteems every day alike. **Let each man be fully assured in his own mind.** ⁶ He that regards the day, regards it to the Lord: and he that eats, eats to the Lord, for he gives God thanks; and he that eats not, to the Lord he eats not, and gives God thanks. ⁷ For none of us lives to himself, and none dies to himself. ⁸ For whether we live, we live to the Lord; or whether we die, we die to the Lord: whether we live therefore, or die, we are the Lord's. ⁹ **For to this end Christ died and lived again, that he might be Lord of both the dead and the living.** ¹⁰ But you, why do you judge your brother? or you again, why do you set at nought your brother? for we shall all stand before the judgment-seat of God. ¹¹ For it is written: As I live, says the Lord, to me every knee shall bow, And every tongue shall confess to God. ¹² **So then each one of us shall give account of himself to God.***

The NASB translation of Rom. 14:1-2 is: '*Now accept the one who is weak in faith, but not to have quarrels over opinions. ² One person has faith that he may eat all things, but the one who is weak [in faith] eats only vegetables.*'
Paul is telling the leaders of the church to not allow what one eats to be a deciding factor. A paraphrase of what Paul is stating is: 'don't get into arguments over the issue of what meat is acceptable and what is not.' What meat, or even whether to eat meat or not, is a personal decision: ⁵ᵇ *Let each man be fully assured in his own mind.*
Paul points out that Christ 'died and lived again' for the purpose of being Lord of those alive and those dead. (⁹ ***For to this end Christ died and lived again, that he might be Lord of both the dead and the living.***)
Is this to be taken literally, Lord of those who have died and those who are still living as others (non-believers) might see it, or is this a reference to being Lord of those still living but who are 'dead to Christ' and as well as to those who are 'alive to Christ'. As Paul ends this passage with ¹² ***So then each one of us shall give account of himself to God*** does that point only to those who are living and yet to die?

Do Not Cause Another to Stumble

14 ¹³ Let us not therefore judge one another anymore: but judge this way, that no man put a stumbling block in his brother's way, or an occasion of falling.
¹⁴ I know, and am persuaded in the Lord Jesus, that nothing is unclean of itself: save that to him who accounts anything to be unclean, to him it is unclean. ¹⁵ For if because of [what] meat [you eat] your brother is grieved, you walk no longer in love. Do not destroy him for whom Christ died because of your [concern for] meat. ¹⁶ Let not then your good be evil spoken of:¹⁷ for the kingdom of God is not [about] eating and drinking, but righteousness and peace and joy in the Holy Spirit. ¹⁸ For he that serves Christ is well-pleasing to God, and approved of men. ¹⁹ So then let us follow after things which make for peace, and things whereby we may edify one another. ²⁰ Overthrow not for meat's sake the work of God. All things indeed are clean; however it is evil for that man who eats with offence. ²¹ It is good not to eat flesh, nor to drink wine, nor to do anything whereby thy brother stumbles.

²² The faith which you have, you have to yourself before God. Happy is he that judges not himself in that which he approves. ²³ But he that doubts is condemned if he eat, because he eats not of faith; and whatsoever is not of faith is sin.

Rom. 14:13-23

In the previous passage Paul posed the question '*¹⁰ **But you, why do you judge your brother?***' and this passage begins with, *¹³ Let us not therefore judge one another anymore: but judge this way, that no man put a stumbling block in his brother's way, or an occasion of falling.*
¹⁴ I know, and am persuaded in the Lord Jesus, that nothing is unclean of itself: save that to him who accounts anything to be unclean, to him it is unclean.
Paul warns that if you disagree with a person over what they should and should not eat, you might cause that person to no longer follow Christ, and that would risk them losing their salvation: *¹⁵ For if because of [what] meat [you eat] your brother is grieved, you walk no longer in love. Do not destroy him for whom Christ died because of your [concern for] meat.*
Paul emphasizes his concern: *¹⁸ For he that serves Christ is well-pleasing to God, and approved of men. ¹⁹ So then let us follow after things which make for peace, and things whereby we may edify one another.*
²⁰ Overthrow not for meat's sake the work of God.
... and Paul finishes up with yet another 'Proverb-like' reminder in verses 22-23.

Self-denial: The Example of Christ

15 Now we that are strong ought to bear the infirmities of the weak, and not to please ourselves. ² Let each one of us please his neighbor for that which is good, unto edifying. ³ For Christ also pleased not himself; but, as it is written, 'The reproaches of them that reproached thee fell upon me.' ⁴ For whatsoever things were written aforetime were written for our learning, that through patience and through comfort of the scriptures we might have hope. ⁵ Now the God of patience and of comfort grant you to be of the same mind one with another according to Christ Jesus: ⁶ that with one accord you may with one mouth glorify the God and Father of our Lord Jesus Christ.

Rom. 15:1-6

Paul references Old Testament prophecy in this passage; *Psalm 69:9 For the zeal of thy house has eaten me up; And the reproaches of them that reproach thee are fallen upon me.* He points out that such writings were written for our benefit – *for our learning* – which Paul explains requires patience but because of our patience we are rewarded with comfort. The final two verses of this passage, 5-6, read as if they were intended to end the letter since they read like a benediction.

Christ is the God of Hope of Jews and Gentiles

15 ⁷ Wherefore receive you one another, even as Christ also received you, to the glory of God. ⁸ For I say that Christ had been made a minister of the circumcision for the truth of God, that he might confirm the promises given to the fathers, ⁹ and that the Gentiles might glorify God for his mercy; as it is written,
Therefore will I give praise unto thee among the Gentiles, And sing to your name.
¹⁰ And again he said, 'Rejoice, you Gentiles, with His people.'
¹¹ And again, 'Praise the Lord, all you Gentiles; And let all the peoples praise him.'
¹² And again, Isaiah said, 'There shall be the root of Jesse, And he that arises to rule over the Gentiles; On him shall the Gentiles hope.'
¹³ Now the God of hope fill you with all joy and peace in believing, that you may abound in hope, in the power of the Holy Spirit.

Rom. 15:7-13

Paul exhorts the people of the Church in Rome to accept one another and explains that Jesus Christ's mission and his (Paul's) purpose is to bring Gentiles to know and accept Christ and quotes Old Testament prophecy to emphasize that the Gentiles are to be reached.
¹⁰ And again he said, 'Rejoice, you Gentiles, with His people.' [Deut. 32:43]
¹¹ "Praise the Lord, all you Gentiles, and let all the peoples extol him." [2 Sam. 22:50]
¹² And again Isaiah says, "The root of Jesse will come, even he who arises to rule the Gentiles; in him will the Gentiles hope." [Is. 11:10]

The final verse of this passage, like that of the prior passage, again sound and feel like a benediction.

The Compiled Teachings of The Apostle Paul

Paul the Minister to the Gentiles — Rom. 15:14-21

15 ¹⁴ And I myself also am persuaded of you, my brethren, that you yourselves are full of goodness, filled with all knowledge, able also to admonish one another. ¹⁵ But I write the more boldly to you in some measure, as putting you again in remembrance, because of the grace that was given me of God, ¹⁶ that I should be a minister of Christ Jesus to the Gentiles, ministering the gospel of God, that the offering up of the Gentiles might be made acceptable, being sanctified by the Holy Spirit. ¹⁷ I have therefore my glorying in Christ Jesus in things pertaining to God. ¹⁸ For I will not dare to speak of any things save those which Christ wrought through me, for the obedience of the Gentiles, by word and deed, ¹⁹ in the power of signs and wonders, in the power of the Holy Spirit; so that from Jerusalem, and round about even to Illyricum, I have fully preached the gospel of Christ; ²⁰ yea, making it my aim so to preach the gospel, not where Christ was already named, that I might not build upon another man's foundation; ²¹ but, as it is written, 'They shall see, those who have never been told of him, And they who have not heard shall understand.'

In this passage Paul makes it clear that he felt called, even commanded, to preach the Gospel of Jesus Christ to the Gentiles and to take the Gospel only to places that it had not previously reached. However, he is writing to the church in Rome; a church that he did not plant, a community that he has not visited, but through this letter he is clearly preaching. He is writing to reprove and correct because he has learned of incorrect understandings and teachings of the Gospel. As he states, '*¹⁵ But I write the more boldly to you in some measure, as putting you again in remembrance, because of the grace that was given me of God, ¹⁶ that I should be a minister of Christ Jesus to the Gentiles, ministering the gospel of God, that the offering up of the Gentiles might be made acceptable, being sanctified by the Holy Spirit.*'

And Paul closes by demonstrating awareness that he was intruding into another missionary's territory, acknowledging that it was someone other than him who had brought the Gospel to Rome, and he quotes Isaiah to emphasize how important their work was: *²¹ but as it is written, "Those who have never been told of him will see, and those who have never heard will understand."*' [Is. 52:15 ESV]

Paul's Plan to Visit Rome — Rom. 15:22-33

15 ²² Wherefore also I was hindered these many times from coming to you: ²³ but now, having no more any place in these regions, and having these many years a longing to come to you, ²⁴ whensoever I am going to Spain (for I hope to see you in my journey, and to be brought on my way thitherward by you, if first in some measure I shall have been satisfied with your company) ²⁵ but now, I say, I go to Jerusalem, ministering to the saints. ²⁶ For it has been the good pleasure of Macedonia and Achaia to make a certain contribution for the poor among the saints that are at Jerusalem. ²⁷ Yea, it has been their good pleasure; and their debtors they are. For if the Gentiles have been made partakers of their spiritual things, they owe it to them also to minister to them in carnal things. ²⁸ When therefore I have accomplished this, and have sealed to them this fruit, I will go on by you to Spain. ²⁹ And I know that, when I come to you, I shall come in the fulness of the blessing of Christ.
³⁰ Now I beseech you, brethren, by our Lord Jesus Christ, and by the love of the Spirit, that you strive together with me in your prayers to God for me; ³¹ that I may be delivered from them that are disobedient in Judaea, and that my ministration which I have for Jerusalem may be acceptable to the saints; ³² that I may come to you in joy through the will of God, and together with you find rest.
³³ Now the God of peace be with you all. Amen.

Briefly referencing other issues that had caused him to not have been able to visit Rome as yet, Paul straightforwardly explains that he had also been planning, or at least desiring, to travel to Spain, but those plans are also on hold as he had reasons to return to Jerusalem before travelling to either Italy (Rome) or Spain.

Paul then asks for those in Rome to pray for him for his safety and he makes specific reference to 'those who are disobedient in Judaea' [15:31], implying that he was expecting to be facing opposition as he performed the duties that he saw before him as one executing the services of a minister of religion, reiterating that it would be after that mission was completed that he would make plans to visit Rome, and in adding the words, 'together with you find rest' suggesting that he intended to remain in Rome.

Personal Greetings — Rom. 16:1-16

16 I commend to you Phoebe our sister, who is a servant of the church that is at Cenchreae: ² that you receive her in the Lord, worthily of the saints, and that you assist her in whatsoever matter she may have need of you: for she herself also has been a helper of many, and of my own self.
³ Salute Prisca and Aquila my fellow-workers in Christ Jesus, ⁴ who for my life laid down their own necks; to whom not only [do] I give thanks, but also all the churches of the Gentiles: ⁵ and salute the church that is in their house. Salute Epaenetus my beloved, who is the first-fruits of Asia to Christ.
⁶ Salute Mary, who bestowed much labor on you. ⁷ Salute Andronicus and Junias, my kinsmen, and my fellow-prisoners,

Paul now mentions a number of those who are active in ministry beginning with Phoebe who is part of the church at Cenchreae, which is a community in the region of Corinthia in Greece. Since Paul is writing from Corinth, Phoebe is most likely a visitor to Paul and others imprisoned in Corinth from where Paul is writing. It would appear that Phoebe is destined to be visiting Rome and Paul asks that she be welcomed and helped 'as she may have need of' [16:2]. Next mentioned are Prisca and Aquila, who Paul also mentions in letters to the Corinthians and Timothy. [Rom. 16:3; 1 Cor. 16:19; 2 Tim. 4:19] *who are of note among the apostles, who also have been in Christ before me. ⁸ Salute Ampliatus my beloved in the Lord. ⁹ Salute Urbanus our fellow-worker in Christ, and Stachys my beloved. ¹⁰ Salute Apelles the approved in Christ. Salute them that are of the household of Aristobulus. ¹¹ Salute Herodion my kinsman. Salute them of the household of Narcissus, that are in the Lord. ¹² Salute Tryphaena and Tryphosa, who labor in the Lord. Salute Persis the beloved, who labored much in the Lord. ¹³ Salute Rufus the chosen in the Lord, and his mother and mine. ¹⁴ Salute Asyncritus, Phlegon, Hermes, Patrobas, Hermas, and the brethren that are with them. ¹⁵ Salute Philologus and Julia, Nereus and his sister, and Olympas, and all the saints that are with them. ¹⁶ Salute one another with a holy kiss. All the churches of Christ salute you.*

Next mentioned is Epaenetus who Paul credits with bringing the first converts in Asia to knowing Christ. As the list continues, mentioning a total of 29 by name and others not being named, e.g. 'all the saints that are with them'. [16:15] and one realizes that these are all with churches in the region of Corinth, or in prison in Corinth, the question is, "why are they being held up in a letter to the church in Rome?" The tone of this passage is one of recognition, praise and thanks rather than a greeting as would be appropriate if those being mentioned were in Rome.

15 ¹⁶ *Greet one another with a holy kiss. All the churches of Christ greet you.*

Final Instructions and Greetings

Rom. 16:17-24

16 ¹⁷ I appeal to you, brothers, to watch out for those who cause divisions and create obstacles contrary to the doctrine that you have been taught; avoid them. ¹⁸ For such persons do not serve our Lord Christ, but their own appetites, and by smooth talk and flattery they deceive the hearts of the naive. [ESV] ¹⁹ For your obedience is come abroad unto all men. I rejoice therefore over you: but I would have you wise to that which is good, and simple to that which is evil. ²⁰ And the God of peace shall bruise Satan under your feet shortly. The grace of our Lord Jesus Christ be with you.

²¹ Timothy my fellow-worker salutes you; and Lucius and Jason and Sosipater, my kinsmen. ²² I Tertius, who write the epistle, salute you in the Lord. ²³ Gaius my host, and of the whole church, salutes you. Erastus the treasurer of the city salutes you, and Quartus the brother.

Paul now returns to the original theme of the early chapters of this epistle, the Book of Romans, for example, Rom. 1:18-32. In Rom. 16:17-20, Paul is exhorting the leaders of the church in Rome to identify those who have caused others to indulge in practices that are not consistent with honoring God, ending with a blessing as though it was the end of the epistle.

Rom. 16:21 begins with a greeting from Timothy, who Paul describes as 'his fellow worker', and Lucius, Jason and Sosipater who Paul describes as being 'fellow kinsmen', placing Timothy in a relationship category that is different from the others.

Rom. 16:22 states, '*I Tertius, who write the epistle, salute you in the Lord.*' Did Tertius write Paul's letter? Is it that maybe Paul simply needed assistance in adding these final greetings that Tertius found himself scribing on behalf of Paul; or might it be that he scribed for Paul throughout?

Doxology

Rom. 16:25-27

16 ²⁵ Now to him that is able to establish you according to my gospel and the preaching of Jesus Christ, according to the revelation of the mystery which has been kept in silence through times eternal, ²⁶ but now is manifested, and by the scriptures of the prophets, according to the commandment of the eternal God, is made known to all the nations to obedience of faith: ²⁷ to the only wise God, through Jesus Christ, to whom be the glory forever. Amen.

The final verses are a benediction that beautifully closes out the epistle, but note that Paul included the phrase, 'according to my gospel and the preaching of Jesus Christ'

Observations:

Timothy is reported in Acts 16:1 as having joined Paul and Silas, and in Acts 17:4, Silas is mentioned as being with Paul in Thessalonica, but neither Timothy or Silvanus (who is not mentioned at all in The Book of Acts) are mentioned, but both may have been in Thessalonica. In Paul's letter to the Romans (Rom. 16:21), Timothy is mentioned, but Silvanus is not. Since neither Paul nor Timothy, nor Silvanus, have visited Rome prior to Paul writing his letter to the church in Rome, one wonders why Timothy would be mentioned, but not Silvanus. Possibly Silvanus was not in Corinth with Paul and Timothy and the time of Paul writing his letter to the Romans. Paul mentions both Timothy and Silvanus as fellow workers in his second letter to the Corinthians (2 Cor. 1:19), and in both the first and second letters to the Thessalonians.

Just an observation!

The Compiled Teachings of The Apostle Paul

1 Thessalonians

Thanksgiving For These Believers 92
Paul's Ministry 92
Encouragement of Timothy's Visit 93
Sanctification and Love 93
Those Who Died in Christ 94
The Day of The Lord 94

Paul's First Letter To The Church In Thessalonica written by Paul at Corinth

Thanksgiving For These Believers

1. Paul, and Silvanus, and Timothy, to the church of the Thessalonians in God the Father and the Lord Jesus Christ: Grace to you and peace.

² We give thanks to God always for you all, making mention of you in our prayers; ³ remembering without ceasing your work of faith and labor of love and patience of hope in our Lord Jesus Christ, before our God and Father; ⁴ knowing, brethren beloved of God, your election, ⁵ how that our gospel came not to you in word only, but also in power, and in the Holy Spirit, and in much assurance; even as you know what manner of men we showed ourselves toward you for your sake. ⁶ And you became imitators of us, and of the Lord, having received the word in much affliction, with joy of the Holy Spirit; ⁷ so that you became an example to all that believe in Macedonia and in Achaia. ⁸ For from you have sounded forth the word of the Lord, not only in Macedonia and Achaia, but in every place your faith to God-ward is gone forth; so that we need not to speak anything. ⁹ For they themselves report concerning us what manner of entering in we had to you; and how you turned to God from idols, to serve a living and true God, ¹⁰ and to wait for his Son from heaven, whom he raised from the dead, even Jesus, who delivered us from the wrath to come.

1 Thess. 1:1-10

Paul opens this first of two letters to the church in Thessalonica (which is in Macedonia) with *'Paul, and Silvanus, and Timothy'* and recognizes and praises the work that those of the church have done in not only the city of Thessalonica but also in the regions of Macedonia and Achaia. *(see comment on prior page.)*

Paul recollects that, *'⁴ knowing, brethren beloved of God, your election, ⁵ how that our gospel came not to you in word only, but also in power, and in the Holy Spirit, and in much assurance'* which strongly suggests that Paul had witnessed the holy spirit falling upon some of the believers in Thessalonica. Paul then states that they *'⁶ ...became imitators of us, and of the Lord, having received the word in much affliction, with joy of the Holy Spirit; ⁷ so that you became an example to all that believe in Macedonia and in Achaia.'*

Paul mentions that they had *'turned to God from idols, to serve a living and true God'* and into believers in Jesus Christ.

In Acts 17:16-32, Luke gives an account of Paul in Athens from which we learn much about the culture of the region.

Paul's Ministry

2. For yourselves, brethren, that our coming to you was not in vain: [ESV] ² but having suffered before and been shamefully treated, as you know, at Philippi, we waxed bold in our God to speak to you the gospel of God in much conflict. ³ For our exhortation is not of error, nor of uncleanness, nor in guile: ⁴ but even as we have been approved of God to be entrusted with the gospel, so we speak; not as pleasing men, but God who proves our hearts. ⁵ For neither at any time were we found using words of flattery, as you know, nor a cloak of covetousness, God is witness; ⁶ nor seeking glory of men, neither from you nor from others, when we might have claimed authority as apostles of Christ. ⁷ But we were gentle in the midst of you, as when a nurse cherishes her own children: ⁸ even so, being affectionately desirous of you, we were well pleased to impart to you, not the gospel of God only, but also our own souls, because you were become very dear to us. ⁹ For you remember, brethren, our labor and travail: working night and day, that we might not burden any of you, we preached to you the gospel of God. ¹⁰ You are witnesses, and God also, how holily and righteously and unblamably we behaved ourselves toward you that believe: ¹¹ as you know how we dealt with each one of you, as a father with his own children, exhorting you, and

1 Thess. 2:1-20

Paul repeats the reminder that he and his co-workers had experience hostility and rejection on their visit to Thessalonica, pointing out that *'we waxed bold in our God to speak to you the gospel of God in much conflict.'* Paul explains that he doesn't preach so as to please men [v4b] and did not resort to *'⁵ ...using words of flattery, as you know, nor a cloak of covetousness'* nor did they make claims regarding their *'authority as apostles of Christ.'* Paul mentions that they were *'⁷...gentle in the midst of you, as when a nurse cherishes her own children'*, and he also points out that they worked night and day so as not to be a burden. By this, Paul means he worked long hours, to the point of exhaustion, and endured hardship in order to preach and teach the gospel. His 'work' may have involved tent

The Compiled Teachings of The Apostle Paul

encouraging you, and testifying, ¹² to the end that you should walk worthily of God, who called you to his own kingdom and glory.

¹³ And for this cause we also thank God without ceasing, that, when you received from us the word of the message, even the word of God, you accepted it not as the word of men, but, as it is in truth, the word of God, which also works in you that believe. ¹⁴ For you, brethren, became imitators of the churches of God which are in Judaea in Christ Jesus: for you also suffered the same things of your own countrymen, even as they did of the Jews; ¹⁵ who both killed the Lord Jesus and the prophets, and drove out us, and please not God, and are contrary to all men; ¹⁶ forbidding us to speak to the Gentiles that they may be saved; to fill up their sins always: but the wrath is come upon them to the uttermost.

¹⁷ But we, brethren, being bereaved of you for a short season, in presence not in heart, endeavored the more exceedingly to see your face with great desire: ¹⁸ because we would fain have come to you, I Paul once and again; and Satan hindered us. ¹⁹ For what is our hope, or joy, or crown of glorying? Are not even you, before our Lord Jesus at his coming? ²⁰ For you are our glory and our joy.

making. Acts 18:1–3 relates that he stayed with Aquila and Priscilla at Corinth because they were tentmakers, as was Paul.[a]

Paul commends the Thessalonians for enduring harsh treatment and he draws a comparison of their experience to that of churches in Judea: '*¹⁴ For you, brethren, became imitators of the churches of God which are in Judaea in Christ Jesus: for you also suffered the same things of your own countrymen, even as they did of the Jews;*' pointing out that the Jews did not want the Gentiles to know that they have the opportunity of salvation.

[a] *Commentary credit: https://www.bibleref.com/*

Encouragement of Timothy's Visit
1 Thess. 3:1-13

3. Wherefore when we could no longer forbear, we thought it good to be left behind at Athens alone; ² and sent Timothy, our brother and God's minister in the gospel of Christ, to establish you, and to comfort you concerning your faith; ³ that no man be moved by these afflictions; for yourselves know that hereunto we are appointed. ⁴ For verily, when we were with you, we told you beforehand that we are to suffer affliction; even as it came to pass, and you know. ⁵ For this cause I also, when I could no longer forbear, sent that I might know your faith, lest by any means the tempter had tempted you, and our labor should be in vain. ⁶ But when Timothy came even now to us from you, and brought us glad tidings of your faith and love, and that you have good remembrance of us always, longing to see us, even as we also to see you; ⁷ for this cause, brethren, we were comforted over you in all our distress and affliction through your faith: ⁸ for now we live, if you stand fast in the Lord. ⁹ For what thanksgiving can we render again to God for you, for all the joy wherewith we joy for your sakes before our God; ¹⁰ night and day praying exceedingly that we may see your face, and may perfect that which is lacking in your faith?

¹¹ Now may our God and Father himself, and our Lord Jesus, direct our way unto you: ¹² and the Lord make you to increase and abound in love one toward another, and toward all men, even as we also do toward you; ¹³ to the end he may establish your hearts unblamable in holiness before our God and Father, at the coming of our Lord Jesus with all his saints.

Paul recounts how Timothy was chosen to be sent to Thessalonica alone leaving Paul and others behind in Athens. Jewish agitators from Thessalonica had stirred up crowds against Paul at Berea, and some Christians at Berea had accompanied Paul to Athens. [Acts 17:13–15]. Timothy and Silas had remained in Berea and Timothy had been sent to Thessalonica from there to strengthen and encourage them in their faith. Paul begins this letter thanking the church in Thessalonica for their faithfulness. Paul relates that Timothy had returned and delivered '*⁶ glad tidings of your faith and love,* ' adding '*and that you have good remembrance of us always, longing to see us, even as we also to see you;*'

Paul finishes this passage of the letter telling the Thessalonians that he and his coworkers pray night and day for them and pray that they will be able to visit again: '*¹⁰ praying exceedingly that we may see your face*' adding '*and may perfect that which is lacking in your faith?*'

Sanctification and Love
1 Thess. 4:1-18

4. Finally then, brethren, we beseech and exhort you in the Lord Jesus, that, as you received of us how you ought to walk and to please God, even as you do walk, – that you abound more and more. ² For you know what charge we gave you through the Lord Jesus. ³ For this is the will of God, even your sanctification, that you abstain from fornication; ⁴ that each one of you know how to possess himself of his own vessel in sanctification and honor, ⁵ not in the passion of lust, even as the Gentiles who know not God; ⁶ that no man transgress, and wrong his brother in the matter: because the Lord is an avenger in all these things, as also we forewarned you and testified. ⁷ For God called us not for uncleanness, but in sanctification. ⁸ Therefore he

Paul begins this passage with a reminder that he had taught them how they should walk and lead a life that pleases God, and reminds them that they should abstain from fornication because each person's body is dedicated to God:

(*In Romans Paul underscored the importance of offering one's body to God "as a living sacrifice, holy and acceptable to God." [Romans 12:1]*)

Paul then exhorts that no man should '*⁶transgress, and wrong his brother in the matter*' referring to '*⁵ the passion of lust*' which Paul points out is a problem that exists with the Gentiles that do not know God, concluding with we must

The Compiled Teachings of The Apostle Paul

that rejects, rejects not man, but God, who gives his Holy Spirit to you.

⁹ But concerning love of the brethren you have no need that one write to you: for you yourselves are taught of God to love one another; ¹⁰ for indeed you do it toward all the brethren that are in all Macedonia. But we exhort you, brethren, that you abound more and more; ¹¹ and that you study to be quiet, and to do your own business, and to work with your hands, even as we charged you; ¹² that you may walk becomingly toward them that are without, and may have need of nothing.

not reject clean living as that is rejecting God, and it is God '⁸ᵇ *who gives his Holy Spirit to you.*'
Paul commends the Thessalonians for already being strong in their ability to show love '¹⁰ *for indeed you do it toward all the brethren that are in all Macedonia.*' and he encourages to excel even more in what they are able to do.
Finally, Paul commands that they should lead peaceful lives, minding their own business, and being industrious and so be self-sufficient.

Those Who Died in Christ
1 Thess. 4:13-8

4. ¹³ But we would not have you ignorant, brethren, concerning them that fall asleep; that you sorrow not, even as the rest, who have no hope. ¹⁴ For if we believe that Jesus died and rose again, even so them also that have fallen asleep in Jesus will God bring with him. ¹⁵ For this we say to you by the word of the Lord, that we that are alive, that are left to the coming of the Lord, shall in no way precede those that have fallen asleep. ¹⁶ For the Lord himself shall descend from heaven, with a shout, with the voice of the archangel, and with the trump of God: and the dead in Christ shall rise first; ¹⁷ then we that are alive, that are left, shall together with them be caught up in the clouds, to meet the Lord in the air: and so shall we ever be with the Lord. ¹⁸ Wherefore comfort one another with these words.

Paul paints a description of resurrection of those '¹⁴ᵇ *that have fallen asleep in Jesus*'. Paul states that God will bring them with Jesus, and adds '*that we that are alive, that are left to (await) the (second) coming of the Lord, shall in no way precede those that have fallen asleep.*'
Paul's description continues reading almost as if he has just read Revelation!!

The Day of The Lord
1 Thess. 5:1-28

5. But concerning the times and the seasons, brethren, you have no need that needs to be written to you. ² For yourselves know perfectly that the day of the Lord will come as a thief in the night. ³ When they are saying, Peace and safety, then sudden destruction comes upon them, as travail upon a woman with child; and they shall in no wise escape. ⁴ But you, brethren, are not in darkness, that that day should overtake you as a thief: ⁵ for you are all sons of light, and sons of the day: we are not of the night, nor of darkness; ⁶ so then let us not sleep, as do the rest, but let us watch and be sober. ⁷ For they that sleep, sleep in the night; and they that are drunken are drunken in the night. ⁸ But let us, since we are of the day, be sober, putting on the breastplate of faith and love; and for a helmet, the hope of salvation. ⁹ For God appointed us not to wrath, but to the obtaining of salvation through our Lord Jesus Christ, ¹⁰ who died for us, that, whether we wake or sleep, we should live together with him. ¹¹ Wherefore exhort one another, and build each other up, even as also you do.

¹² But we beseech you, brethren, to know them that labor among you, and are over you in the Lord, and admonish you; ¹³ and to esteem them exceeding highly in love for their work's sake. Be at peace among yourselves. ¹⁴ And we exhort you, brethren, admonish the disorderly, encourage the faint-hearted, support the weak, be longsuffering toward all. ¹⁵ See that none render to any one evil for evil; but always follow after that which is good, one toward another, and toward all. ¹⁶ Rejoice always; ¹⁷ pray without ceasing; ¹⁸ in everything give thanks: for this is the will of God in Christ Jesus to you-ward. ¹⁹ Quench not the Spirit; ²⁰ despise not prophesyings; ²¹ prove all things; hold fast that which is good; ²² abstain from every form of evil.

²³ And the God of peace himself sanctify you wholly; and may your spirit and soul and body be preserved entire, without blame at the coming of our Lord Jesus Christ. ²⁴ Faithful is he that calls you, who will also do it.

²⁵ Brethren, pray for us.

²⁶ Salute all the brethren with a holy kiss. ²⁷ I adjure you by the Lord that this epistle be read to all the brethren.

²⁸ The grace of our Lord Jesus Christ be with you.

Paraphrasing teaching from Matt. 24 and Luke 12, Paul describes how the second coming of Christ will occur and then references believers as '⁵ *sons of light, and sons of the day: we are not of the night, nor of darkness*' and exhorts the reader to '⁶ *...not sleep, as do the rest, but let us watch and be sober*' before describing what we should wear as armor to protect one's-self; 'putting on' faith, love and hope. Paul exhorts the Thessalonians to '¹³ᵇ *Be at peace among yourselves. ¹⁴ And we exhort you, brethren, admonish the disorderly, encourage the faint-hearted, support the weak, be longsuffering toward all. ¹⁵ See that none render to any one evil for evil; but always follow after that which is good*' and Paul continues his list of encouragement, '¹⁶ *Rejoice always; ¹⁷ pray without ceasing ¹⁸ in everything give thanks: for this is the will of God in Christ Jesus*'. ¹⁹ *Quench not the Spirit; ²⁰ do not despise prophesyings; ²¹ prove all things; hold fast that which is good; ²² abstain from every form of evil.*

Paul makes it clear that the goal is to be sanctified, when the Lord returns, whether one has already died from natural death or is still awake at the time, and finally, Paul requests that this letter be read to all brethren.

The Compiled Teachings of The Apostle Paul

2 Thessalonians

Thanksgiving For These Believers..............................95
Man of Sin...95
Exhortation 96

Paul's Second Letter To The Church In Thessalonica written by Paul at Corinth

Thanksgiving For These Believers
2 Thess. 1:1-10

1. Paul, and Silvanus, and Timothy, to the church of the Thessalonians in God our Father and the Lord Jesus Christ; ² Grace to you and peace from God the Father and the Lord Jesus Christ.

³ We are bound to give thanks to God always for you, brethren, even as it is meet, for that your faith grows exceedingly, and the love of each one of you all toward one another abounds; ⁴ so that we ourselves glory in you in the churches of God for your patience and faith in all your persecutions and in the afflictions which you endure; ⁵ which is a manifest token of the righteous judgment of God; to the end that you may be counted worthy of the kingdom of God, for which you also suffer: ⁶ if so be that it is a righteous thing with God to recompense affliction to them that afflict you, ⁷ and to you that are afflicted rest with us, at the revelation of the Lord Jesus from heaven with the angels of his power in flaming fire, ⁸ rendering vengeance to them that do not know God, and to them that do not obey the gospel of our Lord Jesus: ⁹ who shall suffer punishment, even eternal destruction from the face of the Lord and from the glory of his might, ¹⁰ when he shall come to be glorified in his saints, and to be marveled at in all that believed (because our testimony to you was believed) in that day. ¹¹ To which end we also pray always for you, that our God may count you worthy of your calling, and fulfil every desire of goodness and every work of faith, with power; ¹² that the name of our Lord Jesus may be glorified in you, and you in him, according to the grace of our God and the Lord Jesus Christ.

Again, in this second letter to the Church in Thessalonica, Paul begins by writing, *'Paul, and Silvanus, and Timothy'*, and he extols the *Church of the Thessalonians* as saints for standing steadfast in the faith, enduring persecution and affliction, and he promises them that they will be rewarded and that those who have caused them affliction might be punished. *'⁷ at the revelation of the Lord Jesus from heaven with the angels of his power in flaming fire, ⁸ rendering vengeance to them that do not know God, and to them that do not obey the gospel of our Lord Jesus: ⁹ who shall suffer punishment, even eternal destruction from the face of the Lord and from the glory of his might'*, while they will be rewarded: *'¹⁰ when he shall come to be glorified in his saints, and to be marveled at in all that believed'*.

Paul ends this passage with a prayer that *'¹¹ᵇ God may count you worthy of your calling, and fulfil every desire of goodness and every work of faith, with power'*.

Man of Sin
2 Thess. 2:1-20

2. Now we beseech you, brethren, touching (regarding) the coming of our Lord Jesus Christ, and our gathering together to him; ² to the end that you be not quickly shaken from your mind, nor yet be troubled, either by spirit, or by word, or by epistle as from us, as that the day of the Lord is just at hand; ³ let no man beguile you in any wise: for it will not be, except the falling away come first, and the man of sin be revealed, the son of perdition, ⁴ he that opposes and exalts himself against all that is called God or that is worshipped; so that he sits in the temple of God, setting himself forth as God. ⁵ Remember not, that, when I was yet with you, I told you these things? ⁶ And now you know that which restrains, to the end that he may be revealed in his own season. ⁷ For the mystery of lawlessness does already work: only there is one that restrains now, until he be taken out of the way. ⁸ And then shall be revealed the lawless one, whom the Lord Jesus shall slay with the breath of his mouth, and bring to nought by the manifestation of his coming; ⁹ even he, whose coming is according to the working of Satan with all power and signs and lying wonders, ¹⁰ and with all deceit of unrighteousness

Paul expresses both concern and delight in believing that the second coming of Christ is imminent [1 Thess. 5:1-3] *'²ᶜ as that the day of the Lord is just at hand.'* Paul writes, *'³ᵇ except the falling away come first, and the man of sin be revealed, the son of perdition,'*

The word translated "the falling away," can also be translated, "the rebellion," "the apostasy," or "the departure."

> This 'event' may refer to Israel's revolt against Old Testament teaching when the nation turned to idolatry. It may refer to the state of the world following the departure of the church due to the rapture. It is noteworthy that in verse 1 Paul describes the rapture as "the coming of our Lord Jesus Christ and our being gathering together to him."[6]

Paul is clearly referencing and attacking false teaching that he has learned of; teaching that is being promulgated by false prophets who are

---
[6] Commentary credit: https://www.bibleref.com/

for them that perish; because they received not the love of the truth, that they might be saved. ¹¹ *And for this cause God sends them a working of error, that they should believe a lie:* ¹² *that they all might be judged who did not believe the truth, but had pleasure in unrighteousness.*

¹³ *But we are bound to give thanks to God always for you, brethren beloved of the Lord, for that God chose you from the beginning to salvation in sanctification of the Spirit and belief of the truth:* ¹⁴ *It was for this he called you through our gospel, to the obtaining of the glory of our Lord Jesus Christ.* ¹⁵ *So then, brethren, stand fast, and hold the traditions which you were taught, whether by word, or by epistle of ours.*

¹⁶ *Now our Lord Jesus Christ himself, and God our Father who loved us and gave us eternal comfort and good hope through grace,* ¹⁷ *comfort your hearts and establish them in every good work and word.*

preaching a different gospel; one that promotes unrighteousness *'¹¹ And for this cause God sends them a working of error, that they should believe a lie:* ¹² *that they all might be judged who did not believe the truth, but had pleasure in unrighteousness.'* Paul states that we, he and his coworkers and others that have any connection to those in Thessalonica, give thanks to God for them and he reminds them that Jesus called them to him through the Gospel and exhorts them to remain faithful to the traditions that he, Paul, taught to them, and he then concludes with a benediction.

Exhortation

3. Finally, brethren, pray for us, that the word of the Lord may run (spread rapidly) and be glorified, even as also it is with you; ² *and that we may be delivered from unreasonable and evil men; for not all have faith.* ³ *But the Lord is faithful, who shall establish you, and guard you from the evil one.* ⁴ *And we have confidence in the Lord touching you, that you both do and will do the things which we command.* ⁵ *And the Lord direct your hearts into the love of God, and into the patience of Christ.*

⁶ *Now we command you, brethren, in the name of our Lord Jesus Christ, that you withdraw yourselves from every brother that walks disorderly, and not after the tradition which they received of us.* ⁷ *For yourselves know how you ought to imitate us: for we behaved not ourselves disorderly among you;* ⁸ *neither did we eat bread for no reason at any man's hand, but in labor and travail, working night and day, that we might not burden any of you:* ⁹ *not because we have not the right, but to make ourselves an example to you, that you should imitate us.* ¹⁰ *For even when we were with you, this we commanded you, If any will not work, neither let him eat.* ¹¹ *For we hear of some that walk among you disorderly, that work not at all, but are busybodies.* ¹² *Now them that are such we command and exhort in the Lord Jesus Christ, that with quietness they work, and eat their own bread.* ¹³ *But you, brethren, be not weary in well-doing.* ¹⁴ *And if any man does not obey our word by this epistle, note that man, that you have no company with him, to the end that he may be ashamed.* ¹⁵ *And yet count him not as an enemy, but admonish him as a brother.*

¹⁶ *Now the Lord of peace himself give you peace at all times in all ways. The Lord be with you all.*

¹⁷ *The salutation of me Paul with mine own hand, which is the token in every epistle: so I write.* ¹⁸ *The grace of our Lord Jesus Christ be with you all.*

2 Thess. 3:1-18

Paul asks for prayer that the Gospel will spread, and those who share the *'word of the Lord'* ¹, himself and his coworkers (including those of the church in Thessalonica) will be kept safe as they minister. Paul shares his faith that they will be blessed (*'we have confidence in the Lord touching you'* ⁴) as they *'do and will do the things which we command'* ⁵. This might be the first occasion of Paul using the term 'we' rather than 'I' showing recognition for the importance of his co-workers.

Paul closes out the prayer asking that *'the Lord direct your hearts into the love of God, and into the patience of Christ'* before laying out a command to them: *'in the name of our Lord Jesus Christ, that you withdraw yourselves from every brother that walks disorderly, and not after the tradition which they received of us.'* Paul continues by referencing that he is aware of 'brothers' who *'walk disorderly, and not after the tradition which they received of us'* and he explains that he and his coworkers set an example that should be followed and should earn (work for) their own support: *'If any will not work, neither let him eat.'* And Paul adds, *'we hear of some that walk among you disorderly, that work not at all, but are busybodies.'*

At first it seems as though Paul is saying these need to be cast aside, but he continues to explain by disassociating with them, they will become ashamed and that then they can be counselled and won over: *'¹⁵ And yet count him not as an enemy, but admonish him as a brother.*

The Compiled Teachings of The Apostle Paul

1 Timothy

Misleading Teaching In Doctrine and Living 97
A Call To Prayer 98
Overseers and Deacons 98
Apostasy and A Good Minister's Discipline 99
Treat Others With Respect 99
Concerning Elders 100
Instructions to Those Who Minister 100

Paul's First Letter To Timothy written by Paul at Nicopolis

Misleading Teaching In Doctrine and Living

1 Paul, an apostle of Christ Jesus according to the commandment of God our Savior, and Christ Jesus our hope; 2 to Timothy, my true child in faith: Grace, mercy, peace, from God the Father and Christ Jesus our Lord.

3 As I exhorted you to tarry at Ephesus, when I was going into Macedonia, that you might charge certain men not to teach a different doctrine, 4 neither to give heed to fables and endless genealogies, which minister questionings, rather than a dispensation of God which is in faith; as do I now. 5 But the end of the charge is love out of a pure heart and a good conscience and faith unfeigned: 6 from which things some having swerved have turned aside to vain talking; 7 desiring to be teachers of the law, though they understand neither what they say, nor whereof they confidently affirm. 8 But we know that the law is good, if a man use it lawfully, 9 as knowing this, that law is not made for a righteous man, but for the lawless and unruly, for the ungodly and sinners, for the unholy and profane, for murderers of fathers and murderers of mothers, for manslayers, 10 for fornicators, for abusers of themselves with men, for slave traders, for liars, for false swearers, and if there be any other thing contrary to the sound doctrine; 11 according to the gospel of the glory of the blessed God, which was committed to my trust.

12 I thank him that enabled me, even Christ Jesus our Lord, for that he counted me faithful, appointing me to his service; 13 though I was before a blasphemer, and a persecutor, and injurious: howbeit I obtained mercy, because I did it ignorantly in unbelief; 14 and the grace of our Lord abounded exceedingly with faith and love which is in Christ Jesus. 15 Faithful is the saying, and worthy of all acceptance, that Christ Jesus came into the world to save sinners; of whom I am chief: 16 howbeit for this cause I obtained mercy, that in me as chief might Jesus Christ show forth all his longsuffering, for an example of them that should thereafter believe in him to eternal life. 17 Now to the King eternal, immortal, invisible, the only God, be honor and glory for ever and ever. Amen.

18 This charge I commit to you, my child Timothy, according to the prophecies which led the way to you, that by them you might war the good warfare; 19 holding faith and a good conscience some have rejected and so have suffered shipwreck with regard to the faith: 20 among whom are Hymenaeus and Alexander; whom I delivered to Satan, that they might be taught not to blaspheme.

1 Timothy 1:1-20

This is the first of two letters that Paul wrote to Timothy. This letter, and also the letter to Titus, was written while Paul was in Nicopolis in Macedonia. Timothy and Titus were coworkers to Paul, and studied under him.

Following the greeting paragraph, Paul begins by explaining to Timothy why he had been left behind in Ephesus where Paul had observed *'certain men'* teaching a Gospel that was both different and misleading. Such people, Paul claimed, did not (fully) understand what they said nor what they claimed to be the truth; v7. Paul wrote: *'that law is not made for a righteous man, but for the lawless and unruly, for the ungodly and sinners, for the unholy and profane, for murderers of fathers and murderers of mothers, for manslayers, 10 for fornicators, for abusers of themselves with men, for slave traders, for liars, for false swearers, and if there be any other thing contrary to the sound doctrine;'*

Paul continues by explaining his background and describing the person that he was prior to his encounter with Jesus on the road to Damascus. He refers to himself as the chief of all sinners (being one who persecuted those who were Believers). He admits to having been *'ignorant in unbelief'* (v13) and praises God that *'14 the grace of our Lord abounded exceedingly with faith and love which is in Christ Jesus.'* Paul explains to Timothy that he (believes that) he was chosen as *'an example of them that should thereafter believe in him to eternal life.'* Paul concludes with challenging Timothy to trust in the prophecies so that he might *'by them (you) might war the good warfare, [fight the good fight] 19 holding faith and a good conscience,'* adding to what he has already written a reference to Hymenaeus and Alexander who promoted a false doctrine that was both heresy (contrary) and blasphemous.

The Compiled Teachings of The Apostle Paul

A Call To Prayer

1 Timothy 2:1-15

2 I exhort therefore, first of all, that supplications, prayers, intercessions, thanksgivings, be made for all men; ² for kings and all that are in high place; that we may lead a tranquil and quiet life in all godliness and gravity. ³ This is good and acceptable in the sight of God our Savior; ⁴ who would have all men to be saved, and come to the knowledge of the truth. ⁵ For there is one God, one mediator also between God and men, himself man, Christ Jesus, ⁶ who gave himself a ransom for all; the testimony to be borne in its own times; ⁷ whereunto I was appointed a preacher and an apostle (I speak the truth, I lie not), a teacher of the Gentiles in faith and truth.

⁸ I desire therefore that the men pray in every place, lifting up holy hands, without wrath and disputing. ⁹ In like manner, that women adorn themselves in modest apparel, with decency and sobriety; not with braided hair, and gold or pearls or costly raiment; ¹⁰ but (which becomes women professing godliness) through good works. ¹¹ Let a woman learn in quietness with all subjection. ¹² But I permit not a woman to teach, nor to have dominion over a man, but to be in quietness. ¹³ For Adam was first formed, then Eve; ¹⁴ and Adam was not beguiled, but the woman being beguiled has fallen into transgression: ¹⁵ but she shall be saved through her child-bearing, if they continue in faith and love and sanctification with sobriety.

Paul opens this passage with a request for prayer asking that all men be lifted up, for kings and rulers be prayed for asking that those in high places would come to desire all men to be saved and to know the truth of the Gospel. Paul writes that: *'⁵ For there is one God, one mediator also between God and men, himself man, Christ Jesus'* and he continues to say, *'⁶ who gave himself a ransom for all; the testimony to be borne in its own times'* and he identifies himself and role as: *'⁷...a preacher and an apostle (I speak the truth, I lie not), a teacher of the Gentiles in faith and truth.'*

Paul then continues explaining how he believes men and women should behave concluding with a rationalization as to why women should be quiet and submissive, and that it is through child-bearing that women are saved *'¹⁵ᵇ if they continue in faith and love and sanctification with sobriety.'*

Overseers and Deacons

1 Timothy 3:1-16

3 Faithful is the saying, If a man seeks the office of an overseer (bishop), he desires a good work. ² The overseer therefore must be without reproach, the husband of one wife, temperate, sober-minded, orderly, given to hospitality, apt to teach; ³ no brawler, no striker; but gentle, not contentious, no lover of money; ⁴ one that rules well his own house, having his children in subjection with all gravity; ⁵ (but if a man knows not how to rule his own house, how shall he take care of the church of God?) ⁶ not a novice, lest being puffed up he fall into the condemnation of the devil.

⁷ Moreover, he must have good testimony from them that are without; lest he fall into reproach and the snare of the devil. ⁸ Deacons in like manner must be grave, not double-tongued, not given to much wine, not greedy of filthy lucre. ⁹ holding the mystery of the faith in a pure conscience. ¹⁰ And let these also first be proved; then let them serve as deacons, if they be blameless. ¹¹ Women in like manner must be grave, not slanderers, temperate, faithful in all things. ¹² Let deacons be husbands of one wife, ruling their children and their own houses well. ¹³ For they that have served well as deacons gain to themselves a good standing, and great boldness in the faith which is in Christ Jesus.

¹⁴ These things write I to you, hoping to come to you shortly; ¹⁵ but if I tarry long, that you might know how men ought to behave themselves in the house of God, which is the church of the living God, the pillar and ground of the truth. ¹⁶ And without controversy great is the mystery of godliness;

He who was manifested in the flesh, Justified in the spirit,
  Seen of angels, Preached among the nations,
    Believed on in the world, Received up in glory.

'Seen of the angels' might be a reference to Luke 2:13, since Luke travelled extensively with Paul on his second mission journey, and 'Received up in glory' appears to be a reference to Luke 24:51.

Paul explains necessary qualifications for positions of responsibility, persons who are overseers, and some translations use the term 'bishop' which, of course, is a widely recognized senior position in churches. Perhaps the most significant concern regarding any person selected for such a position is what Paul describes in verse 7: *Moreover, he must have good testimony from them that are without; lest he fall into reproach and the snare of the devil.* By this, Paul means they need to have a good reputation in the community outside of just the believers.

Then Paul addresses another well recognized position, that of deacon. Deacon's, like Bishops must be held to high standards: *⁸ ...grave, not double-tongued, not given to much wine, not greedy of filthy lucre. ⁹ holding the mystery of the faith in a pure conscience.'* And they must also be *'blameless'*. Paul then references women and what qualities they must have although Paul doesn't specify a specific position for them, (or are we to consider them as also candidates for being deacons?) Paul then returns to continue adding to the list of requirements for deacons. They must have more than one wife and they are to be model fathers and husbands, and if their house includes servants, thy should 'rule over' them in a good manner. Paul describes the position of deacon as being one that benefits those who are chosen to serve as deacons as an opportunity to, *" gain to themselves a good standing, and great boldness in the faith which is in Christ Jesus.*

Paul describes the church as:*¹⁵ᵇ the church of the living God, the pillar and ground of the truth* and then Paul then finishes up with an almost poetic summary of Jesus Christ.

Apostacy and A Good Minister's Discipline

4 But the Spirit said expressly, that in later times some shall fall away from the faith, giving heed to seducing spirits and doctrines of demons, ² through the hypocrisy of men that speak lies, branded in their own conscience as with a hot iron; ³ forbidding to marry, and commanding to abstain from meats, which God created to be received with thanksgiving by them that believe and know the truth. ⁴ For every creature of God is good, and nothing is to be rejected, if it be received with thanksgiving: ⁵ for it is sanctified through the word of God and prayer.

⁶ If you put the brethren in mind of these things, you shall be a good minister of Christ Jesus, nourished in the words of the faith, and of the good doctrine which you have followed until now: ⁷ but refuse profane and old wives' fables. And exercise yourself to godliness. ⁸ for bodily exercise is profitable for a little; but godliness is profitable for all things, having promise of the life which now is, and of that which is to come. ⁹ Faithful is the saying, and worthy of all acceptance. ¹⁰ For to this end we labor and strive, because we have our hope set on the living God, who is the Savior of all men, specially of them that believe. ¹¹ These things command and teach. ¹² Let no man despise your youth; but be an example to them that believe, in word, in manner of life, in love, in faith, in purity. ¹³ Till I come, give heed to reading, to exhortation, to teaching. ¹⁴ Neglect not the gift that is in thee, which was given thee by prophecy, with the laying on of the hands of the presbytery. ¹⁵ Be diligent in these things; give thyself wholly to them; that your progress may be manifest to all. ¹⁶ Take heed to yourself, and to your teaching. Continue in these things; for in doing this you shall save both yourself and them that hear you.

1 Timothy 4:1-16

This chapter of the letter to Timothy begins with prophecy that appears in part to be from Matthew 24:11, '*And many false prophets shall arise, and shall lead many astray*' causing believers to reject the Gospel. Paul references that these false prophets will advise against eating meats which Paul says is against God's intention: *⁴ For every creature of God is good, and nothing is to be rejected, if it be received with thanksgiving:⁵ for it is sanctified through the word of God and prayer.*

Paul's challenge to Timothy is to make those in Ephesus aware of the dangers of listening to anyone preaching a different Gospel, reminding him that *'⁸ᵇ godliness is profitable for all things, having promise of the life which now is, and of that which is to come.'*

Paul counsels Timothy to have nothing to do with godless myths and old wives' tales; rather, to train himself to be godly and reminds him that: *'¹⁰ᵇ we have our hope set on the living God, who is the Savior of all men, specially of them that believe.'* Recognizing Timothy's youthfulness, Paul tells him: *'¹² Let no man despise your youth; but be an example to them that believe, in word, in manner of life, in love, in faith, in purity.'*

Paul reminds Timothy of a gift that he has had since hands were laid on him by the presbytery* and also tells him to be diligent in reading, teaching and exhortation and the end result will be that he will save himself and many others, ensuring them all salvation.

* In Acts 6:⁶ 'hands were laid on Stephen, Phillip, Prochorus, Nicanor, Timon, Parmenas and Nicolas.' Paul's reference here, one might presume, is to a similar 'anointing and blessing' event at which Timothy had hands laid on him..

Treat Others With Respect

5 Rebuke not an elder, but exhort him as a father; the younger men as brethren: ² the elder women as mothers; the younger as sisters, in all purity. ³ Honor widows that are widows indeed. ⁴ But if any widow has children or grandchildren, let them learn first to show piety towards their own family, and to requite their parents: for this is acceptable in the sight of God. ⁵ Now she that is a widow indeed, and desolate, has her hope set on God, and continues in supplications and prayers night and day. ⁶ But she that gives herself to pleasure is dead while she lives.

⁷ These things also command, that they may be without reproach. ⁸ But if any provides not for his own, and specially his own household, he has denied the faith, and is worse than an unbeliever.

⁹ Let none be enrolled as a widow under threescore years old, having been the wife of one man, ¹⁰ well reported of for good works; if she has brought up children, if she has used hospitality to strangers, if she has washed the saints' feet, if she has relieved the afflicted, if she has diligently followed every good work. ¹¹ But younger widows refuse: for when they have waxed wanton against Christ, they

1 Timothy 5:1-16

In this passage Paul gives guidance to Timothy on how to deal with various categories of people, especially those that may need charity. *Note that the term 'elder' here is used by Paul in the context of an older person rather than in the context of an appointed Elder of the church which he addresses in the next passage.*

Paul advises that an older-than-you man should be treated respectfully as if he were a father, and treat younger-than-you men as brethren. Older-than-you women should be treated as mothers, and treat younger-than-you women as sisters. Widows that have children or grandchildren should be encouraged to look first to their own family for support, returning favor to their parents as they are able. Paul advises Timothy that widows must have their *⁵ᵇ hope set on God, and continue in supplications and prayers night and day.'* A widow who chooses to *'⁶ᵇgive themself to pleasure is dead while she lives.'*

Paul then writes, *'⁸ But if any provides not for his own, and specially his own household, he has denied the faith, and is worse than an unbeliever'*, and that is something akin to becoming an apostate. Which, because of the use of 'his', is clearly addressing the role that men related to

The Compiled Teachings of The Apostle Paul

desire to marry; ¹² having condemnation, because they have rejected their first pledge. ¹³ And withal they learn also to be idle, going about from house to house; and not only idle, but tattlers also and busybodies, speaking things which they ought not. ¹⁴ I desire therefore that the younger widows marry, bear children, rule the household, give no occasion to the adversary for reviling: ¹⁵ for already some are turned aside after Satan.

¹⁶ If any woman that believes has widows (in her care), let her relieve (continue to help) them, and let not the church be burdened; that it may relieve (help) them that are widows indeed.

a widow must accept; he must provide, or at least participate in providing, for a widow that he is related to. Paul next references an age qualification; that of sixty years old, and then goes on to identify younger widows as likely to fall away, 'wax wanton' meaning they become unrighteous, turning away from godliness, becoming idle (lazy) and engaging themselves in gossip (as tattlers). So Paul writes that he prefers that '¹⁴ younger widows marry, bear children, rule the household.'

The phrase 'Honor widows that are widows indeed' is understood to mean 'widows with no support nor means to support themselves'

Concerning Elders

1 Timothy 5:17-25

5 ¹⁷ Let the elders that rule well be counted worthy of double honor, especially those who labor in the word and in teaching. ¹⁸ For the scripture says, You shall not muzzle the ox when he treads out the corn. And, the laborer is worthy of his hire.

¹⁹ Against an elder receive not an accusation, except at the mouth of two or three witnesses.

²⁰ Them that sin reprove in the sight of all, that the rest also may be in fear. ²¹ I charge you in the sight of God, and Christ Jesus, and the elect angels, that you observe these things without prejudice, doing nothing by partiality. ²² Lay hands hastily on no man, neither be partaker of other men's sins: keep yourself pure. ²³ Be no longer a drinker of (just) water, but use a little wine for your stomach's sake and your often infirmities. ²⁴ Some men's sins are evident, going before to judgment; and some men also they follow after. ²⁵ In like manner also there are good works that are evident; and such as are otherwise cannot be hid.

By writing to Timothy, *'Let the elders that rule well be counted worthy of double honor'* Paul is warning Timothy that there will be Elders that don't perform as well as might be hoped. Rather than suggesting how to discipline or otherwise handle those elders, Paul is suggesting motivating them by rewarding those that meet or exceed expectations, including motivating those that don't teach or preach; *'¹⁷ᵇ labor in the word and in teaching'*. The ox that is harnessed for grinding the corn is rewarded by allowing it to eat freely, and a laborer must be paid.

Paul now turns to discipline for those that sin. He writes that they should be *'²⁰ reprove(d) in the sight of all, that the rest also may be in fear.* This is among the most contentious of all of Paul's teachings; that is, calling out those who have sinned and publicly naming (and shaming) them. Paul advises Timothy that such action must be equally applied to all without any favoritism: *'²¹ I charge you... that you observe these things without prejudice, doing nothing by partiality.'*

Paul includes in this passage some personal health advice for Timothy before closing out advising that some men cannot hide their sins, and similarly 'good works' are also often evident.

Instructions to Those Who Minister

1 Timothy 6:1-21

6 Let as many as are servants under the yoke count their own masters worthy of all honor, that the name of God and the doctrine be not blasphemed. ² And they that have believing masters, let them not despise them, because they are brethren; but let them serve them the rather, because they that partake of the benefit are believing and beloved. These things teach and exhort.

³ If any man teaches a different doctrine, and consents not to sound words, even the words of our Lord Jesus Christ, and to the doctrine which is according to godliness; ⁴ he is puffed up, knowing nothing, but doting about questionings and disputes of words, whereof comes envy, strife, railings, evil surmisings, ⁵ wranglings of men corrupted in mind and bereft of the truth, supposing that godliness is a way of gain. ⁶ But godliness with contentment is great gain: ⁷ for we brought nothing into the world, for neither can we carry anything out; ⁸ but having food and covering we shall be therewith

Paul's words in verse 1 are a directing those who are bond servants (slaves) towards godly behavior, no matter their circumstances. He advises slaves to give their masters honor so that the name of God and the teaching will not be criticized, rejected or insulted.[7]

In verse 2 Paul points out that although the relationship between a slave owner and a slave is not viewed as one of equals, if they are believers they are brothers in Christ, and Paul tells Timothy this is the message he should teach.

Paul goes on the attack against those who are teaching a different doctrine to that of the Gospel of Jesus Christ, criticizing those that pretend to know all but know nothing. He references them as being 'puffed up', that is, having and inflated ego. Paul lists all the things that they claim to know about but really know nothing about. Paul characterizes their teachings as not being

---

[7] Commentary credit: https://www.biblref.com (which uses the word 'reviled').

content. ⁹ But they that desire to be rich fall into temptation and a snare and many foolish and hurtful lusts, such as drown men in destruction and perdition. ¹⁰ For the love of money is a root of all kinds of evil: which some reaching after have been led astray from the faith, and have pierced themselves through with many sorrows.

¹¹ But you, O man of God, flee these things; and follow after righteousness, godliness, faith, love, patience, meekness. ¹² Fight the good fight of the faith, lay hold on the life eternal, whereunto you were called, and did confess the good confession in the sight of many witnesses. ¹³ I charge you in the sight of God, who gives life to all things, and of Christ Jesus, who before Pontius Pilate witnessed the good confession; ¹⁴ that you keep the commandment, without spot, without reproach, until the appearing of our Lord Jesus Christ: ¹⁵ which in its own times he shall show, who is the blessed and only Potentate, the King of kings, and Lord of lords; ¹⁶ who only has immortality, dwelling in light unapproachable; whom no man has seen, nor can see: to whom be honor and power eternal. Amen.

¹⁷ Charge them that are rich in this present world, that they be not high-minded, nor have their hope set on the uncertainty of riches, but on God, who gives us richly all things to enjoy; ¹⁸ that they do good, that they be rich in good works, that they be ready to distribute, willing to communicate; ¹⁹ laying up in store for themselves a good foundation against the time to come, that they may lay hold on the life which is life indeed.

²⁰ O Timothy, guard that which is committed to you, turning away from the profane babblings and oppositions of the knowledge which is falsely so called; ²¹ which some professing have erred concerning the faith.

consistent with godliness which Paul describes as: *6 But godliness with contentment is great gain: 7 for we brought nothing into the world, for neither can we carry anything out; ⁸ but having food and covering we shall be therewith content.* Paul implies that those that promote such ungodliness are motivated by greed. The desire for wealth, the love of money, Paul writes, *'¹⁰ is a root of all kinds of evil: which some reaching after have been led astray from the faith, and have pierced themselves through with many sorrows.'*

Referring to Timothy as being a 'man of God', Paul exhorts him to *'¹¹ flee these things; and follow after righteousness, godliness, faith, love, patience, meekness.'* Paul reminds Timothy of the confession that he made before many witnesses to *'¹² Fight the good fight of the faith, lay hold on the life eternal, whereunto you were called.'* and charges him to *'¹⁴ keep the commandment, without spot (blemish, fault), without reproach, until the appearing of our Lord Jesus Christ:'*

Paul exhorts Timothy to challenge those that have wealth that riches have no certainty, and to use their wealth to do good so that they will be rewarded *'¹⁹ laying up in store for themselves a good foundation against the time to come, that they may lay hold on the life which is life indeed.'*

Finally, Paul concludes the letter with an exhortation to proclaim and defend the kingdom of God, and then a further warning against those who would steer clear of those who teach a doctrine based on false knowledge and shallow arguments.

The Compiled Teachings of The Apostle Paul

Titus

Qualifications of Elders.. 102
Duties of the Older and the Younger..................................... 102
Godly Living... 103
Personal Concerns... 103

Paul's Letter To Titus written by Paul at Nicopolis*

1 Paul, a servant of God, and an apostle of Jesus Christ, according to the faith of God's elect, and the knowledge of the truth which is according to godliness, ² in hope of eternal life, which God, who cannot lie, promised before times eternal; ³ but in his own seasons manifested his word in the message, wherewith I was entrusted according to the commandment of God our Savior; ⁴ to Titus, my true child after a common faith: Grace and peace from God the Father and Christ Jesus our Savior.

Titus 1:1-4

In this greeting to Titus, Paul explains that he was commissioned (trusted) by God to share the message of *'hope of eternal life'*, *³ᵇ wherewith I was entrusted according to the commandment of God our Savior;'* and Paul references Titus as being *'my true child after a common faith'*.

Qualifications of Elders

⁵ For this cause left I you in Crete, that you should set in order the things that were wanting, and appoint elders in every city, as I gave you charge; ⁶ if any man is blameless, the husband of one wife, having children that believe, who are not accused of riot or unruly. ⁷ For the bishop must be blameless, as God's steward; not self-willed, not soon angry, no brawler, no striker, not greedy of filthy lucre; ⁸ but given to hospitality, a lover of good, sober-minded, just, holy, self-controlled; ⁹ holding to the faithful word which is according to the teaching, that he may be able both to exhort in the sound doctrine, and to convict the gainsayers.
¹⁰ For there are many unruly men, vain talkers and deceivers, specially they of the circumcision, ¹¹ whose mouths must be stopped; men who overthrow whole houses, teaching things which they ought not, for filthy lucre's sake.
¹² One of themselves, a prophet of their own, said, Cretans are always liars, evil beasts, idle gluttons.
¹³ This testimony is true. For which cause reprove them sharply, that they may be sound in the faith, ¹⁴ not giving heed to Jewish fables, and commandments of men who turn away from the truth. ¹⁵ To the pure all things are pure: but to them that are defiled and unbelieving nothing is pure; but both their mind and their conscience are defiled. ¹⁶ They profess that they know God; but by their works they deny him, being abominable, and disobedient, and to every good work reprobate (unprincipled).

Titus 1:5-16

Paul explains to Titus that he had left him in Crete to, *'set in order the things that were wanting, and appoint elders in every city'* and he details criteria that need to be met by those considered. Paul also references qualities sure to eliminate a candidate, including those having a negative reputation that is commonly credited to the entire population. Paul advises that strict discipline will be necessary and by quoting what he has been told, that *¹²ᵇ Cretans are always liars, evil beasts, idle gluttons'* and writing *¹³ This testimony is true'* he believes that the Cretans are defiled and *¹⁵ᵇ to them that are defiled and unbelieving nothing is pure; but both their mind and their conscience are defiled'* and Paul adds, *'by their works they deny him, being abominable, and disobedient, and to every good work reprobate'* meaning they are unprincipled, that is they have no morals.

Duties of the Older and the Younger

2 But speak the things which befit the sound doctrine: ² that aged men be temperate, grave, sober-minded, sound in faith, in love, patient: ³ that aged women likewise be reverent in demeanor, not slanderers nor enslaved to much wine, teachers of that which is good; ⁴ that they may train the young women to love their husbands, to love their children, ⁵ to be sober-minded, chaste, workers at home, kind, being in subjection to their own husbands, that the word of God be not blasphemed: ⁶ the younger men likewise exhort to be sober-minded: ⁷ in all things showing yourself an example of good works; in your doctrine showing integrity (uncorruptness), gravity, ⁸ sound speech, that cannot be condemned; that he that is of the contrary part may be ashamed, having no evil thing to say of us. ⁹ Exhort servants to be in subjection to their

Titus 2:1-15

Paul exhorts Titus to preach what is right and good and to teach older men that they must be *² be temperate, grave, sober-minded, sound in faith, in love, (and) patient.'* And teach older women to be *'reverent in demeanor, not slanderers nor enslaved to much wine, teachers of that which is good'* so that they will *'train the young women to love their husbands, to love their children, ⁵ to be sober-minded, chaste, workers at home, kind, being in subjection to their own husbands, that the word of God be not blasphemed'*. Paul explains that if he, Titus, himself being a younger man, should *⁷ in all things show (himself to be) an example of good works'*. Paul exhorts Titus to preach the Gospel in a manner that cannot be criticized or condemned so that those who would criticize are not given opportunity to do so. Then Paul tells Titus to encourage those in service, (bond servants, slaves) to subject

own masters, and to be well-pleasing to them in all things; not gainsaying; ¹⁰ not stealing (purloining), but showing all good fidelity; that they may adorn the doctrine of God our Savior in all things. ¹¹ For the grace of God has appeared, bringing salvation to all men, ¹² instructing us, to the intent that, denying ungodliness and worldly lusts, we should live soberly and righteously and godly in this present world; ¹³ looking for the blessed hope and appearing of the glory of the great God and our Savior Jesus Christ; ¹⁴ who gave himself for us, that he might redeem us from all iniquity, and purify to himself a people for his own possession, zealous of good works.

¹⁵ These things speak and exhort and reprove with all authority. Let no man despise thee.

themselves to their owners, *'to be well-pleasing to them in all things; not gainsaying; ¹⁰ not purloining, but showing all good fidelity; that they may adorn the doctrine of God our Savior in all things.'* and Paul expands on the reasoning for this (often viewed as contentious**) instruction *'¹¹ For the grace of God has appeared, bringing salvation to all men, ¹² instructing us, to the intent that, denying ungodliness and worldly lusts, we should live soberly and righteously and godly in this present world'* Paul begins closing with a reminder that we all surely are *'¹³ looking for the blessed hope and appearing of the glory of the great God and our Savior Jesus Christ, ¹⁴ who gave himself for us, that he might redeem us from all iniquity'* and that is the Gospel message that he must preach.

** It must be acknowledged that in our day and age it is difficult for those of us in the western world who profess to be Christians to understand why Paul would be so supportive of slave owners. In the United States of America most people view slavery as something evil because of the history of the slave trade that brought Africans to America and how they were treated working and living on plantations which was the principal life that most were brought into. Those events are events of the past that must be recognized as being events of the future in Paul's time, and so we must view and understand Paul's writing in the context of the past and not solely in the context of current times.

Godly Living

Titus 3:1-11

3 Put them in mind to be in subjection to rulers, to authorities, to be obedient, to be ready for every good work, ² to speak evil of no man, not to be contentious, to be gentle, showing all meekness toward all men. ³ For we also once were foolish, disobedient, deceived, serving divers lusts and pleasures, living in malice and envy, hateful, hating one another. ⁴ But when the kindness of God our Savior, and his love toward man, appeared, ⁵ not by works done in righteousness, which we did ourselves, but according to his mercy he saved us, through the washing of regeneration and renewing of the Holy Spirit, ⁶ which he poured out upon us richly, through Jesus Christ our Savior; ⁷ that, being justified by his grace, we might be made heirs according to the hope of eternal life. ⁸ Faithful is the saying, and concerning these things I desire that you affirm confidently, to the end that they who have believed God may be careful to maintain good works. These things are good and profitable to men: ⁹ but shun foolish questionings, and genealogies, and strifes, and fightings about the law; for they are unprofitable and vain. ¹⁰ A factious man after a first and second admonition refuse; ¹¹ knowing that such a one is perverted, and sins, being self-condemned.

Paul continues his instructions to Titus reminding him to teach church leaders (and by extension, everyone) to live according to the laws and to be ready for opportunities to do whatever is good. Paul summarizes both positive and negative lifestyle attributes and then reminds Titus that it was through Jesus Christ that God gave man the opportunity to be justified by grace and counsels him to *':⁹ but shun foolish questionings, and genealogies, and strifes, and fightings about the law; for they are unprofitable and vain. ¹⁰ A factious man after a first and second admonition refuse; ¹¹ knowing that such a one is perverted, and sins, being self-condemned.'.*

* As mentioned earlier in Section 3, 'The Chronological Order of Paul's Letters', Nicopolis is mentioned in this letter to Titus (3:12) suggesting that he is at Nicopolis at the time of writing, but that is not fully conclusive. *Paul may not have been in Nicopolis, but rather may have been in Corinth and planning, with the winter coming, to go to Nicopolis.*

Personal Concerns

Titus 3:12-1

3 ¹² When I shall send Artemas to you, or Tychicus, give diligence to come to me to Nicopolis: for there I have determined to winter. ¹³ Set forward Zenas the lawyer and Apollos on their journey diligently, that nothing be wanting to them. ¹⁴ And let our people also learn to maintain good works for necessary uses, that they be not unfruitful.

¹⁵ All that are with me salute you. Salute them that love us in faith.

Grace be with you all.

Paul closes out his letter to Titus referencing future plans telling Titus to be ready to travel to Nicopolis (in Macedonia) where Paul is writing from, and which is where he plans to spend the winter, and in doing so has given Titus some idea of his future plans and also who Paul will be sending to Crete. We also learn that already in Crete are Zenas and Apollos and they are scheduled to be leaving Crete sometime soon.

Finally, Paul sends salutations from himself and others that are with him in Nicopolis*.

The Compiled Teachings of The Apostle Paul

Ephesians

The Blessings of Redemption 104	Be Imitators of God 107
Gratitude and Prayers 104	Marriage Like Christ and the Church 108
Made Alive In Christ 105	Children and Parents 108
Paul's Stewardship 106	Slaves and Masters 109
Unity of the Spirit 106	The Armor of God 109
The Christian's Walk 107	

The Letter To The Ephesians written by Paul at Rome

The Blessings of Redemption

Ephesians 1:1-14

1 Paul, an apostle of Christ Jesus through the will of God, to the saints that are at Ephesus, and the faithful in Christ Jesus: ² Grace to you and peace from God our Father and the Lord Jesus Christ.

³ Blessed be the God and Father of our Lord Jesus Christ, who has blessed us with every spiritual blessing in the heavenly places in Christ: ⁴ even as he chose us in him before the foundation of the world, that we should be holy and without blemish before him in love: ⁵ having foreordained us unto adoption as sons through Jesus Christ unto himself, according to the good pleasure of his will, ⁶ to the praise of the glory of his grace, which he freely bestowed on us in the Beloved: ⁷ in whom we have our redemption through his blood, the forgiveness of our trespasses, according to the riches of his grace, ⁸ which he made to abound toward us in all wisdom and prudence, ⁹ making known unto us the mystery of his will, according to his good pleasure which he purposed in him ¹⁰ unto a dispensation of the fulness of the times, to sum up all things in Christ, the things in the heavens, and the things upon the earth; in him, I say, ¹¹ in whom also we were made a heritage, having been foreordained according to the purpose of him who worked all things after the counsel of his will; ¹² to the end that we should be unto the praise of his glory, we who had before hoped in Christ: ¹³ in whom you also, having heard the word of the truth, the gospel of your salvation, – in whom, having also believed, you were sealed with the Holy Spirit of promise, ¹⁴ which is an earnest (reward) of our inheritance, unto the redemption of God's own possession, unto the praise of his glory.

Following Paul's greeting to the church in Ephesus and his blessing, is a single sentence that summarizes who God is, who Jesus Christ is, what God's plan for us is, and what is promised.

The plan is that we should be holy and expect to be adopted into the '¹²ᵇ *the praise of his glory*' and be '¹³ᵇ *sealed with the Holy Spirit of promise*' and be redeemed.

Gratitude and Prayers

Ephesians 1:15-22

1 ¹⁵ For this cause I also, having heard of the faith in the Lord Jesus which is among you, and the love which you show toward all the saints, ¹⁶ cease not to give thanks for you, making mention of you in my prayers; ¹⁷ that the God of our Lord Jesus Christ, the Father of glory, may give to you a spirit of wisdom and revelation in the knowledge of him; ¹⁸ having the eyes of your heart enlightened, that you may know what is the hope of his calling, what the riches of the glory of his inheritance in the saints, ¹⁹ and what the exceeding greatness of his power to us-ward who believe, according to that working of the strength of his might ²⁰ which he wrought in Christ, when he raised him from the dead, and made Him to sit at his right hand in the heavenly places, ²¹ far above all rule, and authority, and power, and dominion, and every name that is named, not only in this world, but also in that which is to come: ²² and he put all things in subjection under his feet, and gave him to be head over all things to the church, ²³ which is his body, the fulness of him that fills all in all.

Paul expresses his gratitude for the faithfulness and kindness (love) given by the church in Ephesus that supported him and 'all the saints', the term used for those who were believers, but in the context used here, Paul's co-workers. Paul describes that he prays that God will give each of them '¹⁷ᵇ *a spirit of wisdom and revelation in the knowledge of him*', and concludes by describing how God raised Jesus to '²⁰ᵇ *sit at his right hand in the heavenly places, ²¹ far above all rule, and authority, and power, and dominion, and every name that is named, not only in this world, but also in that which is to come:*' '²²ᵇ *and gave him to be head over all things to the church, ²³ which is his body*'.

The Compiled Teachings of The Apostle Paul

Made Alive In Christ

Ephesians 2:1-3

> *2 And you did he make alive, when you were dead through your trespasses and sins, ² wherein you once walked according to the course of this world, according to the prince of the powers of the air, of the spirit that now works in the sons of disobedience; ³ among whom we also all once lived in the lusts of our flesh, doing the desires of the flesh and of the mind, and were by nature children of wrath, even as the rest:*

Paul continues his explanation of who Jesus is beginning with a direct reference to how Jesus, by dying on the cross, being buried and then the resurrection (being raised from the dead), has made us alive because we were dead because of our sins ('*¹ through our trespasses and sins*').

Then Paul uses several unique phrases to describe the world before Christ as: 'we ²ᵇ *once walked according to the course of this world, according to the prince of the powers of the air, of the spirit that now works in the sons of disobedience; ³ among whom we also all once lived in the lusts of our flesh, doing the desires of the flesh and of the mind, and were by nature children of wrath, even as the rest:*'

- 'Walking according to the course of this world,' means following our base-human nature with no conscience;
- '*according to the prince of the powers of the air, of the spirit that now works in the sons of disobedience;*' means the influence of the devil over us;
- '*among whom we also all once lived in the lusts of our flesh, doing the desires of the flesh and of the mind, and were by nature children of wrath,*' means that our base-human nature provided us with temptation upon temptation as to what we would subject our bodies to without conscience; and
- '*even as the rest*' means we were no different from, nor better than, others – and by extension – even though we thought we were good enough by not being as bad, we're still not perfect. (Recall that Jesus said, "even if you have thoughts…" Mark 7:21-23)

Ephesians 2:4-21

> *– ⁴ but God, being rich in mercy, for his great love wherewith He loved us, ⁵ even when we were dead through our trespasses, made us alive together with Christ (for it is by grace that you have been saved), ⁶ and raised us up with him, and made us to sit with him in the heavenly places, in Christ Jesus: ⁷ that in the ages to come he might show the exceeding riches of his grace in kindness toward us in Christ Jesus: ⁸ for by grace you have been saved through faith; and that not of yourselves, it is the gift of God; ⁹ not of works, that no man should glory. ¹⁰ For we are his workmanship, created in Christ Jesus for good works, which God before prepared that we should walk in them.*
>
> *¹¹ Wherefore remember, that once you, the Gentiles in the flesh, who are called Uncircumcision by that which is called Circumcision, in the flesh, made by hands; ¹² that you were at that time separate from Christ, alienated from the commonwealth of Israel, and strangers from the covenants of the promise, having no hope and without God in the world. ¹³ But now in Christ Jesus you that once were far off are made close in the blood of Christ. ¹⁴ For he is our peace, who made both one, and broke down the middle wall of partition, ¹⁵ having abolished in his flesh the enmity, even the law of commandments contained in ordinances; that he might create in himself of the two one new man, so making peace; ¹⁶ and might reconcile them both in one body to God through the cross, having slain the enmity thereby: ¹⁷ and he came and preached peace to you that were far off, and peace to them that were nigh: ¹⁸ for through him we both have our access in one Spirit to the Father. ¹⁹ So then you are no more strangers and sojourners, but you are fellow-citizens with the saints, and of the household of God, ²⁰ being built upon the foundation of the apostles and prophets, Christ Jesus himself being the chief corner stone; ²¹ in whom each several building, fitly framed together, grows into a holy temple in the Lord; ²² in whom you also are built together for a habitation of God in the Spirit.*

Paul, however, explains God's plan by which we can be granted redemption in more detail and it is '⁸*…by grace you have been saved through faith; and that not of yourselves, it is the gift of God*', and Paul adds, '⁹ *not of works, that no man should glory. ¹⁰ For we are his workmanship, created in Christ Jesus for good works, which God before prepared that we should walk in them*' meaning that we should seek to do good works to please God, but doing good works cannot earn redemption; it is through faith that we are saved.

Paul turns to reminding the Ephesians, who are mostly Gentiles, that since they are not circumcised, they were separated from Christ and from Israel, and were outside of the covenants that were given by God through Moses to Israel and, being without God, had no hope. Now, through the blood of Christ (meaning through the truth of Christ's death on the cross, his burial, resurrection and ascension), both Jew and gentile, are reconciled as ¹⁶ᵇ*…in one body to God through the cross, having slain the enmity thereby:* '¹⁸ᵇ *both have our access in one Spirit to the Father.*'

[This is Paul, a Jew, writing to Gentiles.]

Paul's Stewardship — Ephesians 3:1-21

3 For this cause I Paul, the prisoner of Christ Jesus in behalf of you Gentiles, – ² if so be that you have heard of the dispensation of that grace of God which was given to me; ³ how that by revelation was made known to me the mystery, as I wrote before in few words, ⁴ whereby, when you read, you will perceive my understanding in the mystery of Christ; ⁵ which in other generations was not made known to the sons of men, as it has now been revealed to his holy apostles and prophets in the Spirit; ⁶ to wit, that the Gentiles are fellow-heirs, and fellow-members of the body, and fellow-partakers of the promise in Christ Jesus through the gospel, ⁷ whereof I was made a minister, according to the gift of that grace of God which was given me according to the working of his power. ⁸ Unto me, who am less than the least of all saints, was this grace given, to preach unto the Gentiles the unsearchable (boundless ᴺᴬˢᴮ)riches of Christ; ⁹ and to enlighten all people as to what the plan of the mystery is [NASB], which for ages has been hidden in God who created all things ¹⁰ to the intent that now to the rulers and the authorities [NASB] in the heavenly places might be made known through the church the manifold wisdom of God, ¹¹ according to the eternal purpose which he purposed in Christ Jesus our Lord: ¹² in whom we have boldness and access in confidence through our faith in him. ¹³ Wherefore I ask that you may not be discouraged at my tribulations for you, which are your glory.

Paul makes the claim that he is *'the prisoner of Christ Jesus in behalf of you Gentiles',* he wants them to understand that he is a Jew writing to Gentiles. Paul explains that the understanding of the mystery of Christ that he has is because of revelation from God; a revelation that had not previously been made know to anyone else, but which was made first to the Apostles of Jesus Christ and then to him. This revelation, Paul proposes makes the Gentiles *'⁶ᵃfellow-heirs'* to the Jews, becoming *'⁶ᵇ fellow-members of the body'* and, thereby, *'⁶ᶜ fellow-partakers of the promise in Christ Jesus through the gospel.'* Paul then states that it was because of the revelation made to him that he *'⁷ was made a minister, according to the gift of that grace of God which was given me according to the working of his power. ⁸To me, who am less than the least of all saints, was this grace given, to preach to the Gentiles the boundless riches of Christ'.*

Paul continues to describe that God created everything and that it was now God's plan that all of the power of heaven should be made known to all and he then explains that it is through Jesus Christ that he and his coworkers have boldness because of their faith in Jesus. Paul writes that they should not be discouraged by the treatment that he sometimes receives.

¹⁴ For this cause I bow my knees to the Father, ¹⁵ from whom every family in heaven and on earth is named, ¹⁶ that he would grant you, according to the riches of his glory, that you may be strengthened with power through his Spirit in the inward man; ¹⁷ that Christ may dwell in your hearts through faith; to the end that you, being rooted and grounded in love, ¹⁸ may be strong to apprehend with all the saints what is the breadth and length and height and depth, ¹⁹ and to know the love of Christ which surpasses knowledge, that you may be filled to all the fulness of God.

²⁰ Now to him that is able to do exceeding abundantly above all that we ask or think, according to the power that works in us, ²¹ to him be the glory in the church and in Christ Jesus unto all generations for ever and ever. Amen.

Paul concludes this chapter of his letter with a prayer, in which he implores the Ephesians to have Christ *'dwell in your hearts through faith; to the end that you, being rooted and grounded in love,..'* and then, finally, a benediction.

Unity of the Spirit — Ephesians 4:1-17

4 I therefore, the prisoner in the Lord, beseech you to walk worthily of the calling (to which) you were called, ² with all lowliness and meekness, with long-suffering, forbearing one another in love; ³ giving diligence to keep the unity of the Spirit in the bond of peace. ⁴ There is one body, and one Spirit, even as also you were called in one hope of your calling; ⁵ one Lord, one faith, one baptism, ⁶ one God and Father of all, who is over all, and through all, and in all. ⁷ But to each one of us was the grace given according to the measure of the gift of Christ. ⁸ Wherefore he said, when he ascended on high, "he led (many) captives", and gave gifts to men.

⁹ (Now this, He ascended, what is it but that he also descended into the lower parts of the earth? ¹⁰ He that descended is the same also that ascended far above all the heavens, that he might fill all things.)

Paul continues his counselling reminding them that they were called, re-emphasizing the need for them to have the right demeanor in order that the *'³ᵇ the unity of the Spirit in the bond of peace.'* Is maintained. Paul reminds them that there is one God, who is the *'⁶ᵇ Father of all, who is over all, and through all, and in all.'* (creation) *'⁵ one Lord, one faith, one baptism ',* and redemption: *'⁷ to each one of us was the grace given according to the measure of the gift of Christ.'* The next sentence that Paul wrote, translated reads like this: *'when he ascended on high, he led captives, and gave gifts to men'* - which is from Psalm 68:18

¹⁸ Thou hast ascended on high, thou hast led away captives;
Thou hast received gifts among men, Yea, among the rebellious also, that Jehovah God might dwell with them.

Paul appears to have inserted verse 9 for teaching, explaining that Jesus having been crucified and dying, (and then His body being placed in a tomb) descended into *'the lower parts of the earth'* as Jesus said He would (Matt. 12:40).

The Compiled Teachings of The Apostle Paul

¹¹ And he gave some to be apostles; and some, prophets; and some, evangelists; and some, pastors and teachers; ¹² for the perfecting of the saints, to the work of ministering, to the building up of the body of Christ: ¹³ till we all attain the unity of the faith, and of the knowledge of the Son of God, to a full-grown man, to the measure of the stature of the fulness of Christ: ¹⁴ that we may no longer be children, tossed to and fro and carried about with every wind of doctrine, by the sleight of men, in craftiness, after the wiles of error; ¹⁵ but speaking truth in love, may grow up in all things into him, who is the head, even Christ; ¹⁶ from whom all the body fitly framed and knit together through that which every joint supplies, according to the working in due measure of each several part, makes the increase of the body to the building up of itself in love.

Paul mentioned that after He had ascended into heaven, Jesus *'gave gifts to men'*. Here Paul lists those gifts and the purpose of those gifts, with the ultimate goal that *'all attain the unity of the faith, and of the knowledge of the Son of God, to a full-grown man, to the measure of the stature of the fulness of Christ: ¹⁴ that we may no longer be children, tossed to and fro and carried about with every wind of doctrine'*. In other words, the goal is that everyone (all) should come to know Christ, have a full knowledge of who Jesus Christ was and is, such that our faith will become resilient against all challenges. Paul then begins to reference the make a comparison between the body of Christ, with Christ as the head, and the human body.

The Christian's Walk

Ephesians 4:17-30

4 ¹⁷ This I say therefore, and testify in the Lord, that you no longer walk as the Gentiles also walk, in the vanity of their mind, ¹⁸ being darkened in their understanding, alienated from the life of God, because of the ignorance that is in them, because of the hardening of their heart; ¹⁹ who being past feeling gave themselves up to lasciviousness, to work all uncleanness with greediness. ²⁰ But you did not so learn Christ; ²¹ if so be that you heard him, and were taught in him, even as truth is in Jesus: ²² that you put away, as concerning your former manner of life, the old man, that waxes corrupt after the lusts of deceit; ²³ and that you be renewed in the spirit of your mind, ²⁴ and put on the new man, that after God has been created in righteousness and holiness of truth.

²⁵ Wherefore, putting away falsehood, speak truth each one with his neighbor: for we are members one of another. ²⁶ Be angry and sin not: let not the sun go down upon your wrath: ²⁷ neither give place to the devil. ²⁸ Let him that stole steal no more: but rather let him labor, working with his hands the thing that is good, that he may have whereof to give to him that has need. ²⁹ Let no corrupt speech proceed out of your mouth, but such as is good for edifying as the need may be, that it may give grace to them that hear. ³⁰ And grieve not the Holy Spirit of God, in whom you were sealed for the day of redemption. ³¹ Let all bitterness, and wrath, and anger, and clamor, and railing, be put away from you, with all malice: ³² and be kind one to another, tenderhearted, forgiving each other, even as God also in Christ forgave you.

Paul begins to make a case for believing that the Gentiles have become alienated from God because of their vanity, *'¹⁸ darkened in their understanding'*, ignorance, and *'because of the hardening of their heart'*. Paul's understanding of the culture of the Gentiles of Ephesus was that of *'uncleanness and greediness'*, which he said was the reason for their *'lasciviousness'* - crude and offensive sexual behavior. Paul writes, *'²² that you put away, as concerning your former manner of life, the old man, that waxes corrupt after the lusts of deceit; ²³ and that you be renewed in the spirit of your mind, ²⁴ and put on the new man, that after God has been created in righteousness and holiness of truth'* exhorting them to change their ways, to not be angry with one another and do not sin, *'let not the sun go down upon your wrath: ²⁷ neither give place to the devil.'* Paul is in effect saying that the blame lies with the devil who has been sent to corrupt and make man evil, and when you understand this, and you also understand that through grace (given to you by Jesus Christ), we can all be redeemed. From verse 27 through verse 32 Paul lays out a strategy, a recipe if you will, for Christians which he continues in the next chapter.

Be Imitators of God

Ephesians 5:1-21

5 Be you therefore imitators of God, as beloved children; ² and walk in love, even as Christ also loved you, and gave himself up for us, an offering and a sacrifice to God as a fragrant aroma.[NASB]

³ But fornication, and all uncleanness, or covetousness, let it not even be named among you, as becomes saints; ⁴ nor filthiness, nor foolish talking, or jesting, which are not befitting: but rather giving of thanks. ⁵ For this you know of a surety, that no fornicator, nor unclean person, nor covetous man, who is an idolater, has any inheritance in the kingdom of Christ and God. ⁶ Let no man deceive you with empty words: for because of these things cometh the wrath of God upon

Paul continues to articulate his strategy for living a Christian life encouraging in his letter to the Ephesians to become imitators of God, *'² walk in love, even as Christ also loved you.'*

Paul now turns the focus on things that were known to be common practice which must be ceased. Paul begins with fornication, that is sexual intimacy outside of marriage but he expands that from that one specific situation to *'all uncleanness, or covetousness'* and then adds *'⁴ filthiness, nor foolish talking, or jesting, which are not befitting'*. The penalty for any such behavior Paul states is *'⁵ For this you know of a*

> *the sons of disobedience. ⁷ Be not you therefore partakers with them; ⁸ for you were once darkness, but are now light in the Lord: walk as children of light ⁹ (for the fruit of the light is in all goodness and righteousness and truth), ¹⁰ proving what is well-pleasing to the Lord; ¹¹ and have no fellowship with the unfruitful works of darkness, but rather even reprove them; ¹² for the things which are done by them in secret it is a shame even to speak of. ¹³ But all things when they are reproved are made manifest by the light: for everything that is made manifest is light. ¹⁴ Wherefore he said, 'Awake, you that sleeps, and arise from the dead, and Christ shall shine upon you'.*
>
> *¹⁵ Look therefore carefully how you walk, not as unwise, but as wise; ¹⁶ redeeming the time, because the days are evil.*
>
> *¹⁷ Wherefore be not foolish, but understand what the will of the Lord is. ¹⁸ And be not drunken with wine, wherein is riot, but be filled with the Spirit; ¹⁹ speaking one to another in psalms and hymns and spiritual songs, singing and making melody with your heart to the Lord; ²⁰ giving thanks always for all things in the name of our Lord Jesus Christ to God, even the Father; ²¹ subjecting yourselves one to another in the fear of Christ.*

surety, that no fornicator, nor unclean person, nor covetous man, who is an idolater, has any inheritance in the kingdom of Christ and God.'

In verses 6-7 Paul warns against believing those who would preach a different message, something that he refers to as a 'false Gospel'. Verses 8-14 shares encouragement and guidance for each individual and counselling for managing one's relationships.

In verse 14, Paul quotes a scripture which may be from Daniel 12:2, *'And many of them that sleep in the dust of the earth shall awake, some to everlasting life, and some to shame and everlasting contempt'*, which adds a negative not mentioned by Paul for those that have not been redeemed. If Paul had access to Luke's writings, which is quite possible as Luke travelled with Paul extensively, including being jailed together, Luke 9:32 is also a possibility as being the 'scripture source': *'Now Peter and they that were with him were heavy with sleep: but when they were fully awake, they saw his glory, and the two men that stood with him.'*

Paul continues through verses 15-21 sharing advice and guidance for leading a Christian life.

Marriage Like Christ and the Church

Ephesians 5:22-33

> *5 ²² Wives, be in subjection to your own husbands, as to the Lord. ²³ For the husband is the head of the wife, as Christ also is the head of the church, being himself the savior of the body. ²⁴ But as the church is subject to Christ, so let the wives also be to their husbands in everything. ²⁵ Husbands, love your wives, even as Christ also loved the church, and gave himself up for it; ²⁶ that he might sanctify it, having cleansed it by the washing of water with the word, ²⁷ that he might present the church to himself a glorious church, not having spot or wrinkle or any such thing; but that it should be holy and without blemish. ²⁸ Even so ought husbands also to love their own wives as their own bodies. He that loves his own wife loves himself: ²⁹ for no man ever hated his own flesh; but nourishes and cherishes it, even as Christ also the church; ³⁰ because we are members of his body. ³¹ For this cause shall a man leave his father and mother, and shall cleave to his wife; and the two shall become one flesh. ³² This mystery is great: but I speak in regard of Christ and of the church. ³³ Nevertheless do you also severally love each one his own wife even as himself; and let the wife see that she fear (respect) her husband.*

In these next verses, 22-33, Paul gives guidance to those who are married, husbands and wives, including guidance in verse 31: *'³¹ᵇ a man…shall cleave to his wife; and the two shall become one flesh'* and Paul finishes the passage with *'³³ᵇ love each one his own wife even as himself; and let the wife see that she fear her husband'*. Together, these two statements clearly advise that a man should not have more than one wife, and a wife not more than one husband, with the understanding that the word 'fear' in the second of these statements be taken to mean respect, not 'be in fear of'.

Children and Parents

Ephesians 6:1-4

> *6 Children, obey your parents in the Lord: for this is right. ² Honor thy father and mother (which is the first commandment with promise), ³ that it may be well with you, and you may live long on the earth. ⁴ And, fathers, provoke not your children to wrath: but nurture them in the chastening and admonition of the Lord.*

Paul continues giving family advice, advising children to obey and honor their parents, with a reminder that this is according to the first of the great commandments, with verse 4 being sound advice to fathers.

Slaves and Masters

> [5] Servants, be obedient to them that according to the flesh are your masters, with fear and trembling, in singleness of your heart, as to Christ; [6] not in the way of eyeservice, as men-pleasers; but as servants of Christ, doing the will of God from the heart; [7] with good will doing service, as to the Lord, and not to men: [8] knowing that whatsoever good thing each one does, the same shall he receive again from the Lord, whether he be bond or free. [9] And, you masters, do the same things to them, and forbear threatening: knowing that he who is both their Master and yours is in heaven, and there is no respect of persons with him.

The Armor of God

> 6 [10] Finally, be strong in the Lord, and in the strength of his might. [11] Put on the whole armor of God, that you may be able to stand against the wiles of the devil. [12] For our wrestling is not against flesh and blood, but against the principalities, against the powers, against the world-rulers of this darkness, against the spiritual hosts of wickedness in the heavenly places. [13] Wherefore take up the whole armor of God, that you may be able to withstand in the day of evil, and, having done all, to stand. [14] Stand therefore, having girded your loins with truth, and having put on the breastplate of righteousness, [15] and having shod your feet with the preparation of the gospel of peace; [16] in addition taking up the shield of faith, wherewith you shall be able to quench all the fiery darts of the evil one. [17] And take the helmet of salvation, and the sword of the Spirit, which is the word of God: [18] with all prayer and supplication praying at all seasons in the Spirit, and watching thereunto in all perseverance and supplication for all the saints, [19] and on my behalf, that utterance may be given to me in opening my mouth, to make known with boldness the mystery of the gospel, [20] for which I am an ambassador in chains; that in it I may speak boldly, as I ought to speak.
>
> [21] But that you also may know my affairs, how I shall make known to you all things? [22] Tychicus, my beloved brother and faithful minister in the Lord, whom I have sent to you for this very purpose, that you may know our state, and that he may comfort your hearts.
>
> [23] Peace be to the brethren, and love with faith, from God the Father and the Lord Jesus Christ. [24] Grace be with all them that love our Lord Jesus Christ with a love incorruptible.

Ephesians 6:5-24

Now we come to a topic which in the 21st Century is a challenge to the western world; that of slavery and servanthood. Verse 8 reads: '[8b] whether he be bond or free.' For some societies we can reasonably argue that slavery is something of the past, but, regrettably not for all. Reading and properly understanding the intent and purpose of this passage is most important.

Ephesians 6:10-24

This final passage in last chapter of Paul's Letter to The Ephesians is perhaps the most well-known and the most often quoted passage. In earlier passages Paul has used the term body mostly in reference to the church which, as a group of people, represents Christ in the world we live in. Paul switches from a focus on the battle that each person has "*wrestling against flesh and blood*" to a focus on dealing with "*[12b] principalities, against the powers, against the world-rulers of this darkness, against the spiritual hosts of wickedness in the heavenly places.*" It is from '*this darkness*', and '*against the spiritual hosts of wickedness*' that many of the Ephesians have come and all are still living in it. This is where our temptations come from, temptations that we all must fight against. Paul describes a defensive approach of putting on a suit of armor, '*[13b] the whole armor of God*'. Paul asks that all put on this armor and pray for him and '*[18c] for all the saints*', and then Paul concludes with a final greeting and benediction.

Philippians

Thanksgiving 110	*Warnings and Reminders* 112
The Gospel is preached 110	*The Goal of Life* 113
To Live Is Christ 111	*Stand Fast In The Lord* 113
Be Like Christ 111	*God's Provisions* 113
Timothy and Epaphroditus 112	

The Letter To The Church in Philippi written by Paul at Rome

Paul is writing from Rome after having had his life threatened in Jerusalem before he was tried and then imprisoned, then tried again before being transferred to Rome by sea, being shipwrecked on Malta and finally arriving in Rome *'And when we entered into Rome, Paul was suffered to abide by himself with the soldier that guarded him.'*
[Acts 28:16]

Thanksgiving   Philippians 1:1-30

1 Paul and Timothy, servants of Christ Jesus, to all the saints in Christ Jesus that are at Philippi, with the bishops and deacons: 2 Grace to you and peace from God our Father and the Lord Jesus Christ.

3 I thank my God upon all my remembrance of you, 4 always in every supplication of mine on behalf of you all making my supplication with joy 5 for your fellowship in furtherance of the gospel from the first day until now; 6 being confident of this very thing, that he who began a good work in you will perfect it until the day of Jesus Christ: 7 even as it is right for me to be thus minded on behalf of you all, because I have you in my heart, inasmuch as, both in my bonds and in the defense and confirmation of the gospel, you all are partakers with me of grace. 8 For God is my witness, how I long after you all in the tender mercies of Christ Jesus. 9 And this I pray, that your love may abound yet more and more in knowledge and all discernment; 10 so that you may approve the things that are excellent; that you may be sincere and void of offence to the day of Christ; 11 being filled with the fruits of righteousness, which are through Jesus Christ, unto the glory and praise of God.

Following on from his greeting in this letter to the church in Philippi, Paul gives thanks for their support in having met requests that he has made especially in regard to their success in expanding their ministry which he praises and commends them with the phrase, *'6b that he who began a good work in you will perfect it until the day of Jesus Christ'*. Paul tells them that he has them in his heart and that they are, as he is, assured of grace, and Paul states *'8 For God is my witness, how I long for you all 'with the compassion' of Jesus Christ.'*

The Gospel is preached   Philippians 1:12-20

1 12 Now I would have you know, brethren, that the things which happened to me have fallen out rather to (aid) the progress of the gospel; 13 so that my bonds became manifest in Christ throughout the whole praetorian guard, and to all the rest; 14 and that most of the brethren in the Lord, being confident through my bonds, are more abundantly bold to speak the word of God without fear. 15 Some indeed preach Christ even of envy and strife; and some also of good will: 16 the one does it of love, knowing that I am set for the defense of the gospel; 17 but the other proclaim Christ of faction, not sincerely, thinking to raise up affliction for me in my bonds. 18 What then? only that in every way, whether in pretense or in truth, Christ is proclaimed; and therein I rejoice, yea, and will rejoice. 19 For I know that this shall turn out to my salvation, through your supplication and the supply of the Spirit of Jesus Christ, 20 according to my earnest expectation and hope, that in nothing shall I be put to shame, but that with all boldness, as always, so now also Christ shall be magnified in my body, whether by life, or by death.

Paul transitions from encouraging the Philippians in what they have done, and what he asks them to continue doing, to sharing an optimistic view of his challenges, claiming that everything he has experienced has, in some way, strengthened his ministry and so he has been strengthened in his efforts to proclaim Christ.

Paul refers to their support through their prayers for him – *'19 b through your supplication'* – and that is what gives him joy and courage to continue in his efforts.

To Live Is Christ

21 For to me to live is Christ, and to die is gain. 22 But if to live in the flesh, – if this shall bring fruit from my work, then what I shall choose I know not. 23 But I am in a dilemma, caught between the two, having the desire to depart and be with Christ; for it is very far better: 24 yet to abide in the flesh is more needful for your sake. 25 And having this confidence, I know that I shall abide, yea, and abide with you all, for your progress and joy in the faith; 26 that your glorying may abound in Christ Jesus in me through my presence with you again. 27 Only let your manner of life be worthy of the gospel of Christ: that, whether I come and see you or be absent, I may hear of your state, that you stand fast in one spirit, with one soul striving for the faith of the gospel; 28 and in nothing affrighted by the adversaries: which is for them an evident token of perdition, but of your salvation, and that from God; 29 because to you it has been granted in the behalf of Christ, not only to believe on him, but also to suffer in his behalf: 30 having the same conflict which you saw in me, and now hear to be in me.

Philippians 1:21-30

Verse 21 is perhaps one of Paul's most well-known and most often quoted claims – **'For to me to live is Christ, and to die is gain'**. Paul immediately admits that he cannot be sure which will have the greater benefit, giving up his life or continuing to live and minister. It is a dilemma, but he acknowledges that it is probably more helpful to the church of Philippi than death would be. Paul is writing from Rome and, while not in prison is most probably still living with limitations over his freedom: *'Paul was suffered to abide by himself with the soldier that guarded him.'* [Acts 28:16] Such limitations would make it difficult for Paul to make plans for any future travel. However, Paul continues viewing a return to Philippi as a probability rather than just a possibility, let alone an option that doesn't exist. Paul's comment is something of a pragmatic anticipation that he might not be allowed the opportunity of travelling to visit: *'28b that, whether I come and see you or be absent, I may hear of your state'*; and Paul finishes up this passage in his letter with words of encouragement and sound reason *'29 but of your salvation, …because to you it has been granted in the behalf of Christ, not only to believe on him, but also to suffer in his behalf:*

Be Like Christ

2 If there is therefore any exhortation in Christ, if any consolation of love, if any fellowship of the Spirit, if any tender mercies and compassions, 2 make full my joy, that you are of the same mind, having the same love, being of one accord, of one mind; 3 doing nothing through faction or through vainglory, but in lowliness of mind each counting other better than himself; 4 not looking each of you to his own things, but each of you also to the things of others. 5 Have this mind in you, which was also in Christ Jesus: 6 who, existing in the form of God, counted not the being on an equality with God a thing to be grasped, 7 but emptied himself, taking the form of a servant, being made in the likeness of men; 8 and being found in fashion as a man, he humbled himself, becoming obedient even to death, yea, the death of the cross. 9 Wherefore also God highly exalted him, and gave to him the name which is above every name; 10 that in the name of Jesus every knee should bow, of things in heaven and things on earth and things under the earth, 11 and that every tongue should confess that Jesus Christ is Lord, to the glory of God the Father.

12 So then, my beloved, even as you have always obeyed, not as in my presence only, but now much more in my absence, work out your own salvation with fear and trembling; 13 for it is God who works in you both to will and to work, for his good pleasure. 14 Do all things without murmurings and questionings: 15 that you may become blameless and harmless, children of God without blemish in the midst of a crooked and perverse generation, among whom you are seen as lights in the world, 16 holding forth the word of life; that I may have whereof to glory in the day of Christ, that I did not run in vain neither labor in vain. 17 Yea, and if I am offered upon the sacrifice and service of your faith, I joy, and rejoice with you all: 18 and in the same manner do you also joy, and rejoice with me.

Philippians 2:1-18

Paul presents a thought regarding encouragement through believing in Christ, and in living a Christian life there are benefits that we gain. Paul counts fellowship, giving comfort, affection, support of others, and so forth as benefits. If these are obvious, then the results – unity, cooperation, and love – should too be obvious.

Paul reminds the Philippians that Jesus, as we all are, was made in the image of man, but Jesus was the Son of God and He submitted to the will of His father and by dying on the cross glorified God, His father. [In Ephesians 1:20-21 Paul wrote *'when he raised him from the dead, and made Him to sit at his right hand in the heavenly places, 21 far above all rule, and authority, and power, and dominion, and every name that is named, not only in this world, but also in that which is to come'*] and here Paul writes, *'10 that in the name of Jesus every knee should bow, of things in heaven and things on earth and things under the earth, 11 and that every tongue should confess that Jesus Christ is Lord, to the glory of God the Father.'*

As Paul continues with exhortation he writes yet another often quoted, well-known saying, *'12b work out your own salvation with fear and trembling'*, and he emphasizes that this is what they must do on their own without him there and he recognizes that the world is a challenging place; *'a crooked and perverse generation'* in which the church at Philippi is *'seen as lights in the world'* and Paul credits their efforts in spreading the gospel as testament to his success by telling them that he *'16b did not run in vain neither labor in vain'* and together they share in the joy of success.

Timothy and Epaphroditus

2 ¹⁹ But I hope in the Lord Jesus to send Timothy shortly to you, that I also may be of good comfort, when I know your state. ²⁰ For I have no man likeminded, who will care truly for your state. ²¹ For they all seek their own, not the things of Jesus Christ. ²² But you know the proof of him, that, as a child serves a father, so he served with me in furtherance of the gospel. ²³ Him therefore I hope to send forthwith, so soon as I shall see how it will go with me: ²⁴ but I trust in the Lord that I myself also shall come shortly ²⁵ But I counted it necessary to send to you Epaphroditus, my brother and fellow-worker and fellow-soldier, and your messenger and minister to my need; ²⁶ since he longed after you all, and was sore troubled, because you had heard that he was sick: ²⁷ for indeed he was sick nigh to death: but God had mercy on him; and not on him only, but on me also, that I might not have sorrow upon sorrow. ²⁸ I have sent him therefore the more diligently, that, when you see him again, you may rejoice, and that I may be the less sorrowful. ²⁹ Receive him therefore in the Lord with all joy; and hold such in honor:³⁰ because for the work of Christ he came near to death, hazarding his life to supply that which was lacking in your service toward me.

Philippians 2:19-30

After mentioning that he plans on having Timothy come to Philippi and that he, Paul, trusts Timothy more than others, Paul references that he might soon know his own situation (his fate of detention) but still shows optimism about him also being able to travel and return to Philippi. Paul then reflects on having 'sent' Epaphroditus, a younger individual, a *'brother and fellow-worker and fellow-soldier, and your messenger and minister'* adding the phase *'to my need'*. By 'my need' Paul is most likely referring to his desire for the Gospel to be preached without compromise, a reference back to v21 *'For they all seek their own, not the things of Jesus Christ.'*

Paul displays an attribute that many may find surprising when he references that Epaphroditus had been sick, *'sick nigh to death'*, and he continues to express just how much he would have grieved losing him had he not recovered, and concludes the passage with a strong commendation for Epaphroditus and his commitment to preaching the Gospel.

Warnings and Reminders

3 Finally, my brethren, rejoice in the Lord. To write the same things to you, to me indeed is not irksome, but for you it is safe. ² Beware of the dogs, beware of the evil workers, beware of the concision: ³ for we are the circumcision, who worship by the Spirit of God, and glory in Christ Jesus, and have no confidence in the flesh: ⁴ though I myself might have confidence even in the flesh: if any other man thinks to have confidence in the flesh, I yet more: ⁵ circumcised the eighth day, of the stock of Israel, of the tribe of Benjamin, a Hebrew of Hebrews; as touching the law, a Pharisee; ⁶ as touching zeal, persecuting the church; as touching the righteousness which is in the law, found blameless. ⁷ Howbeit what things were gain to me, these have I counted loss for Christ. ⁸ Yea verily, and I count all things to be loss for the excellency of the knowledge of Christ Jesus my Lord: for whom I suffered the loss of all things, and do count them but refuse, that I may gain Christ, ⁹ and be found in him, not having a righteousness of mine own, even that which is of the law, but that which is through faith in Christ, the righteousness which is from God by faith: ¹⁰ that I may know him, and the power of his resurrection, and the fellowship of his sufferings, becoming conformed to his death; ¹¹ if by any means I may attain to the resurrection from the dead. ¹² Not that I have already obtained, or am already made perfect: but I press on, if so be that I may lay hold on that for which also I was laid hold on by Christ Jesus. ¹³ Brethren, I count not myself yet to have laid hold: but one thing I do, forgetting the things which are behind, and stretching forward to the things which are before, ¹⁴ I press on toward the goal to the prize of the high calling of God in Christ Jesus. ¹⁵ Let us therefore, as many as are perfect, be thus minded: and if in anything you are otherwise minded, this also shall God reveal to you: ¹⁶ only, whereunto we have attained, by that same rule let us walk.

¹⁷ Brethren, be therefore imitators together of me, and mark them that so walk even as you have us for an example. ¹⁸ For many walk, of whom I told you often, and now tell you even weeping, that they are the enemies of the cross of Christ: ¹⁹ whose end is perdition, whose god is the belly, and whose glory

Philippians 3:1-16

Oddly, Paul begins this chapter of his letter with the word 'finally', suggesting this would be the final passage of the letter prior only to final greetings and a benediction. However, this is the third of four chapters.

Paul writes that writing for him is not 'irksome' and he does so because *'for you it is safe'*. By this Paul is referring to them being armed with sound teaching to which they are likely to need to resort to given that Paul has real concerns about those who would teach a false doctrine. Paul then references many things that the Philippians need to be aware of with a gentle reminder that *'we are the circumcision, who worship by the Spirit of God'*, and he relates his own background as being of the tribe of Benjamin and is himself circumcised, and of having persecuted Christians. He explains that he, however, has given up – *'^{8b} suffered the loss of all things, and do count them but refuse, that I may gain Christ'* – and has found *'^{9b} faith in Christ, the righteousness which is from God by faith: ¹⁰ that I may know him, and the power of his resurrection ¹¹ if by any means I may attain to the resurrection from the dead.'*

In verse 14, Paul writes, *'¹⁴ I press on toward the goal to the prize of the high calling of God in Christ Jesus. ¹⁵ Let us therefore, as many as are perfect, be thus minded'* by which he means to have the 'mind of Christ'; a phrase used by Paul in his letter to the Corinthians; 1 Cor. 2:16[b].

Paul is also referencing his earlier comments: *'even as it is right for me to be thus minded on behalf of you all'* [Philipp. 1:7] and *'that you are of the same mind, having the same love, being of one accord, of one mind; ³ doing nothing through faction or through vainglory, but in lowliness of*

is in their shame, who mind earthly things. ²⁰ For our citizenship is in heaven; whence also we wait for a Savior, the Lord Jesus Christ: ²¹ who shall fashion anew the body of our humiliation, that it may be conformed to the body of his glory, according to the working whereby he is able even to subject all things to himself.

mind each counting other better than himself; ⁴ not looking each of you to his own things, but each of you also to the things of others. ⁵ Have this mind in you, which was also in Christ Jesus:' [Philipp. 2:2-5]

Paul exhorts the Philippians to become as imitators, and for each to recognize those that do and to use them, including himself, as examples to follow. Paul calls out those who would be enemies of the cross *'whose end is perdition'* and he reminds the Philippians that the goal for all Christians is *'citizenship is in heaven'*.

The Goal of Life

Philippians 3:17-21

3 ¹⁷ Brethren, be therefore imitators together of me, and mark them that so walk even as you have us for an example. ¹⁸ For many walk, of whom I told you often, and now tell you even weeping, that they are the enemies of the cross of Christ: ¹⁹ whose end is perdition, whose god is the belly, and whose glory is in their shame, who mind earthly things. ²⁰ For our citizenship is in heaven; whence also we wait for a Savior, the Lord Jesus Christ: ²¹ who shall fashion anew the body of our humiliation, that it may be conformed to the body of his glory, according to the working whereby he is able even to subject all things to himself.

Paul exhorts the Philippians to become as imitators, and for each to recognize those that do and to use them, including himself, as examples to follow. Paul calls out those who would be enemies of the cross *'whose end is perdition'* and he reminds the Philippians that the goal for all Christians is *'citizenship is in heaven'*.

Stand Fast In The Lord

Philippians 4:1-9

4 Wherefore, my brethren beloved and longed for, my joy and crown, so stand fast in the Lord, my beloved.
² I exhort Euodia, and I exhort Syntyche, to be of the same mind in the Lord. ³ Yes, I ask you also, true yokefellow, help these women, for they labored with me in the gospel, with Clement also, and the rest of my fellow-workers, whose names are in the book of life.
⁴ Rejoice in the Lord always: again I will say, Rejoice. ⁵ Let your forbearance be known to all men. The Lord is at hand. ⁶ In nothing be anxious; but in everything by prayer and supplication with thanksgiving let your requests be made known to God. ⁷ And the peace of God, which passes all understanding, shall guard your hearts and your thoughts in Christ Jesus.
*⁸ Finally, brethren, **whatsoever things are true, whatsoever things are honorable, whatsoever things are just, whatsoever things are pure, whatsoever things are lovely, whatsoever things are of good report; if there be any virtue, and if there be any praise, think on these things**. ⁹ The things which you both learned and received and heard and saw in me, these things do: and the God of peace shall be with you.*
²³ The grace of the Lord Jesus Christ be with your spirit.

Paul describes the Philippians as *'my joy and crown'* and exhorts them to *'stand fast in the Lord'*. He then names Euodia and Syntyche and asks the Philippians to help them. Paul also mentions Clement another who had helped Paul with his ministry.

Paul offers reassurance: *'⁵ᵇ The Lord is at hand. ⁶ In nothing be anxious; but in everything by prayer and supplication with thanksgiving let your requests be made known to God. ⁷ And the peace of God, which passes all understanding, shall guard your hearts and your thoughts in Christ Jesus'*, which are words we hear often used, especially in benedictions, and those words are followed by another often quoted saying; Philipp. 4:8ᵇ.

God's Provisions

Philippians 4:10-23

4 ¹⁰ But I rejoice in the Lord greatly, that now at length you have revived your thought for me; wherein you did indeed take thought, but you lacked opportunity. ¹¹ Not that I speak in respect of want: for I have learned, in whatsoever state I am, therein to be content. ¹² I know how to be abased, and I know also how to abound: in everything and in all things have I learned the secret both to be filled and to be hungry, both to abound and to be in want. ¹³ I can do all things in him that strengthens me. ¹⁴ Howbeit you did well that you had fellowship with my affliction. ¹⁵ And you yourselves also know, you Philippians, that in the beginning of the gospel, when I departed from Macedonia, no church had fellowship with me in the matter of giving and receiving but you only; ¹⁶ for even in Thessalonica you sent once and again to my need. ¹⁷ Not that I seek for the gift; but I seek for the fruit that increases to your account. ¹⁸ But I have all things, and abound: I am filled, having received from Epaphroditus the things that came from you, an odor of a sweet smell, a sacrifice acceptable, well-pleasing to God. ¹⁹ And every need of yours according to his riches in glory in Christ Jesus. ²⁰ Now to our God and Father be the glory forever and ever. Amen.
²¹ Salute every saint in Christ Jesus. The brethren that are with me salute you. ²² All the saints salute you, especially they that are of Caesar's household.

In this final passage of Paul's letter to the Church in Philippi, he lavishes thanks and praise for the support that he has received from the Philippians, both support while he was with them and also support that they sent to him when he was in Macedonia and in Thessalonica, (one of the cities in east Macedonia such which are west of Philippi which is in the region of Thrace). Paul reminds the Philippians of how they had sent support via Epaphroditus to him and expresses his gratitude.

Paul concludes with an assurance that God will provide whatever their needs might be 'God will provide whatever their needs might be *'¹⁹ᵇ according to his riches in glory in Christ Jesus"*

The Compiled Teachings of The Apostle Paul

Colossians

Thankfulness for Spiritual Attainments 114
You Are Built Up in Christ 115
Put On the New Self 116
Family Relations 117
Speak With Grace 117

The Letter To The Colossians written by Paul at Rome

This letter to the Church in Colossae, like Paul's letters to the churches in Corinth (2 Corinthians) and Thessalonica both include Timothy's name in the initial greeting indicating that Timothy had ministered in both Corinth and Thessalonica and so was known to them. However, as there is no record of Paul visiting Colossae, as mentioned in the 2nd chapter, Paul mentions Laodicea which is close to Colossae but that doesn't confirm that Paul visited either city. As Timothy is referenced in the initial greeting it is possible (probable?) that Timothy had ministered in both Colossae and Laodicea, quite possibly visiting both on the way from Macedonia (Berea) to Corinth where he and Silas 'caught up with Paul': **Acts 18:**5 *When Silas and Timothy arrived from Macedonia.*

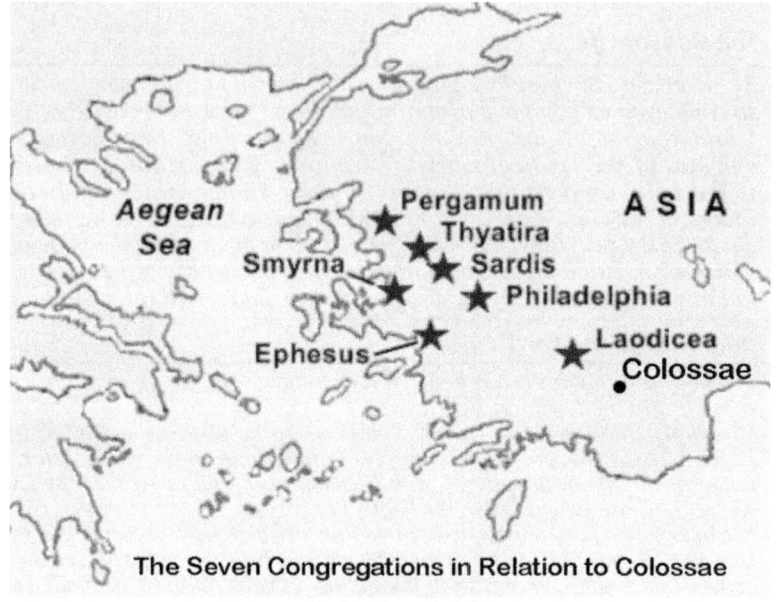

The Seven Congregations in Relation to Colossae

Thankfulness for Spiritual Attainments

Colossians 1:1-29

1 Paul, an apostle of Christ Jesus through the will of God, and Timothy our brother, 2 to the saints and faithful brethren in Christ that are at Colossae: Grace to you and peace from God our Father.

3 We give thanks to God the Father of our Lord Jesus Christ, praying always for you, 4 having heard of your faith in Christ Jesus, and of the love which you have toward all the saints, 5 because of the hope which is laid up for you in the heavens, whereof you heard before in the word of the truth of the gospel, 6 which is come to you; even as it is also in all the world bearing fruit and increasing, as it does in you also, since the day you heard and knew the grace of God in truth; 7 even as you learned from Epaphras our beloved fellow-servant, who is a faithful minister of Christ on our behalf, 8 who also declared to us your love in the Spirit.

The Incomparable Christ

1 9 For this cause we also, since the day we heard it, do not cease to pray and make request for you, that you may be filled with the knowledge of his will in all spiritual wisdom and understanding, 10 to walk worthily of the Lord to all pleasing, bearing fruit in every good work, and increasing in the knowledge of God; 11 strengthened with all power, according to the might of his glory, to all patience and longsuffering with joy; 12 giving thanks to the Father, who made us meet to be partakers of the inheritance of the saints in light; 13 who delivered us out of the power of darkness, and translated us into the kingdom of the Son of his love; 14 in whom we have our redemption, the forgiveness of our sins: 15 who is the image of the invisible God, the firstborn of all

A key to understanding that Paul had never ministered in Colossae beyond there being no record in the Book of Acts, is that Paul states, *4 'having heard of your faith in Christ Jesus, and of the love which you have toward all the saints'* [Col. 1:4]. In addition to the possibility that Timothy had ministered in Colossae, in v7 Paul also names Epaphras: *'7 even as you learned from Epaphras our beloved fellow-servant, who is a faithful minister of Christ on our behalf, 8 who also declared to us your love in the Spirit'* making it clear that it was Epaphras who had taught the Gospel to the Colossians.

After expressing his joy and gratitude that they understand and have embraced the Gospel, Paul transitions into a prayer for the Colossians; that they will continue to increase in *'spiritual wisdom and understanding'* of Jesus Christ *'15 who is the image of the invisible God, the firstborn of all creation'* is supreme and that because of His perfect sacrifice the penalty for sin has been completely removed: *19 For it was the good pleasure of the Father that in him should all the fulness dwell; 20 and through him*

creation; ¹⁶ *for in him were all things created, in the heavens and upon the earth, things visible and things invisible, whether thrones or dominions or principalities or powers; all things have been created through him, and to him;* ¹⁷ *and he is before all things, and in him all things consist.* ¹⁸ *And he is the head of the body, the church: who is the beginning, the firstborn from the dead; that in all things he might have the preeminence.* ¹⁹ *For it was the good pleasure of the Father that in him should all the fulness dwell;* ²⁰ *and through him to reconcile all things to himself, having made peace through the blood of his cross; through him, I say, whether things upon the earth, or things in the heavens.* ²¹ *And you, being in time past alienated and enemies in your mind in your evil works,* ²² *yet now has he reconciled in the body of his flesh through death, to present you holy and without blemish and unreproveable before him:* ²³ *if so be that you continue in the faith, grounded and steadfast, and not moved away from the hope of the gospel which you heard, which was preached in all creation under heaven; whereof I Paul was made a minister.*

1 ²⁴ *Now I rejoice in my sufferings for your sake, and fill up on my part that which is lacking of the afflictions of Christ in my flesh for his body's sake, which is the church;* ²⁵ *whereof I was made a minister, according to the dispensation of God which was given me to you-ward, to fulfil the word of God,* ²⁶ *even the mystery which had been hidden for ages and generations: but now has been manifested to his saints,* ²⁷ *to whom God was pleased to make known what is the riches of the glory of this mystery among the Gentiles, which is Christ in you, the hope of glory:* ²⁸ *whom we proclaim, admonishing every man and teaching every man in all wisdom, that we may present every man perfect in Christ;* ²⁹ *whereunto I labor also, striving according to his working, which works in me mightily.*

You Are Built Up in Christ

2 For I would have you know how greatly I strive for you, and for them at Laodicea, and for as many as have not seen my face in the flesh; ² *that their hearts may be comforted, they being knit together in love, and to all riches of the full assurance of understanding, that they may know the mystery of God, even Christ,* ³ *in whom are all the treasures of wisdom and knowledge hidden.* ⁴ *This I say, that no one may delude you with persuasiveness of speech.* ⁵ *For though I am absent in the flesh, yet am I with you in the spirit, joying and beholding your order, and the steadfastness of your faith in Christ.*
⁶ *As therefore you received Christ Jesus the Lord, so walk in him,* ⁷ *rooted and built up in him, and established in your faith, even as you were taught, abounding in thanksgiving.*
⁸ *Take heed lest there shall be any one that makes spoil of you through his philosophy and vain deceit, after the tradition of men, after the rudiments of the world, and not after Christ:* ⁹ *for in him dwelleth all the fulness of the Godhead bodily,* ¹⁰ *and in him you are made full, who is the head of all principality and power:* ¹¹ *in whom you were also circumcised with a circumcision not made with hands, in the putting off of the body of the flesh, in the circumcision of Christ;* ¹² *having been buried with him in baptism, wherein you were also raised with him through faith in the working of God, who raised him*

Paul reminds the Colossians that by continuing in the faith our pasts will be reconciled and our sins forgiven: ²¹ *And you, being in time past alienated and enemies in your mind in your evil works,* ²² *yet now has he reconciled in the body of his flesh through death, to present you holy and without blemish and unreproveable before him.*

Paul concludes his prayer with a warning to not allow themselves to move '*away from the hope of the gospel*' followed by a reminder that he had been made a minister of the Gospel which was to be preached to all nations.

Paul continues, referencing experiences of his ministry and explains that his task – the reason he was made a minister – was to bring the Gospel to all.

Paul claims that he had suffered for the sake of those at Colossae [Col. 1:24] which could be taken to understand that he had ministered in Colossae; but he had shared God's Word [Col. 1:25] and served as a missionary among the Gentiles [Col. 1:27]. As referenced [Col. 1:28] Paul has proclaimed Christ with all of his energy [Col. 1:29], and he sees this suffering as a service done for the sake of Christ.

Colossians 2:1-23

Paul references Laodicea, a city close to Colossae in the region of Phrygia, and Paul writes, '*1a for as many as have not seen my face in the flesh*' a phrase which suggests that either Paul had not visited either city, or, if he had, it may have been a very short-stay visit. If Paul hadn't ever visited Colossae, then he would be relying on reports from Timothy (who Paul mentioned in the greeting) and Epaphras [Col. 1:7b], and maybe others.

Paul exhorts the Colossians to '*7b walk in him,* ⁷ *rooted and built up in him, and established in your faith, even as you were taught, abounding in thanksgiving.*' and then Paul spells out a warning: ⁸ *Take heed lest there shall be any one that makes spoil of you through his philosophy and vain deceit, after the tradition of men, after the rudiments of the world, and not after Christ.* What Paul is saying here is, there are those who are teaching of the flesh but claiming and making it seem as though they are teaching the Gospel,

from the dead. ^{13} And you, being dead through your trespasses and the uncircumcision of your flesh, you, I say, did he make alive together with him, having forgiven us all our trespasses; ^{14} having blotted out the bond written in ordinances that was against us, which was contrary to us: and he has taken it out of the way, nailing it to the cross; ^{15} having despoiled the principalities and the powers, he made a show of them openly, triumphing over them in it.

2 ^{16} Let no man therefore judge you in meat, or in drink, or in respect of a feast day or a new moon or a sabbath day: ^{17} which are a shadow of the things to come; but the body is Christ's. ^{18} Let no man rob you of your prize by a voluntary humility and worshipping of the angels, dwelling in the things which he has seen, vainly puffed up by his fleshly mind, ^{19} and not holding fast the Head, from whom all the body, being supplied and knit together through the joints and bands, increases with the increase of God. ^{20} If you died with Christ from the rudiments of the world, why, as though living in the world, you subject yourselves to ordinances ^{21} Handle not, nor taste, nor touch ^{22} (all which things are to perish with the using), after the precepts and doctrines of men? ^{23} Which things have indeed a show of wisdom in will-worship, and humility, and severity to the body; but are not of any value against the indulgence of the flesh.

but they are not teaching the full truth of Jesus Christ.

A second warning that Paul gives them is that of who they should allow themselves to be judged by. Paul tells them that what they choose to eat and drink are not for anyone who is not in Christ to judge, and that those not in Christ advocating feast days based on the moon or other worldly events: *^{17} which are a shadow of the things to come.'* Paul explains that we should not be restricted by what other people think or believe especially when they have only a grasp of 'fleshly', aka earthly, thinking.

Paul hits hard against practices which he describes as *'indulgence of the flesh'*. He points to restrictions that he calls *'precepts and doctrines of men'* that are practices of worship which are merely superstitious observance that have no divine authority, but which people foolishly accept as having a redeeming value, but don't.

Put On the New Self

3 If then you were raised together with Christ, seek the things that are above, where Christ is, seated on the right hand of God. ^{2} Set your mind on the things that are above, not on the things that are upon the earth. ^{3} For you died, and your life is hidden with Christ in God. ^{4} When Christ, who is our life, shall be manifested, then shall you also with him be manifested in glory.

^{5} Put to death therefore your earthly body: putting aside fornication, uncleanness, passion, evil desire, and covetousness, which is idolatry; ^{6} for which things' sake comes the wrath of God upon the sons of disobedience: ^{7} wherein you also once walked, when you lived in these things; ^{8} but now do you put them all away also: anger, wrath, malice, railing, shameful speaking out of your mouth: ^{9} lie not one to another; seeing that you have put off the old man with his doings, ^{10} and have put on the new man, that is being renewed to a true knowledge according to the image of him that created him: ^{11} where there cannot be Greek and Jew, circumcision and uncircumcision, barbarian, Scythian*, bondman, freeman; but Christ is all, and in all.

^{12} Put on therefore, as God's elect, holy and beloved, a heart of compassion, kindness, lowliness, meekness, longsuffering; ^{13} forbearing one another, and forgiving each other, if any man has a complaint against another; even as the Lord forgave you, so you do also: ^{14} and above all these things put on love, which is the bond of perfectness. ^{15} And let the peace of Christ rule in your hearts, to the which also you were called in one body; and be thankful. ^{16} Let the word of Christ dwell in you richly; in all wisdom teaching and admonishing one another with psalms and hymns and spiritual songs, singing with grace in your hearts to God. ^{17} And whatsoever you do, in word or in deed, do all in the name of the Lord Jesus, giving thanks to God the Father through him.

Col 3:1-17

Paul begins to explain that if you are in Christ – *'were raised together with Christ'* – then, when Christ returns and is manifested in glory, then you too will be with Him in glory.

Paul tells them to put aside activities that do not honor God, which he describes as putting off the old man and his ways and, instead, putting on the new self, *'that is being renewed to a true knowledge according to the image of the One who created him'*, and this, without exception, is available for everyone.

Paul next 'preaches' a message of being holy, of having compassion, tolerance, forgiveness, love, and thankfulness which, by doing so, will give you the peace of Christ. Paul reminds them of the importance of the word of Christ, and as a community teaching and encouraging one another and *'^{16c} singing with grace in your hearts to God.'*

* *Scythians were closely related to ancient Iranian peoples who had migrated west and north to live in the western Asia/eastern Europe region north and west of The Black Sea and north of Macedonia and Thrace. Their religion included mythology, ritual practices and other beliefs. In contrast the Thracians were closely related to ancient Indo-European peoples. Their religions also included mythology, ritual practices and other beliefs.*

The Compiled Teachings of The Apostle Paul

Family Relations

Col 3:18-25

3 *18 Wives, be in subjection to your husbands, as is fitting in the Lord. 19 Husbands, love your wives, and be not bitter against them. 20 Children, obey your parents in all things, for this is well-pleasing in the Lord. 21 Fathers, provoke not your children, that they be not discouraged. 22 Servants, obey in all things them that are your masters according to the flesh; not with eye-service, as men-pleasers, but in singleness of heart, fearing the Lord: 23 whatsoever you do, work heartily, as to the Lord, and not to men; 24 knowing that from the Lord you shall receive the recompense of the inheritance: you serve the Lord Christ. 25 For he that does wrong shall receive again for the wrong that he has done: and there is no respect of persons.*

Here, Paul gives guidance for living as families. Included in families are servants who Paul exhorts to live '22c *fearing the Lord*' and Paul finishes by stating that if you wrong another, you will (should expect to) receive wrong against you, regardless of who you are.

Speak With Grace

Col 4:1-18

4 Masters, render to your servants that which is just and equal; knowing that you also have a Master in heaven.

2 Continue steadfastly in prayer, watching therein with thanksgiving; 3 additionally praying for us also, that God may open to us a door for the word, to speak the mystery of Christ, for which I am also in bonds; 4 that I may make it manifest, as I ought to speak. 5 Walk in wisdom toward them that are without, redeeming the time. 6 Let your speech be always with grace, seasoned with salt, that ye may know how you ought to answer each one.

7 All my affairs shall Tychicus make known to you, the beloved brother and faithful minister and fellow-servant in the Lord: 8 whom I have sent to you for this very purpose, that you may know our state, and that he may comfort your hearts; 9 together with Onesimus, the faithful and beloved brother, who is one of you. They shall make known to you all things that are done here.

10 Aristarchus my fellow-prisoner salutes you, and Mark, the cousin of Barnabas (touching whom you received commandments; if he comes to you, receive him), 11 and Jesus that is called Justus, who are of the circumcision: these only are my fellow-workers to the kingdom of God, men that have been a comfort to me. 12 Epaphras, who is one of you, a servant of Christ Jesus, salutes you, always striving for you in his prayers, that you may stand perfect and fully assured in all the will of God. 13 For I bear him witness, that he has much labor for you, and for them in Laodicea, and for them in Hierapolis. 14 Luke, the beloved physician, and Demas salute you. 15 Salute the brethren that are in Laodicea, and Nymphas, and the church that is in their house. 16 And when this epistle has been read among you, cause that it be read also in the church of the Laodiceans; and that you also read the epistle from Laodicea. 17 And say to Archippus, Take heed to the ministry which you have received in the Lord, that you fulfil it.

18 The salutation of me Paul with mine own hand. Remember my bonds. Grace be with you.

Paul now gives instructions to masters, that they their treatment should be '1 *just and equal,*' adding a reminder that they have a master in heaven.

Paul exhorts them to pray and to be sure to recognize when and how their prayers are met, giving thanks accordingly. Paul then switches from having a focus of their own needs to having a focus on his needs and the needs of his coworkers specifically asking them to pray for God to open a door for them to be able to preach the word.

Paul references Tychicus* who Paul states '*Shall make all my affairs known to you; I have sent (him) to you for this very purpose, that you may know our state, and that he may comfort your heart*'

*Tychicus is among those listed in Acts 20:4 who were with Paul in Macedonia and who travelled with Silas and others to Troas where they met up with Paul again. Tychius is also mentioned in 2 Tim. 4:12 as being sent by Paul to Ephesus.

Paul also mentions Onesimus, who is himself a Colossian, and then also mentions Aristarchus and '*Mark, the cousin of Barnabas*' who Paul exhorts to the Colossians; '10b *if he comes to you, receive him*'. Paul then again mentions Epaphras who he identifies as also being a co-worker who, like Onesimus, is a Colossian. Next Paul passes along greetings from Luke and Demas, and then he asks to be remembered to the churches in Laodicea and Nymphas and the church that meets in the house of Nymphas. Paul references an epistle from Laodicea and he mentions Archippus who might be the person who wrote the epistle from Laodicea.

The Compiled Teachings of The Apostle Paul

2 Timothy

Timothy Charged to Guard His Trust..................................... 118
Be Strong... 118
Difficult Times Will Come.. 119
Preach the Word.. 120

Paul's Second Letter To Timothy written by Paul at Rome

Timothy Charged to Guard His Trust

1 Paul, an apostle of Christ Jesus through the will of God, according to the promise of the life which is in Christ Jesus, ² to Timothy, my beloved child: Grace, mercy, peace, from God the Father and Christ Jesus our Lord.
³ I thank God, whom I serve from my forefathers in a pure conscience, how unceasing is my remembrance of you in my supplications, night and day ⁴ longing to see you, remembering your tears, that I may be filled with joy; ⁵ having been reminded of the unfeigned faith that you have; which dwelt first in your grandmother Lois, and your mother Eunice; and, I am persuaded, in you also. ⁶ For which cause I put you in remembrance that you stir up the gift of God, which is in you through the laying on of my hands. ⁷ For God gave us not a spirit of fearfulness; but of power and love and discipline. ⁸ Be not ashamed therefore of the testimony of our Lord, nor of me his prisoner: but suffer hardship with the gospel according to the power of God; ⁹ who saved us, and called us with a holy calling, not according to our works, but according to his own purpose and grace, which was given us in Christ Jesus before times eternal, ¹⁰ but has now been manifested by the appearing of our Savior Christ Jesus, who abolished death, and brought life and immortality to light through the gospel, ¹¹ whereunto I was appointed a preacher, and an apostle, and a teacher. ¹² For which cause I suffer also these things: yet I am not ashamed; for I know him whom I have believed, and I am persuaded that he is able to guard that which I have committed to him against that day. ¹³ Hold the pattern of sound words which you have heard from me, in faith and love which is in Christ Jesus. ¹⁴ That good thing which was committed to you guard through the Holy Spirit which dwells in us.
¹⁵ This you know, that all that are in Asia turned away from me; of whom are Phygelus and Hermogenes. ¹⁶ The Lord grant mercy to the house of Onesiphorus: for he often refreshed me, and was not ashamed of my chain; ¹⁷ but, when he was in Rome, he sought me diligently, and found me ¹⁸ (the Lord grant to him to find mercy of the Lord in that day); and in how many things he ministered at Ephesus, you know very well.

2 Tim. 1:1- 18

Paul wrote his first letter to Timothy written while Paul was in Nicopolis* while on his second missionary trip, but now he is writing from Rome, some considerable while later.
Paul follows his opening greeting lauding praise on Timothy, recalling that Timothy's grandmother, Lois, and his mother, Eunice, were both women of great faith. Paul also recalls how he anointed Timothy by the laying of his hands on him and then states '⁷ *For God gave us not a spirit of fearfulness; but of power and love and discipline.*'
Paul then exhorts Timothy to not be ashamed of the Gospel and to endure whatever hardships he may encounter, because, Paul says, it's because Jesus Christ who he has personally encountered (¹²ᵇ *for I know him whom I have believed*) which is the reason that he endures and is not ashamed. Then Paul adds advice that Timothy should stay true to what he, Paul, has taught him; '¹³ *Hold the pattern of sound words which you have heard from me, in faith and love which is in Christ Jesus. ¹⁴ That good thing which was committed to you guard through the Holy Spirit which dwells in us.*'
Paul then explains to Timothy, or rather reminds Timothy, that some of his co-workers in Asia turned away from Paul's teaching, and then Paul praises Onesiphorus for standing by him and coming to Rome and searching for him while was in prison until he found him; which confirms that Paul was in Rome in prison or at least under restrictions of parole when he wrote this letter.

Be Strong

2 You therefore, my child, be strengthened in the grace that is in Christ Jesus. ² And the things which you have heard from me among many witnesses, the same commit yourself to faithful men, who shall be able to teach others also. ³ Suffer hardship with me, as a good soldier of Christ Jesus. ⁴ No soldier on service entangles himself in the affairs of this life; that he may please him who enrolled him as a soldier. ⁵ And if also a man contends in the games, he is not crowned, except he has contended lawfully. ⁶ The husbandman that labors must be the first to partake of the fruits. ⁷ Consider what I say; for the Lord shall give you understanding in all things. ⁸ Remember Jesus Christ, risen from the dead, of the seed of David, according to my gospel: ⁹ wherein I suffer hardship of bonds, as a

2 Timothy 2:1-26

Paul writes this passage to Timothy inviting him to share in the ministry that he has personally committed to, inviting him to '*Suffer hardship*' with him. Hinting at the rewards Paul explains that '*The husbandman that labors must be the first to partake of the fruits*', and shares reassurance that God will help him understand all things, and explains why he accepts suffering, '⁹ *wherein I suffer hardship of bonds, as a malefactor; but the*

- 118 -

malefactor; but the word of God is not bound. ¹⁰ Therefore I endure all things for the elect's sake, that they also may obtain the salvation which is in Christ Jesus with eternal glory. ¹¹ Faithful is the saying: For if we died with him, we shall also live with him: ¹² if we endure, we shall also reign with him: if we shall deny him, he also will deny us: ¹³ if we are faithless, he abides faithful; for he cannot deny himself.

word of God is not bound. ¹⁰ Therefore I endure all things for the elect's sake, that they also may obtain the salvation which is in Christ Jesus with eternal glory.'

An Unashamed Worker

2 ¹⁴ Of these things put them in remembrance, charging them in the sight of the Lord, that they strive not about words, to no profit, to the subverting of them that hear. ¹⁵ Give diligence to present thyself approved unto God, a workman that needs not to be ashamed, handling aright the word of truth. ¹⁶ But shun profane babblings: for they will proceed further in ungodliness, ¹⁷ and their word will eat as does a gangrene: of whom is Hymenaeus and Philetus; ¹⁸ men who concerning the truth have erred, saying that the resurrection is past already, and overthrow the faith of some. ¹⁹ Howbeit the firm foundation of God stands, having this seal, The Lord knows them that are his: and, Let everyone that names the name of the Lord depart from unrighteousness. ²⁰ Now in a great house there are not only vessels of gold and of silver, but also of wood and of earth; and some unto honor, and some unto dishonor. ²¹ If a man therefore purge himself from these, he shall be a vessel unto honor, sanctified, meet for the master's use, prepared unto every good work. ²² But flee youthful lusts, and follow after righteousness, faith, love, peace, with them that call on the Lord out of a pure heart. ²³ But foolish and ignorant questionings refuse, knowing that they gender strifes. ²⁴ And the Lord's servant must not strive, but be gentle towards all, apt to teach, forbearing, ²⁵ in meekness correcting them that oppose themselves; if peradventure God may give them repentance unto the knowledge of the truth, ²⁶ and they may recover themselves out of the snare of the devil, having been taken captive by him unto his will.

2 Timothy 2:14-25

Paul reminds Timothy that a workman who is doing the right things does not need to be ashamed, and he warns Timothy of the danger of 'profane babblings' which are just the beginning of decline. Paul references two individuals who have begun preaching a false gospel regarding the resurrection, saying it is past already; but only the resurrection of Christ is past.

Paul them proclaims that *'the firm foundation of God stands, having this seal, The Lord knows them that are his: and, Let everyone that names the name of the Lord depart from unrighteousness'*, he warns Timothy to *'flee youthful lusts, and follow after righteousness, faith, love, peace, with them that call on the Lord out of a pure heart.' '²⁴ And the Lord's servant must not strive, but be gentle towards all, apt to teach, forbearing, ²⁵ in meekness correcting them that oppose themselves'*, and finally offering hope that *'they may recover themselves out of the snare of the devil, having been taken captive by him…'*

Difficult Times Will Come

3 But know this, that in the last days grievous times shall come. ² For men shall be lovers of self, lovers of money, boastful, haughty, railers, disobedient to parents, unthankful, unholy, ³ without natural affection, implacable, slanderers, without self-control, fierce, no lovers of good, ⁴ traitors, headstrong, puffed up, lovers of pleasure rather than lovers of God; ⁵ holding a form of godliness, but having denied the power thereof: from these also turn away. ⁶ For of these are they that creep into houses, and take captive silly women laden with sins, led away by divers lusts, ⁷ ever learning, and never able to come to the knowledge of the truth. ⁸ And even as Jannes and Jambres withstood Moses, so do these also withstand the truth; men corrupted in mind, reprobate concerning the faith. ⁹ But they shall proceed no further: for their folly shall be evident to all men, as theirs also came to be. ¹⁰ But you followed my teaching, conduct, purpose, faith, longsuffering, love, patience, ¹¹ persecutions, sufferings; what things befell me at Antioch, at Iconium, at Lystra; what persecutions I endured: and out of them all the Lord delivered me. ¹² Yea, and all that would live godly in Christ Jesus shall suffer persecution. ¹³ But evil men and impostors shall wax worse and worse, deceiving and being deceived. ¹⁴ But abide in the things which you have learned and have been assured of, knowing of whom you have learned them; ¹⁵ and that from a babe you have known the sacred writings which are able to make you wise unto salvation through faith which is in Christ Jesus. ¹⁶ Every scripture inspired of God is also profitable for teaching, for reproof, for correction, for instruction which is in righteousness: ¹⁷ that the man of God may be complete, furnished completely unto every good work.

2 Timothy 3:1-17

Paul transitions to prophecy, warning that people will become ungodly, becoming greedy, self-indulgent, disobedient, narcissistic, immoral and debased in many ways. Paul warns Timothy that *'all that (who) would live godly in Christ Jesus shall suffer persecution,'* [2 Tim. 3:12] Paul then catalogs many of the persecutions that he has suffered and endured before referencing that from a very young age he, Timothy, has been taught about salvation and faith in Christ. Paul ends this passage with a single sentence that is so often quoted by ministers, preachers and teachers of the Gospel, *'Every scripture inspired of God is also profitable for teaching, for reproof, for correction, for instruction which is in righteousness: ¹⁷ that the man of God may be complete, furnished completely unto every good work.'*

[2 Tim. 3:16-17]

Preach the Word

4 I charge thee in the sight of God, and of Christ Jesus, who shall judge the living and the dead, and by his appearing and his kingdom: ² preach the word; be urgent in season, out of season; reprove, rebuke, exhort, with all longsuffering and teaching. ³ For the time will come when they will not endure the sound doctrine; but, having itching ears, will heap to themselves teachers after their own lusts; ⁴ and will turn away their ears from the truth, and turn aside unto fables. ⁵ But be sober in all things, suffer hardship, do the work of an evangelist, fulfil thy ministry. ⁶ For I am already being offered, and the time of my departure is come. ⁷ I have fought the good fight, I have finished the course, I have kept the faith: ⁸ henceforth there is laid up for me the crown of righteousness, which the Lord, the righteous judge, shall give to me at that day; and not to me only, but also to all them that have loved his appearing.

Personal Concerns

⁹ Give diligence to come shortly to me: ¹⁰ for Demas forsook me, having loved this present world, and went to Thessalonica; Crescens to Galatia, Titus to Dalmatia. ¹¹ Only Luke is with me. Take Mark, and bring him with you; for he is useful to me for ministering. ¹² But Tychicus I sent to Ephesus. ¹³ When you come, bring the cloak that I left at Troas with Carpus, and the books, especially the parchments. ¹⁴ Alexander the coppersmith did me much evil: the Lord will render to him according to his works: ¹⁵ of whom do thou also beware; for he greatly withstood our words. ¹⁶ At my first defense no one took my part, but all forsook me: may it not be laid to their account. ¹⁷ But the Lord stood by me, and strengthened me; that through me the message might be fully proclaimed, and that all the Gentiles might hear: and I was delivered out of the mouth of the lion. ¹⁸ The Lord will deliver me from every evil work, and will save me unto his heavenly kingdom: to whom be the glory for ever and ever. Amen.

¹⁹ Salute Prisca and Aquila, and the house of Onesiphorus. ²⁰ Erastus remained at Corinth: but Trophimus I left at Miletus sick. ²¹ Give diligence to come before winter. Eubulus saluteth thee, and Pudens, and Linus, and Claudia, and all the brethren.

²² The Lord be with thy spirit. Grace be with you.

2 Timothy 4:1-22

Paul now gives Timothy his commission, that is to preach the Word, instructing him to '*be urgent in season, out of season; reprove, rebuke, exhort, with all longsuffering and teaching*' and shares further warnings regarding teachers of false gospels. In verse 6, Paul acknowledges that he has only a short time left stating, '*I have fought the good fight, I have finished the course, I have kept the faith*' and references that he believes that, '*there is laid up for me the crown of righteousness, which the Lord, the righteous judge, shall give to me at that day; and not to me only, but also to all them that have loved his appearing.*'

Paul then begins to close out his letter by mentioning the names of some that he hopes will be able to visit him, being unable to travel himself because of his house arrest confinement. Paul specifically mentions that Luke is the only one there with him, and in the next verse he asks Timothy to come and visit him and bring Mark with him and to bring a coat that he left at Troas and '*especially the parchments*'.

Paul references Alexander the coppersmith who had stood against him warning Timothy that this was a person to be wary of. While Paul states that he expects the '*the Lord will render to him (Alexander) according to his works*' (v14), he hopes that for others that did not stand by him, '*may it not be laid to their account.*' Again, Paul repeats that his faith in God was justified because the '*Lord stood by*' him and he expects that '*The Lord will deliver me from every evil work, and will save me to his heavenly kingdom: to whom be the glory for ever and ever. Amen.*' [2 Tim. 4:18]

Finally, Paul concludes the letter with greetings and a brief doxology.

The Compiled Teachings of The Apostle Paul

Philemon

Philemon's Love and Faith..121
Plea for Onesimus, a Free Man..................................121

Paul's Letter To Philemon written by Paul at Rome

Philemon's Love and Faith

Philemon 1:1-3

> **Salutation**
>
> 1 *Paul, a prisoner of Christ Jesus, and Timothy our brother,*
> *To Philemon our beloved brother and fellow worker,* ² *and to Apphia our sister, and to Archippus our fellow soldier, and to the church in your house:* ³ *Grace to you and peace from God our Father and the Lord Jesus Christ.*

In this epistle, which is addressed from Paul and Timothy to Philemon, Apphia and Archippus, Paul refers to Philemon as a *'beloved fellow worker'*. We know from Colossians 4:17 that Archippus is a prominent leader in the church in Colossae, and from that and other sources we understand Philemon to also be with the church in Colossae where he hosts a church in his home. That this final letter written by Paul states that it is from Paul and Timothy suggests that Paul's wish for Timothy to come and visit him in Rome [2 Tim. 4:18] was fulfilled. That the letter reached Philemon perhaps suggests that Timothy made another visit to Colossae.

Philemon's Love and Faith

Philemon 1:4-9

> *1* ⁴ *I thank my God always, making mention of you in my prayers,* ⁵ *because I hear of your love and of the faith which you have toward the Lord Jesus and toward all the saints;* ⁶ *and I pray that the fellowship of your faith may become effective through the knowledge of every good thing which is in you for the sake of Christ.* ⁷ *For I have had great joy and comfort in your love, because the hearts of the saints have been refreshed through you, brother.*
>
> ⁸ *Therefore, though I have enough confidence in Christ to order you to do what is proper,* ⁹ *yet for love's sake I rather appeal to you – since I am such a person as Paul, an old man, and now also a prisoner of Christ Jesus –*

After giving thanks, Paul states, *'though I have enough confidence in Christ to order you to do what is proper,* ⁹ *yet for love's sake I rather appeal to you – since I am such a person as Paul, an old man, and now also a prisoner of Christ Jesus –'* [Philn. 1: 8] and he explains that he is *'a prisoner of Christ Jesus'*, which could be a reference to being in detention in Rome rather than them both being servants of the Lord.

Plea for Onesimus, a Free Man

Philemon 1:10-25

> ¹⁰ *I appeal to you for my son Onesimus, whom I fathered in my imprisonment,* ¹¹ *who previously was useless to you, but now is useful both to you and to me.* ¹² *I have sent him back to you in person, that is, sending my very heart,* ¹³ *whom I wanted to keep with me, so that in your behalf he might be at my service in my imprisonment for the gospel;* ¹⁴ *but I did not want to do anything without your consent, so that your goodness would not be, in effect, by compulsion, but of your own free will.* ¹⁵ *For perhaps it was for this reason that he was separated from you for a while, that you would have him back forever,* ¹⁶ *no longer as a slave, but more than a slave, a beloved brother, especially to me, but how much more to you, both in the flesh and in the Lord.*
>
> ¹⁷ *If then you regard me as a partner, accept him as you would me.* ¹⁸ *But if he has wronged you in any way or owes you anything, charge that to my account;* ¹⁹ *I, Paul, have written this with my own hand, I will repay it (not to mention to you that you owe to me even your own self as well).* ²⁰ *Yes, brother, let me benefit from you in the Lord; refresh my heart in Christ.*
>
> ²¹ *Having confidence in your obedience, I write to you, since I know that you will do even more than what I say.*
>
> ²² *At the same time also prepare me a guest room, for I hope that through your prayers I will be given to you.*
>
> ²³ *Epaphras, my fellow prisoner in Christ Jesus, greets you,* ²⁴ *as do Mark, Aristarchus, Demas, and Luke, my fellow workers.*
>
> ²⁵ *The grace of the Lord Jesus Christ be with your spirit.*

Paul is about to make a special request on behalf of Onesimus is most likely the reason for emphasizing that he is making a request and is not issuing an order or directive. Onesimus, Paul explains, *'previously was useless to you, but now is useful both to you and to me.'* [Philn. 1: 8]

Onesimus was a slave in the household of Philemon and who ran away and became attached to Paul and his companions. Paul clearly believes that Onesimus has changed for the better and deserves to be given a second chance rather than punished for being a runaway.

Paul states *'I, Paul, have written this with my own hand'* and proceeds to offer to compensate Philemon but also points out to Philemon, *'(not to mention to you that you owe to me even your own self as well).'*

Paul finishes up with greetings from Epaphras who Paul refers to as a *'fellow prisoner in Christ Jesus'*, and greetings too from *'Mark, Aristarchus, Demas, and Luke, my fellow workers.'*

The Compiled Teachings of The Apostle Paul

Section 4
Quick Reference Listing of The Teachings of Paul **122**
An Expanded Summarization of The Teachings of Paul **124**

By including additional text to provide context, this fourth section is intended to add explanation to the detailed reference listing of the major topics that Paul teaches that are provided in the Section 1.

See 1st section for 'quick reference' listing of the major topics that Paul teaches on.
See 2nd section for the full account of Paul provided by Luke in the Book of Acts with commentary.
See 3rd section for the documented teachings of Paul, letter-by-letter.

Quick Reference Listing of The Teachings of Paul The Apostle
See Section 2 for the full account of Paul's Mission Trips provided by Luke in the Book of Acts, with commentary.
See Section 3 for the documented teachings of Paul, letter-by-letter, with commentary.

Admonish, Admonishing, Admonishment
Acts 20:31
1 Cor. 4:14
Rom. 15:14
1 Thess. 5:12; 5:13
2 Thess. 3:15
Col. 1:27; Col. 3:16

Adulterer, Adulteress
1 Cor. 6:9
Rom. 1:3

Adultery (see also Fornication)
Rom. 2:22; Rom. 13:9

Anointing – see Laying on of hands

Apostle(s)
Acts 9:27; Acts 14:4; Acts 14:14; Acts 15:2; Acts 15:4; Acts 15:6; Acts 15:22; Acts 16:4
Gal. 1:1; Gal. 1:17; Gal. 1:19; Gal. 2:8
1 Cor. 1:1; 1 Cor. 4:9; 1 Cor. 9:1; 1 Cor. 9:2; 1 Cor. 12:28; 1 Cor. 14:7
2 Cor. 11:5; 2 Cor. 11:13; 2 Cor. 12:11^b; 2 Cor. 1:1
Rom. 1:1; Rom. 1:4^b; Rom. 1:5; Rom. 11:13; Rom. 16:7
1 Thess. 2:5^b
1 Tim. 1:1
Titus 1:1
Col. 1:1
2 Tim. 1:1; 2 Tim. 1:11

Bishop(s)
Phile. 1:1
Titus 1:5^b

Circumcise, Circumcision, Circumcised
Acts 7:8; Acts 7:51; Acts 15:1; Acts 15:5; Acts 16:3; Acts 20:21
Gal. 2:9; Gal. 2:12; Gal. 5:2; Gal. 5:6; Gal. 5:11; Gal. 6:12, Gal. 12:3; Gal. 12:7;
1 Cor. 7:18
Rom. 2:25; Rom. 3:1; Rom. 3:29^b; Rom. 4:9; Rom. 15:8
Eph. 2:11
Philipp. 3:2
Col. 2:11; Col. 3:11; Col. 4:11
Titus 1:10

Daughter(s)
Acts 2:16; Acts 7:21; Acts 21:9
1 Cor. 7:36
2 Cor. 6:18; 2 Cor. 6:37

Deacons
1 Tim. 3:8
Philipp. 1:1

Elders
Acts 6:12; Acts 11:29; Acts 14:23; Acts 15:2; Acts 15:4; Acts 15:6; Acts 15:22; Acts 16:4; Acts 20:17; Acts 20:17; Acts 4:1; Acts 23:12; Acts 24:1; Acts 25:13
Rom. 9:12
1 Tim. 5:1; 1 Tim. 5:17
Titus 1:5

Emasculation (Castration)
Gal. 4:11

Encourage(d), Encouragement, Exhort
Rom. 1:12; 1 Thess. 5:14; Col. 4:10-11

Faith
2 Cor. 1:23^b, 2 Cor. 4:13, 2 Cor. 5:6, 2 Cor. 8:7, 2 Cor. 10:15^b, 2 Cor. 13:4,
Rom. 1:8, Rom. 1:17, Rom. 2:3, Rom. 3:22, Rom. 3:24, Rom. 3:27, Rom. 3:28, Rom. 3:30, Rom. 3:31, Rom. 4:5, Rom. 4:9, Rom. 4:11, Rom. 4:13, Rom. 4:16, Rom. 4:18, Rom. 5:1, Rom. 9:10, Rom. 10:6, Rom. 11:20, Rom. 12:3^b, Rom. 12:6^b, Rom. 14:1, Rom. 14:22, Rom. 16:26^b,
1 Thess. 1:3, 1 Thess. 1:8, 1 Thess. 3:2, 1 Thess. 3:4, 1 Thess. 3:6, 1 Thess. 3:9, 1 Thess. 5:8,
2 Thess. 1:3^b, 2 Thess. 1:11, 2 Thess. 3:2^b
1 Tim. 1:2, 1 Tim. 4:4, 1 Tim. 4:14, 1 Tim. 4:18^b, 1 Tim. 2:7, 1 Tim. 2:14^b, 1 Tim. 3:8, 1 Tim. 3:13, 1 Tim. 4:1, 1 Tim. 4:6^b, 1 Tim. 4:12
Titus 3:15^b
Ephes. 1:15, Ephes. 2:8, Ephes. 3:11, Ephes. 3:17, Ephes. 4:4^b, Ephes. 4:12^b, Ephes. 6:16, Ephes. 6:23
1 Philipp. 1:25^b, 1 Philipp. 1:27^b, 1 Philipp. 2:17, 1 Philipp. 3:9^b
1 Col. 1:3

Faithful(ness)
Acts 16:15,
1 Cor. 1:9, 1 Cor. 4:1^b, 1 Cor. 10:13,
2 Cor. 1:18,
1 Thess. 5:24^b,
2 Thess. 3:3, 1 Tim. 1:12,
1 Tim. 1:15, 1 Tim. 3:1, 1 Tim. 3:11, 1 Tim. 4:9,
1 Tim. 5:8, 1 Tim. 6:10,
1 Titus 1:4, 1 Titus 1:13^b, 1 Titus 2:2, 1 Titus 3:8,
Ephes. 6:22,
1 Coloss. 1:7

Father(s)
Acts 16:1; Acts 22:1; Acts 28:8; Acts 28:17; Acts 28:25
Gal. 1:14
1 Cor. 4:15; 1 Cor. 5:1; 1 Cor. 10:1
1 Thess. 2:10
1 Tim. 1:9; 1 Tim. 5:5
Eph. 5:29; Eph. 6:1
Philipp. 2:20
Col. 3:20

Father, Abraham
2 Cor. 12:4.
Rom. 4:16; Rom. 9:7

Forgave, Forgive, Forgiving, Forgiveness
Acts 26:16^b
Eph. 1:7
2 Cor. 2:5; 2 Cor. 12:12
Rom. 4:4^b
Eph. 1:3; Eph. 4:31
Col. 1:10; Col. 1:13; Col 2:12; Col 3:12

Fornication (see also Adultery), Fornicator(s)
1 Cor. 5:1; 1 Cor. 5:9;
1 Cor. 6:9; 1 Cor. 6:13; 1 Cor. 6:15
1 Tim. 1:9
1 Cor. 7:1; 1 Cor. 9:7; 1 Cor. 12:19^b
1 Tim. 1:8;
Eph. 5:3
Col. 3:3

The Compiled Teachings of The Apostle Paul

God (Father), God of our Fathers
*Acts 2:32; Acts 13:16; Acts 13:32; Acts 13:36;
Acts 15:10; Acts 22:14; Acts 23:14; Acts 26:5b
Gal. 1:1; Gal. 4:2
1 Cor. 8:5; 1 Cor. 15:24
2 Cor. 1:3; 2 Cor. 6:17; 2 Cor. 11:30
Rom. 6:4; Rom. 8:15; Rom. 9:3; Rom. 11:28;
Rom. 14:6; Rom. 15:7
Eph. 1:1; Eph. 1:2; Eph. 1:3; Eph. 1:16; Eph. 2:17;
Eph. 3:14; Eph. 4:4; Eph. 4:18; Eph. 6:23
Philipp. 1:3; Philipp. 2:10; Philipp. 4:19
Col. 1:1; Col. 1:2b; Col. 1:3; Col. 1:9b; Col. 3:16
1 Tim. 1:1
2 Tim. 1:1
1 Thess. 1; 1 Thess. 1:4; 1 Thess. 3:11
2 Thess. 1; 2 Thess. 2:16
1 Titus 1:4
2 Tim. 1:2
Phile. 1:3*

Grace of God
*Acts 14:24
1 Cor. 3:10; 1 Cor. 1:4; 1 Cor. 15:10
2 Cor. 6:1; 2 Cor. 6:6; 2 Cor. 8:1; 2 Cor. 9:12;
2 Cor. 9:14
Eph. 3:1; Eph. 3:2; Eph. 3:7
Col. 1:3; Col. 1:6; Titus 2:11*

Gossip – see also Tattlers
Rom. 1:28

Husband(s)
*Gal. 4:24b
1 Cor. 3:8
1 Cor. 7:1; 1 Cor. 7:10; 1 Cor. 7:13; 1 Cor. 7:32b;
1 Cor. 7:39; 1 Cor. 14:33b
2 Cor. 1:1
Rom. 7:1b
1 Tim. 3:1; 1 Tim. 3:12
Titus 1:5b; Titus 2:3b
Eph. 5:22; Eph. 5:28; Col. 3:18*

Laying On of Hands
*Acts 9:11b; Acts 9:17; Acts 9:10;
Acts 13:2; Acts 14:3; Acts 19:4;
Acts 21:27; Acts 28:8
1 Tim. 2:8; 1 Tim. 4:14; 1 Tim. 5:21
2 Tim 1:6*

Marriage
*1 Cor. 7:1b; 1 Cor. 7:26; 1 Cor. 7:3; 1 Cor. 7:36
Rom. 7:7
1 Tim. 4:1; 1 Tim. 5:9
Eph. 5:22*

Minister(ing) – *verb*
*2 Cor. 3:1; 2 Cor. 8:1; 2 Cor. 9:9
Rom. 15:22
Eph. 3:11
2 Tim. 4:9*

Minister(s) – *Noun*
*1 Cor 3:4; 1 Cor. 4:1; 2 Cor. 11:12
2 Cor. 6:6; 2 Cor. 8:16; 2 Cor. 11:18
Rom. 13:1; Rom. 15:15
Gal. 2:15
1 Thess. 3:1
1 Tim. 4:4
Eph. 3:1; Eph. 6:10
Col. 1:3; Col. 1:19; Col. 4:2*

Ministration
*1 Cor. 12:4
2 Cor. 9:12*

Ministry
*Acts 20:17; Acts 21:17
2 Cor. 4:1; 2 Cor. 5:14
Rom. 11:11; Rom. 12:3
Col. 4:10
2 Tim. 2:15; 2 Tim. 4:1
Phile. 1:8*

Pastor(s), **Preacher**(s)
*Acts 17:16
1 Cor. 9:13; 1 Cor. 15:15
Rom. 10:14
2 Tim. 1:8
Rom. 10:11
1 Tim. 2:5
2 Tim. 1:8*

Prophecy, Prophetic, Prophet(s)
*Acts 11:27; Acts 13:1; Acts 13:6; Acts 13:36;
Acts 15:30; Acts 19:6; Acts 21:10
1 Cor. 12:7; 1 Cor. 13:1
Rom. 1:1
1 Tim. 1:18*

Redeem(ed), **Redemption**
*Gal. 3:11; Gal. 4:4
Rom. 3:21; Rom. 8:22
Eph. 1:4b
Col. 1:13
Titus 2:11
Eph. 1:3; Eph. 4:25; Eph. 4:15
Col. 1:9; Col. 4:1*

Son(s) – except Sons of God; see next section below:
*Acts 16:1; Acts 19:13; Gal. 3:6; Gal. 4:28;
Rom. 9:6; 1 Thess. 5:4*

Son of God
*Acts 9:19b; Acts 13:17; Acts 13:26
1 Cor. 15:27
2 Cor. 15:18
Rom. 1:8; Rom. 5:8; Rom. 8:2; Rom. 8:19;
Rom. 8:29; Rom. 8:31
Gal. 2:19*

Sons of God – except Son (singular) of God
*Rom. 8:12
Gal. 3:23; Gal. 4:4; Gal. 4:21
1 Thess. 1:9*

Son of Perdition, Son of The Devil
*Acts 13:9
2 Thess. 2:3b*

Sons of The Lord
*Acts 7:30; Acts 9:1; Acts 9:28; Acts 9:31;
Acts 11:20; Acts 13:9b; Acts 13:46; Acts 15:6;
Acts 15:32; Acts 15:36; Acts 15:39b; Acts 16:29;
Acts 18:4; Acts 19:1; Acts 19:8; Acts 19:13;
Acts 20:35; Acts 21:13
1 Cor. 2:10; 1 Cor. 5:2; 1 Cor. 7:25; 1 Cor. 7:32b;
1 Cor. 9:4; 1 Cor. 10:9; 1 Cor. 10:20; 1 Cor. 11:23;
1 Cor. 11:31; 1 Cor. 14:37; 1 Cor. 15:58;
1 Cor. 16:10; 1 Cor. 16:22
2 Cor. 3:17; 2 Cor. 5:11; 2 Cor. 5:19 b;
2 Cor. 11:30; 2 Cor. 12:1; 2 Cor. 13:14
Rom. 10:12; Rom. 10:34*

Sons of The Lord (Cont'd)
*1 Thess. 1:6; 1 Thess. 4:15; 1 Thess. 5:1;
1 Thess. 5:5b;
2 Thess. 2:1b; 2 Thess. 2:13; 2 Thess. 3:1b;
2 Thess. 3:17b
Eph. 6:1; Eph. 4:14
Philipp. 4:23
Col. 1:9; Col. 3:16*

Tattler(s) – see also Gossip
1 Tim. 4:11

Teacher(s)
Acts 13:1

Temptation
*Gal. 5:19-21
1 Cor. 10:13
1 Tim. 6:10-11*

Tongues
*Acts 12:8; Acts 19:6
1 Cor. 12:6; 1 Cor. 12:28; 1 Cor. 13:1;
1 Cor. 14:4; 1 Cor. 14:6; 1 Cor. 14:16;
1 Cor. 14:21; 1 Cor. 14:37*

Virgin(s)
*1 Cor. 7:25; 1 Cor. 7:34b; 1 Cor. 7:36
2 Cor. 11:2*

Widow(s), Widowed
*1 Cor. 7:7b;
1 Tim. 5:3; 1 Tim. 5:9; 1 Tim. 5:14; 1 Tim. 5:16*

Wife, Wives
*Acts 18:1; Acts 24:24
1 Cor. 5:1; 1 Cor. 7:1b; 1 Cor. 7:4; 1 Cor. 7:5;
1 Cor. 7:12; 1 Cor. 7:14; 1 Cor. 7:16; 1 Cor. 7:26;
1 Cor. 7:32b; 1 Cor. 7:39; 1 Cor. 9:5
1 Tim. 3:2; 1 Tim. 3:12; 1 Tim. 5:9
Titus 1:5
Eph. 5:23; Eph. 5:25; Eph. 5:28; Eph. 5:31*

Wisdom
*1 Cor. 1:17; Col. 1:9; 1 Cor. 2:1b; 1 Cor. 2:12;
1 Cor. 3:19; 1 Cor.11:7
Rom. 11:33
Eph. 1:7; Eph. 3:10b
Col. 1:9b; Col. 1:27; Col. 2:1b; Col. 2:23;
Col. 3:16; Col. 4:5*

Women
*Acts 8:1; Acts 9:1; Acts 16:1; Acts 16:13;
Acts 17:3 b; Acts 17:11b; Acts 17:33;
Acts 17:4
Gal. 1:15; Gal. 4:4; Gal. 4:22; Gal. 4:27;
Gal. 4:30
1 Cor. 7:1; 1 Cor. 7:12b; 1 Cor. 7:1b; 1 Cor. 7:32b;
1 Cor. 11:3; 1 Cor. 14:34
Rom. 1:26; Rom. 7:2
1 Thess. 5:2
1 Tim. 2:8; 1 Tim. 3:10; 1 Tim. 5:1; 1 Tim. 5:16
Titus 2:3
Philipp. 4:2
2 Tim. 3:6*

The Compiled Teachings of The Apostle Paul

An Expanded Summarization of The Teachings of Paul

The Key words list of the Quick Reference Listing of The Teachings of Paul The Apostle is duplicated here, but a summarization for each word or term reference in the text of Acts or in any of the Epistles has been added.

... of The Lord

This passage in Acts 7 is from Stephen's speech. In this speech [Acts 7:1-53] Stephen reminds the Jews of their heritage and of the treatment that their fathers had given the prophets of God.

Acts 7:30...a voice of the Lord
*And when forty years were fulfilled, an angel appeared to him in the wilderness of mount Sinai, in a flame of fire in a bush. [31] And when Moses saw it, he wondered at the sight: and as he drew near to behold, there came **a voice of the Lord**, [32] I am the God of thy fathers, the God of Abraham, and of Isaac, and of Jacob. And Moses trembled, and dared not behold.*

Saul, who had heard Stephen's speech, and who was trained by Gamaliel [Acts 5:31-39; 22:3], began persecuting those who were believers in Jerusalem [Acts 8:1-3; 9:1–2]. In this passage Luke refers to the believers as 'disciples of the Lord'.

Acts 9:1 ...the disciples of the Lord
*"Saul, still breathing threats and murder against **the disciples of the Lord**, went to the High Priest, and asked for letters from him (the High Priest) to the synagogues at Damascus, so that if he found any belonging to The Way, both men and women, he might bring them bound to Jerusalem."*

This passage is about Saul, who having had an encounter with Jesus on the road to Damascus [Acts 93-27] is now a changed person, and he has returned to Jerusalem.

Acts 9:28 ... in the name of the Lord
*And he (Saul) was with them going in and going out at Jerusalem, [29] preaching boldly **in the name of the Lord**: and he spoke and disputed against the Grecian Jews; but they were seeking to kill him.*

As Saul had left Judea and had gone to Tarsus, the anger against the church subsided and the calm the church in Judea and Samaria are witnessing was the direct work of the Holy Spirit.
For believers, the "fear of the Lord" combines a deep respect for God with the understanding that He hates sin. Comfort" is from the Greek root word *paraklēsis*, meaning "solace and refreshment." [www.bibleref.com/Acts/9/Acts-9-31.html]

Acts 9:31 ...the fear of the Lord
*So the church throughout all Judaea and Galilee and Samaria had peace, being edified; and, walking in **the fear of the Lord** and in the comfort of the Holy Spirit, was multiplied.*

Acts 11:20 ... the hand of the Lord
*But there were some of them, men of Cyprus and Cyrene, who, when they had come to Antioch, spoke to the Greeks also, preaching the Lord Jesus. [21] And **the hand of the Lord** was with them: and a great number that believed turned to the Lord.*

Jews who regularly interacted with Gentiles had much less resistance to the idea that Jesus had come for the Gentiles as well as the Jews. They saw no reason why their friends wouldn't be interested in Jesus and even less doubt that Jesus would be interested in their friends.

In this passage we see Paul invoking the hand of the Lord as he accuses Elymas, a sorcerer (magician) who opposed Paul and his companions, of being 'full of all guile and all villainy' and calls him 'son of the devil' and 'enemy of all righteousness' because he was seeking to turn the proconsul away from believing.

Acts 13:9[b]   ...the right ways of the Lord   ... the hand of the Lord
*But Saul, who is also called Paul, filled with the Holy Spirit, fastened his eyes on him, [10] and said, "O full of all guile and all villainy, you son of the devil, you enemy of all righteousness, will you not cease to pervert **the right ways of the Lord**? [11] And now, behold, **the hand of the Lord** is upon you, and you shall be blind, not seeing the sun for a season. And immediately there fell upon him a mist and a darkness; and he went about seeking some to lead him by the hand. [12] Then the proconsul, when he saw what was done, believed, being astonished at **the teaching of the Lord**.*

Acts 13:46 ... the word of God
*And Paul and Barnabas spoke out boldly, and said, It was necessary that **the word of God** should first be spoken to you. Seeing you thrust it from you, and judge yourselves unworthy of eternal life, lo, we turn to the Gentiles. [47] For so has the Lord commanded us, saying, I have set thee for a light of the Gentiles, that you shouldest be for salvation unto the uttermost part of the earth. [48] And as the Gentiles heard this, they were glad, and **glorified the word of God**: and as many as were ordained to eternal life believed. [49] And **the word of the Lord** was spread abroad throughout all the region.*

Paul and Barnabas berate the Jews for rejecting the Gospel, the Word of God, in this passage – the synagogue leaders had rejected the Gospel because they were jealous of the following that Paul and Barnabas had attracted – and they (Paul and Barnabas) explain why they chose to take the message (the Gospel) to the Gentiles [v47], and they report that 'the Word of the Lord' was gladly received by the Gentiles who '*glorified the word of God*', and '*the word of the Lord was spread throughout the region*' (of Asia Minor).

The Compiled Teachings of The Apostle Paul

In this passage, Peter, with Paul and others of the church in Jerusalem, explains to the leaders of the Jews why he (Peter) was chosen to take *'the word of the gospel'* to the Gentiles; that God *'made no distinction between us and them'* and that He (God) had *'cleansed their hearts by faith'*. Peter then challenges the Jews by asking why they were putting God to the test when Jews know all too well that the Scriptures tell them not to put God to the test [Deut. 6:16; Exodus 17:1-7] except as regards putting God first [Mal. 3:10], and Peter finishes by stating, *'¹¹ But we believe that we (Jews) will be saved through **the grace of the Lord Jesus**, just as they will'*, implying that the Gentiles do not need to live under the Law with regard to such requirements as circumcision.

If, as the text suggests, Paul was there hearing this speech he might have felt that Peter was taking away something that he had a right to, namely that he had been chosen to be the one to take the Gospel to the Gentiles. Peter, however, also had a legitimate claim – see Acts 10:9-33.

Acts 15:6   ...the word of the gospel
*Peter stood up and said to them, "Brothers, you know that in the early days God made a choice among you, that by my mouth the Gentiles should hear **the word of the gospel** and believe. ⁸ And God, who knows the heart, bore witness to them, by giving them the Holy Spirit just as he did to us, ⁹ and he made no distinction between us and them, having cleansed their hearts by faith. ¹⁰ Now, therefore, why are you putting God to the test by placing a yoke on the neck of the disciples that neither our fathers nor we have been able to bear? ¹¹ But we believe that we will be saved through **the grace of the Lord Jesus**, just as they will."*

Acts 15:32   ...the word of the Lord
*And Judas and Silas, who were themselves prophets, encouraged and strengthened the brothers with many words. ³³ And after they had spent some time, they were sent off in peace by the brothers to those who had sent them. ³⁵ But Paul and Barnabas remained in Antioch, teaching and preaching **the word of the Lord**, with many others also.*

In these next two passages we see Paul and Barnabas separating, each with a new partner setting off in different geographical directions. Paul travelled first to Derbe and Lystra which are in the Asia Minor region of Lycaonia, between Syria and the region of Pisidia.

Acts 15:39ᵇ   ... the grace of the Lord
*Barnabas took Mark with him and sailed away to Cyprus, ⁴⁰ but Paul chose Silas and departed, having been commended by the brothers to **the grace of the Lord**. ⁴¹ And he went through Syria and Cilicia, strengthening the churches.*

Acts 16:29 ... the word of the Lord
*And the jailer called for lights and rushed in, and trembling with fear he fell down before Paul and Silas. ³⁰ Then he brought them out and said, "Sirs, what must I do to be saved?" ³¹ And they said, "Believe in the Lord Jesus, and you will be saved, you and your household." ³² And they spoke **the word of the Lord** to him and to all who were in his house. ³³ And he took them the same hour of the night and washed their wounds; and he was baptized at once, he and all his family.*

An Observation: It appears to be that it is Troas that Luke joined Paul. (In Acts 16:7 and 8, Luke writes 'they', whereas in verse 10, Luke writes 'we'. This might indicate that it was in Troas that Luke joined Paul and his other companions.

In this passage we are introduced to Apollos. Apollos was a disciple of John The Baptist who *'knew only the baptism of John'* but he knew of Jesus. Which most likely means he did not preach that Christ died for our sins but taught, as John taught, about repenting and being baptized.

Acts 18:24   ... the way of the Lord
*Now a Jew named Apollos, a native of Alexandria, came to Ephesus. He was an eloquent man, competent in the Scriptures. ²⁵ He had been instructed in **the way of the Lord**. And being fervent in spirit, he spoke and taught accurately the things concerning Jesus, though he knew only the baptism of John. (See also Acts 19:4-7)*

Paul, like Apollos, went to Ephesus, and he learned from some disciples he found there that they had been baptized, but they did not know about the Holy Spirit.

Acts 19:1   ... the name of the Lord Jesus
*And it happened that while Apollos was at Corinth, Paul passed through the inland country and came to Ephesus. There he found some disciples. ² And he said to them, "Did you receive the Holy Spirit when you believed?" And they said, "No, we have not even heard that there is a Holy Spirit." ³ And he said, "Into what then were you baptized?" They said, "Into John's baptism." ⁴ And Paul said, "John baptized with the baptism of repentance, telling the people to believe in the one who was to come after him, that is, Jesus." ⁵ On hearing this, they were baptized in **the name of the Lord Jesus**. ⁶ And when Paul had laid his hands on them, the Holy Spirit came on them, and they began speaking in tongues and prophesying. ⁷ There were about twelve men in all.*

The Compiled Teachings of The Apostle Paul

Paul stayed and preached in Ephesus for about three months by which time the Jews who were leaders at the synagogue rejected the Gospel, so Paul stopped going to the synagogue and moved his ministry to a different location, the Hall of Tyrannus, where he continued ministering for about two years.
(Paul refused to shut down or shut up!)

Acts 19:8   ... the word of the Lord
*And he entered the synagogue and for three months spoke boldly, reasoning and persuading them about the kingdom of God. ⁹ But when some became stubborn and continued in unbelief, speaking evil of the Way before the congregation, he withdrew from them and took the disciples with him, reasoning daily in the hall of Tyrannus. ¹⁰ This continued for two years, so that all the residents of Asia heard **the word of the Lord**, both Jews and Greeks.*

Paul performed many extraordinary miracles of healing while he was in Ephesus [Acts 19:11-12].

Luke, in this next passage, writes that some Jewish exorcists (sorcerers) were invoking Christ referencing Paul's name, and one of the spirits that they were attempting to exorcize (remove) from a man leaped from the man's body and turned on the priests, who were the seven sons of a Jewish high priest named Sceva, overpowering and wounding them such that the seven priests fled out of the house.

Acts 19:13   ... the name of the Lord Jesus   ... the word of the Lord
*Then some of the itinerant Jewish exorcists undertook to invoke **the name of the Lord Jesus** over those who had evil spirits, saying, "I adjure you by the Jesus whom Paul proclaims." ¹⁴ Seven sons of a Jewish high priest named Sceva were doing this. ¹⁵ But the evil spirit answered them, "Jesus I know, and Paul I recognize, but who are you?" ¹⁶ And the man in whom the evil spirit was leaped on them, mastered all of them and overpowered them, so that they fled out of that house naked and wounded. ¹⁷ And this became known to all the residents of Ephesus, both Jews and Greeks. ...²⁰ So **the word of the Lord** continued to increase and prevail mightily.*

Paul travelled from Ephesus which was in the region of Lydia in Asia Minor (modern day Turkey) to Macedonia and to Greece, and then returned to Miletus in Lydia where he summoned the church leaders from Ephesus to come to him. In his discussion with them he told them *'remember the words of the Lord Jesus, how he himself said, 'It is more blessed to give than to receive.'*

Acts 20:35 ... the words of the Lord Jesus
*In all things I have shown you that by working hard in this way we must help the weak and remember **the words of the Lord Jesus**, how he himself said, 'It is more blessed to give than to receive.'" ³⁶ And when he had said these things, he knelt down and prayed with them all.*

When Paul had returned to Judea, to Caesarea, The prophet Agabus came to visit Paul and warned him of what might happen to him if he went to Jerusalem and Paul's friends tried to persuade him to not go to Jerusalem.

Acts 21:13 ... the name of the Lord Jesus
*Then Paul answered, "What are you doing, weeping and breaking my heart? For I am ready not only to be imprisoned but even to die in Jerusalem for **the name of the Lord Jesus**." ¹⁴ And since he would not be persuaded, we ceased and said, "Let the will of the Lord be done."*

---

1 Cor. 2:10   ... the things of God   ... the Spirit of God   ... the mind of Christ

*But to us God revealed them through the Spirit: for the Spirit searches all things, yea, the deep things of God. ¹¹ For who among men knows the things of a man, save the spirit of the man, which is in him? even so **the things of God none knows, save the Spirit of God**. ¹² But we did not receive the spirit of the world, but the spirit which is from God; that we might know the things that were freely given to us of God.*

This passage in Paul's first letter to the church in Corinth is part of Paul's teaching on the Holy Spirit. [1 Cor. 2:1-16; 3:1-23;]

Paul describes how if the rulers had understood God's wisdom they would not have crucified Jesus, who Paul references as the Lord of Glory. [1 Cor. 2:6-9]

*... ¹⁶ For who has known the mind of the Lord, that he should instruct him? But we have **the mind of Christ**.*

---

1 Cor. 5:2-5 ... the name of our Lord Jesus   ... the power of our Lord Jesus   ... the day of the Lord Jesus

In this passage Paul is berating the Corinthian church leaders for setting a poor example when it comes to moral issues, and he is referencing the report that one of them has taken his father's wife as his own. Paul acknowledges that he has reached judgment without being physically present in Corinth, and implores the other leaders to investigate and correct the individual concerned so that *'the spirit (of the Lord) may be saved in the day of the Lord Jesus'*, meaning that this individual's soul might be saved.

*1 Cor. 5:2 And you are puffed up (arrogant), and did not rather mourn, that he that had done this deed might be taken away from among you. ³ For I verily, being absent in body but present in spirit, have already as though I were present judged him that has so wrought this thing, ⁴ in **the name of our Lord Jesus**, you being gathered together, and my spirit, with **the power of our Lord Jesus**, ⁵ to deliver such a one to Satan for the destruction of the flesh, that the spirit may be saved in **the day of the Lord Jesus**.*

The Compiled Teachings of The Apostle Paul

1 Cor. 7:25-28 ... commandment of the Lord ... mercy of the Lord

The 7th chapter in Paul's First Letter to the church in Corinth is focused on teaching on marriage. In this chapter Paul acknowledges that he has not received 'guidance from the lord' of some issues, and in this passage, 1 Cor. 25-28 Paul candidly states he has not *'received a **commandment of the Lord'***. He also states that he is *'one that has obtained **mercy of the Lord** to be trustworthy'*. Paul states that *'it is good for a man to be as he is.'* This would seem logical for him to state as he is a single, unmarried (never been married as far as we know) male, but then he gives guidance for those who are married and have a wife telling them to not consider separation. Then, for those that might be widowed (as Paul is primarily addressing men) or those who might have become separated, to stay as they are; *'seek not a wife.'* Then Paul addresses those who would wish to be married and have a wife; *'28But should you marry, you have not sinned;'* and also addresses the female, *'if a virgin marry, she has not sinned.'* which, by exception, leads one to the conclusion that if she is not a virgin, she has sinned.

*1 Cor. 7:25 Now concerning virgins I have not (received a) **commandment of the Lord**: but I give my judgment, as one that has obtained **mercy of the Lord** to be trustworthy. 26I think therefore that this is good by reason of the distress that is upon us, namely, that it is good for a man to be as he is. 27Are you bound to a wife? seek not to be freed. Are you freed from a wife? seek not a wife. 28But should you marry, you have not sinned; and if a virgin marry, she has not sinned.*

In this next passage, Paul points out that it is difficult to serve two masters, a theme that Jesus addressed. You cannot be focused entirely on God if you have a wife and a family. There are clearly times when a man with a family has to spend time with his family or else he is leaving them abandoned. Paul is basically saying that only the unmarried, including the virgin, are able to give themselves 100 per cent to the Lord.

1 Cor. 7:32b   ...things of the Lord
*He that is unmarried is careful for the **things of the Lord**, how he may please the Lord: 33but he that is married is careful for the things of the world, how he may please his wife, 34 and is divided. So also the woman that is unmarried and the virgin is careful for the **things of the Lord**, that she may be holy both in body and in spirit: but she that is married is careful for the things of the world, how she may please her husband.*

In Cor. 9:3, Paul uses the phrase, *"my defense to those that examine me is this:"* which immediately suggest that he is responding to criticism. In the chapter that this passage is taken from, Paul quotes from Deuteronomy [Deut. 25:4] and he references *'those who perform sacred services'* [1 Cor. 9:13-14] and explains that the Lord directed those who proclaim the Gospel to get their living from the Gospel which appears to be a reference to Matt. 10:10 and Luke 10:7 in which Jesus gives direction to his disciples as he sends them out to minister.

1 Cor. 9:4   ... brethren of the Lord
*Have we no right to eat and to drink? 5 Have we no right to lead about a wife that is a believer, even as the rest of the apostles, and the **brethren of the Lord**, and Cephas (Peter)? 6 Or I only and Barnabas, have we not a right to forbear working? 7 What soldier ever serves at his own charges? who plants a vineyard, and eats not the fruit thereof? or who feeds a flock, and eats not of the milk of the flock?*

Paul is referencing Numbers 21:5-9 in this passage when the people of Israel were in the wilderness and complained to Moses that he had brought them out to die where there was no food and showed their anger against God when 'fiery serpents' (poisonous snakes) caused many of them to die. Paul is telling the Corinthians not to complain otherwise they too might perish.

1 Cor. 10:9 ... make trial of the Lord
***Neither let us make trial of the Lord**, as some of them made trial, and perished by the serpents. 10 Neither murmur, as some of them murmured, and perished by the destroyer. 11 Now these things happened to them by way of example; and they were written for our admonition, upon who the ends of the ages are come.*

Paul is endeavoring to make the distinction between paying homage to God and worshipping demons, gods of pagans. Paul is telling the church in Corinth that they must set aside completely any and all idol worship. When Paul states, *'21 You cannot drink **the cup of the Lord**'* he is making a reference to Jesus when he was in the Garden of Gethsemane the night before his betrayal asking God, *"take this cup from me"*. Paul has already in the prior verses (1 Cor. 10:16-17) referenced the practice of sharing the cup and the bread which are not sacrifices but rather are symbolic acts of worship that connect each believer to God and also to each other.

1 Cor. 10:20
*But I say, that the things which the Gentiles sacrifice, they sacrifice to demons, and not to God: and I would not that you should have communion with demons. 21 You cannot drink **the cup of the Lord**, and [also drink of] the cup of demons: you cannot partake of the table of the Lord, and [also] of the table of demons.*

The Compiled Teachings of The Apostle Paul

Chapter 11 of Paul's first letter to the church in Corinth is a written review of the practices for each meeting. In verse 23 Paul begins the explanation of the sacrament or communion 'meal'. The communion meal is not intended to be a meal that is part of one's nutrition program, but rather is part of one's spiritual program. Paul shares with the Corinthians what many know as 'the words of institution', meaning reciting the words that Jesus spoke when he instituted what we know as 'the Lord's supper' which we find written in the gospels (Mark 14:22-24; Matt. 26:26-28; Luke 22:17-20). Paul has expanded the words of institution adding verses 27, 28 and 29 which are not in any of the Gospels.

1 Cor. 11:23   ... received of the Lord   ... the cup of the Lord
*For I **received of the Lord** that which also I delivered to you, that the Lord Jesus in the night in which he was betrayed took bread; ^{24} and when he had given thanks, he broke it, and said, This is my body, which is for you: this do in remembrance of me. ^{25} In like manner also the cup, after supper, saying, This cup is the new covenant in my blood: this do, as often as you drink it, in remembrance of me. ^{26} For as often as you eat this bread, and drink the cup, you proclaim the Lord's death till he comes. ^{27} Wherefore whosoever shall eat the bread or drink **the cup of the Lord** in an unworthy manner, shall be guilty of the body and the blood of the Lord. ^{28} But let a man prove himself, and so let him eat of the bread, and drink of the cup.* [1 Cor. 11:23]

1 Cor. 11:31   ... disciplined by the Lord
*But if we discerned ourselves, we should not be judged. ^{32} But when we are judged, we are **disciplined by the Lord**, that we might not be condemned along with the world.*

Paul directly addresses those in the church in Corinth who receive revelation from God or who are spiritual people (1 Cor. 2:14), telling them that they read and understand all that he has written are commands from God, being delivered to them by one who was called by God, who indeed had a personal encounter with Jesus. They should sense from God, from His Spirit, that what he, Paul, is telling them is right and is true. [Credit : www.bibleref.com]

1 Cor. 14:37   ... the commandment of the Lord
*If any man thinks himself to be a prophet, or spiritual, let him take knowledge of the things which I write to you, that they are **the commandment of the Lord**. ^{38} But if any man is ignorant, let him be ignorant. ^{39} Wherefore, my brethren, desire earnestly to prophesy, and forbid not to speak with tongues. ^{40} But let all things be done decently and in order.*

This next passage, verse 58, one might think this is a benediction, and in a way it is. It is, however, not marking the end of Paul's letter but simply the end of a section. Immediately following, Cor. 16:1, Paul turns to issue a reminder that he, even though he cannot travel to Corinth, he is still on a mission to raise financial support for the saints in Jerusalem.

1 Cor. 15:58   ... the work of the Lord
*Wherefore, my beloved brethren, be steadfast, unmovable, always abounding in **the work of the Lord**, forasmuch as you know that your labor is not vain in the Lord.*

Paul is hopeful that Timothy will visit Corinth and spend time there helping with the church, however, Corinth will be just a short stayover for in Corinth for Timothy because Paul wants him to come and visit him in Ephesus where he has been detained.

1 Cor. 16:10   ... the work of the Lord
*Now if Timothy comes, see that he is with you without fear; for he works **the work of the Lord**, as I also do: ^{11} let no man therefore despise him. But set him forward on his journey in peace, that he may come to me: for I expect him with the brethren.*

1 Cor. 16:22   ... grace of the Lord
If any man loves not the Lord, let him be anathema. Maranatha.
*^{23} **The grace of the Lord Jesus Christ** be with you.*

Anathema means 'disliked, detested or loathed', and Maranatha means "the Lord is coming" or "come, O Lord".

The Compiled Teachings of The Apostle Paul

In the second of his two letters to the church in Corinth, Paul uses the phrases *'the Spirit of the Lord'* and *'the glory of the Lord'*, neither of which he has used previously, but he does use both phrases later in this same letter, but not elsewhere.

2 Cor. 3:17-18
Now the Lord is the Spirit: and where **the Spirit of the Lord** *is, there is liberty.* [18] *But we all, with unveiled face beholding as in a mirror* **the glory of the Lord**, *are transformed into the same image from glory to glory, even as from the Lord the Spirit.*

Paul begins by declaring that the Lord is a Spirit, that is the Holy Spirit, one of the three members of the Trinity: God the Father, God the Son (which is Christ), and God the Spirit. When one turns to the Lord by trusting in Christ's death for the forgiveness of their sin, the Spirit of God (God the Spirit) becomes revealed, and with that comes freedom; freedom from guilt and freedom from death. But until each of us can realize this we struggle because of our hardened minds and don't see the glory of God clearly. It is through faith in Christ and the power of the Spirit that we each become free from spiritual blindness.   2 Cor. 3:16 [ESV]

But when one turns to the Lord, the veil is removed.

2 Cor. 5:11   ... the fear of the Lord
It because of a strong belief that salvation from sin and hell is a gift given freely by God to all who trust in Christ, that Paul and his coworkers work hard in sharing the Gospel. Paul hopes the Corinthians are fully convinced about the genuineness of the work Paul and those with him have done among them, and also about the work that they themselves have done and continue to do.

Knowing therefore **the fear of the Lord**, *we persuade men, but we are made manifest unto God; and I hope that we are made manifest also in your consciences.*

The next passage is part of an explanation by Paul regarding helpers who are being sent to Corinth. The helpers are Titus, whom Paul refers to as his partner and fellow worker [2 Cor. 8:23] and two brothers, neither of which are named. First is the brother *'whose fame in the things of the Gospel'* has spread through all the churches, and second *'our brother whom we have often tested and found diligent'*. The first of these two unnamed brothers is about whom the reference in this passage is made; a brother who was sent out by the church in Jerusalem.

2 Cor. 8:19[b]- 21   ... the glory of the Lord   ... in the sight of the Lord
...but who was also appointed by the churches to travel with us in the matter of this grace, which is ministered by us to **the glory of the Lord**, *and to show our readiness:* [20] *avoiding this, that any man should blame us in the matter of this bounty which is ministered by us:* [21] *for we take thought for things honorable, not only in* **the sight of the Lord**, *but also in the sight of men.*

In this passage there are two references to the Lord; the *'glory of the Lord'* and the *'sight of the Lord'*. In 2 Cor. 3:18 the term *'glory of the Lord'* is used, but seemingly in a different manner to the same phrase in this sentence.
In 2 Cor. 3:18 Paul references seeing the glory of the Lord with the veil (which has previously prevented us from seeing it) removed. But in this passage, 2 Cor. 8:19, the works that Paul and his coworkers do is done to glorify the Lord; their ministry works are performed as a testament to the glory of the Lord.
Paul continues in the next two verses to emphasize that they take their ministry work seriously; in the NIV the verse reads: *'for we have regard for what is honorable, not only in the sight of the Lord, but also in the sight of other people.'* [2 Cor. 3:21]

Paul continues in this passage (which, here, is focused on the phrase 'God and Father of the Lord') referencing glory, which in this passage Paul is talking about being boastful. "If I am to brag about something, how about how I escaped capture that most likely would have meant death?" That is what he talks about in verse 23, but, no, it is pointing out the glory of God the Father who gave the disciples in that city the idea that allowed him (at that time known as Saul) to escape.

2 Cor. 11:30   ... The God and Father of the Lord
If I must needs glory, I will glory of the things that concern my weakness. [31] **The God and Father of the Lord Jesus**, *He who is blessed for evermore know that I lie not.* [32] *In Damascus the governor under Aretas the king guarded the city of the Damascenes in order to take me:* [33] *and through a window was I let down in a basket by the wall, and escaped his hands.*

2 Cor. 12:1   ... revelations of the Lord
...but I will tell about (go on to) visions and **revelations of the Lord**. [2] *I know a man in Christ, fourteen years ago (whether in the body, I know not; or whether out of the body, I know not; God knows), such a one caught up even to the third heaven.* [3] *And I know such a man (whether in the body, or apart from the body, I know not; God knows),* [4] *how that he was caught up into Paradise, and heard unspeakable words, which it is not lawful for a man to utter.* [5] *On behalf of such a one will I glory: but on mine own behalf I will not glory, save in my weaknesses.*

Regarding boasting and bragging, Paul says it might be necessary, but it is not profitable. [2 Cor. 12:1[a]] Instead, he says, *'I will tell about to visions and revelations of the Lord.'* Paul then relates his own personal story of a vision that he experienced. Paul, being humble, doesn't say, "I had this vision in which I had revealed to me." He could have as this is clearly his own personal experience rather than one related to him by some other person. Even at the end of this story he uses the phrase, *'On behalf of such a one will I glory: but on mine own behalf I will not glory'*.

- 129 -

In regard to the passage referenced above, Paul mentions 'the third heaven'. In the Old Testament, the third heaven is often referred to as the highest heaven, a place created by God where He lives and where angels praise Him (1 Kings 8:27; Nehemiah 9:6; Psalm 148:4). Most commentators understand the first heaven—or first heavens—to be the sky above the earth. The second would be the realm of the sun, moon, and stars: what we would now refer to as outer space. [Credit: www.bibleref.com] Paul emphasizes that only God knows whether he physically travelled to the third heaven in his body or whether it was an out-of-body experience. Paul wrote that this happened 14 years before the time of his writing the Second Letter to the church in Corinth. That would put the experience sometime around AD 42-44; prior to his first missionary journey.

This last verse in Paul's Second Letter to the church in Corinth is a benediction in which Paul invokes Jesus, God the Father, and The Holy Spirit.

2 Cor. 13:14 ... love of God
*The grace of the Lord Jesus Christ, and the **love of God**, and **the communion of the Holy Spirit**, be with you all.*

Rom. 10:12 ... the name of the Lord
*For there is no distinction between Jew and Greek: for the same Lord is Lord of all, and is rich unto all that call upon Him: ¹³ for, **whosoever shall call upon the name of the Lord shall be saved**. ¹⁴ How then shall they call on Him in someone they have not believed?*

The verse prior to this passage quotes Isaiah 28:16 - *Whosoever believes in Him shall not be put to shame.* [ASV] This prophecy passage refers to a foundation stone, and the NASB version Bible reads: *'the Lord GOD says: 'Behold, I am laying a stone in Zion, a tested stone, A precious cornerstone for the foundation, firmly placed. The one who believes in it will not be disturbed.'*

Rom. 11:34 ... the mind of the Lord
*For who has known **the mind of the Lord**? or who has been his counsellor? ³⁵ or who has first given to him, and it shall be recompensed to him again? ³⁶ For of him, and through him, and to him, are all things.*

Romans 11:34 is a quote from Isaiah 40:13; *'Who has directed the Spirit of the Lord, or who gave him counsel?'* One might argue these are two non-sensical questions. Who, or what kind of being, could ever comprehended the mind of the Lord, or who could be knowledgeable enough or wise enough to give God counsel? Then in verse 35 we have another non-sensical question; *'Who gave Him understanding and taught Him the paths of justice such that He should need to repay or reward them'** Then finally, in verse 35, Paul gives the answers. * *Paraphrase based on more than one translation/version.*

In this passage in Paul's First letter to the Thessalonian's Paul claims himself, his coworkers, and also the Lord as the role models that the leaders, teachers, and members of the church have followed and copied. As Paul emphasizes, their sharing, preaching and teaching the word of the Lord, that is the Gospel, has become an example to all that believe, and their faith is so evident that often their example has superseded their need to even speak.

1 Thess. 1:6 ... of the Lord ... the word of the Lord
*And you became imitators of us, **and of the Lord**, having received the word in much affliction, with joy of the Holy Spirit; ⁷ so that you became an example to all that believe in Macedonia and in Achaia. ⁸ For from you have sounded forth **the word of the Lord**, not only in Macedonia and Achaia, but in every place your faith to God-ward is gone forth; so that we need not to speak anything.*

This passage in the first of the two letters that Paul wrote to the church in Thessalonica is teaching by Paul regarding the second coming of Christ and the periods of tribulation, rapture and Armageddon that Jesus warned His disciples of [Matt. 24:15-28; Luke 17:22-37], which shows that not only was Paul well studied in the Scriptures (of the Old Testament) which he learned as a pharisee, but he had learned well about Christ from 'studying' with the Apostles and other disciples. -- See also 1 Cor. 15:12-34.

1 Thess. 4:14-18 ... the word of the Lord ... the coming of the Lord
¹⁴ *For if we believe that Jesus died and rose again, even so them also that have fallen asleep in Jesus will God bring with him.* ¹⁵ *For this we say to you by **the word of the Lord**, that we that are alive, that are left to **the coming of the Lord**, shall in no way precede those that have fallen asleep.* ¹⁶ *For the Lord himself shall descend from heaven, with a shout, with the voice of the archangel, and with the trump of God: and the dead in Christ shall rise first;* ¹⁷ *then we that are alive, that are left, shall together with them be caught up in the clouds, to meet the Lord in the air: and so shall we ever be with the Lord.* ¹⁸ *Wherefore comfort one another with these words.*

Paul references *'the word of the Lord'* and *'the coming of the Lord'* in this passage and in the following passage, 1 Thess. 5, he references *'the Day of The Lord'* which will come immediately after the period of rapture [Matt. 24:29] and which, in the Book of Revelation, is followed by Armageddon; which is either immediately or at a later time.

Matt. 24:29-31 describes 'The Return of Christ' for us:
²⁹ *But immediately after the tribulation of those days the sun shall be darkened, and the moon shall not give her light, and the stars shall fall from heaven, and the powers of the heavens shall be shaken:* ³⁰ *and then shall appear the sign of the Son of man in heaven: and then shall all the tribes of the earth mourn, and they shall see the Son of man coming on the clouds of heaven with power and great glory.* ³¹ *And he shall send forth his angels with a great sound of a trumpet, and they shall gather together his elect from the four winds, from one end of heaven to the other.*

The Compiled Teachings of The Apostle Paul

Paul most likely did not have any of the Gospel accounts available to him, however, in this passage he writes as if he had copies of Matthew's or Luke's writings. [Matt. 24:42-44; Luke 12:35-40]

1 Thess. 5:1   ... the day of the Lord
*But concerning the times and the seasons, brethren, you have no need that needs to be written to you. ² For yourselves know perfectly that **the day of the Lord** will come as a thief in the night. ³ When they are saying, Peace and safety, then sudden destruction comes upon them, as travail upon a woman with child; and they shall in no wise escape. ⁴ But you, brethren, are not in darkness, that that day should overtake you as a thief; ⁵ for you are all sons of light, and sons of the day: we are not of the night, nor of darkness; ⁶ so then let us not sleep, as do the rest, but let us watch and be sober.*

---

2 Thess. 1:5ᵇ-10   ... the revelation of the Lord   ... the face of the Lord

Referencing *'Jesus (coming) from heaven with the angels of his power in flaming fire'*, Paul writes that God will render *'vengeance to them that do not know God, and to them that do not obey the gospel of our Lord Jesus'* and that they will be punished *'even eternal destruction from the face of the Lord and from the glory of his might'*. Paul adds a parenthetic comment at the end of the verse 10; *'because our testimony to you was believed'*; a comment that might be viewed as a somewhat grandiose claim that, to some extent, goes against the characterization of Paul as being a humble individual. However, if not bold in himself, Paul is certainly bold in the Lord.

*2 Thess. 1:5ᵇ ...to the end that you may be counted worthy of the kingdom of God, for which you also suffer: ⁶ if so be that it is a righteous thing with God to recompense affliction to them that afflict you, ⁷ and to you that are afflicted rest with us, at **the revelation of the Lord Jesus** from heaven with the angels of his power in flaming fire, ⁸ rendering vengeance to them that do not know God, and to them that do not obey the gospel of our Lord Jesus: ⁹ who shall suffer punishment, even eternal destruction from **the face of the Lord** and from the glory of his might, ¹⁰ when he shall come to be glorified in his saints, and to be marveled at in all that believed (because our testimony to you was believed) in that day.*

---

2 Thess. 2:1ᵇ   ... the coming of our Lord   ... the day of the Lord

*...regarding) **the coming of our Lord Jesus Christ**, and our gathering together to him; ² to the end that you be not quickly shaken from your mind, nor yet be troubled, either by spirit, or by word, or by epistle as from us, as that **the day of the Lord** is just at hand; ³ let no man beguile you in any wise: for it will not be, except the falling away come first, and the man of sin be revealed, the son of perdition, ⁴ he that opposes and exalts himself against all that is called God or that is worshipped; so that he sits in the temple of God, setting himself forth as God.*

This passage is a further reference to the order in which the events of the Second Coming of Christ must take place. The phrase *'except the falling away come first'* is a reference to apostasy, which is *'a total desertion of or departure from one's religion, principles, party, cause, etc.'* [per dictionary.com]

Paul uses the phrase *'beloved of the Lord'* as if there might be something specific and special about the church in Thessalonica. Paul then adds *'for that God chose you from the beginning...'* perhaps, as the ESV and NIV translations read, that they were 'first fruits'; 'because God chose you as the firstfruits to be saved', however, Thessalonica was not the first city that Paul visited and preached the Gospel to, either Antioch in the region of Pisidia or one of the cities en route to Pisidian Antioch would surely have been the firstfruits. Nevertheless, the church leaders and others who read or heard Paul's letter would most likely have been encouraged by such words, and those word would probably not have been questioned.

2 Thess. 2:13   ... beloved of the Lord
*But we are bound to give thanks to God always for you, brethren **beloved of the Lord**, for that God chose you from the beginning to salvation in sanctification of the Spirit and belief of the truth: ¹⁴ It was for this he called you through our gospel, to the obtaining of the glory of our Lord Jesus Christ. ¹⁵ So then, brethren, stand fast, and hold the traditions which you were taught, whether by word, or by epistle of ours.*

---

2 Thess. 3:17ᵇ-21   ... the will of the Lord
*...be not foolish, but understand what **the will of the Lord** is. ¹⁸ And be not drunken with wine, wherein is riot, but be filled with the Spirit; ¹⁹ speaking one to another in psalms and hymns and spiritual songs, singing and making melody with your heart to the Lord; ²⁰ giving thanks always for all things in the name of our Lord Jesus Christ to God, even the Father; ²¹ subjecting yourselves one to another in the fear of Christ.*

In this passage Paul gives direction regarding what to do and what not to do to be sure that you are living your life righteously, that is according to His will.

The Compiled Teachings of The Apostle Paul

2 Thess. 3:1b ... the word of the Lord   ... Lord is faithful ... the love of God

This passage references the Lord God in three different ways. First *'the word of the Lord'* meaning the Gospel, the message of redemption through Christ. Second, *'the Lord is faithful'* meaning we can trust in God, and third, *'the love of God'*. Paul couples this phrase with *'and into the patience of Christ.'* Paul is making it clear that it is us that have to reach out to God and to Jesus Christ and not the other way around, but Paul's prayer is that the Lord will in some way direct their hearts toward him and to Jesus which the Jews will only do if they believe Paul's teaching and accept Jesus as the Messiah.

*...pray for us, that **the word of the Lord** may run (spread rapidly) and be glorified, even as also it is with you; ² and that we may be delivered from unreasonable and evil men; for not all have faith. ³ But **the Lord is faithful**, who shall establish you, and guard you from the evil one. ⁴ And we have confidence in the Lord touching you, that you both do (are doing) and will do the things which we command. ⁵ And the Lord direct your hearts into **the love of God**, and into the patience of Christ.*

This next passage is from Paul's letter to the Ephesians, and it bears much resemblance to the passage from 2 Thess. 3:17-21

Eph. 5:14
*Wherefore he said, 'Awake, you that sleeps, and arise from the dead, and Christ shall shine upon you'. ¹⁵ Look therefore carefully how you walk, not as unwise, but as wise; ¹⁶ redeeming the time, because the days are evil. ¹⁷ Wherefore be not foolish, but understand what **the will of the Lord** is. ¹⁸ And be not drunken with wine, wherein is riot, but be filled with the Spirit;*

Paul gives direction to both parents and children regarding what to do and what not to do to...

Eph. 6:1 ... in the Lord   ... admonition of the Lord
*Children, obey your parents **in the Lord**: for this is right. ² Honor thy father and mother (which is the first commandment with promise), ³ that it may be well with you, and you may live long on the earth. ⁴ And, fathers, provoke not your children to wrath: but nurture them in the chastening and **admonition of the Lord**.*

In the benediction in this last verse in Paul's Letter to the church in Philippi, Paul invokes the *'grace of the Lord Jesus Christ.*

Philipp. 4:23
The grace of the Lord Jesus Christ be with your spirit.

In this next passage Paul teaches about walking with the Lord and uses the phrase, *'walk worthily of the Lord'* and the directions he gives leads to a statement of belief that is not found elsewhere in Paul's Letters or teachings: *'¹² giving thanks to the Father, who made us meet to be partakers of the inheritance of the saints in light; ¹³ who delivered us out of the power of darkness, and translated us into the kingdom of the Son of his love; ¹⁴ in whom we have our redemption, the forgiveness of our sins: ¹⁵ who is the image of the invisible God, the firstborn of all creation; ¹⁶ for in him were all things created, in the heavens and upon the earth, things visible and things invisible, whether thrones or dominions or principalities or powers; all things have been created through him, and to him; ¹⁷ and he is before all things, and in him all things consist.'* Also, verses 15-17 summarize the personage of Jesus Christ and his relationship to God the father.

Col. 1:9 ... worthily of the Lord   ... the knowledge of God
*For this cause we also, since the day we heard it, do not cease to pray and make request for you, that you may be filled with the knowledge of his will in all spiritual wisdom and understanding, ¹⁰ to **walk worthily of the Lord** to all pleasing, bearing fruit in every good work, and increasing in **the knowledge of God**; ¹¹ strengthened with all power, according to the might of his glory, unto all patience and longsuffering with joy; ¹² giving thanks to the Father, who made us meet to be partakers of the inheritance of the saints in light; ¹³ who delivered us out of the power of darkness, and translated us into the kingdom of the Son of his love; ¹⁴ in whom we have our redemption, the forgiveness of our sins: ¹⁵ who is the image of the invisible God, the firstborn of all creation; ¹⁶ for in him were all things created, in the heavens and upon the earth, things visible and things invisible, whether thrones or dominions or principalities or powers; all things have been created through him, and to him; ¹⁷ and he is before all things, and in him all things consist.*

Col. 3:16 ... the word of Christ   ... the name of the Lord Jesus
Let the word of Christ *dwell in you richly; in all wisdom teaching and admonishing one another with psalms and hymns and spiritual songs, singing with grace in your hearts to God. ¹⁷ And whatsoever you do, in word or in deed, do all in **the name of the Lord Jesus**, giving thanks to God the Father through him.*

This passage which references both *'the word of Christ'* and the *'name of the Lord Jesus'* closes out a teaching passage in Colossians 3:12-17 that is both a complement and a contrast to the passage in Ephesians 6:10-16; one speaks to gentleness and peace while the other speaks to being strong and being prepared for battle. Both speak to becoming the 'new self', and both are tied in with teaching about family relationships.

The Compiled Teachings of The Apostle Paul

Admonish
Admonish means to 'warn or reprimand someone firmly' or 'to advise or urge (someone) earnestly'. It's an archaic definition referenced in modern dictionaries is 'to warn (someone) of something to be avoided', which means that back in Paul's time it probably meant more than just slap someone's wrist or give them a verbal rap over the knuckles. Paul preached the Gospel without compromise and there are references to Paul admonishing in Acts 21:3; 1 Cor. 4:14; Rom. 15:14; 1 Thess. 5:12,13; 2 Thess. 3:15; Col. 1:27, and Col. 3:16.
The opposite of admonish is praise.

Adulterer, Adulteress
An adulterer or adulteress is a person who has, while married, had a sexual relationship with another other than their spouse. Paul preaches that adultery is a sin which may in part be based upon being told by one of Jesus disciples Jesus preached, "I say unto you, that every one that looks on a woman to lust after her has committed adultery with her already in his heart." [Matt. 5:28] This teaching is echoed by Paul in Romans 13:9.

Adultery   (see also Fornication)
Paul teaches on adultery in Romans [Rom. 2:22; Rom. 13:9] The book of Romans might be being singled out simply because the word 'adultery' is used only in Romans. Elsewhere, in Paul's writings, the word 'fornication' is used. An example of Paul's teaching is found in 1 Cor. 6:18[b] *'he that commits **fornication** sins against his own body.'* (See 'Fornication)
By this Paul is clearly admonishing any who are slaves to sexual perversion, meaning anything other than what is essential for procreation.

*Rom. 2:22 You that preaches a man should not steal, do you steal? ²² You that says a man should not commit **adultery**, do you commit **adultery**? You that abhors idols, do you rob temples?*

*Rom. 13:8-9 Owe no man anything, save to love one another: for he that loves his neighbor has fulfilled the law. ⁹ For this, You shall not commit **adultery**, You shall not kill, You shall not steal, You shall not covet, and if there be any other commandment, it is summed up in this word, namely, You shall love thy neighbor as thyself.*

Anointing   (see Laying on of hands)
There are three occasions of the word 'anoint' in *Acts; Acts 4:26; Acts 4:27, and Acts 10:38*. All three are anointings delivered by Peter, and none delivered by Paul. The term 'Laying on of hands' is used elsewhere rather than the term anointing in *Acts 9:12[b]; Acts 9:17; Acts 9:10; Acts 13:2; Acts 14:3; Acts 19:4; Acts 21:27; Acts 28:8; 1 Tim. 2:8; 1 Tim. 4:14; 1 Tim. 5:21; 2 Tim 1:6*.

Apostle(s)
There are many times that the term apostle is mentioned in both the Book of Acts and in Paul's letters, but most times simply as a reference to (the) apostles as a group or to individuals. In his letters Paul offers some teaching:

*Gal. 1:1 Paul, an **apostle**—not from men nor through man, but through Jesus Christ and God the Father, who raised him from the dead.* Here Paul is stating that because he was encountered by Jesus Christ on the road to Damascus, he was chosen to be an apostle as were the other apostles except for Matthias who was chosen by lot.

*1 Cor. 4:9 For, I think, God has set forth us the **apostles** last of all, as men doomed to death: for we are made a spectacle to the world, both to angels and men.* Here Paul is stating that one who is chosen to be an apostle has been chosen to sacrifice themselves.

*1 Cor. 9:2 If to others I am not an **apostle**, yet at least I am to you; for the seal of my **apostleship** are you in the Lord. ³ My defense to them that examine me is this. ⁴ Have we no right to eat and to drink? ⁵ Have we no right to lead about a wife that is a believer, even as the rest of the **apostles**, and the brethren of the Lord, and Cephas (Peter)?*

Here Paul is again defending his right to claim that he is an apostle, equal to those chosen before him, but he is also restating the expectation of sacrifice. In this next reference to apostles, Paul demarks the hierarchy of those who preach the gospel, placing apostles at the head of the list.

*1 Cor. 12:28 And God has set some in the church, first **apostles**, secondly prophets, thirdly teachers, then miracles, then gifts of healings, helps, governments, diverse kinds of tongues.*

Paul shows awareness of others who claim themselves to be apostles, but who are teaching a different gospel, and Paul describes them as deceitful:

*2 Cor. 11:13 For such men are false apostles, deceitful workers, fashioning themselves into **apostles** of Christ. ¹⁴ And no marvel; for even Satan fashions himself into an angel of light.*

*2 Cor. 12:12 Truly the signs of an **apostle** were wrought among you in all patience, by signs and wonders and mighty works.*

The Compiled Teachings of The Apostle Paul

Paul references the healings and other miracles that have been performed by other apostles such as Peter and James stating that those are the sign of a true apostle, and Paul had performed a number of signs: The blinding of Elymas the sorcerer [Acts 13:6-11], The healing of the slave girl who had a spirit of divination [Acts 16:16-18], Paul and Silas released from jail by the Holy Spirit [Acts 16:25-27], *And God was doing extraordinary miracles by the hands of Paul, *^{12}* so that even handkerchiefs or aprons that had touched his skin were carried away to the sick, and their diseases left them and the evil spirits came out of them.* [Acts 19:11-12], the restoring to life of Eutychus [Acts 20:9-12], and the healings and miracles that he performed when the ship became wrecked by the storm off Malta. [Acts 28:1-9]

Paul in his letter to the Romans makes two references about apostles. First he categorized himself as an apostle of Gentiles, and second he appears to be crediting two of his coworkers with being apostles.

Rom. 11:13 *But I speak to you that are Gentiles. Inasmuch then as I am an **apostle** of Gentiles, I glorify my ministry*

Romans 16:7 *Salute Andronicus and Junias, my kinsmen, and my fellow-prisoners, who are of note among the apostles, who also have been in Christ before me.*

Believe, Believed, Believer(s)

Quite surprisingly the term 'believer' does not appear in any of the Letters of Paul prior to his Letter to the church in Thessalonica. Related terms, believe and believed, also are not in Galatians, 1 Corinthians, 2 Corinthians, or Romans. The three uses in 1 Thessalonians are: (1) believers [1 Thess. 1:7], (2) believed [1 Thess. 1:10] twice, and (3) believe [2 Thess. 1:10].

1 Thess. 1:7 *so that you became an example to all the **believers** in Macedonia and in Achaia.*

1 Thess. 1:10 *when he comes on that day to be glorified in his saints, and to be marveled at among all who have **believed**, because our testimony to you was **believed**.*

1 Thess. 2:10 *You are witnesses, and God also, how holily and righteously and unblamably we behaved ourselves toward you that **believe**:*

There are more than 20 references to **coming to believe**, **believing**, **believed**, and **believer**(s) in Acts. These are listed below. Some are not 'teachings of Paul' per se, but most are in one way or another related to Paul. The notable exceptions are the references in Acts 11:21, Acts 15:5; 15:7 and 15:11 which relate to Peter and the other apostles.

Acts 11:21 *And the hand of the Lord was with them: and a great number that **believed** turned unto the Lord.*

Acts 13:12 *Then the proconsul, when he saw what was done, **believed**, being astonished at the teaching of the Lord.*

Acts 13:38b *... that through this man is proclaimed unto you remission of sins: *^{39}* and by Him every one that **believes** is justified from all things, from which you could not be justified by the law of Moses.*

Acts 13:48 *And as the Gentiles heard this, they were glad, and glorified the word of God: and as many as were ordained to eternal life **believed**.*

Acts 14:23 *And when they had appointed elders for them in every church, with prayer and fasting they committed them to the Lord in whom they had **believed**.*

Acts 15:5 *But some **believers** who belonged to the party of the Pharisees rose up and said, "It is necessary to circumcise them and to order them to keep the law of Moses."*

Acts 15:7 *And after there had been much debate, Peter stood up and said to them, "Brothers, you know that in the early days God made a choice among you, that by my mouth the Gentiles should hear the word of the gospel and **believe**.*

Acts 15:11 *But we **believe** that we will be saved through the grace of the Lord Jesus, just as they will."*

Acts 16:1 *Paul came also to Derbe and to Lystra. A disciple was there, named Timothy, the son of a Jewish woman who was a **believer**, but his father was a Greek.*

Acts 16:31 *And they said, "**Believe** in the Lord Jesus, and you will be saved, you and your household." *^{32}* And they spoke the word of the Lord to him and to all who were in his house. *^{33}* And he took them the same hour of the night and washed their wounds; and he was baptized at once, he and all his family. *^{34}* Then he brought them up into his house and set food before them. And he rejoiced along with his entire household that he had **believed** in God.*

Acts 17:12 *Many of them therefore believed, with not a few Greek women of high standing as well as men.*

Acts 17:33 *So Paul went out from their midst. *^{34}* But some men joined him and **believed**, among whom also were Dionysius the Areopagite and a woman named Damaris and others with them.*

Acts 18:8 *Crispus, the ruler of the synagogue, **believed** in the Lord, together with his entire household. And many of the Corinthians hearing Paul believed and were baptized.*

Acts 18:27 *And when he (Apollos) wished to cross to Achaia, the brothers encouraged him and wrote to the disciples to welcome him. When he arrived, he greatly helped those who through grace had **believed**, *^{28}* for he powerfully refuted the Jews in public, showing by the Scriptures that the Christ was Jesus.*

Acts 19:1 *Paul passed through the inland country and came to Ephesus. There he found some disciples. *^{2}* And he said to them, "Did you receive the Holy Spirit when you **believed**?" And they said, "No, we have not even heard that there is a Holy Spirit." *^{3}* And he said, "Into what then were you baptized?" They said, "Into John's baptism." *^{4}* And Paul said, "John baptized with the baptism of repentance,*

The Compiled Teachings of The Apostle Paul

telling the people to **believe** in the one who was to come after him, that is, Jesus." ⁵ On hearing this, they were baptized in the name of the Lord Jesus.

Acts 19:17 And this became known to all the residents of Ephesus, both Jews and Greeks. And fear fell upon them all, and the name of the Lord Jesus was extolled. ¹⁸ Also many of those who were now **believers** came, confessing and divulging their practices.

Acts 20:20 And when they heard it, they glorified God. And they said to him, "You see, brother, how many thousands there are among the Jews of those who have **believed**. They are all zealous for the law, ²¹ and they have been told about you that you teach all the Jews who are among the Gentiles to forsake Moses, telling them not to circumcise their children or walk according to our customs.

Acts 20:25 But as for the Gentiles who have **believed**, we have sent a letter with our judgment that they should abstain from what has been sacrificed to idols, and from blood, and from what has been strangled, and from sexual immorality."

Acts 21:17 "When I had returned to Jerusalem and was praying in the temple, I fell into a trance ¹⁸ and saw him saying to me, 'Make haste and get out of Jerusalem quickly, because they will not accept your testimony about me.' ¹⁹ And I said, 'Lord, they themselves know that in one synagogue after another I imprisoned and beat those who **believed in you**. ²⁰ And when the blood of Stephen your witness was being shed, I myself was standing by and approving and watching over the garments of those who killed him.

Acts 26:25 But Paul said, "I am not out of my mind, most excellent Festus, but I am speaking true and rational words. ²⁶ For the king knows about these things, and to him I speak boldly. For I am persuaded that none of these things has escaped his notice, for this has not been done in a corner. ²⁷ King Agrippa, **do you believe the prophets?** I know that you **believe**." ²⁸ And Agrippa said to Paul, "In a short time would you persuade me to be a Christian?"

Acts 28:23 When they had appointed a day for him, they came to him at his lodging in greater numbers. From morning till evening he expounded to them, testifying to the kingdom of God and trying to convince them about Jesus both from the Law of Moses and from the Prophets. ²⁴ And **some were convinced** by what he said, but others **disbelieved**.

In 1 Tim. 1:15 Paul writes that Christ Jesus came into this world to save sinners, and he describes himself as the foremost sinner because of how he persecuted members of the Way, and here he writes that he was given mercy so that '*Christ might demonstrate his perfect patience*'. [NASB]	**1 Tim. 1:16** But I received mercy for this reason, that in me, as the foremost, Jesus Christ might display his perfect patience as an example to those who were to **believe** in him for eternal life.

Titus 1:6 ....if anyone is above reproach, the husband of one wife, and his children are **believers** and not open to the charge of debauchery or insubordination.	This passage addresses the topic (challenge) of selecting elders to serve the church. There are four qualification requirements according to this verse. First, he must be beyond reproach (meaning the individual must be of strong moral character); second, is a husband who has only one wife (meaning he should be known for being faithfully commitment to one wife); third, he has children who believe (meaning any children an elder has must not reject God); and fourth, he is not accused of 'dissipation or rebellion'. [NASB]
Eph. 1:13 *In him you also, when you heard the word of truth, the gospel of your salvation, and believed in him, were sealed with the promised Holy Spirit,*	Paul is telling the church in Ephesus (where he revealed the Holy Spirit to them - Acts 19:1-5) that when they became believers they "were sealed with the promised Holy Spirit." [A "seal" was a mark indicating a letter or scroll was closed, or completed. A king or dignitary would seal a letter with a resin imprint of his ring. The Holy Spirit likewise shows that believers belong to the Lord.]

In Philipp. 1:27 Paul explains that, whether he is able to visit Philippi or not, he hopes to hear that they are '*standing fast in one spirit, with one soul striving for the faith of the gospel; ²⁸ and in nothing affrighted by the adversaries (not afraid of being opposed)*. Paul is explaining that the reward for suffering is salvation.	**Philipp. 1:28ᵇ-29** but of your salvation, and that from God; ²⁹ because to you it has been granted on behalf of Christ, not only to believe in him, but also to suffer in his behalf:

This next verse reads almost as if it is from the same letter as the prior verse in this list, but it is not. Paul is explaining why he endures suffering.	**2 Tim. 1:12** which is why I suffer as I do. But I am not ashamed, for I know whom I have believed, and I am convinced that he is able to guard until that day what has been entrusted to me.

The translation shown here is from the ASV – American Standard Version, and gives us the phrase, '*what has been entrusted to me*', which suggests Paul is the custodian of something that he has been assigned to look after. Other translations suggest that Paul has given the custodian responsibility to Christ.
The NASB – New American Standard Bible, reads 'I am convinced that He is able to protect what I have entrusted to Him until that day.'
The NIV – New International Version, reads '(I) am convinced that he is able to guard what I have entrusted to him until that day.
The NKJV – New King James Version, reads, '(I) am persuaded that he is able to keep that which I have committed unto him against that day'.

One commentary (www.Bibleref.com) states, *"There is some uncertainty about what Paul is referring to when he says that Christ "is able to guard until that Day what has been entrusted to me."*

Since Paul is expecting to one day stand before the Lord – Jesus Christ who Paul has already met once – my own leaning is toward Paul saying he was commission to preach (trusted with preaching) the Gospel, and he is able to endure suffering because God is guarding over him.

Bishop(s)

Paul makes just one specific reference to bishops, in which he lists out the qualities and abilities that bishops should have:

See other categories (Leader, Ministers, etc.) for additional teaching on qualifications and selection.

At first reading it seems that Paul is referencing back to previously given instruction, either written or orally – or both, and that may well be the case but Paul, however, 'reminds' Titus of what that instruction was:

Titus 1:6

*if any man is blameless, the husband of one wife, having children that believe, who are not accused of riot or unruly. ⁷ For the **bishop** must be blameless, as God's **steward**; not self-willed, not soon angry, no brawler, no striker, not greedy of filthy lucre; ⁸ but given to hospitality, a lover of good, sober-minded, just, holy, self-controlled; ⁹ holding to the faithful word which is according to the teaching, that he may be able both to exhort in the sound doctrine, and to convict the gainsayers. ¹⁰ For there are many unruly men, vain talkers and deceivers, specially they of the circumcision, ¹¹ whose mouths must be stopped; men who overthrow whole houses, teaching things which they ought not, for filthy lucre's sake. ¹² One of themselves, a prophet of their own, said, Cretans are always liars, evil beasts, idle gluttons.*

Circumcise(d) / Circumcision

On circumcision, Paul preaches first that Abraham was not circumcised when God established a covenant with him; the promise that he would be the father of a great nation. Abraham agreed to be circumcised in order that the covenant be established [Gen. 17:11]

1 Chronicles 16:16 / Psalm 105:9 [ASV]
¹⁴ He is Jehovah our God; His judgments are in all the earth.
¹⁵ Remember His covenant forever, The word which He commanded to a thousand generations,
¹⁶ The covenant which He made with Abraham, and His oath to Isaac,
¹⁷ And confirmed the same to Jacob for a statute to Israel for an everlasting covenant,
¹⁸ Saying, To you will I give the land of Canaan, the lot of your inheritance.

In Acts...

Peter Preaches In The Temple

And you are heirs of the prophets and of the **covenant** God made with your fathers. He said to **Abraham**, 'Through your offspring all peoples on earth will be blessed.' [Acts 3:25 / Gen. 22:18]

Stephen Preaches To The High Priest

...And he gave him the covenant of **circumcision**: and so *Abraham* begat Isaac, and **circumcised** him the eighth day; and Isaac *begat* Jacob, and Jacob the twelve patriarchs. Then he gave **Abraham** the **covenant** of **circumcision**, and **Abraham** became the father of Isaac and **circumcised** him eight days after his birth. Later Isaac became the father of Jacob, and Jacob became the father of the twelve patriarchs. [Acts 7:8 NASB]

In Paul's Epistles (Letters)... *For a quick review study of Paul's teachings on circumcision and references to this topic, see the study notes in the Addenda.*

Daughter(s)

Paul gives guidance regarding family relationships in 1 Cor. 7 and in verse 36 he references unmarried daughters and cites the possibility of a father wishing to marry one of his daughters. To repeat the comments in the notes for 1 Cor. 7 which provides the full text, at face value in modern terms, it seems that when Paul says, 'Let them marry' he is giving approval to incest and possibly also to bigamy. However, how likely might it have been that a daughter would be prepared to marry her father if her mother was still alive? Not likely, but perhaps what was quite likely is that the elder daughter has become a surrogate for her deceased mother; quite likely a mother who died in childbirth or from some other cause. The older daughter would in almost all cases step up and take care of her siblings including a new-born. Paul began by stating, *³⁶But if any man thinks that he behaves himself unseemly (inappropriately) toward his virgin daughter, if she be past the flower of her age, and if need so requires, let him do what he will; he sins not; let them marry.* In other words, the father is finding his own daughter as attractive to him as he found her mother and she has in some shown her love for him, and so Paul says '*let them marry*'.

1 Cor. 7:36-38

³⁶ But if any man thinks that he is behaving himself inappropriately is past the flower of her age, and if need so requires, let him do what he will; he sins not; let them marry.

The Compiled Teachings of The Apostle Paul

In verses 37 and 38 Paul explains that where there is no desire on the part of the father to have his daughter marry him, then it is good for either the daughter to be given in marriage or to not be given in marriage, finally expressing the view that if she is not given in marriage, then the father does better that if he gives his daughter in marriage. (My own thinking here is that this guidance would relate to only the oldest daughter in the family, and not to all daughters.)

37 But he that stands steadfast in his heart, having no necessity, but has power as touching his own will, and has determined this in his own heart, to keep his own virgin daughter, shall do well.

*38 So then both he that giveth his own virgin **daughter** in marriage does well; and he that giveth her not in marriage shall do better.*

2 Cor. 6:18

...AND WILL BE TO YOU A FATHER, AND YOU SHALL BE SONS AND **DAUGHTERS** TO ME, says the Lord Almighty.

In 2 Cor. 6:18 Paul offers up a quote that is credited to God; the Lord Almighty. But where is this quote from? In Acts 2, Peter quoted Joel which references sons and daughters, but this clearly is not quote that of 2 Cor. 6:18 'AND IT SHALL BE IN THE LAST DAYS,' God says, 'THAT I WILL POUR OUT MY SPIRIT ON ALL MANKIND, AND YOUR SONS AND YOUR DAUGHTERS WILL PROPHESY AND YOUR YOUNG MEN WILL SEE VISIONS, AND YOUR OLD MEN WILL HAVE DREAMS; [Acts 2:17]

Deacons

Paul makes just two specific teaching references to deacons, which as he did with bishops, he lists qualities and abilities that are relevant to what he expects of deacons. The first of these list presents the requirements more in terms of what they should *not* (must not) have rather than what they should have as he did with bishops, with just one exception given in verse 9.

The second reference, which follows the first, but the two are separated by a reference to women which may or may not be interpreted as relating to women serving as deacons, lists additional qualifications and abilities, this time in a 'should have/must have' listing:

So combining these together in a positive 'should have/must have' we see that deacons must be serious (grave), straightforward and always honest, speaking cleanly and clearly without hidden meanings, sober individuals that moderate their drinking of alcohol, has no doubts regarding the belief that Jesus of Nazareth was indeed the Christ who was crucified to death, was buried in a sealed tomb and who was raised from the dead and who was witnessed ascending into heaven to return to our heavenly father from whom he came, is married but to only one wife, teaching and managing his family and their household affairs in a manner without reproach, and serving the community of believers to the very best of their ability so as to be recognized and respected and, finally, are bold on sharing the Gospel.

1 Tim. 3:8-10

Deacons in like manner must be grave, not double-tongued, not given to much wine, not greedy of filthy lucre (ill-gotten wealth). 9 holding the mystery of the faith in a pure conscience. 10 And let these also first be proved; then let them serve as deacons, if they be blameless.

1 Tim. 3:12-13

Let deacons be husbands of one wife, ruling their children and their own houses well. 13 For they that have served well as deacons gain to themselves a good standing, and great boldness in the faith which is in Christ Jesus.

Elders

Elders are referenced in The Book of Acts first as being members of the Jewish leadership of the Temple in Jerusalem and the Sanhedrin in, and then in connection with Stephen in Acts 6:12.

Acts 4:1 - I persecuted this Way to the death, binding and delivering to prison both men and women, 5 as the high priest and the whole council of **elders** can bear me witness.

Acts 6:12 - And they stirred up the people, and the **elders**, and the scribes, and came upon him, and seized him, and brought him into the council, 13 and set up false witnesses.

The next reference to elders is to elders of the churches in Judea including the church in Jerusalem. This was in regard to the church in Antioch – where people of The Way were first called Christians – choosing to send support to churches in Judea.

Saul, who by now was becoming known as Paul travelled to the regions of Pisidia and Phrygia in Asia Minor where they began establishing churches in Pisidian Antioch and surrounding communities – Iconium, Lycaonia, Lystra, Derbe and Attalia – setting up leadership by appointing **elders**.

Acts 11:29 - And the disciples, every man according to his ability, determined to send relief to the brethren that dwelt in Judaea: 30 which also they did, sending it to the **elders** by the hand of Barnabas and Saul.

Acts 14:23 - And when they had appointed **elders** for them in every church, with prayer and fasting they committed them to the Lord in whom they had believed.

The Compiled Teachings of The Apostle Paul

Acts 15:1 records that some were teaching that circumcision was essential in order to be saved, but Paul and Barnabas did not agree with that teaching. Support for those insisting that circumcision was necessary and all must be directed to observe the Law of Moses came from Pharisees, which resulted in 'much debate'.

*Acts 15:1 - 'some men came down from Judea and were teaching the brothers, "Unless you are circumcised according to the custom of Moses, you cannot be saved..."' ² And after Paul and Barnabas had no small dissension and debate with them, Paul and Barnabas and some of the others were appointed to go up to Jerusalem to the apostles and the **elders** about this question. ⁴ When they came to Jerusalem, they were welcomed by the church and the apostles and the **elders**, and they declared all that God had done with them.*

Acts 15 ⁷ And after there had been much debate, Peter stood up and said to them, "Brothers, you know that in the early days God made a choice among you, that by my mouth the Gentiles should hear the word of the gospel and believe. ⁸ And God, who knows the heart, bore witness to them, by giving them the Holy Spirit just as he did to us, ⁹ and he made no distinction between us and them, having cleansed their hearts by faith. ¹⁰ Now, therefore, why are you putting God to the test by placing a yoke on the neck of the disciples that neither our fathers nor we have been able to bear? ¹¹ But we believe that we will be saved through the grace of the Lord Jesus, just as they will."
¹² And all the assembly fell silent, and they listened to Barnabas and Paul as they related what signs and wonders God had done through them among the Gentiles.

While it was Peter that made the first response (Acts 15:7-12), after the debate had reached a point where many for both viewpoints had expressed their views which resulted in a silence that James (the brother of Jesus) took advantage of:

Acts 15:13 After they finished speaking, James replied, "Brothers, listen to me. ¹⁴ Simeon has related (to us) how God first visited the Gentiles, to take from them a people for his name. ¹⁵ And with this the words of the prophets agree, just as it is written, ¹⁶ "'After this I will return, and I will rebuild the tent of David that has fallen; I will rebuild its ruins, and I will restore it, ¹⁷ that the remnant of mankind may seek the Lord, and all the Gentiles who are called by my name, says the Lord, who makes these things ¹⁸ known from of old.'

¹⁹ Therefore my judgment is that we should not trouble those of the Gentiles who turn to God, ²⁰ but should write to them to abstain from the things polluted by idols, and from sexual immorality, and from what has been strangled, and from blood. ²¹ For from ancient generations Moses has had in every city those who proclaim him, for he is read every Sabbath in the synagogues."

*Acts 15:22 Then it seemed good to the apostles and the **elders**, with the whole church, to choose men from among them and send them to Antioch with Paul and Barnabas. They sent Judas called Barsabbas, and Silas, leading men among the brothers, ²³ with the following letter: "The brothers, both the apostles and the **elders**, to the brothers who are of the Gentiles in Antioch and Syria and Cilicia, greetings.*

While we have no report back on Judas called Barsabbas and Silas (Acts 15:22), we do have a report on Paul and Barnabas.

*Acts 16:4 - As they went on their way through the cities, they delivered to them for observance the decisions that had been reached by the apostles and **elders** who were in Jerusalem.*

These next passages are the first references to 'elders' in Paul's epistles:

Titus 1:5
*This is why I left you in Crete, so that you might put what remained into order, and appoint **elders** in every town as I directed you*

Rom. 9:12
*...it was said to her, The **elder** shall serve the younger. ¹³ Even as it is written, Jacob I loved, but Esau I hated.*

This passage from Acts help us understand how Paul would have worked with the Gentile communities as he travelled, and help us understand how Paul met with and worked with those who had been appointed elders both in Asia and in Judea:

Acts 20:17
*Now from Miletus he (Paul) sent to Ephesus and called the **elders** of the church to come to him. ¹⁸ And when they came to him, he said to them: "You yourselves know how I lived among you the whole time from the first day that I set foot in Asia.*

Paul not only worked with the Gentile communities in Asia to spread the Gospel, he also raised financial support from them that he brought back to the church in Jerusalem (Acts 11:29; Cor. 16:1-4) although there are no reports of the collections made being received or distributed in Jerusalem.

Acts 21:17
*When we had come to Jerusalem, the brothers received us gladly. ¹⁸ On the following day Paul went in with us to James, and all the **elders** were present.*

The Compiled Teachings of The Apostle Paul

These next passages relate how elders among the leadership of the Jews sought to remove Paul and stop his ministry, but it is important to read the full chapter(s) in order to gain a more complete understanding:

Acts 23:12
*When it was day, the Jews made a plot and bound themselves by an oath neither to eat nor drink till they had killed Paul. ¹³ There were more than forty who made this conspiracy. ¹⁴ They went to the chief priests and **elders** and said, "We have strictly bound ourselves by an oath to taste no food till we have killed Paul.*

Acts 24:1
*And after five days the high priest Ananias came down with some **elders** and a spokesman, one Tertullus. They laid before the governor their case against Paul.*

Acts 25:13
*"There is a man left prisoner by Felix, ¹⁵ and when I was at Jerusalem, the chief priests and the **elders** of the Jews laid out their case against him, asking for a sentence of condemnation against him.*

1 Tim. 5:1
*Rebuke not an **elder**, but exhort him as a father; the younger men as brethren: ² the **elder** women as mothers; the younger as sisters, in all purity.*

1 Tim. 5:17
*Let the **elders** that rule well be counted worthy of double honor, especially those who labor in the word and in teaching. ¹⁸ For the scripture says, You shall not muzzle the ox when he treads out the corn. And, the laborer is worthy of his hire. ¹⁹ Against an **elder** receive not an accusation, except at the mouth of two or three witnesses.*

Titus 1:5
*For this cause left I you in Crete, that you should set in order the things that were wanting, and appoint **elders** in every city, as I gave you charge.*

Emasculation (Castration)

In Galatians 5:12 Paul writes: ¹²*I would that they that unsettle you would even go beyond **circumcision***.
NASB: '*would even emasculate themselves*.'
NLT: *I just wish that those troublemakers who want to mutilate you by circumcision would mutilate themselves.*
By this statement, "go beyond circumcision", Paul is suggesting that mutilation of the male genitals, aka emasculation, be justified and is appropriate in certain circumstances. Paul is specifically referring to agitators and troublemakers who were (still) preaching that circumcision is a requirement for all.

Encourage(d), Encouragement, Exhort

In Acts 15:30-32 Luke writes of Paul and his co-workers that they were encouraged by the response of the congregation at the church in Antioch on hearing the letter that they had brought from Jerusalem, and they were also given much encouragement by Judas and Silas:

Acts 15:30-32 ³⁰ *So when they were sent off, they went down to Antioch, and having gathered the congregation together, they delivered the letter. ³¹ And when they had read it, they rejoiced because of its encouragement. ³² And Judas and Silas, who were themselves prophets, encouraged and strengthened the brothers with many words.*
Rom. 1:12 *...that is, that we may be mutually **encouraged** by each other's faith, both yours and mine.*

1 Thess. 5:14 *And we exhort you, brethren, admonish the disorderly, **encourage** the faint-hearted, support the weak, be longsuffering toward all.*
Col. 4:10-11 ¹⁰ *Aristarchus, my fellow prisoner, sends you his greetings; and also Barnabas's cousin Mark (about whom you received instructions; if he comes to you, welcome him); ¹¹ and also Jesus who is called Justus; these are the only fellow workers for the kingdom of God who are from the circumcision, and they have proved to be an **encouragement** to me.*

The Compiled Teachings of The Apostle Paul

Faith

2 Cor. 1:23[b] ...I refrained to come to Corinth. [24] Not that we have **lordship over your faith**, but are helpers of your joy: for in faith you stand fast.

2 Cor. 4:13 But **having the same spirit of faith**, according to that which is written, I believed, and therefore did I speak; we also believe, and therefore also we speak; [14] knowing that He that raised up the Lord Jesus shall raise up us also with Jesus, and shall present us with you.

2 Cor. 5:6 Being therefore always of good courage, and knowing that, whilst we are at home in the body, we are absent from the Lord [7] (**for we walk by faith, not by sight**); [8] we are of good courage, I say, and are willing rather to be absent from the body, and to be at home with the Lord.

2 Cor. 8:7 But as you abound in everything, **in faith**, and utterance, and knowledge, and in all earnestness, and in your love to us, see that you abound in this grace also.

2 Cor. 10:15[b] ... having hope that, **as your faith grows**, we shall be magnified in you according to our province to further abundance, [16] so as to preach the gospel even to the parts beyond you, and not to glory in another's province in regard of things ready to our hand.

2 Cor. 13: 4 Try your own selves, whether you **are in the faith**; prove your own selves. Or know you not as to your own selves, that Jesus Christ is in you? unless indeed you fail the test.

Romans 1:5 ...through whom **we have received grace and apostleship to bring about the obedience of faith for the sake of his name among all the nations**, [6] including you who are called to belong to Jesus Christ,

Romans 1:8 First, I thank my God through Jesus Christ for all of you, because **your faith is proclaimed in all the world**.

Romans 1:12 ...that is, that we may be mutually encouraged by each other's faith, both yours and mine

Romans 1:17 For in it the righteousness of God is revealed from faith for faith, as it is written, "The righteous shall live by faith."

Romans 2:3 For what if some were without faith? shall their want of faith make of none effect the faithfulness of God? [4] God forbid:

Romans 3:22 ...even **the righteousness of God through faith in Jesus Christ** to all them that believe; for there is no distinction; [23] for all have sinned, and fall short of the glory of God;

Romans 3:24 ...being justified freely by his grace through the redemption that is in Christ Jesus: [25] whom God set forth to be a propitiation, **through faith, in his blood**, to show his righteousness because of the passing over of the sins done aforetime, in the forbearance of God; [26] for the showing, I say, of his righteousness at this present season: **that he might himself be just, and the justifier of him that has faith in Jesus.**

Romans 3:27 Where then is the glorying? It is excluded. By what manner of law? of works? Nay: **but by a law of faith**.

Romans 3:28 We reckon therefore that a **man is justified by faith apart from the works of the law**.

Romans 3:30 ...if so be that God is one, and **he shall justify the circumcision by faith, and the uncircumcision through faith**.

Romans 3:31 Do we then make the law of none effect (non-effective) through faith? God forbid: nay, we establish the law.

Romans 4:5 But to him that works not, but believes in him that justifies the ungodly, **his faith is reckoned for righteousness**.

Romans 4:9 "To Abraham **his faith was reckoned for righteousness**."

Romans 4:11 ...and he received the sign of circumcision, **a seal of the righteousness of the faith** which he had while he was in uncircumcision.

Romans 4:12 ...and the father of circumcision to them who not only are of the circumcision, **but (also those) who also walk in the steps of that faith** of our father Abraham which he had in uncircumcision.

Romans 4:13 For not through the law was the promise to Abraham or to his seed that he should be heir of the world, **but through the righteousness of faith**. [14] For if those that are of the law are heirs, **faith is made void**, and the promise is made of no effect:

Romans 4:16 For this cause it is of faith, that it may be according to grace; to the end that the promise may be sure to all the seed; not to that only which is of the law, but to that also **which is of the faith of Abraham**, who is the father of us all [17] (as it is written, A father of many nations have I made thee) before him whom he believed, even God, who gives life to the dead, and calls the things that are not, as though they were.

Romans 4:18 Who in hope believed against hope, to the end that he might become a father of many nations, according to that which had been spoken, 'So shall thy seed be'. [19] And **without being weakened in faith** he considered his

The Compiled Teachings of The Apostle Paul

own body now as good as dead (he being about a hundred years old), and the deadness of Sarah's womb; [20] yet, looking to the promise of God, he wavered not through unbelief, **but waxed strong through faith, giving glory to God**.

Romans 5:1 Being therefore **justified by faith**, we have peace with God through our Lord Jesus Christ; [2] through whom also we have had our access by faith into this grace wherein we stand; and we rejoice in hope of the glory of God.

Romans 9:10 ...the Gentiles, who followed not after righteousness, attained to righteousness, **even the righteousness which is of faith**: [31] but Israel, following after a law of righteousness, did not arrive at that law. [32] Why? Because they sought it **not by faith, but as it were by works**. They stumbled at the stone of stumbling; [33] even as it is written: Behold, I lay in Zion a stone of stumbling and a rock of offence: And he that believeth in Him shall not be put to shame. *(Is. 28:16)*

Romans 10:6 But **the righteousness which is of faith** says thus, Say not in your heart, Who shall ascend into heaven? (that is, to bring Christ down:) [7] or, Who shall descend into the abyss? (that is, to bring Christ up from the dead.) [8] But what does it say? The word is in you, in your mouth, and in your heart: **this is, the word of faith [that] which we preach**: [9] because if you confess with your mouth Jesus as Lord, and believe in your heart that God raised Him from the dead, you will be saved: [10] for with the heart man believes unto righteousness; and with the mouth confession is made into salvation.

Romans 11:20 Well; by their unbelief they were broken off, and **you stood by your faith**.

Romans 12:3[b] ...but so to think as to think soberly, according as God hath dealt **to each man a measure of faith**.

Romans 12:6[b] ...whether prophecy, let us prophesy **according to the proportion of our faith**; [7] or ministry, let us give ourselves to our ministry; or he that teaches, to his teaching;

Romans 14:1 But him that is **weak in faith** receives you, yet not for decision of scruples. [2] One man **has faith to eat all things**: but he that is **weak [in faith] eats herbs**. [3] Let not him that eats sit with him that eats not; and let not him that eats not judge him that eats: for God has received him.

Romans 14:22 The faith which you have, you have to yourself before God. Happy is he that judges not himself in that which he approves. [23] But he that doubts is condemned if he eat, **because he eats not of faith**; and **whatsoever is not of faith is sin**.

Romans 16:26b ...according to the commandment of the eternal God, is made known to all the nations **to obedience of faith**

1 Thess. 1:3 ...remembering without ceasing **your work of faith and labor of love** and patience of hope in our Lord Jesus Christ

1 Thess. 1:8 For from you have sounded forth the word of the Lord, not only in Macedonia and Achaia, but in every place **your faith to God-ward is gone forth**; so that we need not to speak anything.

1 Thess. 3:2 ...and sent Timothy, our brother and God's minister in the gospel of Christ, to establish you, and to comfort you **concerning your faith**; [3] that no man be moved by these afflictions; for yourselves know that hereunto we are appointed.

1 Thess. 3:4 For verily, when we were with you, we told you beforehand that we are to suffer affliction; even as it came to pass, and you know. [5] For this cause I also, when I could no longer forbear, sent **that I might know your faith**, lest by any means the tempter had tempted you, and our labor should be in vain.

1 Thess. 3:6 But when Timothy came even now to us from you, and brought us **glad tidings of your faith and love**, and that you have good remembrance of us always, longing to see us, even as we also to see you; [7] for this cause, brethren, we were comforted over you in all our distress and affliction through your faith: [8] for now we live, if you stand fast in the Lord.

1 Thess. 3:9 For what thanksgiving can we render again to God for you, ... [10b] and **may perfect that which is lacking in your faith**?

1 Thess. 5:8 But let us, since we are of the day, be sober, putting on **the breastplate of faith and love**; and for a helmet, the hope of salvation.

2 Thess. 1:3[b] ...that your faith grows exceedingly, and the love of each one of you all toward one another abounds; [4] so that we ourselves glory in you in the churches of God **for your patience and faith in all your persecutions** and in the afflictions which you endure; [5] which is a manifest token of the righteous judgment of God;

2 Thess. 1:11 To which end we also pray always for you, that our God may count you worthy of your calling, and fulfil every desire of goodness and **every work of faith, with power**; [12] that the name of our Lord Jesus may be glorified in you, and you in him

2 Thess. 3:2[b] ...that we may be delivered from unreasonable and evil men; **for not all have faith**. [3] But the Lord is faithful, who shall establish you, and guard you from the evil one.

1 Tim. 1:2 ...to Timothy, **my true child in faith**

The Compiled Teachings of The Apostle Paul

1 Tim. 4:4 ...*neither to give heed to fables and endless genealogies, which minister questionings, rather than **a dispensation of God which is in faith**; as do I now.* [5] *But the end of the charge is love out of a pure heart and a good conscience and **faith unfeigned**:* [6] *from which things some having swerved have turned aside to vain talking;* [7] *desiring to be teachers of the law, though they understand neither what they say, nor whereof they confidently affirm.*

1 Tim. 4:14 ...*and **the grace of our Lord abounded exceedingly with faith and love** which is in Christ Jesus.*

1 Tim. 4:18[b] ...*that by them you might war the good warfare;* [19] ***holding faith and a good conscience*** *some have rejected and so have suffered shipwreck with regard to the faith:* [20] *among whom are Hymenaeus and Alexander*

1 Tim. 2: 7 ...*whereunto I was appointed a preacher and an apostle (I speak the truth, I lie not), **a teacher of the Gentiles in faith and truth**.*

1 Tim. 2: 14[b] ...*but the woman being beguiled has fallen into transgression:* [15] *but she shall be saved through her child-bearing, **if they continue in faith and love and sanctification** with sobriety.*

1 Tim. 3:8 *Deacons in like manner must be grave, not double-tongued, not given to much wine, not greedy of filthy lucre.* [9] ***holding the mystery of the faith in a pure conscience**.*

1 Tim. 3:13 *For they that have served well as deacons gain to themselves a good standing, and great **boldness in the faith which is in Christ Jesus**.*

1 Tim. 4:1 ...*in later times **some shall fall away from the faith**, giving heed to seducing spirits and doctrines of demons,*

1 Tim. 4:6[b] ...*be a good minister of Christ Jesus, **nourished in the words of the faith**, and of the good doctrine which you have followed until now:* [7] *but refuse profane and old wives' fables.*

1 Tim. 4:12 *Let no man despise your youth; but be an example to them that believe, in word, in manner of life, in love, **in faith**, in purity.*

1 Titus 3:15[b] *Salute them that **love us in faith**.*

Ephes. 1:15 *For this cause I also, **having heard of the faith in the Lord Jesus which is among you**, and the love which you show toward all the saints,* [16] *cease not to give thanks for you*

Ephes. 2:8 ...*for by grace **you have been saved through faith**; and that not of yourselves, it is the gift of God;* [9] *not of works, that no man should glory.*

Ephes. 3:11 ...*according to the eternal purpose which he purposed in Christ Jesus our Lord:* [12] *in whom we have boldness and access in confidence through our faith in him.*

Ephes. 3:17 ...*that Christ may dwell in your hearts through faith; to the end that you, being rooted and grounded in love,* [18] *may be strong*

Ephes. 4:4[b] ...*even as also you were called in one hope of your calling;* [5] *one Lord, one faith, one baptism,* [6] *one God and Father of all, who is over all, and through all, and in all.*

Ephes. 4:12[b] ...*to the building up of the body of Christ:* [13] *till we all **attain the unity of the faith**, and of the knowledge of the Son of God, to a full-grown man, to the measure of the stature of the fulness of Christ*

Ephes. 6:16 *in addition **taking up the shield of faith**, wherewith you shall be able to quench all the fiery darts of the evil one.* [17] *And take the helmet of salvation, and the sword of the Spirit, which is the word of God*

Ephes. 6:23 *Peace be to the brethren, and **love with faith**, from God the Father and the Lord Jesus Christ.*

1 Philipp. 1:25[b] ...*I know that I shall abide, yea, and abide with you all, for **your progress and joy in the faith**;* [26] *that your glorying may abound in Christ Jesus in me through my presence with you again*

1 Philipp. 1:27[b] ...*that you stand fast in one spirit, with one soul **striving for the faith of the gospel***

1 Philipp. 2:17 ...*if I am offered upon **the sacrifice and service of your faith**, I joy, and rejoice with you all*

1 Philipp. 3:9[b] *not having a righteousness of mine own, even that which is of the law, **but that which is through faith** in Christ, the righteousness **which is from God by faith***

1 Coloss. 1:3 *We give thanks to God the Father of our Lord Jesus Christ, praying always for you,* [4] ***having heard of your faith in Christ Jesus**, and of the love which you have toward all the saints*

The Compiled Teachings of The Apostle Paul

Faithful(ness)

Acts 16:15 *And after she was baptized, and her household as well, she urged us, saying,* ***"If you have judged me to be faithful to the Lord, come to my house and stay."*** *And she prevailed upon us.*

1 Cor. 1:9 ***God is faithful****, by whom you were called into the fellowship of his Son, Jesus Christ our Lord.*

Gal 5:22 *But the fruit of the Spirit is love, joy, peace, forbearance, kindness, goodness****, faithfulness****, [23] gentleness and self-control. Against such things there is no law.*

1 Cor. 4:1[b] *Let a man so account of us, as of ministers of Christ, and stewards of the mysteries of God.* [2] *Here, moreover,* ***it is required in stewards, that a man be found faithful****.*

1 Cor. 10:13 *No temptation has taken you but such as man can bear: but God is faithful, who will not suffer you to be tempted above that you are able; but will with the temptation make also the way of escape, that you may be able to endure it.*

2 Cor. 1:18 ***But as God is faithful****, our word toward you is not yea and nay.* [19] *For the Son of God, Jesus Christ, who was preached among you by us, even by me and Silvanus and Timothy, was not yea and nay, but in Him is yea.* [20] *For however many are the promises of God, in Him is the yea: wherefore also through Him is the Amen, to the glory of God through us.*

1 Thess. 5: [24b] *at the coming of our Lord Jesus Christ.* [24] ***Faithful is he that calls you****, who will also do it.*

2 Thess. 3:3 ***But the Lord is faithful****, who shall establish you, and guard you from the evil one.*

1 Tim. 1:12 *I thank him that enabled me, even Christ Jesus our Lord, for that* ***he counted me faithful****, appointing me to his service;* [13] *though I was before a blasphemer, and a persecutor, and injurious: howbeit I obtained mercy, because I did it ignorantly in unbelief;*

1 Tim. 1:15 ***Faithful is the saying****, and worthy of all acceptance, that Christ Jesus came into the world to save sinners; of whom I am chief:* [16] *howbeit for this cause I obtained mercy*

1 Tim. 3:1 ***Faithful is the saying****, If a man seeks the office of an overseer (bishop), he desires a good work.*

1 Tim. 3:11 *Women in like manner must be grave, not slanderers, temperate,* ***faithful in all things****.*

1 Tim. 4:9 ***Faithful is the saying****, and worthy of all acceptance.* [10] *For to this end we labor and strive, because we have our hope set on the living God, who is the Savior of all men, specially of them that believe.*

1 Tim. 5:8 *But if any provides not for his own, and specially his own household,* ***he has denied the faith****, and is worse than an unbeliever.*

1 Tim. 6:10 *For the love of money is a root of all kinds of evil: which some reaching after have been* ***led astray from the faith****, and have pierced themselves through with many sorrows.* [11] *But you, O man of God, flee these things; and follow after righteousness, godliness,* ***faith****, love, patience, meekness.* [12] ***Fight the good fight of the faith****, lay hold on the life eternal, whereunto you were called, and did confess the good confession in the sight of many witnesses.*

1 Titus 1: 4 *to Titus, my true child after a common* ***faith****:*

1 Titus 1:9 ***holding to the faithful*** *word which is according to the teaching, that he may be able both to exhort in the sound doctrine, and to convict the gainsayers.*

1 Titus 1: 13[b] *For which cause reprove them sharply, that they may be sound in the faith,* [14] *not giving heed to Jewish fables, and commandments of men who turn away from the truth.*

1 Titus 2:2 *that aged men be temperate, grave, sober-minded, sound in faith, in love, patient:* [3] *that aged women likewise be reverent in demeanor,*

1 Titus 3:8 ***Faithful is the saying****, and concerning these things I desire that you affirm confidently, to the end that they who have believed God may be careful to maintain good works.*

Ephes. 6:22 *Tychicus, my beloved brother and* ***faithful minister*** *in the Lord, whom I have sent to you for this very purpose, that you may know our state, and that he may comfort your hearts.*

1 Coloss. 1:7 *even as you learned from Epaphras our beloved fellow-servant, who is a faithful minister of Christ*

The Compiled Teachings of The Apostle Paul

False Gospel / False Teaching

Paul references teaching of a false Gospel several times in his epistles. The accusation of false is also used in connection with false witnesses in the Book of Acts:

Acts 6:12
And they stirred up the people, and the **elders**, and the scribes, and came upon him, and seized him, and brought him into the council, ¹³ and set up false witnesses

Acts 13:6
And when they had gone through the whole island to Paphos, they found **a certain sorcerer, a false prophet**, a Jew, whose name was Bar-Jesus; ⁷ who was with the proconsul, Sergius Paulus, a man of understanding. The same called to him Barnabas and Saul, and sought to hear the word of God. ⁸ But Elymas the sorcerer (for so is his name by interpretation) withstood them, seeking to turn aside the proconsul from the faith. ⁹ But Saul, who is also called Paul, filled with the Holy Spirit, fastened his eyes on him, ¹⁰ and said, **"O full of all guile and all villainy, you son of the devil, you enemy of all righteousness, will you not cease to pervert the right ways of the Lord?** ¹¹ And now, behold, the hand of the Lord is upon you, and you shall be blind, not seeing the sun for a season. And immediately there fell upon him a mist and a darkness; and he went about seeking some to lead him by the hand.

Here are the references regarding false teaching of the Gospel made by Paul in his epistles:

Gal. 2:3
³ But not even Titus who was with me, being a Greek, was compelled to be circumcised: ⁴ and that because of the **false brethren** privately brought in, who came in privately to spy out our liberty which we have in Christ Jesus, that they might bring us into bondage: ⁵ to whom we gave place in the way of subjection, no, not for an hour; that the truth of the gospel might continue with you.

1 Cor. 15:13
¹³ But if there is no resurrection of the dead, neither has Christ been raised: ¹⁴ and if Christ has not been raised, then is our preaching vain, your faith also is vain. ¹⁵ Yea, and we are **found false witnesses of God**; because we witnessed of God that he raised up Christ: whom he raised not up, if so be that the dead are not raised. ¹⁶ For if the dead are not raised, neither has Christ been raised: ¹⁷ and if Christ has not been raised, your faith is vain; you are yet in your sins.

2 Cor. 11:12-15
But what I do, that I will do, that I may cut off occasion from them that desire an occasion; that wherein they glory, they may be found even as we. ¹³ For such men are **false apostles**, deceitful workers, fashioning themselves into apostles of Christ. ¹⁴ And no marvel; for even Satan fashions himself into an angel of light. ¹⁵ It is no great thing therefore if his ministers also fashion themselves as ministers of righteousness; whose end shall be according to their works.

2 Cor. 11:26
²³ **Are they ministers of Christ?** (I speak as one beside himself) I more; in labors more abundantly, in prisons more abundantly, in stripes above measure, in deaths oft. ²⁴ Of the Jews, five times received I forty stripes save one. ²⁵ Thrice was I beaten with rods, once was I stoned, thrice I suffered shipwreck, a night and a day have I been in the deep; ²⁶ in journeyings often, in perils of rivers, in perils of robbers, in perils from my countrymen, in perils from the Gentiles, in perils in the city, in perils in the wilderness, in perils in the sea, **in perils among false brethren**; ²⁷ in labor and travail, in watchings often, in hunger and thirst, in fastings often, in cold and nakedness

1 Tim. 1:9
...as knowing this, that law is not made for a righteous man, but for the lawless and unruly, for the ungodly and sinners, for the unholy and profane, for murderers of fathers and murderers of mothers, for manslayers, ¹⁰ for fornicators, for abusers of themselves with men, for slave traders, for liars, **for false swearers**, and if there be any other thing contrary to the sound doctrine;

1 Tim. 1:18-20
¹⁸ᵇ according to the prophecies which led the way to you, that by them you might war the good warfare; ¹⁹ holding faith and a good conscience some have rejected and so have suffered shipwreck with regard to the faith: ²⁰ among whom are Hymenaeus and Alexander; whom I delivered to Satan, that they might be taught not to blaspheme. (Because they promoted a **false doctrine** that was both heresy (contrary) and blasphemous.)

1 Tim. 4:1-3
¹ᵇ some shall fall away from the faith, giving heed to seducing spirits and doctrines of demons, ² through the hypocrisy of men that **speak lies**, branded in their own conscience as with a hot iron; ³ forbidding to marry, and commanding to abstain from meats, which God created to be received with thanksgiving by them that believe and know the truth.

1 Tim. 6:20-21
²⁰ O Timothy, guard that which is committed to you, turning away from the profane babblings and oppositions of the knowledge **which is falsely so called**; ²¹ which some professing have erred concerning the faith.

Eph. 4:25-27
²⁵ Wherefore, **putting away falsehood, speak truth each one with his neighbor**: for we are members one of another. ²⁶ Be angry and sin not: let not the sun go down upon your wrath: ²⁷ neither give place to the devil.

Phillip. 3:2
² Beware of the dogs, **beware of the evil workers, beware of the concision**:

> **Concision**: A term relating to over-zealous circumcision, related to emasculation.

The Compiled Teachings of The Apostle Paul

Father(s)

In Acts 2 and Acts 3 Peter, in his sermon, makes several references to fathers and forefathers, and in Acts 7, there are references to fathers and forefathers made by Stephen in his sermon showing that both Stephen and Peter were knowledgeable regarding the Jewish scriptures.

In Acts 13:16-43 Paul delivers a sermon in which he too makes references to fathers and forefathers, many of which are the same as those preached by Peter and Stephen, and in that sermon – in verses 32-39 – Paul preaches that God, as father, has delivered His son to humanity fulfilling a promise that Paul references as being from Psalm 2.

Acts 13:32-39 [32] *And we bring you good tidings of the promise made unto the fathers,* [33] **that God has fulfilled the same unto our children, in that he raised up Jesus; as also it is written in the second psalm, Thou art my Son, this day have I begotten thee.** [34] *And as concerning that he raised him up from the dead, now no more to return to corruption, he has spoken on this wise, I will give you the holy and sure blessings of David.* [35] *Because he said also in another psalm, 'You will not allow your Holy One to see corruption.* [36] **For David, after he had in his own generation served the counsel of God, fell asleep, and was laid with his fathers**, *and saw corruption (decay):* [37] **but he whom God raised up saw no corruption** *(decay).* [38] *Be it known to you therefore, brethren, that* **through this man is proclaimed to you remission of sins:** [39] **and by Him every one that believes is justified from all things**, *from which you could not be justified by the law of Moses.*

Later, Peter addressing the disciples – which most likely included some of the apostles and possibly Luke who wrote the Book of Acts – gives us a fairly clear account of his view that the Gospel should be taken to the Gentiles and on what terms it should be delivered to them, that is to say, without the requirement of circumcision.

The yoke that Peter is referencing is the challenge of persuading Gentiles to agree to circumcision should circumcision be considered mandatory.

Acts 15:7ᵇ Peter stood up and said to them, "Brothers, you know that in the early days God made a choice among you, that by my mouth the Gentiles should hear the word of the gospel and believe. [8] *And God, who knows the heart, bore witness to them, by giving them the Holy Spirit just as he did to us,* [9] *and he made no distinction between us and them, having cleansed their hearts by faith.* [10] *Now, therefore, why are you putting God to the test by placing a yoke on the neck of the disciples that neither our* **fathers** *nor we have been able to bear?* [11] *But we believe that we will be saved through the grace of the Lord Jesus, just as they will.*

Continuing to work through the Book of Acts, the next reference to fathers provides us with some background information about Timothy.

Acts 16 [1]*Paul came also to Derbe and to Lystra. A disciple was there, named Timothy, the son of a Jewish woman who was a believer, but his* **father** *was a Greek.*

In Acts 21:27-36, Paul was seized in Jerusalem by the crowd when Jews from Asia (Ephesus) made accusations against him, and it was only the action of the commander of the Roman cohort that prevented Paul from being beaten to death. After Paul pleaded with the Commander that he should be allowed to address the people (the crowd) publicly, the Commander permitted him to do so. Here is Paul's address:

Acts 22 "Brothers and **fathers**, *hear the defense that I now make before you."* [2] *And when they heard that he was addressing them in the Hebrew language, they became even more quiet. And he said:* [3] *"I am a Jew, born in Tarsus in Cilicia, but brought up in this city, educated at the feet of Gamaliel according to the strict manner of the law of our fathers, being zealous for God as all of you are this day.*

Paul has shared some background information about himself identifying that he is as much a Jew as any of those who had made accusations against him and even those who had attacked him: "*being zealous for God as all of you are this day*".

The next reference to fathers we encounter in Acts is a reference to '*The God of our fathers.*' In this passage Paul is explaining what occurred on the road to Damascus.

Acts 21:13ᵇ And at that very hour I received my sight and saw him. [14] *And he said, '***The God of our fathers** *appointed you to know his will, to see the Righteous One and to hear a voice from his mouth;* [15] *for you will be a witness for him to everyone of what you have seen and heard.*

It is from this passage that we understand that Paul had experienced an encounter with Jesus in which he both heard Jesus's voice and saw him, and also that Paul had been given the mission of being a witness for Jesus Christ.

In Acts 26, Paul is on trial being heard by the new Jewish king, Herod Agrippa and Paul is referencing the scriptures that prophesied about the Messiah, and he directly references the resurrection of Jesus Christ.

Acts 26:6 And now I stand here on trial **because of my hope in the promise made by God to our fathers,** [7] *to which our twelve tribes hope to attain, as they earnestly worship night and day.* **And for this hope I am accused by Jews, O king!** [8] **Why is it thought incredible by any of you that God raises the dead?**

The Compiled Teachings of The Apostle Paul

The next reference to fathers is in Acts 28, the last chapter in the Book of Acts, verse 8. Paul and his companions along with the crew of their ship are on the island of Malta having been ship-wrecked off the shore of Malta. Much of the land of this small island belong to a man named Publius:	*Acts 28:8* [8] *It happened that **the father of Publius lay sick with fever and dysentery. And Paul visited him and prayed, and putting his hands on him, healed him**.* [9] *And when this had taken place, the rest of the people on the island who had diseases also came and were cured.*

We don't generally associate Paul with miracle healings, but this is not the only time he is reported as having cured illness or brought a person back to life (Acts 20:7-12).

There is one final reference to fathers in the Book of Acts, in verse 23 (read Acts 28:17-29) Paul is preaching to both Jews and Gentiles when he referenced a scripture that prophesied that people would not accept the Gospel:	*Acts 28: 24* [24b] *(others were) disagreeing among themselves, they departed after Paul had made one statement:* **"The Holy Spirit was right in saying to your fathers through Isaiah the prophet:** [26] *"'Go to this people, and say, "You will indeed hear but never understand, and you will indeed see but never perceive."*
In his letter to the Galatians Paul states very directly that God was the father of Jesus and it was God who raised Jesus from the tomb.	*Gal. 1:1 Paul, an apostle – not from men nor through man, but through Jesus Christ and **God the Father**, who raised him from the dead.*
Paul relates to the Galatians the harsh truth about his past in Gal. 1:13-14. Paul acknowledges that he was one who was a zealous Pharisee who opposed and went after the disciples of Jesus – he uses the term 'the church of God' – persecuting them and approving of imprisonment, even some being sentenced to death, believing that he was faithfully defending the traditions of 'his fathers'.	*Gal 1:13 For you have heard of my manner of life in time past in the Jews' religion, how that beyond measure I persecuted the church of God, and made havoc of it:* [14] *and I advanced in the Jews' religion beyond many of mine own age among my countrymen, being more exceedingly zealous for **the traditions of my fathers**.*

The next references that Paul makes to fathers are all opening greetings in the letters he wrote to the churches in Corinth, Ephesus, Thessalonica, and Philippi, and in the letters he wrote to Timothy, Titus and Philemon.

In these opening sentences Paul references 'God our Father', 'God and Father', 'God The Father', God, the father of our Lord Jesus Christ.

In his letter to the Galatians Paul states very directly that God was the father of Jesus and it was God who raised Jesus from the tomb.	*Gal. 1:1 Paul, an apostle – not from men nor through man, but through Jesus Christ and **God the Father**, who raised him from the dead.*
The two observations we can make regarding the opening lines of the two letters to the Corinthians is that Paul used the same description of 'God the Father' in both letters, but the first letter was a prayer, 'Grace to you and peace to…" to the church in Corinth, while the second letter offered a praise to the God the Father followed by a recognition that what God is.	1 Cor. 1:3 Grace to you and peace from **God our Father** and the Lord Jesus Christ. 2 Cor. 1:3 **Blessed be the God and Father** of our Lord Jesus Christ, **the Father** of mercies and God of all comfort,

Eph. 1:2-4
*Grace to you and peace from **God our Father** and the Lord Jesus Christ.* [3] *Blessed be **the God and Father** of our Lord Jesus Christ, who has blessed us with every spiritual blessing in the heavenly places in Christ:* [4] *even as he chose us in him before the foundation of the world, that we should be holy and without blemish before him in love.*

1 Thess. 1:1
*Paul, and Silvanus, and Timothy, To the church of the Thessalonians in **God the Father** and the Lord Jesus Christ: Grace to you and peace.*

1 Thess. 1:2
We give thanks to God always for all of you, constantly mentioning you in our prayers, [3] *remembering before our **God and Father** your work of faith and labor of love and steadfastness of hope in our Lord Jesus Christ.*

1 Thess. 1:1
*Paul, and Silvanus, and Timothy, To the church of the Thessalonians in **God the Father** and the Lord Jesus Christ: Grace to you and peace.*

2 Thess. 1:1
*Paul, and Silvanus, and Timothy, To the church of the Thessalonians **in God the Father** and the Lord Jesus Christ: Grace to you and peace from **God our Father** and the Lord Jesus Christ.*

1 Tim. 1:3
*Grace, mercy, and peace from **God the Father** and Christ Jesus our Lord.*

1 Titus 1:4[b]
*Grace and peace from **God the Father** and Christ Jesus our Savior.*

The Compiled Teachings of The Apostle Paul

Philipp. 1:2
Grace to you and peace from God our Father and the Lord Jesus Christ

Coloss. 1:3
We always thank God, the father of our Lord Jesus Christ, *when we pray for you, ⁴ since we heard of your faith in Christ Jesus and of the love that you have for all the saints, ⁵ because of the hope laid up for you in heaven.*

Coloss. 1: 11[b]
*being strengthened with all power, according to his glorious might, for all endurance and patience with joy; ¹² **giving thanks to the Father**, who has qualified you to share in the inheritance of the saints in light.*

2 Tim. 1:2[b]
*Grace, mercy, and peace from **God the Father** and Christ Jesus our Lord.*

In Paul's letter to Philemon, Paul references himself as having become as a father to Onesimus, even referring to Onesimus as a child. One must presume from this reference that Onesimus was a youth whom Paul describes as '*was formerly useless to you*' [NASB], but who now '*is both useful both to you and me*'. (Phile. 1:10-16)

Phil. 4:10 I appeal to you for my child, Onesimus, **whose father I became** in my imprisonment.

---

1 Tim. 1:9[b] the law is not laid down for the just but for the lawless and disobedient, for the ungodly and sinners, for the unholy and profane, for those who strike their **fathers and mothers**, for murderers, ¹⁰ the sexually immoral, men who practice homosexuality, enslavers, liars, perjurers, and whatever else is contrary to sound doctrine.

Finally, in this reference that Paul makes to fathers. In 1 Timothy 1:9 Paul addresses the reason for and purpose of the law:

Father Abraham — See also 'God of Our Fathers'

Paul preaches that **Abraham** would be the father of a great nation. [Gen. 17:11], and **Isaac** would father twelve patriarchs [Acts 7:8 NASB], and **Ishmael** too will be blessed and will father twelve princes and will be made into a great nation. [Gen. 17:20b]

In **Romans 4:9-12** Paul preaches of **Abraham** that:
⁹ᵇ *Faith was reckoned for righteousness, ... ¹¹ and **he received the sign of circumcision while he was in uncircumcision that he might be the father of all them that believe**... ¹²ᵇ**to all who walk in the steps of that faith of our father Abraham**...*

[Also see comment regarding Col.2:13-14 on 'Forgiveness' below.]

Forgave, Forgive, Forgiving

Paul teaches about forgiving and being forgiven on two levels; first on how we should forgive others and about being forgiven, which is receiving forgiveness. Between each of as individuals, we can forgive others for anything by which they might have wronged us, and be forgiven by others who we may have wronged. We only have control over how we determine when and how to forgive others. Other than making an outright plea to someone we have wronged we have no control over when, how, or if we might be forgiven.

2 Cor. 2:6 *Sufficient to such a one is this punishment which was inflicted by the many; ⁷ **so that you should rather forgive him otherwise and comfort him**, lest by any means such a one should be swallowed up with his overmuch sorrow. ⁸ Wherefore I ask you to confirm your love toward him. ⁹ For to this end also did I write, that I might know the proof of you, whether you are obedient in all things. ¹⁰ But **to whom you forgive anything, I forgive also: for what I also have forgiven, if I have forgiven anything, for your sakes have I forgiven it in the presence of Christ**; ¹¹ that no advantage may be gained over us by Satan: for we are not ignorant of his devices.*

Paul writes in 2 Corinthians, Ephesians and Colossians on forgiving others and receiving forgiveness from others. In 2 Cor. 12:13, Paul also writes asking for forgiveness not for being a burden to the church in Corinth, but for not being a burden, a reference to his ability to earn his own living as a tent maker, something that he was able to do in Corinth because of Aquila and Priscilla [2 Cor. 18:3].

2 Cor. 12:13 *For what is there wherein you were made inferior to the rest of the churches, except it be that I myself was not a burden to you? **forgive me this wrong**.*

Eph. 4:31 *Let all bitterness, and wrath, and anger, and clamor, and railing, be put away from you, with all malice: ³² and be kind one to another, tenderhearted, **forgiving each other, even as God also in Christ forgave you**.*

The Compiled Teachings of The Apostle Paul

Regarding forgiveness of sins, the second level, Paul writes in Acts 26, Romans 4, Ephesians 1, and Colossians 1 & Colossians 2 *(See 'Forgiveness' below)*.

In Rom. 4:6 Paul writes, *"Even as David also pronounced blessing upon the man, to whom God reckoned righteousness apart from works"*, Paul clearly understood that forgiveness of sins can only come from God, and only comes from God through believing in Jesus Christ. [John 14:6]

In Col. 2:13-14 Paul writes: *"And you, being dead through your trespasses and the uncircumcision of your flesh, you, I say, did he make alive together with him, **having forgiven us all our trespasses**; ¹⁴ having blotted out the bond written in ordinances that was against us, which was contrary to us: and he has taken it out of the way, nailing it to the cross"*, by which Paul is making it clear that the requirement of circumcision for those who are under the law of Moses, is not a requirement for Gentiles.

***Col. 3:12** Put on therefore, as God's elect, holy and beloved, a heart of compassion, kindness, lowliness, meekness, longsuffering; ¹³ **forbearing one another, and forgiving each other**, if any man has a complaint against another; **even as the Lord forgave you, so you do also**: ¹⁴ and above all these things put on love, which is the bond of perfectness.*

Forgiveness

Acts 26:15 *And I said, 'Who are you, Lord?' And the Lord said, 'I am Jesus whom you are persecuting. ¹⁶ But rise and stand upon your feet, for I have appeared to you for this purpose, to appoint you as a servant and witness to the things in which you have seen me and to those in which I will appear to you, ¹⁷ delivering you from your people and from the Gentiles—to whom I am sending you ¹⁸ to open their eyes, so that they may turn from darkness to light and from the power of Satan to God, **that they may receive forgiveness of sins** and a place among those who are sanctified by faith in me.'*

Rom. 4:6 *Even as David also pronounced blessing upon the man, to whom God reckoned righteousness apart from works, ⁷ saying, "Blessed are they **whose iniquities are forgiven**, And whose sins are covered. ⁸ Blessed is the man to whom the Lord will not reckon sin."*

Eph. 1:5 *having foreordained us unto adoption as sons through Jesus Christ unto himself, according to the good pleasure of his will, ⁶ to the praise of the glory of his grace, which he freely bestowed on us in the Beloved: ⁷ in whom we have our redemption through his blood, **the forgiveness of our trespasses**, according to the riches of his grace, ⁸ which he lavished upon us, in all wisdom and insight.*

Col. 1:12 *giving thanks to the Father, who made us meet to be partakers of the inheritance of the saints in light; ¹³ who delivered us out of the power of darkness, and translated us into the kingdom of the Son of his love; ¹⁴ **in whom we have our redemption, the forgiveness of our sins**: ¹⁵ who is the image of the invisible God, the firstborn of all creation; ¹⁶ for in him were all things created, in the heavens and upon the earth, things visible and things invisible, whether thrones or dominions or principalities or powers; all things have been created through him, and to him; ¹⁷ and he is before all things, and in him all things consist.*

Col 2:13 *And you, being dead through your trespasses and the uncircumcision of your flesh, you, I say, did he make alive together with him, **having forgiven us all our trespasses**; ¹⁴ having blotted out the bond written in ordinances that was against us, which was contrary to us: and he has taken it out of the way, nailing it to the cross; ¹⁵ having despoiled the principalities and the powers, he made a show of them openly, triumphing over them in it.*

Fornication, Fornicator(s)   - see also Adultery

Addressing sexual activity sinning, aka fornication, is a common theme in Paul's preaching recorded both in Paul's epistles, the Letters, and also in Acts (which was written by Luke). Part of the challenge for us is looking at it through the lens of the 21st century is being able to recognize and relate to how Paul would have viewed things through the lens of the first century.

To begin with, we have no knowledge of Paul ever being married, or ever in a relationship, although there was a period after he was converted when he left Jerusalem and went away to Arabia, to return a number of years later [Gal. 1:17] during which he could have been in a relationship, married or otherwise, during that time? We know that his defense before Festus, the Roman Governor over Palestine, included a very detailed explanation about who he was; that he was an ardent student of the Jewish law, trained under one of the most respected teachers of the time [Acts 22:1]. Apart from the perspective Paul would have gained from being a Pharisee, was there any other personal awareness that Paul had that would qualify him to become a counselor on the matter of infidelity or of sexual activity of the unmarried?

As far as I am aware there is nothing in Paul's past that suggests that he was other than always single. Furthermore, there are his own statements about "wishing that certain other men were as he is" [Acts 26:29b; Gal. 4:12a] as well as his statement that he wished that certain others "would emasculate themselves" [Gal. 4:12b]. Is it possible that Paul himself had chosen that route in order to control his own human emotions?

What Paul actually preached was directly targeted at infidelity by either spouse, but he also addressed the issue of the unmarried, especially of virgins. In 1 Cor. 7:8 Paul

The Compiled Teachings of The Apostle Paul

writes: *⁸But I say to the unmarried and to **widows**, it is good for them if they abide even as I.*

There is little doubt that any Christian today who reflects Paul's teaching is almost certain to encounter the charge of moralizing when counseling another, so the question is, to what extent is Paul's teaching on this topic of fornication still fully relevant?

1 Cor. 5:1 It is actually reported that **there is fornication among you, and such fornication as is not even among the Gentiles**, that one of you has his father's wife.

1 Cor. 6: 13ᵇ **But the body is not for fornication**, but for the Lord; and the Lord for the body: ¹⁴and God both raised the Lord, and will raise up us through his power.

1 Cor. 6: 18 Flee **fornication**. Every sin that a man does is without the body; but **he that commits fornication sins against his own body**. ¹⁹Or know you not that your body is a temple of the Holy Spirit which is in you, which you have from God?

1 Cor. 7:1 Now concerning the things whereof you wrote: It is good for a man not to touch a woman. ²But, **because of fornications**, let each man have his own wife, and let each woman have her own husband.

1 Cor. 10:7 Neither be idolaters, as were some of them; as it is written, The people sat down to eat and drink, and rose up to play. ⁸ **Neither let us commit fornication, as some of them committed**, and fell in one day three and twenty thousand. ⁹ Neither let us make trial of the Lord, as some of them made trial, and perished by the serpents.

1 Cor. 12:21 lest again when I come my God should humble me before you, and I should mourn for many of them that have sinned heretofore, and **repented not of the uncleanness and fornication and lasciviousness** which they committed.

Thess. 4:3 For this is the will of God, even your sanctification, **that you abstain from fornication**; ⁴ that each one of you know how to possess himself of his own vessel in sanctification and honor, ⁵ not in the passion of lust, even as the Gentiles who know not God; ⁶ that no man transgress, and wrong his brother in the matter: because the Lord is an avenger in all these things, as also we forewarned you and testified. ⁷ For God called us not for uncleanness, but in sanctification. ⁸ Therefore he that rejects, rejects not man, but God, who gives his Holy Spirit to you.

Eph. 5:3 But **fornication**, and all uncleanness, or covetousness, let it not even be named among you, as becomes saints; ⁴ nor filthiness, nor foolish talking, or jesting, which are not befitting: but rather giving of thanks.

Col. 3:5 Put to death therefore your earthly body: putting aside fornication, uncleanness, passion, evil desire, and covetousness, which is idolatry; ⁶ for which things' sake comes the wrath of God upon the sons of disobedience;

God (of our Fathers) – See also earlier listing for 'Fathers'

Acts 2:32-33
Peter addresses the other apostles, *This Jesus did **God** raise up, whereof we all are witnesses. Being therefore by the right hand of **God** exalted, and having received of the **Father** the promise of the Holy Spirit, he has poured forth this, which you see and hear.*

Acts 26:5b
*... I lived as a Pharisee. ⁶ And now I stand here to be judged for **the hope of the promise made of God to our fathers**; ⁷ to which promise our twelve tribes, **earnestly serving God night and day**, hope to attain. And concerning this hope I am accused by the Jews, O king! ⁸ Why is it judged incredible with you, if God does raise the dead?*

Acts 26:16
But arise, and stand up on your feet: for to this end have I appeared to you, to appoint you a minister and a witness both of the things wherein you have seen me, and of the things wherein I will appear to you; ¹⁷ delivering you from the people, and from the Gentiles, to whom I am sending you, ¹⁸ to open their eyes, that they may turn from darkness to light and from the power of Satan to God, that they may receive remission of sins and an inheritance among them that are sanctified by faith in me.

Acts 26:22
*Having therefore obtained **the help that is from God**, I stand to this day testifying both to small and great, saying nothing but what the prophets and Moses did say should come; ²³ how **that the Christ must suffer, and how that He first by the resurrection of the dead should proclaim light both to the people and to the Gentiles**.*

Grace of God

In this first use of the term 'grace of God', Luke writing about Paul's first missionary trip, Paul had responded to an invitation to 'share' in the synagogue in Antioch of Pisidia:

Acts 13:15 *And after the reading of the law and the prophets the rulers of the synagogue sent to them, saying, Brethren, if you have any word of exhortation for the people, say on.*

At the end of Paul's preaching, Luke writes:

Acts 13:42-43 *And as they went out, they besought that these words might be spoken to them the next sabbath. ⁴³ Now when the synagogue broke up, many of the Jews and of the devout proselytes followed Paul and Barnabas; who, speaking to them, urged them to continue **in the grace of God**.*

The Compiled Teachings of The Apostle Paul

Having won the confidence of the Gentiles as well as many Jews in Antioch of Pisidia, Paul and Barnabas travelled throughout the region (Acts 14) ministering and then return to Antioch in Syria where their trip had begun, and Luke writes that they had been *'commended to the grace of God.'*

Acts 14:26
*Then they passed through Pisidia and came to Pamphylia. ²⁵ And when they had spoken the word in Perga, they went down to Attalia, ²⁶ and from there they sailed to Antioch, where they had been **commended to the grace of God** for the work that they had fulfilled.*
There is, however, no explanation given by Luke as to how this was manifested.

Paul writes in his first of two letters to the church in Corinth a note of thanks that God has given them grace; the 'grace of God'. Paul had visited Corinth and ministered there but was writing from Ephesus where he was in jail. There are three references to the grace of God in this letter.

1 Cor. 1:4
*I give thanks to my God always for you **because of the grace of God** that was given you in Christ Jesus, ⁵ that in every way you were enriched in him in all speech and all knowledge – ⁶ even as the testimony about Christ was confirmed among you.*

The first reference uses the term *'because of the grace of God'* which is communicating that Paul could see changes in those in Corinth which were in some way extraordinary. Paul does not elaborate specifically but he does reference that they had gained and advanced in knowledge and also in speech, i.e. the ability to speak publicly in order to share their knowledge and understanding. Paul also references that they are *'not lacking in any gift'* [Cor. 1: 7] implying that perhaps there are among them some who are prophesying, interpreting or healing.

The second reference uses the term *'according to the grace of God'* clearly referring to his personal encounter with Christ through which Paul, previously known as Saul, completely changed the direction of his life.

1 Cor. 3:10
According to the grace of God *which was given to me, as a wise master-builder I laid a foundation; and another builds thereon. But let each man take heed how he builds thereon. ¹¹ For other foundation can no man lay than that which is laid, which is Jesus Christ.*

The third reference uses two terms, *'because of the grace of God'* and *'but the grace of God'*. Again Paul is making a personal reference to his changed life, and he then gives full credit to the grace of God *'which was with me'* for all that he has accomplished in taking the Gospel message to the Gentiles.

1 Cor. 15:10
But by the grace of God *I am what I am: and **his grace** which was bestowed upon me was not found vain; but I labored more abundantly than they all: yet not I, **but the grace of God** which was with me. ¹¹ Whether then it be I or they, so we preach, and so you believed.*

2 Cor. 6:1
*And working together with him we entreat also that you do not receive **the grace of God** in vain ² (for he said, AT AN ACCEPTABLE TIME I LISTENED TO YOU, AND IN A DAY OF SALVATION I HELPED YOU: [Is. 49:8] Behold, now is the acceptable time; behold, now is the day of salvation).*

At first this verse seems rather confusing as the sentiment is mentioned in a negative sentence structure which should be taken to mean that we want you to receive the grace of God and for it not to be taken seriously or wasted.

In the verse that follows this passage, Paul explains that those in the churches in Macedonia gave of their own free will. In verse 14 Paul references that they in Corinth have an abundance, and he directly suggest that their abundance is also the supply for the needs of those in Macedonia. In other words, Paul is preaching a hard-hitting sermon on giving, that the grace of God should be in them to provide for those in need.

2 Cor. 8:1
*Moreover, brethren, we make known to you **the grace of God** which has been given in the churches of Macedonia; ² how that in much proof of affliction the abundance of their joy and their deep poverty abounded to the riches of their liberality.*

Following on from the previous passage, although separated by more than 20 verses, Paul closes out chapter 9 with an additional reference and reminder that one of the purposes of his letter was to secure financial support from the church in Corinth for the churches in Macedonia.

2 Cor. 9:14-15
*while they themselves also, with supplication on your behalf, long after you **by reason of the exceeding grace of God** in you. ¹⁵ Thanks be to God for his unspeakable gift.*

The Compiled Teachings of The Apostle Paul

Eph. 3:1-4
*For this cause I Paul, the prisoner of Christ Jesus in behalf of you Gentiles, — [2] if so be that you have heard of **the dispensation (stewardship) of the grace of God** (God's grace) which was given to me; [3] how that by revelation was made known to me the mystery, as I wrote before in few words, [4] whereby, when you read, you will perceive my understanding in the mystery of Christ.*

As Paul wrote in his first letter to the church in Corinth, he also writes to the church in Ephesus with direct reference to himself in mentioning the grace of God. He refers to himself as having been made a steward of God's grace. (Paul also references that he had written before, *'as I wrote before in few words'*, but, as there are no references in this letter to his encounter with Christ, he must be referring to an earlier letter.

Paul begins to explain that the Gentiles are now included in God's plan rather than being excluded as they were understood to be under the Laws of Moses and the prophets, and he references that the grace of God was afforded to him.

Eph. 3:7
[5] *which in other generations was not made known to the sons of men, as it has now been revealed to his holy apostles and prophets in the Spirit;* [6] *to wit, that the Gentiles are fellow-heirs, and fellow-members of the body, and fellow-partakers of the promise in Christ Jesus through the gospel,* [7] *whereof I was made a minister, **according to the gift of that grace of God** which was given me according to the working of his power.*

Col. 1:6
[5] *because of the hope which is laid up for you in the heavens, whereof you heard before in the word of the truth of the gospel,* [6] *which is come to you; even as it is also in all the world bearing fruit and increasing, as it does in you also, since the day you heard and knew **the grace of God in truth**;* [7] *even as you learned from Epaphras our beloved fellow-servant, who is a faithful minister of Christ on our behalf,* [8] *who also declared to us your love in the Spirit.*

Paul uses the phrase *'the grace of God in truth'* in this passage. This is a reference to being saved by grace through faith in Jesus. [Eph. 2:8]
Romans 8:[24] *For in hope we were saved: but hope that is seen is not hope: for who hopes for that which he sees?*

Paul writes that *'the grace of God has appeared, bringing salvation to all men'*. Paul tells us that the grace of God instructs us in how to live Godly lives.

Titus 2:11
[9] *Exhort servants to be in subjection to their own masters, and to be well-pleasing to them in all things; not gainsaying;* [10] *not stealing (purloining), but showing all good fidelity; that they may adorn the doctrine of God our Savior in all things.* [11] *For **the grace of God has appeared**, bringing salvation to all men,* [12] *instructing us, to the intent that, denying ungodliness and worldly lusts, we should live soberly and righteously and godly in this present world.*

Husband(s)

This first passage is included here because Aquila was the husband of Priscilla and this is of relevance in confirming that husband and wife teams were an important aspect of Paul's ministry. Recall that Paul had grown up, educated and trained as a Pharisee. This almost certainly meant that women would not have been considered by Paul as being in any leadership role in the temple.

Acts 18 *After this Paul left Athens and went to Corinth.* [2] *And he found a Jew named Aquila, a native of Pontus, recently come from Italy with his wife Priscilla, because Claudius had commanded all the Jews to leave Rome. And he went to see them.*

In Galatians, Paul references the scriptures that reference Abraham by referring to the mothers of Isaac and Ishmael as being Jerusalem (Sarah) and Mount Sinai in Arabia (Hagar). This prophecy predicts that there would be more descendants of Hagar than there would be of Sarah. [Gen. 21:10-13]

Gal. 4:26 [26] *But the Jerusalem that is above is free, and she is our mother.* [27] *For it is written: "Be glad, barren woman, you who never bore a child; shout for joy and cry aloud, you who were never in labor; **because more (numerous) are the children of the desolate woman than of her who has a husband**."*

The Compiled Teachings of The Apostle Paul

The next references to husband are in 1 Corinthians 7. The first of these addresses sexual activity and Paul begins by stating that the woman's body should not be touched, but since human reproduction relies on intimacy between a male and a female, Paul explains that a man should have a wife, and each woman a husband; that is Paul defines monogamy as meeting God's approval. Then Paul explains that in the marriage relationship neither controls the other's body and neither control their own body, but both are subject to each other.

*1 Cor. 7:1 It is good for a man not to touch a woman. ² But, because of fornications, let each man have his own wife, and **let each woman have her own husband**. ³Let the husband render to the wife her due: and likewise also the wife to the husband. ⁴The wife has not power over her own body, but the husband: and likewise also the husband has not power over his own body, but the wife.*

Paul explains that it is not him that is setting the rules, but the rules are those given by God. Wives should not leave their husbands and husbands should not leave their wives, but if they do separate they should not marry another.

*1 Cor. 7:10 But to the married I give charge, yea not I, but the Lord¹, **That the wife depart not from her husband** ¹¹(but should she depart, **let her remain unmarried, or else be reconciled to her husband**); and that **the husband leave not his wife**.* [¹ See Mark 10:12, Luke 16:18[

Paul addresses the challenge of being unequally yoked as regards belief in God. First Paul states that if the wife in not a believer but she is happy to remain with her husband, the husband should accept that and himself choose not to leave, and the same applies if the husband is not a believer, the believing wife should not leave him. Paul then states that an unbelieving spouse is sanctified by the believing spouse, and explains that is so that their children are sanctified otherwise they would be considered unclean.

Having stated his beliefs firmly, Paul then calls into question the certainty of what he has just written by questioning whether or not a believing spouse can sanctify an unbelieving spouse.

*1 Cor. 7:12 If any brother has an unbelieving wife, and she is content to dwell with him, let him not leave her. ¹³ And **the woman that has an unbelieving husband, and he is content to dwell with her, let her not leave her husband**. ¹⁴ For **the unbelieving husband** is sanctified in the wife, and the unbelieving wife is sanctified in the brother [her husband]: else were your children unclean; but now are they holy. ¹⁵Yet if the unbelieving departs, let them depart: the brother or the sister is not under bondage in such cases: but God has called us in peace. ¹⁶**For how knows you, O wife, whether you shall save your husband**? or **how do you know, O husband, whether you shall save thy wife**?*

These next two passages refer to making the choice of whether to marry or not. Paul cautions that becoming a husband or a wife is a balancing act; for once married one must not only please God but also please their spouse.

1 Cor. 7:32b He that is unmarried is careful for the things of the Lord, how he may please the Lord: ³³but he that is married is careful for the things of the world, how he may please his wife, ³⁴ and is divided.

1 Cor. 7:34b …but she that is married is careful for the things of the world, how she may please her husband.

On the topic of becoming widowed, Paul writes:
Paul addresses this topic again in his letter to the Church in Rome (Rom. 7).

*Cor. 7:39 ³⁹A wife is bound for so long time as her **husband** lives; but **if the husband be dead, she is free** to be married to whom she will; only in the Lord.*

The next reference to 'husbands' comes in a passage of 'Instructions for the church' that addresses issues of 'public behavior' in church such as speaking in tongues, interpretation of tongues, and prophesying before addressing women speaking in church. [1 Cor. 20-40]. On women speaking in church, Paul says, 'no', they should remain silent and if they have questions they should address those questions to their husbands at home.

*1 Cor. 14:34 ³⁴ let the women keep silent in the churches: for it is not permitted to them to speak; but let them be in subjection, as also says the law. ³⁵ And if they would learn anything, **let them ask their own husbands at home**: for it is shameful for a woman to speak in the church.*

In Paul's second letter to the church in Corinth, he references what he had written previously in the first letter, but this is an allegorical reference that he uses to address the issue of false witnessing by others who preach a False Gospel *(see 'False Gospel / False Teaching')*.

*2 Cor. 11:2 For I am jealous over you with a godly jealousy: **for I espoused you to one husband, that I might present you as a pure virgin to Christ**. ³ But I fear, lest by any means, as the serpent beguiled Eve in his craftiness, your minds should be corrupted from the simplicity and the purity that is toward Christ.*

Rom. 7:7
*Or are you ignorant, brethren (for I speak to men who know the law), that the law has had dominion over a man for as long as he lives? ² For the woman that has a husband is bound by law to the husband while he lives; but if the husband dies, she is discharged from the law of the husband. ³ So then if, while the husband lives and she is joined to another man (**married**), she shall be called an adulteress: but if the husband dies, she is free from the law, so that she is not an adulteress and [even though] she may be joined to another man.*

The Compiled Teachings of The Apostle Paul

The next four passages in which husbands are referenced – two in Paul's first letter to Timothy and two in his letter to Titus – are in relation to church leadership. Paul spells it out, consistent with guidance given to churches, that married leaders – who Paul addresses as overseers, deacons, and elsewhere, Elders – should have only one wife and also meet other criteria. In 1 Tim. 3, Paul twice addresses church leaders, first those who are overseers and second those who are deacons:

*1 Tim. 3:2 The **overseer** therefore must be without reproach, **the husband of one wife**, temperate, sober-minded, orderly, given to hospitality, apt to teach; ³ no brawler, no striker; but gentle, not contentious, no lover of money; ⁴ one that rules well his own house, having his children in subjection with all gravity; ⁵ (but **if a man knows not how to rule his own house, how shall he take care of the church of God?**) ⁶ not a novice, lest being puffed up he fall into the condemnation of the devil.*

*1 Tim. 3:12 Let deacons be **husbands of one wife**, ruling their children and their own houses well. ¹³ For they that have served well as **deacons** gain to themselves a good standing, and great boldness in the faith which is in Christ Jesus.*

In Titus 1, Paul relates the same message regarding having only one wife but takes a somewhat different view to the children of the overseer church leadership position, the children must not be associated with excessive indulgence in sensual pleasures (aka debauchery) nor be defiant of authority; insubordinate.

In Titus 2, Paul provides a lengthy list of criteria for older men and a second list for older women, and for women also charges the older women with the responsibility of training younger women.

*Titus 1:6 ...if anyone is above reproach, **the husband of one wife**, and his children are believers and not open to the charge of debauchery or insubordination. ⁷ For an **overseer**, as God's steward, must be above reproach.*

*Titus 2:2 ...that aged men be temperate, grave, sober-minded, sound in faith, in love, patient: ³ that aged women likewise be reverent in demeanor, not slanderers nor enslaved to much wine, teachers of that which is good; ⁴ **that they may train the young women to love their husbands**, to love their children, ⁵ to be sober-minded, chaste, workers at home, kind, **being in subjection to their own husbands**, that the word of God be not blasphemed.*

In Paul's Letter to the Church in Ephesus, in Ephesians 5, Paul addresses the husband-wife relationship. Paul describes the husbands as the head of the household and he exhorts wives to honor their husbands. Paul balances this seemingly one-sided, male-oriented (chauvinistic) view by then telling husbands to love their wives, and puts them on the same level as the church, which is all who believe, who are loved by Christ.

In Eph. 5:31-33, Paul addresses the basis for marriage, that a man leaves his own parents in order to take a wife to whom he commits to be bonded to, and that he should love her as much as he loves himself and in return should expect to be respected.

*Eph. 5:22 **Wives, be in subjection to your own husbands**, as to the Lord. ²³ **For the husband is the head of the wife**, as Christ also is the head of the church, being himself the savior of the body. ²⁴ But as the church is subject to Christ, **so let the wives also be to their husbands in everything**. ²⁵ Husbands, love your wives, even as Christ also loved the church, and gave himself up for it; ²⁶ that he might sanctify it, having cleansed it by the washing of water with the word, ²⁷ that he might present the church to himself a glorious church, not having spot or wrinkle or any such thing; but that it should be holy and without blemish. ²⁸ **Even so ought husbands also to love their own wives as their own bodies**.*

Eph. 5:31 For this cause shall a man leave his father and mother, and shall cleave to his wife; and the two shall become one flesh. ³² This mystery is great: but I speak in regard of Christ and of the church. ³³ Nevertheless do you also severally love each one his own wife even as himself; and let the wife see that she fear (respect) her husband.

Marriage, (Married, Unmarried)
Acts 21:4, 8-9

*⁴ And having sought out the disciples, we stayed there for seven days. ⁸ᵇ ...we entered the house of Philip the evangelist, who was one of the seven, and stayed with him. ⁹ He had four **unmarried daughters**, who prophesied.*

That Philip's daughters were able to prophesy is perhaps an indication of the genuineness of Philip's spiritual gifts.

(The two references to disciples and seven days in Acts 21 appears to mean that seven disciples were found who were willing to provide accommodation for Paul and his coworkers, each for a single night.)

1 Cor. 7:7ᵇ

*Howbeit each man has his own gift from God, one after this manner, and another after that. ⁸But I say to the **unmarried** and to widows, it is good for them if they abide even as I. ⁹But if they have not self-control, let them **marry**: for it is better to marry than to burn.*

Speaking to the elders about women who are single because they either have never been married or they were married but are now widowed Paul suggest that it is best they remain single but if they are unable to control their desires to be married, then let them marry for if they don't and they give into the temptation to engage in sexual activity outside of being married, they will be dammed and will burn in hades.

The Compiled Teachings of The Apostle Paul

In referencing 'will burn in Hades', is Paul referring to Malachi 4:1-3? Or, perhaps to John the Baptist claiming, *'His winnowing fork is in his hand, and he will clear his threshing floor, gathering his wheat into the barn and burning up the chaff with unquenchable fire.'* (Matthew 3:12)?

Paul himself also makes reference to punishment for sin in at least three of his Letters: *'All who sin apart from the law will also perish apart from the law, and all who sin under the law will be judged by the law.'* (Romans 2:12)	*'He will punish those who do not know God and do not obey the gospel of our Lord Jesus. They will be punished with everlasting **destruction** and shut out from the presence of the Lord and from the glory of his might.'* (2 Thess. 2:3) *'Their destiny is **destruction**, their god is their stomach, and their glory is in their shame.'* (Philippians 3:19)

In this verse, Paul offers assurance that marriage is not sinful.	**1 Cor. 7:28** ²⁸But should you **marry**, you have not sinned; and **if a virgin marry**, she has not sinned.

Somewhat akin to Jesus' teaching that you cannot serve two masters, Paul warns that remaining single and a virgin is more holy that being married because of the conflicting interests between giving yourself wholly to God and being married and having responsibilities *'for the things of the world'*.	**1 Cor. 7:32ᵇ** *He that is unmarried is careful for the **things of the Lord**, how he may please the Lord: ³³but he that is married is careful for the things of the world, how he may please his wife, ³⁴ and is divided. So also the woman that is unmarried and the virgin is careful for the **things of the Lord**, that she may be holy both in body and in spirit: but she that is married is careful for the things of the world, how she may please her husband.*

1 Cor. 7:34ᵇ
So also **the woman that is unmarried and the virgin is careful for the things of the Lord**, that she may be holy both in body and in spirit: but she that is married is careful for the things of the world, how she may please her husband.

1 Cor. 7:38

So then both he that giveth his own **virgin daughter** in **marriage** does well; and he that giveth her not in **marriage** shall do better.	This passage appears to be addressing the father of a virgin daughter regarding whether to or not commit his daughter to being betrothed and subsequently married. Paul writes that *'the father of the potential bride does well whether he gives her in marriage (to allow her to marry) or not give her in marriage.'*

Some commentaries, citing that there are differing views on how to translate the two previous verses 1 Cor. 7:36-37 as well as v38; *'Are these verses written to Christian men who are engaged to be married or to the Christian fathers of young women who are engaged to be married? Bible scholars differ'*. [www.bibleref.com] Those that feel that Paul is writing to the single male who is betrothed but who has decided against marriage and those that feel Paul is writing to the father of the virgin daughter. This is likely because either only the single male who is betrothed or the father of a virgin daughter can agree to dissolve the betrothal commitment. In the either case Paul cites two conditions; the first condition is that the young woman will not be dishonored by an unseemly end to the engagement. The second one is that the man—or the young woman if the father is being addressed—has the gift of celibacy, with his or her sexual desire under control.

1 Cor. 7:39

³⁹A wife is bound for so long time as her husband lives; but if the husband be dead, she is free to be **married** to whom she will; only in the Lord.	In this passage Paul is addressing a wife and what her commitment is while her husband is alive and what her rights to being released if she is widowed are. Paul states that she is *'free to be married to whom she will'* if her husband dies. Here Paul is endeavoring the establish clear guidelines for widows. In other places Paul references 'widows of childbearing age', but here he does not distinguish between younger and older.

Paul has disdain for those who would teach a false Gospel. Paul's reference to hypocrisy may mean that he believes (or even knows) that these teachers neither practice what they preach nor even truly believe what they are teaching. His reference to being branded with a hot iron could mean several different things. First, they have committed themselves to being identified with certain aspects of what they are teaching, such as claims that they know are untrue. Second, branding with a hot iron numbs not only the skin, but also the nerves, and so those who have been branded, especially by their own teaching, have lost sensitivity; in this case sensitivity to what is true and what is false. With regard to being married, Gnosticism is one example of a false teaching that caused its followers to adopt unreasonable restrictions including marriage.

The Compiled Teachings of The Apostle Paul

Paul comments that these things were made by God, therefore these things are good.	**1 Tim. 4:1-3** *But the Spirit said expressly, that in later times some shall fall away from the faith, giving heed to seducing spirits and doctrines of demons, [2] through the hypocrisy of men that speak lies, branded in their own conscience as with a hot iron; [3] forbidding to **marry**, and commanding to abstain from meats, which God created to be received with thanksgiving by them that believe and know the truth.*

1 Tim. 5:11-12
*But younger widows refuse: for when they have waxed wanton against Christ, they desire to **marry**; [12] having condemnation, because they have rejected their first pledge.*

This passage is referenced under 'Tattlers', and Paul is suggesting that younger widows are likely to fall away as they *'wax wanton'* meaning they become unrighteous, turning away from godliness, becoming idle (lazy) and engaging themselves in gossip (as tattlers). However, Paul is stating that many have had associations with men outside of their marriage after becoming widowed *'desiring to marry'*. Their 'first pledge' that Paul mentions, was to be a 'one-man woman' for life.

Following on from the prior passage, Paul suggests (states) that younger widows should marry, and he details duties and responsibilities that they should accept, and suggest that this is so that the adversary (Satan) might be resisted.	**1 Tim. 5:14-15** *I desire therefore that the younger widows **marry**, bear children, rule the household, give no occasion to the adversary for reviling: [15] for already some are turned aside after Satan.*

Eph. 5:22-33
Marriage Like Christ and the Church

These words are not wording of any verse in Ephesians 5, but are words that are offered as a heading for verses 22-33, of Ephesians 5.

In the prior verse, Eph. 5:21, Paul mentions the importance of mutual submission between all believers, which is important as one begins to understand the next three verses. Ephesians 5:22–24 is often taken drastically out of context, and grossly misinterpreted. Beginning in Eph. 5:22, Paul specifically applies this principle within the context of marriage, beginning with wives. Wives, he states, are to submit to their own husband. This does not mean that women are commanded to submit in a similar way to all men; but only to their husbands. As given verse 21, all believers are called to practice a form of humble submission to one another, but most definitely not in the way that *'a man leaves his father and mother, and shall cleave to his wife'* [Matt. 19:5] as commanded by Jesus. Those in dating relationships, in social or in employment contexts, or a woman with respect to another woman's husband are not included as those male-female relationships do not carry the same level of expectation. Also, it should be noted that nothing in Paul's teachings, here or elsewhere in the Bible, commands a woman to keep herself or her children physically (or mentally) available for spousal abuse.

[Credit: www.bibleref.com]

Prophecy, Prophetic, Prophet(s)

This passage in Acts introduces us to Agabus who perhaps reminds us of Joseph, and we also read about in Acts 21:10 in which Agabus proves that he does have the gift of prophecy should anyone not given him the benefit of any doubt regarding the prophecy in this passage. After all, Agabus could have just been lucky by coincidence.	**Acts 11:27** *Now in these days there came down prophets from Jerusalem to Antioch. [28] And one of them named Agabus stood up, and signified by the Spirit that there should be a great famine over all the world: which came to pass in the days of Claudius. [29] And the disciples, every man according to his ability, determined to send relief to the brethren that dwelt in Judaea: [30] which also they did, sending it to the elders by the hand of Barnabas and Saul.*

Acts 13:1 Barnabas is someone that we read fairly extensively about in Acts, and he is also mentioned in 1 Corinthians, Galatians and Colossians showing that he was a long-term co-worker and travelling with Paul and also making his own mission trips (see Acts 15:36). Barnabas is one of the four prophets mentioned together with Paul in this passage.	*Now there were at Antioch, in the church that was there, **prophets and teachers**, Barnabas, and Simeon that was called Niger, and Lucius of Cyrene, and Manaen the foster-brother of Herod the tetrarch, and Saul. [2] And as they ministered to the Lord, and fasted, the Holy Spirit said, "Separate [for] me Barnabas and Saul for the work whereunto I have called them." [3] Then, when they had fasted and prayed and laid their hands on them, they sent them away.*

The Compiled Teachings of The Apostle Paul

In this passage Paul establishes beyond doubt that he has spiritual powers. He prophesies that Elymas will become blind 'for a season' and immediately Elymas was unable to see.

Acts 13:6 - And when they had gone through the whole island to Paphos, they found **a certain sorcerer, a false prophet**, a Jew, whose name was Bar-Jesus; [7] who was with the proconsul, Sergius Paulus, a man of understanding. The same called to him Barnabas and Saul, and sought to hear the word of God. [8] But Elymas **the sorcerer** (for so is his name by interpretation) withstood them, seeking to turn aside the proconsul from the faith. [9] But Saul, who is also called Paul, filled with the Holy Spirit, fastened his eyes on him, [10] and said, "O full of all guile and all villainy, you son of the devil, you enemy of all righteousness, will you not cease to pervert the right ways of the Lord? [11] And now, behold, the hand of the Lord is upon you, and you shall be blind, not seeing the sun for a season. And immediately there fell upon him a mist and a darkness; and he went about seeking some to lead him by the hand.

Paul is explaining that Jesus was raised from the grave and through His death, Jesus took away our sin for all who will believe in him, and even sin that could not be justified by the law of Moses is now justified by Christ.

Acts 13:36
(And Paul spoke...) For David, after he had in his own generation served the counsel of God, fell asleep, and was laid to his fathers, and saw corruption: [37] but he whom God raised up saw no corruption. [38] Be it known to you therefore, brethren, that through this man is proclaimed unto you remission of sins: [39] and by Him every one that believes is justified from all things, from which you could not be justified by the law of Moses. [40] **Beware therefore, lest that come upon you which is spoken in the prophets**: 'For I work a work in your days, A work which you shall in no way believe, if one declares it to you.'

The first question one might raise regarding the next passage in Acts 15 is, 'Which Antioch?' There are two Antiochs mentioned in the Book of Acts, both of which Paul visited and spent time at ministering. There is the city of Antioch in Syria, north of Palestine (The Holy Land), and there is another city of Antioch in the region of Pisidia in Asia Minor, which is modern day Turkey. That Antioch was visited by Paul on his first missionary trip, but all three of Paul's missionary trips were started from Antioch in Syria, which is the Antioch mention in this passage, and timewise, this visit was after the first missionary trip and prior to the second missionary trip.

Acts 15:30
So when they were sent off, they went down to Antioch, and having gathered the congregation together, they delivered the letter. [31] And when they had read it, they rejoiced because of its encouragement. [32] And Judas and Silas, who were themselves **prophets**, encouraged and strengthened the brothers with many words. [33] And after they had spent some time, they were sent off in peace by the brothers to those who had sent them. [35] But Paul and Barnabas remained in Antioch, teaching and preaching the word of the Lord, with many others also.

Acts 19:6 ...they began **speaking in tongues and prophesying**.

In this passage Paul is in Ephesus, a city in Asia Minor that Apollos (a disciple and a prophet) had also visited and baptized many, but Apollos was now in Corinth, in Greece.

In Ephesus Paul encountered some of the disciples that Apollos had baptized and asked them if they had received the Holy Spirit when they were baptized, and they answered him, 'No," and told Paul they had not heard of the Holy Spirit so Paul asked them, [3]"Into what then were you baptized?" They said, "Into John's Baptism." [4] Paul said, "John baptized with the baptism of repentance, telling the people to believe in the one who was to come after him, that is, Jesus." [5]When they heard this they were baptized in the name of the Lord Jesus. [6] And when Paul had laid his hands on them, the Holy Spirit came on them, and they began **speaking in tongues and prophesying**. [7] There were about twelve men in all.

Agabus is first mentioned in Acts 11 when he visited Antioch (in Syria) and prophesied that there would be a famine, and the famine came about as he had said it would.

Paul is now arriving in Caesarea on the return from his third missionary trip heading to Jerusalem. The prophesy by Agabus, who came and visited Paul at the home of Philip the evangelist, in this passage was perhaps intended to deter Paul from going to Jerusalem.

Acts 21:10
On the next day we departed and came to Caesarea, and we entered the house of Philip the evangelist, who was one of the seven, and stayed with him. [9] **He had four unmarried daughters, who prophesied.** [10] **While we were staying for many days, a prophet named Agabus came down from Judea.** [11] And coming to us, he took Paul's belt and bound his own feet and hands and said, "Thus says the Holy Spirit, 'This is how the Jews at Jerusalem will bind the man who owns this belt and deliver him into the hands of the Gentiles.'" [12] When we heard this, we and the people there urged him not to go up to Jerusalem. [13] Then Paul answered, "What are you doing, weeping and breaking my heart? For I am ready not only to be imprisoned but even to die in Jerusalem for the name of the Lord Jesus." [14] And since he would not be persuaded, we ceased and said, "Let the will of the Lord be done."

The Compiled Teachings of The Apostle Paul

Paul in this chapter of his first letter to the church in Corinth is explaining spiritual gifts. He first references their pagan worship; '*² You know that when you were Gentiles you were led away to those dumb idols, howsoever you might be led. ³ Wherefore I make known to you, that no man speaking in the Spirit of God said, Jesus is anathema* [disliked, loathed, accursed]*; and no man can say, Jesus is Lord, except in the Holy Spirit.*' Paul is pointing out there is only one God, not many gods, and only those who have received the Holy Spirit are able to speak in the Spirit of God, and he continues to explain that people receive the Holy Spirit in different ways. [1 Cor. 12:1-11]

1 Cor. 12:7
But to each one is given the manifestation of the Spirit to profit likewise. ⁸ For to one is given through the Spirit the word of wisdom; and to another the word of knowledge, according to the same Spirit: ⁹ to another faith, in the same Spirit; and to another gifts of healings, in the one Spirit; ¹⁰ and to another workings of miracles; **and to another prophecy**; *and to another discerning of spirits: to another diverse kinds of tongues; and to another the interpretation of tongues: ¹¹ but all these are of the one and the same Spirit, dividing to each one severally even as he will.*

---

1 Cor. 13:1
If I speak with the tongues of men and of angels, but have not love, I am become sounding brass, or a clanging cymbal. **² And if I have the gift of prophecy, and know all mysteries and all knowledge**; *and if I have all faith, so as to remove mountains, but have not love, I am nothing…. ⁴ Love suffers long, and is kind; love envies not; love vaunts not itself, is not puffed up, ⁵ does not behave itself unseemly, seeks not its own, is not provoked, takes not account of evil; ⁶ rejoices not in unrighteousness, but rejoices with the truth; ⁷ bears all things, believes all things, hopes all things, endures all things. ⁸ Love never fails: but* **whether there be prophecies, they shall be done away**; *whether there be tongues, they shall cease; whether there be knowledge*

Chapter 13 of Paul's first letter to the church in Corinth is often referred to as the 'Love chapter'. With regard to prophecy and other spiritual gifts, Paul is explain if his the motivation and actions, and those of those who have these gifts, are not grounded in love (caring), then he understands everything is meaningless; '*profits me nothing*' '⁶ *rejoices not in unrighteousness, but rejoices with the truth;*' '⁹ *For we know in part, and we prophesy in part; ¹⁰ but when that which is perfect is come, that which is in part shall be done away*', meaning it has come to pass and has been fulfilled.

In his introduction of himself in the opening verses in his letter to the church in Rome – a church that he had not personally taken the Gospel to and had not visited yet (he was writing this during his second missionary trip from Corinth) – Paul makes the statement that he was foreordained to be an apostle: '*called to be an apostle, set apart for the gospel of God, ² which he promised beforehand through his prophets in the holy Scriptures,*'

Rom. 1:1
Paul, a servant of Christ Jesus, called to be an apostle, set apart for the gospel of God, **² which he promised beforehand through his prophets in the holy Scriptures**, *³ concerning his Son, who was descended from David according to the flesh ⁴ and was declared to be the Son of God in power according to the Spirit of holiness by his resurrection from the dead, Jesus Christ our Lord, ⁵ through whom we have received grace and apostleship to bring about the obedience of faith for the sake of his name among all the nations, ⁶ including you who are called to belong to Jesus Christ.*

Some translations do not mention 'the Way' and only reference, '*prophecies previously made concerning you*'[NASB] (as an example) or similar. Timothy is introduced in *Acts 16: ¹ Paul came also to Derbe and to Lystra. A disciple was there, named Timothy, the son of a Jewish woman who was a believer, but his father was a Greek. ² He was well spoken of by the brothers at Lystra and Iconium.* From this introduction we know that he was by parentage both Jew and Gentile. The reference to 'the Way' is Paul saying that Timothy was led by the spirit to the first Christians who were known initially as a sect called the Way: **Acts 24:14** *But this I confess to you, that according to the Way, which they call a sect, I worship the* **God of our fathers**… What the prophecies were, we aren't told by Paul, but they may well have been prophesies that were reported to Timothy.

1 Tim. 1:18
This charge I commit to you, my child Timothy, **according to the prophecies which led the Way to you**, *that by them you might war the good warfare; ¹⁹ holding faith and a good conscience some have rejected and so have suffered shipwreck with regard to the faith: ²⁰ among whom are Hymenaeus and Alexander; whom I delivered to Satan, that they might be taught not to blaspheme.*

Redeem(ed), Redemption

In his letter to the church in Galatia, Paul, speaking to the Jews primarily, explains why he has faith that Jesus Christ is the Messiah and that redemption is for the Gentiles as well as the Jews.

This is the first use of the term redemption by Paul that we have record of.

Gal. 3:11 Now that no man is justified by the law before God, is evident: for, The righteous shall live by faith; **12** and the law is not of faith; but, He that does, they shall live in them. **13 Christ redeemed us from the curse of the law**, having become a curse for us; for it is written, Cursed is every one that hangs on a tree: **14** that upon the Gentiles might come the blessing of Abraham in Christ Jesus; that we might receive the promise of the Spirit through faith.

Again, Paul is speaking primarily to the Jews in his letter to the church in Galatia in Gal. 4:4.

Gal. 4:4
But when the set time had fully come, God sent his Son, born of a woman, born under the law, **5 to redeem those under the law**, *that we might receive adoption to sonship.*

In Romans 3:20, the verse prior to this next passage, Paul explains that the Law speaks only to those under the law, that is those who are descended from Jacob, and that through the law comes knowledge of sin, meaning that the commandments of Moses and other prophets establish what is acceptable and what is not acceptable.

Rom. 3:21
But now apart from the law a righteousness of God has been manifested, being witnessed by the law and the prophets; **22** *even **the righteousness of God** through faith in Jesus Christ to all them that believe; for there is no distinction;* **23** *for all have sinned, and fall short of the glory of God;* **24** *being justified freely by his grace through the redemption that is in Christ Jesus:* **25** *whom God set forth to be a propitiation, through faith, in his blood, to show his righteousness because of the passing over of the sins done aforetime, in the forbearance of God.*

Paul explains that through Jesus Christ, everyone can be redeemed, and that is in believing by faith that Jesus Christ was of God, was born as man, lived as man, and was predestined according to the prophets to give His life so that all should be saved. *(For an explanation of atonement and how God gave Jesus to the world, see 2 Corinthians 5:18-19, '18 But all things are of God, who reconciled us to himself through Christ, and gave to us the ministry of reconciliation; 19 to wit, that God was in Christ reconciling the world to himself').*

Paul appears to use the word redemption in this passage as if he believes that our early body will be traded-in and we will be given a replacement body, one that we believe will be glorious, something that, he is saying, is worth waiting for, even though we may complain about our present circumstances.

Rom. 8:22
For we know that the whole creation groans and travails in pain together until now. **23** *And not only so, but ourselves also, who have the first-fruits of the Spirit, even we ourselves groan within ourselves, waiting for our adoption, to wit,* **the redemption of our body**.

The claim made by Paul in this passage is that we will be redeemed from all our transgressions, but then there is the word 'might'. 'Might be' is not the same as will be.
Referencing Romans 6, the theme of that chapter is that believers are dead to sin, but are alive to God:
Rom. 2:2 May it never be! How shall we who died to sin still live in sin?
Paul states that *'the grace of God has appeared' bringing salvation to all men,* [Titus 2:11] which appears to mean that the grace of God is Jesus Christ, and certainly it is Jesus Christ who has brought *'salvation to all men'.*

Titus 2:11
*For the **grace of God** has appeared, bringing salvation to all men,* **12** *instructing us, to the intent that, denying ungodliness and worldly lusts, we should live soberly and righteously and godly in this present world;* **13** *looking for the blessed hope and appearing of the glory of the great God and our Savior Jesus Christ;* **14** *who gave himself for us,* **that he might redeem us from all iniquity**, *and purify to himself a people for his own possession, zealous of good works.*

In his letter to the church in Ephesus, Paul states very firmly *'7 In him we have redemption through his blood.',* and Paul adds by way of explanation: *'7b the forgiveness of our trespasses',* making it clear what he expects us to understand by redemption.

Eph. 1:4b
In love **5** *he predestined us for adoption to himself as sons through Jesus Christ, according to the purpose of his will,* **6** *to the praise of his glorious grace, with which he has blessed us in the Beloved.* **7 In him we have redemption through his blood, the forgiveness of our trespasses**, *according to the riches of his grace,* **8** *which he lavished upon us, in all wisdom and insight* **9** *making known to us the mystery of his will, according to his purpose, which he set forth in Christ* **10** *as a plan for the fullness of time, to unite all things in him, things in heaven and things on earth.*

The Compiled Teachings of The Apostle Paul

This passage in Paul's letter to the church in Ephesus provides solid advice about how to conduct oneself and be a better person, and the passage ends with '*grieve not the Holy Spirit of God*' meaning do not cause grief; do not cause the Holy Spirit to grieve.

Eph. 4:25
Wherefore, putting away falsehood, speak truth each one with his neighbor: for we are members one of another. [26] *Be angry and sin not: let not the sun go down upon your wrath:* [27] *neither give place to the devil.* [28] *Let him that stole steal no more: but rather let him labor, working with his hands the thing that is good, that he may have whereof to give to him that has need.* [29] *Let no corrupt speech proceed out of your mouth, but such as is good for edifying as the need may be, that it may give grace to them that hear.* [30] *And grieve not the Holy Spirit of God,* **in whom you were sealed for the day of redemption.**

Eph. 5:15
Look therefore carefully how you walk, not as unwise, but as wise; [16] **redeeming** *the time, because the days are evil.*

Most other references to redemption mention sin, but this passage references time, '*because the days are evil.*' When one redeems a voucher or token we are exchanging the value of that voucher for something that we receive in return. Such a transaction is known as purchasing, and Jesus Christ purchased our sins when he went to the cross, and if we live wisely as this passage advises, we are exchanging days in which we could be sinful for days in which we are righteous.

In this passage in the early part of Paul's letter to the church in Colossae, Paul makes the statement that we, that is humanity, has been delivered out from under the control of the powers of evil (darkness), and that we have a place in the kingdom of the Son of God who has already made the sacrifice that redeems those who believe. Then Paul summarizes the personage of Jesus Christ and his relationship to God the father.

Col. 1:13-17
[13] *who delivered us out of the power of darkness, and translated us into the kingdom of the Son of his love;* [14] **in whom we have our redemption,** *the forgiveness of our sins:* [15] *who is the image of the invisible God, the firstborn of all creation;* [16] *for in him were all things created, in the heavens and upon the earth, things visible and things invisible, whether thrones or dominions or principalities or powers; all things have been created through him, and to him;* [17] *and he is before all things, and in him all things consist.*

When Paul speaks to the Ephesian Elders [Acts 20:32[b]] he uses the term '*inheritance among all those who are sanctified*', from which, we can take '*those who are sanctified*' to mean the same as '*the saints in light*' referenced in this passage.

As mentioned earlier, in Ephesians 1:7, Paul writes, '*In him we have redemption through his blood, the forgiveness of our trespasses.*' Here in Colossians, we see the same exact phrase.
Putting the two together we have both the plan and the implementation of the plan described:

Eph. 1:5-7
...he predestined us for adoption to himself as sons through Jesus Christ, according to the purpose of his will, [6] *to the praise of his glorious grace, with which he has blessed us in the Beloved.*

Col. 1:13-14
He has delivered us from the domain of darkness and transferred us to the kingdom of his beloved Son,

in whom we have redemption, *the forgiveness of sins.* [Eph. 1:7; Col. 1:14]

This is the second passage in the letter to the Colossians that refers to 'redeeming the time' (The other passage is *Eph. 5:15*
Look therefore carefully how you walk, not as unwise, but as wise; [16] *redeeming the time, because the days are evil.*)

Also, again, there is a reference to walking. The instruction in this passage is to '*walk toward them who are without*' (meaning outside) '*in wisdom*', which compares closely to the instruction in Ephesians to '*walk, not as unwise, but as wise*'.

Col. 4:1
Masters, render to your servants that which is just and equal; knowing that you also have a Master in heaven. [2] *Continue steadfastly in prayer, watching therein with thanksgiving;* [3] *additionally praying for us also, that God may open to us a door for the word, to speak the mystery of Christ, for which I am also in bonds;* [4] *that I may make it manifest, as I ought to speak.* [5] **Walk in wisdom toward them that are without, redeeming the time.** [6] *Let your speech be always with grace, seasoned with salt, that you may know how you ought to answer each one.*

The Compiled Teachings of The Apostle Paul

Salvation

In Acts there are several references to salvation. In the first, Paul makes reference to John the Baptist, second he refers to the commission that he has been given by Jesus Christ, third Luke reports on an event in Phillippi, and fourth, in Acts 28, when Paul and his companions, together with the crew of their ship, have arrived in Rome and Paul is in custody under house arrest and he calls the leaders of the Jewish community to meet with him.

Acts 13:25
*And as John was fulfilling his course, he said, What suppose you that I am? I am not he. But behold, there cometh one after me the shoes of whose feet I am not worthy to unloose. ²⁶ Brethren, children of the stock of Abraham, and those among you that fear God, to us is the word of this **salvation** sent forth.*

Acts 13:47
*For so has the Lord commanded us, saying, I have set thee for a light of the Gentiles, that you shouldest be for **salvation** unto the uttermost part of the earth.*

Acts 16:17
*She followed Paul and us, crying out, "These men are servants of the Most High God, who proclaim to you the way of **salvation**."*

Acts 28:28
*Therefore let it be known to you that this **salvation** of God has been sent to the Gentiles; they will listen."*

In Paul's second letter to the churches in Corinth, Paul explains that '*it is for their comfort and salvation*' that they suffer for Christ and later references the scriptures to point out that the time of '*a day of salvation*' has now come.

In 2 Cor. 7: ¹⁰, Paul offers reassurance that repentance to salvation brings no regrets while the '*sorrow of the world*' brings death.

2 Cor. 1:5 *For as we share abundantly in Christ's sufferings, so through Christ we share abundantly in comfort too. ⁶ If we are afflicted, **it is for your comfort and salvation**; and if we are comforted, it is for your comfort, which you experience when you patiently endure the same sufferings that we suffer.*

2 Cor. 6:1-2
*And working together with him we entreat also that you do not receive the grace of God in vain ² (for he said, AT AN ACCEPTABLE TIME I HEARKENED UNTO THEE, AND IN **A DAY OF SALVATION** DID I SUCCOR THEE: [Is. 49:8] behold, now is the acceptable time; behold, **now is the day of salvation**)*

2 Cor. 7:10
*For godly sorrow works **repentance to salvation**, a repentance which brings no regret: but the sorrow of the world works death.*

Paul describes the 'word of truth' – the gospel of Jesus Christ – as being 'the gospel of their salvation' because they have chosen to believe in Jesus.

Eph. 1:13
*In him you also, when you heard the word of truth, **the gospel of your salvation**, and believed in him, were sealed with the promised Holy Spirit, ¹⁴ who is the guarantee of our inheritance until we acquire possession of it, to the praise of his glory.*

The first reference to salvation in Paul's letter to the church in Rome is a reassurance that all who believe, both Jews and Gentiles, that is those who speak the Greek language, will receive salvation, provided that they live righteous lives, and in Romans 10, Paul explains that it is by spoken confession that we receive salvation. In Romans 11, Paul, who is writing primarily to the leadership of the Jews explains that the Jews, God's chosen people have fallen and it because of their fall that the Gentiles, those who are recognized as those who speak Greek and other languages, have been given equal status for salvation in the eyes of God.

Finally, in Romans 13 Paul expresses urgency pointing out that salvation is near, '*nearer that when we first believed.*'

Romans 1:16
*For I am not ashamed of the gospel, for **it is the power of God for salvation to everyone who believes**, to the Jew first and also to the Greek. ¹⁷ For in it the righteousness of God is revealed from faith for faith, as it is written, "The righteous shall live by faith."*

Romans 10:9
*...because if you confess with your mouth Jesus as Lord, and believe in your heart that God raised Him from the dead, you will be saved: ¹⁰ for with the heart man believes unto righteousness; and **with the mouth confession is made into salvation**. ¹¹ For the scripture says, Whosoever believes in Him shall not be put to shame.*

Romans 11:11
*I say then, Did they stumble that they might fall? God forbid: **but by their fall salvation is come to the Gentiles**, to provoke them to jealousy. ¹² Now if their fall is the riches of the world, and their loss the riches of the Gentiles; how much more their fulness?*

Romans 13:11
*And this, knowing the season, that already it is time for you to wake out of sleep: **for now is salvation nearer** to us than when we first believed.*

The Compiled Teachings of The Apostle Paul

In Paul's first letter to the church in Thessalonica, Paul draws an analogy to being military – 'soldiers for Christ' – wearing helmets and breastplates, but pointing out that we are not to live by waring but to live in hope with the goal of obtaining salvation *'through our Lord, Jesus Christ'*. In his second letter to the Thessalonians, Paul states that each person (who believes in Christ) has been chosen by God to receive salvation.

1 Thess. 5:8
*But let us, since we are of the day, be sober, putting on the breastplate of faith and love; and for a helmet, **the hope of salvation**. ⁹ For God appointed us not to wrath, but to the **obtaining of salvation through our Lord Jesus Christ**, ¹⁰ who died for us, that, whether we wake or sleep, we should live together with him.*

2 Thess. 2:13
*But we are bound to give thanks to God always for you, brethren beloved of the Lord, for that God chose you from the beginning **to salvation in sanctification of the Spirit** and belief of the truth.*

Paul takes a very direct approach in his letter to Titus, simply stating that *'the grace of God has appeared'* – that is Jesus Christ – and it is Jesus Christ that has brought salvation *'to all men'*, but receiving salvation is not automatic; it is not available to the ungodly, nor to those who cannot deny worldly lusts. Paul states that we must live sober lives and be righteous and godly in spite of all of the temptations of the world.

Titus 2:11
*For the grace of God has appeared, **bringing salvation to all men**, ¹² instructing us, to the intent that, denying ungodliness and worldly lusts, we should live soberly and righteously and godly in this present world; ¹³ looking for the blessed hope and appearing of the glory of the great God and our Savior Jesus Christ*

Paul implies in his letter to the church in Ephesus that they are now equals, he and his companions coming as believers and those in Ephesus having now also become believers have been granted the promise of salvation. Paul also uses the same analogy of being deployed as military as he used in his letter to the Thessalonians, wearing helmets and breastplates, but now also armed with *'the sword of the spirit'* and wearing *'the helmet of salvation'* and *'praying at all times'*.

Eph. 1:12ᵇ
*we who had before hoped in Christ: ¹³ in whom you also, having heard the word of the truth, **the gospel of your salvation**, – in whom, having also believed, you were sealed with the Holy Spirit of promise*

Eph. 6:17
*And take **the helmet of salvation**, and the sword of the Spirit, which is the word of God: ¹⁸ with all prayer and supplication praying at all seasons in the Spirit,*

In the NASB version of the Bible, the term 'In Him" is used rather than 'in whom' used in the ASV. Paul's teaching is always focused on the belief that Jesus Christ is the son of God.

NASB – New American Standard Bible; ASV – American Standard Version

---

In his letter to the church in Philippi, Paul first references his salvation and that he does not expect to be put to shame, and in the second reference, he focuses on their salvation, that they need to believe in in Jesus Christ but also expect to suffer hardships because of Him. They must stand together in the face of whatever adversities that they might be confronted by.

Confirming that he is not just somewhere away from Philippi, but is not expecting to be able to visit them any time soon, Paul tells them to focus on working out their salvation *'with fear and trembling'*.

Philip. 1:19
*For I know that this shall turn out to **my salvation**, through your supplication and the supply of the Spirit of Jesus Christ, ²⁰ according to my earnest expectation and hope, that in nothing shall I be put to shame*

Philip. 1:27b
*that you stand fast in one spirit, with one soul striving for the faith of the gospel; ²⁸ and in nothing affrighted by the adversaries: which is for them an evident token of perdition, but **of your salvation**, and that from God; ²⁹ because to you it has been granted in the behalf of Christ, not only to believe on him, but also to suffer in his behalf*

Philip. 2:12
*So then, my beloved, even as you have always obeyed, not as in my presence only, but now much more in my absence, **work out your own salvation** with fear and trembling; ¹³ for it is God who works in you both to will and to work, for his good pleasure.*

Writing to Timothy, Paul states that his goal is that others will gain salvation, and he advises Timothy that he must live by what he has been taught so that he stays *'wise unto salvation'*.

*2 Tim. 2: ¹⁰ Therefore I endure all things for the elect's sake, that they also **may obtain the salvation which is in Christ Jesus** with eternal glory.*
*2 Tim. 3: ¹⁴ But abide in the things which you have learned and have been assured of, knowing of whom you have learned them; ¹⁵ and that from a babe you have known the sacred writings which are able to make you wise **unto salvation through faith** which is in Christ Jesus.*

The Compiled Teachings of The Apostle Paul

Son(s), Son of God
— except Sons of God; see next section below.

In this passage Luke introduces Timothy. Lystra is one of the first cities in Asia Minor after travelling through Tarsus, and this is the second visit that Paul is making to Lystra. By parentage Timothy is both Jew and Gentile and Luke refers to him as a disciple. On his previous missionary trip, Paul had travelled with Barnabas, but he had chosen Silas to accompany him on this trip. Timothy was invited by Paul to join them and he agreed to being circumcised as that would make him more accepted in the synagogues.

Acts 16:1
Paul came also to Derbe and to Lystra. **A disciple was there, named Timothy, the son of a Jewish woman who was a believer, but his father was a Greek.** ² He was well spoken of by the brothers at Lystra and Iconium. ³ Paul wanted Timothy to accompany him, and he took him and circumcised him because of the Jews who were in those places, for they all knew that his father was a Greek.

The sons that we read of in this passage are described by Luke as being exorcists in many Bible translations and they were invoking Jesus's name along with Paul's name in performing exorcisms and Luke records that one of the evil spirits that they were attempting to exorcise turned on one of the sons of the Jewish high priest overpowering him causing both him and his brothers to flee.

Acts 19:13
Then some of the itinerant Jewish exorcists undertook to invoke the name of the Lord Jesus over those who had evil spirits, saying, "I adjure you by the Jesus whom Paul proclaims." ¹⁴ **Seven sons of a Jewish high priest named Sceva** were doing this. ¹⁵ But the evil spirit answered them, "Jesus I know, and Paul I recognize, but who are you?" ¹⁶ And the man in whom was the evil spirit leaped on them, mastered all of them and overpowered them, so that they fled out of that house naked and wounded. ¹⁷ And this became known to all the residents of Ephesus, both Jews and Greeks. And fear fell upon them all, and the name of the Lord Jesus was extolled.

This passage in Paul's letter to the churches in Galatia appears to be a response to disbelief by either the Jews in Galatia or the Gentiles, or both, that Gentiles cannot be redeemed because they are not descendants of Abraham, Isaac and Jacob. Paul is pointing out the scriptures record that God told Abraham that he would be the father of many nations and in him all nations will be blessed.

Gal. 3:6
Even as Abraham believed God, and it was reckoned to him for righteousness. ⁷ Know therefore that they that are of faith, the same are **sons of** Abraham. ⁸ And the scripture, foreseeing that God would justify the Gentiles by faith, preached the gospel beforehand to Abraham, saying, In thee shall all the nations be blessed.

Paul is speaking directly to the Jews in the next two passages explaining that as children descended from Abraham, they are covered under the Law. Both passages reference Isaac, with the passage in Romans referring to him as 'our father Isaac' pointing out that his wife Rebecca (Rebekah) conceived. *(The records in Genesis 27 -32 follow only Jacob's life and only reference Esau in Genesis 33.)*

The passage in Galatians concludes with Paul stating that 'we are not children of the slave woman (Hagar), but of the free woman (Sarah).

Gal. 4:28
Now you, brothers and sisters, like Isaac, are children of promise. ²⁹ At that time the son born according to the flesh persecuted the son born by the power of the Spirit. It is the same now. ³⁰ But what does Scripture say? "Get rid of the **slave woman and her son, for the slave woman's son** will never share in the inheritance with the **free woman's son**." [Gen. 21:10-13] ³¹ Therefore, brothers and sisters, we are not children of the slave woman, but of the free woman.

Rom. 9:6
For they are not all Israel, that are of Israel:⁷ neither, because they are Abraham's seed, are they all children: but, in Isaac shall thy seed be called. ⁸ That is, it is not the children of the flesh that are children of God; but the children of the promise are reckoned for a seed. ⁹ For this is a word of promise, According to this season will I come, and **Sarah shall have a son**. ¹⁰ And not only so; but Rebecca also having conceived by one, even by our father Isaac.

This passage from Paul's letter to the church in Thessalonica sounds reminiscent of Jesus's teachings (John 12:36).
1 Thess. 5:4
But you, brethren, are not in darkness, that that day should overtake you as a thief: ⁵ **for you are all sons of light, and sons of the day**: we are not of the night, nor of darkness; ⁶ so then let us not sleep, as do the rest, but let us watch and be sober.

The Compiled Teachings of The Apostle Paul

Son of God

Paul began his ministry in Damascus, the city he was travelling to with authority to find any who were members of 'The Way' as those who believed in Christ were known, and *'if he found any belonging to The Way, both men and women, he might bring them bound to Jerusalem.'* [Acts 9:1-2] but before he reached Damascus he encountered Jesus and became a believer [Acts 9:3-19]. At that time, he was still known as Saul, and those who heard him proclaim that Jesus of Nazareth who had been crucified was the Son of God recalled that he had been causing havoc in Jerusalem [Acts 5:34-42; 8:1-3], and so they were amazed (and probably confused and skeptical).

Acts 9:19[b]
For some days he was with the disciples at Damascus. ²⁰ *And immediately he proclaimed Jesus in the synagogues, saying, "He is* **the Son of God**.*"* ²¹ *And all who heard him were amazed and said, "Is not this the man who made havoc in Jerusalem of those who called upon this name?*

In this passage which is from Paul's testimony when he preached in the synagogue in Antioch in Pisidia (in Asia Minor), and in it he references two sons, Saul, son of Kish who became King Saul, and David, son of Jesse who became King David.

Acts 13:17
The God of this people Israel chose our fathers, and exalted the people when they sojourned in the land of Egypt, and with a high arm led he them forth out of it. ¹⁸ *And for about the time of forty years as a nursing-father bare he them in the wilderness.* ¹⁹ *And when he had destroyed seven nations in the land of Canaan, he gave them their land for an inheritance, for about four hundred and fifty years:* ²⁰ *and after these things he gave them judges until Samuel the prophet.* ²¹ *And afterward they asked for a king: and God gave them Saul the* **son** *of Kish, a man of the tribe of Benjamin, for the space of forty years.* ²² *And when he had removed him, he raised up David to be their king; to whom also he bare witness and said, I have found David the* **son** *of Jesse, a man after my heart, who shall do all my will.* ²³ *Of this man's seed has God according to promise brought unto Israel a Savior, Jesus;* ²⁴ *when John (John The Baptist) had first preached before his coming the baptism of repentance to all the people of Israel.* ²⁵ *And as John was fulfilling his course, he said, What suppose you that I am? I am not he. But behold, there comes one after me, the shoes of whose feet I am not worthy to unloose.*

Paul transitioned from the Old Testament (The Prophets) to the New Testament in the previous passage and he continues ending with a passage from the Book of Psalms being referenced as prophecy fulfilled.

Acts 13:26
³⁰ *But God raised him from the dead:* ³¹ *and he was seen for many days of them that came up with him from Galilee to Jerusalem, who are now his witnesses unto the people.* ³² *And we bring you good tidings of the promise made to the fathers,* ³³ *that God has fulfilled the same unto our children, in that he raised up Jesus; as also it is written in the second psalm, Thou art my* **Son**, *this day have I begotten thee.*

1 Cor. 15:27
For, He put all things in subjection under his feet. But when he said, All things are put in subjection, it is evident that He is excepted who did subject all things to him. ²⁸ *And when all things have been subjected to him, then shall the* **Son** *also himself be subjected to him that did subject all things to him, that God may be all in all.*

In this first reference to 'son' in the Letters that Paul wrote, *'He (God) put all things in subjection under his (Jesus's) feet'*, but while Jesus was alive – while he had powers to heal and perform other miracles, God the Father, who put all things in subjection to Him, did not put himself under the subjection of the Son *'it is evident that He is excepted who did subject all things to him'*; so 'all' does not mean all yet because all at this time (still) does not include God himself. While it would be only after Jesus had been crucified and God had raised him from the grave, had ascended into heaven – all of which has been completed – it will still only be after God's plan has been fully completed that all things, including the Father himself coming under subjection. This means, one day, everything will be fully submissive to Christ; that will be when *'God may be all in all'*.

Gal. 2:19-21
For I through the law died unto the law, that I might live unto God. ²⁰ *I have been crucified with Christ; and it is no longer I that live, but Christ lives in me: and that life which I now live in the flesh I live in faith,* **the faith which is in the Son of God**, *who loved me, and gave himself up for me.* ²¹ *I do not make void the grace of God: for if righteousness is through the law, then Christ died for no purpose.*

In this passage in the Letter written by Paul to the church in Galatia, Paul explains that having been released from the law because of his faith in Christ, who Paul states, *'loved me, and gave himself up for me.'*

The Compiled Teachings of The Apostle Paul

Paul uses the term, '*Son of God*' for the first time in his letters in this, his second letter, the first letter to the church in Corinth. When Paul began preaching in Damascus he used the term 'Son of God' [Acts 9:20] so it not a new term to him, and in his letter to the Galatians (the prior passage) Paul refers to 'the Son', and from the context it is clear that he is writing about 'the Son of God'. Paul is emphasizing that there is no doubt about Jesus of Nazareth is the Christ and He is the Son of God.

2 Cor. 1:18-20
But as God is faithful, our word toward you is not yea and nay. [19] *For **the Son of God, Jesus Christ**, who was preached among you by us, even by me and Silvanus and Timothy, was not yea and nay, but in Him is yea.* [20] *For however many are the promises of God, in Him is the yea: wherefore also through Him is the Amen, to the glory of God through us.*

In this letter to the church in Rome, his fourth letter (after Galatians and the two letters to the Corinthians), Paul is writing to a church that he did not establish as he has not yet visited Rome.
Paul makes it clear why we can believe that Jesus was the Son of God: '*[4] was declared to be the Son of God in power according to the Spirit of holiness by his resurrection from the dead.*'

Rom. 1:1-7
Paul, a servant of Christ Jesus, called to be an apostle, set apart for the gospel of God, [2] *which he promised beforehand through his prophets in the holy Scriptures,* [3] *concerning his Son, who was descended from David according to the flesh* [4] *and **was declared to be the Son of God** in power according to the Spirit of holiness by his resurrection from the dead, Jesus Christ our Lord,* [5] *through whom we have received grace and apostleship to bring about the obedience of faith for the sake of his name among all the nations,* [6] *including you who are called to belong to Jesus Christ,* [7] <u>*To all those in Rome*</u> *who are loved by God and called to be saints*

Paul writes '*your faith is proclaimed in all the world.*' which communicates to the church in Rome that their efforts to spread the Gospel are succeeding and he also writes that he holds them up in prayer, all intended to be words of encouragement, and, embedded in this passage, is another firm statement of his belief and commitment to Christ. Finally, as a reminder that Paul has not yet visited the church in Rome, Paul ends this opening passage by writing: '*that somehow by God's will, I may now at last succeed in coming to you.*'

Rom. 1:8-10
First, I thank my God through Jesus Christ for all of you, because your faith is proclaimed in all the world. [9] *For God is my witness, **whom I serve with my spirit in the gospel of his Son**, that without ceasing I mention you* [10] *always in my prayers, asking that somehow by God's will, I may now at last succeed in coming to you.*

This next reference to 'Son' is prefaced by Paul referencing God's love and then a reminder that our pasts are less than perfect which leads into another firm statement of belief, '*Christ died for us.*' This is followed by Paul stating why Christ died; was crucified; that He died to save us from the wrath of God.
Paul uses the term 'enemies' to describe how we are seen when we are not following God's will, and then states that '*we were reconciled to God through the death of his Son,*' and so we are saved because of Jesus's sacrifice, and Paul ends up making the proclamation that we can '*rejoice in God through our Lord Jesus Christ*' because we have been reconciled to God by him.

Rom. 5:8-11
But God commends his own love toward us, in that, while we were yet sinners, Christ died for us. [9] *Much more then, being now justified by his blood, shall we be saved from the wrath of God through him.* [10] *For if, while we were enemies, **we were reconciled to God through the death of his Son**, much more, being reconciled, shall we be saved by his life;* [11] *and not only so, but we also rejoice in God through our Lord Jesus Christ, through whom we have now received the reconciliation.*

Although this passage is separated from the prior passage by more than two chapters, it almost reads as if it was the follow-on passage. Paul explains what reconciliation has done for him personally, and points out that Jesus was God incarnate and that all mankind was condemned in sin under the Law. He concludes that the Law has not been abolished but rather it has been fulfilled if we choose to '*live according to the Spirit*'. [NIV]

Rom. 8:2-4
For the law of the Spirit of life in Christ Jesus made me free from the law of sin and of death. [3] *For what the law could not do, in that it was weak through the flesh, **God, sending his own Son in the likeness of sinful flesh and for sin**, condemned sin in the flesh:* [4] *that the ordinance of the law might be fulfilled in us, who walk not after the flesh, but after the Spirit.*

The Compiled Teachings of The Apostle Paul

Rom. 8:29
²⁸ *And we know that to them that love God all things work together for good, even to them that are called according to his purpose. For whom he foreknew, **he also foreordained to be conformed to the image of his Son, that he might be the firstborn among many brethren**; ³⁰ and whom he foreordained, them he also called: and whom he called, them he also justified: and whom he justified, them he also glorified.*

Paul is writing about God's unfathomable greatness and that God, even in advance of His Son (Jesus) being born, knew who His Son would be, and He chose those that His Son chose (His disciples), to become like (conformed to the image of) his Son, and each of those His son called, were justified by their faith in Christ, and then they were glorified.

Paul continues to offer encouragement to the church because, even though they are having much success in sharing the Gospel, Paul is aware that they are suffering, as indeed all of creation is, because we cannot be glorified and be with God forever until we, ourselves, end our earthly lives. The fact that we suffer, though, does not mean that God is not with us or for us. Paul is stressing that we should ask ourselves, "Who is against us?" When God gave up His own Son, we too, through Christ becoming our intermediary who intercedes on our behalf, were also delivered up to God, justified.

Rom. 8:31
What then shall we say to these things? ***If God is for us, who is against us?*** *³² **He that spared not his own Son, but delivered him up for us all, how shall he not also with him freely give us all things?** ³³ Who shall lay anything to the charge of God's elect? It is God that justifies;* ³⁴ *who is he that condemned? It is Christ Jesus that died, yea rather, that was raised from the dead, who is at the right hand of God, who also makes intercession for us.*

Sons of God — except singular Son of God

Paul in writing to the church in Galatia in this passage uses the analogy that those who are under the Law are as if being tutored (for the Law guides those who are observant to it in what to do and what not to do). The Law was necessary because there was no redemption even though worship, sacrifices and other rituals (cleansing, for example) were practiced. These practices were not exclusive to those under the Law for even pagans worshipped and sacrificed to their gods. But God had revealed through the prophets a plan for salvation through the one known as the Messiah about whom John The Baptist preached. When the Messiah came, which was in the personage of Jesus of Nazareth, that was when faith had come, and the prophecies of the Scriptures began to be fulfilled.

Gal. 3:23-26
But before faith came, we were kept in ward under the law, shut up to the faith which should afterwards be revealed. ²⁴ *So that the law is become our tutor to bring us to Christ, that we might be justified by faith.* ²⁵ *But now that faith is come, we are no longer under a tutor.* ²⁶ *For you are all **sons of God**, through faith, in Christ Jesus.* ²⁷ *For as many of you as were baptized into Christ did put on Christ.* ²⁸ *There can be neither Jew nor Greek, there can be neither bond nor free, there can be no male and female; for you all are one man in Christ Jesus.*

Paul summarizes the birth of Christ and states the reason for God's Son being born as made, God incarnate; that we might be redeemed, and Paul uses the phrase '*that we might receive adoption to sonship*' in this passage. Paul also quotes the phrase, '*Abba, Father*', [Mark 14:36] words that were uttered by Christ in the final moments before He died.

Gal. 4:4-6
*But when the set time had fully come, God sent **his Son**, born of a woman, born under the law,* ⁵ *to redeem those under the law, that we might receive **adoption to sonship**.* ⁶ *Because you are **his sons, God sent the Spirit of his Son** into our hearts, the Spirit who calls out, "Abba, Father."*

Gal. 4:21
Tell me, you who want to be under the law, are you not aware of what the law says? ²² *For it is written that **Abraham had two sons**, one by the slave woman and the other by the free woman.* ²³ *His son by the slave woman was born according to the flesh, but his son by the free woman was born as the result of a divine promise.*

The passage from the scriptures that Paul is quoting here acknowledges that Abraham was a father to two sons; one born of his wife's handmaid, and a second born to his wife, Sarah. Paul references Hagar the handmaid as a slave woman and describes Sarah as a free woman. God had told Abraham that he would become the father of His people, however, he did not tell Abraham that he would not recognize the children that were descendants of Hagar as his (Abraham's) children. However, this was the reality that had developed as the Laws of Moses was applicable only to those descended of Isaac, and only to those of the circumcision, an arrangement that meant females could only be justified under the Law by males.

The Compiled Teachings of The Apostle Paul

Prior to Christ's resurrection, the term 'sons of God' meant those who were descended from Abraham and Isaac, both male and female. Some would add the restriction of having to be a descendant of Jacob, thus shutting off those descended from Esau. However, after Christ was raised from the grave, those that believed in the resurrection of Jesus and that he was the Christ, also became recognized as being children of God, that is also sons of God. As Paul writes in his Letter to the church in Rome, those that *'are led by the Spirit of God, these are sons of God.'*

Rom. 8:12-14
So then, brethren, we are debtors, not to the flesh, to live after the flesh: [13] for if you live after the flesh, you must die; but if by the Spirit you put to death the deeds of the body, you shall live. **[14] For as many as are led by the Spirit of God, these are sons of God**.

Paul made clear in the prior passage that those in Christ by faith are already the children of God (although we continue to appear on the surface the same as everyone else.) We look forward to a time when those in Christ will be glorified and it will become impossible to deny that we are God's children at which time God's righteousness, and our faith in Him, will be vindicated to the world, and all the world is looking to the future, with or without expectation.

Rom. 8:19
For the earnest expectation of the creation waits for the **revealing of the sons of God**. [20] For the creation was subjected to vanity, not of its own will, but by reason of him who subjected it, in hope [21] that the creation itself also shall be delivered from the bondage of corruption into the liberty of the glory of the children of God.

1 Thess. 1:9-10
*For they themselves report concerning us what manner of entering in we had to you; and how you turned to God from idols, to serve a living and true God, [10] and to **wait for his Son from heaven**, whom he raised from the dead, even Jesus, who delivered us from the wrath to come.*

Paul is commending the church in Thessalonica for changing their ways from idol worship and for their good work in sharing the Gospel: '[6] And you became imitators of us, and of the Lord, having received the word in much affliction, with joy of the Holy Spirit; [7] so that you became an example to all that believe in Macedonia and in Achaia. [8] For from you have sounded forth the word of the Lord, not only in Macedonia and Achaia, but in every place your faith to God-ward is gone forth; so that we need not to speak anything.'

Son of Perdition, Son of The Devil

Perdition: *eternal punishment and damnation*

Paul is in Paphos, a city on the island of Cyprus, when he encounters Elymas, a sorcerer (magician) who, seeking to turn the proconsul away from believing, opposed Paul and his companions.

Acts 13:9
*But Saul, who is also called Paul, filled with the Holy Spirit, fastened his eyes on him, [10] and said, "O full of all guile and all villainy, you **son of the devil, you enemy of all righteousness**, will you not cease to pervert the right ways of the Lord? [11] And now, behold, the hand of the Lord is upon you, and you shall be blind, not seeing the sun for a season. And immediately there fell upon him a mist and a darkness; and he went about seeking some to lead him by the hand.*

2 Thess. 2:3
*Let no man deceive you in any way: for it will not be, except the falling away come first, and the man of sin be revealed, the **son of perdition**, [4] he that opposes and exalts himself against all that is called God or that is worshipped; so that he sits in the temple of God, setting himself forth as God.*

Paul shares a concern with the church in Thessalonica that there are imposters who are likely to pretend to be from Paul, or otherwise communicate with them by letter or other message that the Day of The Lord has come, and so Paul is letting them know that both tribulation and rapture must both come before the Day of The Lord.

In the following passage written to Timothy, Paul makes a statement or saying of wisdom that is often quoted, both inside the church and outside in the secular world; *'the love of money is a root of all kinds of evil.'*

1 Timothy 6:9
*[9] But they that desire to be rich fall into temptation and a snare and many foolish and hurtful lusts, **such as drown men in destruction and perdition**. [10] For the love of money is a root of all kinds of evil: which some reaching after have been led astray from the faith, and have pierced themselves through with many sorrows.*

The Compiled Teachings of The Apostle Paul

Paul, in writing to the church in Philippi, is encouraging the people of the church to live like Christ. In Philip. 1:21 Paul writes, *'For to me to live is Christ, and to die is gain.'* and he debates between the choice of dying so that he can be with Christ and staying in the flesh alive so he can minister. Paul then exhorts the Philippians to conduct themselves *'in a manner worthy of the Gospel'* [NASB] in effect telling them do not let God down and do not let yourselves down; *'stand firm with one mind striving together for the faith of the Gospel.'*

Philippians 1:27-30
*²⁷ Only let your manner of life be worthy of the gospel of Christ: that, whether I come and see you or be absent, I may hear of your state, that you stand fast in one spirit, with one soul striving for the faith of the gospel; ²⁸ and in nothing affrighted by the adversaries: which is for them **an evident token of perdition** (a sign of destruction), but of your salvation, and that from God; ²⁹ because to you it has been granted in the behalf of Christ, not only to believe in him, but also to suffer on his behalf: ³⁰ having the same conflict which you saw in me, and now hear to be in me.*

One might say, as a suggested strategy, in Philippians 2, Paul exhorts the Philippians to imitate him; and in Philippians 2, he describes who he is, a circumcised Hebrew of the tribe of Benjamin, a Pharisee and a (former) persecutor of the church, but now he is a minister of the Gospel, 'pressing onward toward the goal for the prize for the call of God in Christ Jesus.' [Philipp. 2:14 NASB] and in Philipp. 2:19 he makes it clear that many become enemies of the cross because they choose earthly things rather than Godly things.

Philippians 3:17-21
*¹⁷ Brethren, be therefore imitators together of me, and mark them that so walk even as you have us for an example. ¹⁸ For many walk, of whom I told you often, and now tell you even weeping, that they are the enemies of the cross of Christ: ¹⁹ **whose end is perdition** (destruction), whose god is the belly, and whose glory is in their shame, who mind earthly things.*

Speaking in Tongues – See Tongues

Steward(s), Stewardship

Paul gives counselling to the church in Corinth regarding leaders, specifically ministers who he refers to as *'stewards of the mysteries of God'*. Paul adds a second comment about stewards, advising that they must be faithful.

1 Cor. 4:1-2
*Let a man so account of us, as of ministers of Christ, and **stewards of the mysteries of God**. ² Here, moreover, it is required in **stewards**, that a man be found faithful.*

1 Cor. 9:17
*¹⁷ For if I do this of mine own will, I have a reward: but if not of mine own will, I have a **stewardship entrusted to me**.*

The reward that Paul is talking about is the winning of souls to Christ, both those who are under the Law (Jews) and those who are not under the Law (Gentiles). [1 Cor. 16-21]

This instruction to Timothy suggests that there are some in leadership positions at the church in Ephesus that he feels uncertain of, that they might not yet have put aside fully their past practices.

1 Tim. 1:3ᵇ-4
*…remain on in Ephesus and instruct certain persons not to teach any different doctrine, ⁴ nor to devote themselves to myths and endless genealogies, which promote speculations rather than the **stewardship** from God that is by faith.*

Paul makes just one specific reference to bishops, in which he lists out the qualities and abilities that bishops should have. An alternate term for 'bishop' used in some Bible translations is 'overseer' (1 Tim. 3:2, Titus 1:6):

Titus 1:7-10
*For the bishop must be blameless, as God's **steward**; not self-willed, not soon angry, no brawler, no striker, not greedy of filthy lucre; ⁸ but given to hospitality, a lover of good, sober-minded, just, holy, self-controlled;*

⁹ holding to the faithful word which is according to the teaching, that he may be able both to exhort in the sound doctrine, and to convict the gainsayers.

The Compiled Teachings of The Apostle Paul

*This passage is entitled '**Paul's Stewardship**' in the NASB (New American Standard Bible) but the word 'stewardship' does not appear in the text in all translations. Alternative words include 'ministration' and 'dispensation'.*

Paul wants to make it clear that he has been tasked with the responsibility of bringing both Jews and Gentiles to Christ, those under the Law (the laws of Moses) and those not under the Law.

Eph. 3:1-7
*For this cause I Paul, the prisoner of Christ Jesus in behalf of you Gentiles, – ² if so be that you have heard of the dispensation (stewardship) of that grace of God which was given to me; ³ how that by revelation was made known to me the mystery, as I wrote before in few words, ⁴ whereby, when you read, you will perceive my understanding in the mystery of Christ; ⁵ which in other generations was not made known to the sons of men, as it has now been revealed to his holy apostles and prophets in the Spirit; ⁶ to wit, that the Gentiles are fellow-heirs, and fellow-members of the body, and fellow-partakers of the promise in Christ Jesus through the gospel, ⁷ whereof **I was made a minister**, according to the gift of that grace of God which was given me according to the working of his power.*

Tattler(s) / Gossip

There are just three references that Paul makes to gossips, aka tattlers. The first of these references 'they' - *They were filled with all manner of unrighteousness* – but there is no specificity as to who 'they' are. In verse 18 Paul writes *'¹⁸ For the wrath of God is revealed from heaven against all ungodliness and unrighteousness of men'* which suggest that 'they' are everyone and anyone who is not Godly and who are unrighteous, but in verses 22-25 Paul writes, *'²² Claiming to be wise, they became fools, ²³ and exchanged the glory of the immortal God for images resembling mortal man and birds and animals and creeping things. ²⁴ Therefore God gave them up in the lusts of their hearts to impurity, to the dishonoring of their bodies among themselves, ²⁵ because they exchanged the truth about God for a lie and worshiped and served the creature rather than the Creator'* which defines 'they' somewhat more precisely to those who knew God but have rejected Him.

Rom. 1:29-31 ²⁹ *They were filled with all manner of unrighteousness, evil, covetousness, malice. They are full of envy, murder, strife, deceit,* **maliciousness. They are gossips**, ³⁰ **slanderers**, *haters of God, insolent, haughty, boastful, inventors of evil, disobedient to parents,* ³¹ *foolish, faithless, heartless, ruthless.*

The second reference identifies issues relating to younger widows:

1 Tim. 5:11-15 ¹¹ *But younger widows refuse: for when they have waxed wanton against Christ, they desire to marry; ¹² having condemnation, because they have rejected their first pledge. ¹³ And withal they learn also to be idle, going about from house to house; and not only idle, but **tattlers also and busybodies, speaking things which they ought not**. ¹⁴ I desire therefore that the younger widows marry, bear children, rule the household, give no occasion to the adversary for reviling: ¹⁵ for already some are turned aside after Satan.*

The third reference to gossiping, aka tattling, is found in 1 Timothy 5 is a specific charge against younger widows who Paul describes as *'they learn also to be idle, going about from house to house; and not only idle, but tattlers also and busybodies, speaking things which they ought not.'*

Paul references the younger widows as having *'waxed wanton against Christ'* which, in the NASB translation reads, *'for when they feel sensual desires in disregard of Christ'* in other words, they wish to remarry in order to be in a new relationship with a new husband which Paul says he encourages: ¹⁴ *I desire therefore that the younger widows marry, bear children.*

Teacher(s)

The Antioch mentioned here is the city of Antioch in Syria, and Paul (still known at that time as Saul) and Barnabas are about to begin their first missionary trip.

Acts 13:1
*Now there were at Antioch, in the church that was there, prophets and **teachers**, Barnabas, and Simeon that was called Niger, and Lucius of Cyrene, and Manaen the foster-brother of Herod the tetrarch, and Saul. ² And as they ministered to the Lord, and fasted, the Holy Spirit said, "Separate [for] me Barnabas and Saul for the work whereunto I have called them." ³ Then, when they had fasted and prayed and laid their hands on them, they sent them away.*

The Compiled Teachings of The Apostle Paul

Temptation

Gal. 5:19-21
¹⁹ The acts of the flesh are obvious: sexual immorality, impurity and debauchery; ²⁰ idolatry and witchcraft; hatred, discord, jealousy, fits of rage, selfish ambition, dissensions, factions ²¹ and envy; drunkenness, orgies, and the like. I warn you, as I did before, that those who live like this will not inherit the kingdom of God.

Although the word 'temptation' does not appear in the text, the text contains a listing of many things that we recognize as temptations. Paul states, '*I warn you, as I did before,*' but having not been able to find such prior warning in his writings, I presume that he must be referring to warnings he gave while visiting Galatia. Paul firmly states that the destiny for those that live according to the 'acts of the flesh', temptations, '*will not inherit the kingdom of God*'.

1 Cor. 10:13
¹³ No **temptation** has taken you but such as man can bear: but God is faithful, **who will not suffer you to be tempted above that you are able**; but will with **the temptation** make also the way of escape, that you may be able to endure it.

1 Tim. 6:9-10
⁹ But they that desire to be rich fall into **temptation** and a snare and many foolish and hurtful lusts, such as drown men in destruction and perdition. ¹⁰ For the love of money is a root of all kinds of evil: which some reaching after have been led astray from the faith, and have pierced themselves through with many sorrows.

Tongues

Paul teaches about tongues, about speaking in tongues, which is speaking out loud in a spiritual manner, and interpretation of tongues, only in Acts and in I Corinthians.

In general, we understand that people of different countries (from different lands) and of different origins do not all speak the same language, and that one person speaking in their language will not be understood by those who do not know that language. I myself, although familiar with three languages other than my 'mother tongue' (but I am not adequately proficient in those other three languages to lay claim that I can 'speak' them). In fact, if I ask a question in the language of someone who speaks one of those languages, the likelihood that I will understand their response is minimal. In other words, I have to admit that I am monolingual. Paul was not monolingual, he spoke at least two languages, Greek and Hebrew, the language of the Jews. But Paul from his teachings clearly also spoke in tongues. In both Acts and in 1 Corinthians Paul teaches about tongues: '*to another **diverse kinds of tongues**; and to another **the interpretation of tongues**.*'

Acts 12:8
For to one is given through the Spirit the word of wisdom; and to another the word of knowledge, according to the same Spirit: ⁹ to another faith, in the same Spirit; and to another gifts of healings, in the one Spirit; ¹⁰ and to another workings of miracles; and to another prophecy; and to another discerning of spirits: to another **diverse kinds of tongues**; and to another the **interpretation of tongues**: ¹¹ but all these are of the one and the same Spirit, dividing to each one severally even as he will.

Acts 19:6
The Holy Spirit came on them, and they began **speaking in tongues** and prophesying. ⁷ There were about twelve men in all.

1 Cor. 12:6
And there are diversities of workings, but the same God, who works all things in all. ⁷ But to each one is given the manifestation of the Spirit to profit likewise. ⁸ For to one is given through the Spirit the word of wisdom; and to another the word of knowledge, according to the same Spirit: ⁹ to another faith, in the same Spirit; and to another gifts of healings, in the one Spirit; ¹⁰ and to another workings of miracles; and to another prophecy; and to another discerning of spirits: to another **diverse kinds of tongues**; and to another **the interpretation of tongues**: ¹¹ but all these are of the one and the same Spirit, dividing to each one severally even as he will.

1 Cor. 12:28
And God has set some in the church, first apostles, secondly prophets, thirdly teachers, then miracles, then gifts of healings, helps, governments, **diverse kinds of tongues**. ²⁹ Are all apostles? are all prophets? are all teachers? are all workers of miracles? ³⁰ have all gifts of healings? **do all speak with tongues**? do all interpret?

The Compiled Teachings of The Apostle Paul

1 Cor. 13:1
If I **speak with the tongues of men and of angels**, but have not love, I am become sounding brass, or a clanging cymbal. [2] And if I have the gift of prophecy, and know all mysteries and all knowledge; and if I have all faith, so as to remove mountains, but have not love, I am nothing. [3] And if I bestow all my goods to feed the poor, and if I give my body to be burned, but have not love, it profits me nothing. [4] Love suffers long, and is kind; love envies not; love vaunts not itself, is not puffed up, [5] does not behave itself unseemly, seeks not its own, is not provoked, takes not account of evil; [6] rejoices not in unrighteousness, but rejoices with the truth; [7] bears all things, believes all things, hopes all things, endures all things. [8] Love never fails: but whether there be prophecies, they shall be done away; **whether there be tongues, they shall cease**; whether there be knowledge, it shall be done away.

1 Cor. 14:4
He that speaks in a tongue edifies himself; but he that prophesies edifies the church. [5] Now I would have you all **speak with tongues**, but rather that you should prophesy: and greater is he that prophesies than he that **speaks with tongues**, except he interprets, that the church may receive edifying.

1 Cor. 14:6
But now, brethren, if I come to you **speaking with tongues**, what shall I profit you, unless I speak to you either by way of revelation, or of knowledge, or of prophesying, or of teaching. [7] Even things without life, giving a voice, whether pipe or harp, if they give not a distinction in the sounds, how shall it be known what is piped or harped?

1 Cor. 14:16
Else if you bless with the spirit, how shall he that fills the place of the unlearned say the Amen at your giving of thanks, seeing he knows not what you say? [17] For you verily give thanks well, but the other is not edified. [18] I thank God, **I speak with tongues** more than you all: [19] howbeit in the church I had rather speak five words with my understanding, that I might instruct others also, than ten thousand **words in a tongue**.

1 Cor. 14:21
In the law it is written, By **men of strange tongues** and by the lips of strangers will I speak to this people; and not even thus will they hear me, says the Lord. [22] Wherefore **tongues are for a sign**, not to them that believe, but to the unbelieving: but prophesying is for a sign, not to the unbelieving, but to them that believe. [23] If therefore the whole church be assembled together and all **speak with tongues**, and there come in men unlearned or unbelieving, will they not say that ye are mad? [24] But if all prophesy, and there come in one unbelieving or unlearned, he is reproved by all, he is judged by all; [25] the secrets of his heart are made manifest; and so he will fall down on his face and worship God, declaring that God is among you indeed.

1 Cor. 14:37
If any man thinks himself to be a prophet, or spiritual, let him take knowledge of the things which I write to you, that they are the commandment of the Lord. [38] But if any man is ignorant, let him be ignorant. [39] Wherefore, my brethren, desire earnestly to prophesy, and **forbid not to speak with tongues**. [40] But let all things be done decently and in order.

Transgression

Gal. 3:19
What then is the law? It was added **because of transgressions**, till the seed should come to whom the promise has been made; and it was ordained through angels by the hand of a mediator.

Rom. 2:23
You who glories in the law, (but who) **through your transgression of the law**, (do you not) dishonor God? [24] For the name of God is blasphemed among the Gentiles because of you, even as it is written.

Rom. 4:9:14
For if those that are of the law are heirs, faith is made void, and the promise is made of no effect: [15] for the law worketh wrath; but where there is no law, **neither is there transgression**. [16] For this cause it is of faith, that it may be according to grace; to the end that the promise may be sure to all the seed; not to that only which is of the law, but to that also which is of the faith of Abraham, who is the father of us all

The Compiled Teachings of The Apostle Paul

Rom. 5:13^b-15
...for until the law sin was in the world; but sin is not imputed when there is no law. ^{14}*Nevertheless death reigned from Adam until Moses, even over them that had not sinned* **after the likeness of Adam's transgression**, *who is a figure of him that was to come.* ^{15}*But not as the trespass, so also is the free gift.*

---

1 Tim. 2:13-15
For Adam was first formed, then Eve; ^{14}*and Adam was not beguiled, but the woman* **being beguiled has fallen into transgression**: ^{15}*but she shall be saved through her child-bearing.*

Col. 2:13
When you were dead in your transgressions *and the uncircumcision of your flesh, He made you alive together with Him, having* **forgiven us all our transgressions**, ^{14}*having canceled out the certificate of debt.*

Virgin(s)

Paul begins this passage on this topic by stating that he has not received a commandment (any words of guidance) from God regarding virgins, nevertheless, he proceeds to share his advice:

1 Cor. 7:25
Now concerning **virgins** *I have not (received a) commandment of the Lord: but I give my judgment, as one that has obtained mercy of the Lord to be trustworthy.* ^{26}*I think therefore that this is good by reason of the distress that is upon us, namely, that it is good for a man to be as he is.* ^{27}*Are you bound to a wife? seek not to be freed. Are you freed from a wife? seek not a wife.* ^{28}*But should you marry, you have not sinned; and* **if a virgin marry**, *she has not sinned. Yet such shall have tribulation in the flesh: and I would spare you.*

Paul's first comment, speaking to men, of course, is if you are single, stay single, followed by, if you are married, stay married.

If you have been married but are now freed from your wife, either you are a widower or your wife left you for another man, don't look for another wife; stay single.

If you feel compelled to get married again, seek a virgin, but beware there are bound to be challenges ahead.

Paul has explained in the prior verses that:
'He that is unmarried is careful for the things of the Lord, how he may please the Lord: ^{33}*but he that is married is careful for the things of the world, how he may please his wife,* ^{34}*and is divided.*

1 Cor. 7:34b
So also **the woman that is unmarried and the virgin is careful for the things of the Lord**, *that she may be holy both in body and in spirit: but she that is married is careful for the things of the world, how she may please her husband.*

For a comment on this passage see the Summarization notes on 'Daughters' earlier in this section. (My own thinking here is that this guidance relates to only the oldest daughter in the family, and not to all daughters.)

1 Cor. 7:36
But if any man thinks that he behaves himself unseemly toward his **virgin daughter**, *if she be past the flower of her age, and if need so requires, let him do what he will; he sins not; let them marry.* ^{37}*But he that stands steadfast in his heart, having no necessity, but has power as touching his own will, and has determined this in his own heart, to keep his own* **virgin daughter**, *shall do well.* ^{38}*So then both he that giveth his own* **virgin daughter** *in marriage does well; and he that giveth her not in marriage shall do better.* ^{39}*A wife is bound for so long time as her husband lives; but if the husband be dead, she is free to be married to whom she will; only in the Lord.*

A note on the culture of Paul's time for the Jews, if not also for the Gentiles in Corinth, from 'Bibleref.com' suggests that the betrothal period was much more binding than the modern concept of an engagement. A father would betroth his daughter to a man to be married months or years in the future. The father's responsibility, in part, was to protect his daughter's virginity and well-being until she was safely married to her husband.

With that background in mind, Paul is talking to each one of the Corinthians as if he was their father who had betrothed each one of them to God, and he is endeavoring to protect them from the false teachings of others.

This second passage on the topic of virgins reflects a different usage of the word. Virgin, of course, means untouched, pure.

2 Cor. 11:2
For I am jealous over you with a godly jealousy: for I espoused you to one husband, that I might present you as **a pure virgin to Christ**. ^{3}*But I fear, lest by any means, as the serpent beguiled Eve in his craftiness, your minds should be corrupted from the simplicity and the purity that is toward Christ.*

The Compiled Teachings of The Apostle Paul

Widow(s), Widowed

Determining that widows are now unmarried and considered to again be single, Paul's guidance is that it is good if they stay single, but those that have a need and do not have self-control over their physical emotions, then they should marry, emphasizing that intimate sex outside of a marriage relationship is sin.

1 Cor. 7:7b
*Howbeit each man has his own gift from God, one after this manner, and another after that. ⁸But I say to the unmarried and to **widows**, it is good for them if they abide even as I. ⁹But if they have not self-control, let them marry: for it is better to marry than to burn.*

Paul defines the category of widow as one who not only has lost her husband to death, but who also has been left with neither children nor grandchildren to support them, which he qualifies as being desolate. [1 Tim. 5:5]. These he refers to these as widows indeed.

In 1 Tim. 5:9, Paul further qualifies widows based on their age, married only once and having a good reputation, and adds further qualification guidelines for younger widows who are still of child-bearing age in 1 Tim. 5:14.

1 Tim. 5:3
*Honor widows that are widows indeed. ⁴ But **if any widow has children or grandchildren**, let them learn first to show piety towards their own family, and to requite their parents: for this is acceptable in the sight of God. ⁵ Now she that is **a widow indeed, and desolate**, has her hope set on God, and continues in supplications and prayers night and day. ⁶ But she that gives herself to pleasure is dead while she lives.*

1 Tim. 5:9
Let none be enrolled as a widow under threescore years old, having been the wife of one man, ¹⁰ well reported of for good works;

1 Tim. 5:14
*I desire therefore that the **younger widows marry**, bear children, rule the household, give no occasion to the adversary for reviling: ¹⁵ for already some are turned aside after Satan.*

1 Tim. 5:16
*If any woman that believes has widows (in her care), let her relieve (continue to help) them, and let not the church be burdened; that it may relieve (provide help to) **them that are widows indeed**.*

In this passage addressing widows, Paul writes that any woman in whose family that there is a widow that needs to be cared for, let her care for that widow and not let the church be burdened as the church has enough of a challenge providing care for widows who are desolate.

Wife, Wives

This first references to a wife is in Acts 18:1; the wife of Jew who had recently come to Corinth from Italy who invited Paul to stay and work with them.

Acts 18:1
After this Paul left Athens and went to Corinth. ² And he found a Jew named Aquila, a native of Pontus, recently come from Italy with his <u>wife</u> Priscilla, ³ and because he was of the same trade he stayed with them and worked, for they were tentmakers by trade.

The next wife mentioned is the wife of Felix, the Roman Governor over the province of Palestine, who was a Jewess. Not because of anything she is on record for having done, but just because she was a Jew and a non-believer, she might be considered to have been a stumbling block. In part, because of her, Paul remained in prison for two years.

Acts 24:24
After some days Felix came with his wife Drusilla, who was Jewish, and he sent for Paul and heard him speak about faith in Christ Jesus. [And desiring to do the Jews a favor, Felix left Paul in prison.]

In the First of the two Letters that Paul wrote to the church in Corinth, Paul finds himself responding to a very negative and troubling report. There are some notes on this issue in the review of this passage in Acts in 'The Teachings In The Letters' section.

1 Cor. 5:1
*It is actually reported that there is <u>fornication</u> among you, and such <u>fornication</u> as is not even among the Gentiles, that one of you has **his father's wife**.*

For comments on each of the following passages in 1 Cor. 7, <u>see the comments under 'Husband'</u>, and also the notes for 1 Corinthians 7 in Section 3:

1 Cor. 7:1b
*It is good for a man not to touch a woman. ²But, because of <u>fornications</u>, **let each man have his own wife**, and let each woman have her own <u>husband</u>. ³Let the **husband render to the wife** her due: and like-wise **also the wife** to the <u>husband</u>.*

1 Cor. 7:4
***The wife has not power** over her own body, but the <u>husband</u>: and like-wise also the <u>husband</u> has not power over his own body, **but the wife**.*

The Compiled Teachings of The Apostle Paul

1 Cor. 7:5
But to the married I give charge, yea not I, but the Lord, That **the wife depart not** from her husband ¹¹(but should she depart, let her remain unmarried, or else be reconciled to her husband); and that the husband **leave not his wife**.

1 Cor. 7:12
If any brother has **an unbelieving wife**, and she is content to dwell with him, let him not leave her.

In this passage, 1 Cor. 7:12ᵇ-14, Paul gives guidance for those that have a spouse who is not a believer. However, in 1 Cor. 7:16 Paul cautions: 'For how knows you, **O wife**, whether you shall save your husband? or how do you know, O husband, whether you shall save **thy wife**?' which leaves us perhaps less than certain.

1 Cor. 7:13
If any brother has an unbelieving wif*e*, and she is content to dwell with him, let him not leave her. ¹³ And the **woman** that has an unbelieving husband, and he is content to dwell with her, let her not leave her husband.

1 Cor. 7:14
For **the unbelieving husband is sanctified in the wife,** and the **unbelieving wife is sanctified in [her husband]**: else were your children unclean; but now are they holy.

1 Cor. 7:16
For how knows you, **O wife**, whether you shall save your husband? or how do you know, O husband, whether you shall save **thy wife**?

1 Cor. 7:26
I think therefore that this is good by reason of the distress that is upon us, namely, that it is good for a man to be as he is. ²⁷Are you **bound to a wife**? seek not to be freed. Are you **freed from a wife**? **seek not a wife**. ²⁸But should you marry, you have not sinned; and if a virgin marry, she has not sinned.

Cor. 7:32ᵇ
He that is unmarried is careful for the things of the Lord, how he may please the Lord: ³³but he that is married is careful for the things of the world, how he may **please his wife**, ³⁴ and is divided.

1 Cor. 7:39
A wife is bound for so long time as her husband lives; but if the husband be dead, she is free to be married to whom she will; only in the Lord.

1 Cor. 9:5
Have we no right to **lead about a wife** that is a believer, even as the rest of the apostles, and the brethren of the Lord, and Cephas (Peter)?

For comments on this passage, see the notes for 1 Corinthians 9 in Section 3:

For comments on these two passages in Timothy, see the notes for Titus 1:6 and Titus 2:2-3 in Section 3.

1 Tim. 3:2 (Titus 1:6)
The overseer therefore must be without reproach, the husband of **one wife**, temperate, sober-minded, orderly, given to hospitality,

1 Tim. 3:12 (Titus 2:2-3)
Let deacons be husbands of **one wife**, ruling their children and their own houses well. ¹³ For they that have served well as deacons gain to themselves a good standing, and great boldness in the faith which is in Christ Jesus.

For comments on this passage, see the notes under 'Widows' above.
1 Tim. 5:9   Let none be enrolled as a widow under threescore years old, having been the **wife** of one man,

For comments on this passage in Titus, see the notes for Paul's Letter to Titus in Section 3.

Titus 1:5
This is why I left you in Crete, so that you might put what remained into order, and appoint elders in every town as I directed you – ⁶ if anyone is above reproach, the husband of **one wife**, and his children are believers and not open to the charge of debauchery or insubordination.

For comments on each of the following passages in Eph. 5, see the comments under 'Husband' in this section, and also the notes for Paul's Letter to the church in Ephesus in Section 3:

Eph. 5:23
For the husband is **the head of the wife**, as Christ also is the head of the church, being himself the savior of the body. ²⁴ But as the church is subject to Christ, so **let the wives also be** to their husbands in everything.

Eph. 5:25
Husbands, **love your wives**, even as Christ also loved the church, and gave himself up for it;

Eph. 5:28
Even so ought husbands also to **love their own wives** as their own bodies. **He that loves his own wife loves himself**:

Eph. 5:31
For this cause shall a man leave his father and mother, and shall **cleave to his wife**; and the two shall become one flesh. ³² This mystery is great: but I speak in regard of Christ and of the church. ³³ Nevertheless do you also severally **love each one his own wife** even as himself; and **let the wife see that she fear (respect) her** husband.

Wisdom

1 Cor. 1:17
*For Christ did not send me to baptize but to preach the gospel, and not with words of eloquent **wisdom**, lest the cross of Christ be emptied of its power.*

Paul states that he wasn't sent to preach with *'words of eloquent wisdom'* and he gives his reasoning as *'lest the cross of Christ be emptied of its power'*, meaning that he was very aware that one of the values of this era was *rhetoric*, speeches that were recognized for their brilliant use of words and phrasing to wow an audience and overwhelm a debate opponent on a given topic. We know that as a writer, Paul was capable of being eloquent and wise in his presentation of the gospel, but to just be eloquent would be to risk devalue the importance of the cross of Christ. In 1 Cor. 1 Paul is striving to make it clear that baptism is not the gospel; that Baptism is a step of obedience and a public declaration that a believer belongs to Christ. Paul's teaching of the gospel makes it clear that faith in Christ is the only path to God's grace and eternal salvation from sin (Ephesians 2:8-9), baptized or not, although he expected that all who came to Christ to be baptized, just as Christ commanded His followers to both make disciples and baptize all who believed (Matthew 28:19).

1 Cor. 2:1b
*...when I came to you, came not with excellency of speech or of **wisdom**, proclaiming to you the testimony of God. ² For I determined not to know anything among you, save Jesus Christ, and him crucified. ³ And I was with you in weakness, and in fear, and in much trembling. ⁴ And my speech and my preaching were not in persuasive words of **wisdom**, but in demonstration of the Spirit and of power: ⁵ that your faith should not stand in the wisdom of men, but in the power of God. ⁶ We speak **wisdom**, however, among them that are full-grown: yet a **wisdom** not of this world, nor of the rulers of this world, who are coming to nought: ⁷ but we speak **God's wisdom** in a mystery, even **the wisdom that has been hidden**, which God foreordained before the worlds to our glory.*

Paul reminds them of when he first came to Corinth and began proclaiming the testimony of God. Paul spent over a year and a half in Corinth leading people to faith in Christ and helping to establish the church there. Many of his readers would remember when he first showed up; his arrival marked a significant change in their lives as they began a relationship with God. Paul wants them to remember that he did not preach the gospel to them as if he were performing – see the notes above for *1 Cor. 1:17*. Paul presented the Gospel to them as plain truth; his mission was to simply deliver Christ's message to them.

Paul is endeavoring to explain that there is the spirit of the world and there is the spirit which is from God. If we only know the spirit of the world we cannot understand the things that are of the Spirit of God. (perhaps, for us, a reminder of Nicodemus who came to visit Jesus by night [John 3:1-21], not that Paul necessarily knew that Nicodemus met Jesus).

1 Cor. 2:12
*But we did not receive the spirit of the world, but the spirit which is from God; that we might know the things that were freely given to us of God. ¹³ Which things also we speak, not in words which **man's wisdom teaches, but which the Spirit teaches**; combining spiritual things with spiritual words.*

Human wisdom and God's wisdom contradict each other in that human wisdom is limited, and God's wisdom has no limits. Paul quotes scripture [Job 5:3] that tells us that God knows the wisdom of the world to be folly or foolish, and so all who trust in Christ should be aware of human wisdom.

1 Cor. 3:19
For the wisdom of this world is foolishness with God. For it is written, He that takes the wise in their craftiness: ²⁰ and again, The Lord knows the reasonings of the wise, that they are vain.

(**Job 5:3** I've seen it myself—seen fools putting down roots, and then, suddenly, their houses are cursed.)

Paul has identified that there are different 'services' or 'ministrations' of the spirit [1 Cor. 12:4], and there are different spiritual gifts, but they all come from the same Holy Spirit. *...there are diversities of workings, but the same God, who works all things in all.* [1 Cor. 12:6]. The term translated 'services' here is diakoniōn, alternatively translated as *'ministries.'* Some are given through the Spirit the gift of wisdom. All spiritual gifts given by the Spirit are intended for serving others in the body of Christ. None of the spiritual gifts are given as a way of enriching or serving just the one who is gifted.

1 Cor. 12:7
*But to each one is given the manifestation of the Spirit to profit likewise. ⁸ For to one is given through the Spirit the word of **wisdom**; and to another the word of knowledge, according to the same Spirit: ⁹ to another faith, in the same Spirit; and to another gifts of healings, in the one Spirit;*

The Compiled Teachings of The Apostle Paul

Rom. 11:33
*O the depth of the riches both of **the wisdom and the knowledge of God**! how unsearchable are his judgments, and his ways past tracing out!* ³⁴ *For who has known the mind of the Lord? or who has been his counsellor?*

Paul expresses awe at the depth of God's wisdom; God's judgments are unfathomable. God's ways are said to be inscrutable, not easily understood; mysterious. Knowing that human beings simply lack the capacity to understand why God decides what He does, Paul asks 'who knows the mind of the Lord?'.

Eph. 1:7-9
in whom we have our redemption through his blood, the forgiveness of our trespasses, according to the riches of his grace, ⁸ *which he made to abound toward us **in all wisdom and prudence*** ⁹ *making known to us the mystery of his will, according to his good pleasure.*

In Eph. 1:7 Paul refers to Christ's death on the cross as being the payment for the sins of all who believe; *'we have our redemption through his blood'*. This redemption paid for by Christ's death, released us from an eternal penalty. It was not "free" to us, but not free for Christ; His sacrifice cost Him everything. For the believer, the price has already been paid. This is grace: the ability to become a child of God, because God provided a free way to know Him by faith. Paul uses the term *'mystery'* not to mean some mystical or self-contradictory approach, but is referring to something which was previously unknown. A mystery of the past has now been revealed, with Gentiles coming to faith through the coming of and the resurrection of Christ (1 Cor. 15:3–11). God's planned *'in all wisdom and prudence'*, (prudence meaning 'wise in practical affairs, as by providing for the future') *'making known to us the mystery of his will'*.

Regarding the 'mystery' referenced in Eph. 3:9ᵇ-11, *'...and to enlighten all people as to what the plan of the mystery is* [NASB], *which for ages has been hidden in God who created all things* ¹⁰ *to the intent that now to the rulers and the authorities* [NASB] *in the heavenly places might be made known through the church the manifold wisdom of God,* ¹¹ *according to the eternal purpose which he purposed in Christ Jesus our Lord'*.

Paul writes that revealing this mystery was done *'according to his good pleasure (purpose)'*; something which was not of human creation or wisdom. Only God could design and implement such an amazing, well-orchestrated plan to bring forth His plans and ultimately bring greater glory to Himself. (Credit: Bibleref.com)

Eph. 3:10ᵇ
... now to the rulers and the authorities [NASB] *in the heavenly places might be made known through the church **the manifold wisdom of God**,*

Col. 1:9-10
*And so, from the day we heard, we have not ceased to pray for you, asking that you may be filled with the knowledge of his will in all **spiritual wisdom and understanding**,* ¹⁰ *so as to walk in a manner worthy of the Lord, fully pleasing to him.*

In 1 Thessalonians 5:16–18, Paul speaks about prayer without ceasing as part of God's will for all Christians. In this passage, he presents this as part of his ministry on behalf of the Colossian believers. That he and Timothy, are praying asking for knowledge among the Colossian believers which is just one of the qualities Paul prays for that are not only helpful, they are part of becoming more like Christ. Jesus was known for His wisdom [Matthew 13:54; Mark 6:2], and His followers are to walk with wisdom as well.

The faith of the Colossian Christians was not based on worldly thinking, but rather the power of God [1 Cor. 2:5]. At the same time, Paul also desires wisdom among believers including the importance of "wisdom toward outsiders" [Colossians 4:5]. (Credit: Bibleref.com)

Col. 1:27-28
...to whom God was pleased to make known what are the riches of the glory of this mystery among the Gentiles, which is Christ in you, the hope of glory: ²⁸ *whom we proclaim, admonishing every man and **teaching every man in all wisdom**, that we may present every man perfect in Christ.*

Paul explains that he and his coworkers, which includes many in the church in Colossae, carry the message of this mystery *'which is Christ in you, the hope of glory.'* Christ came to earth and also now lives in those who believe. He seeks to make the gospel message very personal for these Colossian Christians, whom he has never personally met. With Christ in you, as a saved believer, you have the "hope of glory." In other words, a believer can be confident of eternity with Christ in heaven when he or she knows Christ is already in them now. [Credit: www.bibleref.com]

Paul is writing while a prisoner under house arrest in Rome and so, although he has visited the church in Colossae in the past, he knows there are many who know of him but have not met him and he is speaking of them and praying for them, that will come to know Christ. Paul writes, *'that they may know the mystery of God, even Christ,* ³ *in whom are all the treasures of wisdom and knowledge hidden'*, and he adds a comment that shares his concern about not being able to be there in person to persuade (protect) them from those that preach false gospels, especially from those that preach a distorted or diluted version of Christianity.

Col. 2:1ᵇ-4
...for as many as have not seen my face in the flesh; ² *that their hearts may be comforted, they being knit together in love, and to all riches of the full assurance of understanding, that they may know the mystery of God, even Christ,* ³ *in whom are all **the treasures of wisdom and knowledge** hidden.* ⁴ *This I say, that no one may delude you with persuasiveness of speech.*

The Compiled Teachings of The Apostle Paul

Col. 2:23
*Which things have indeed **a show of wisdom in will-worship**, and humility, and severity to the body; but are not of any value against the indulgence of the flesh.*

The NASB translation of this passage is: *'These are matters which, to be sure, have the appearance of wisdom in self-made religion and humility and severe treatment of the body, but are of no value against fleshly indulgence.'*

Paul is attacking asceticism which is the practice of rigorous self-denial; self-mortification, or extreme abstinence. Those who practice such restrictions promote the appearance of being 'holier than thou', and those who follow such practices have been led astray.

Paul teaches against false teachers by again noting how deceptive their approach is. Following restrictive religious rules makes a person look holy to others, Paul specifically says these teachings are self-made; they are not actually anything from God, their practices are merely human rules based on principles which don't come from Christ.

Paul highlights the futility of these teachings. These attempts at denying the flesh, through human efforts, don't actually stop sinful desires.

Because Gospel-based Christian practices include fasting and avoiding certain foods, those who are still seeking are easily attracted to Gnosticism, an early heresy plaguing the church, and other alternative religions that, like Gnosticism, rely on mysticism and complex philosophies even to the extreme of insisting that the physical world is entirely evil, so all physical pleasures must be eliminated. The Bible teaches that believers are given forgiveness of sin only through Christ, and it is acknowledged that believers continue to struggle with sin (Romans 7:14–20), requiring the power of God's Spirit to overcome temptation.

Paul advocates that all types of music were to be used to *'let the word of Christ dwell richly within us'*. Singing was to be done with an attitude of thanksgiving. Singing praise to God is largely associated with showing our gratitude to Him, rather than focusing on ourselves or our own desires.

Col. 3:16
*Let the word of Christ dwell in you richly; **in all wisdom teaching and admonishing** one another with psalms and hymns and spiritual songs, singing with grace in your hearts to God.*

Col. 4:5-6
***Walk in wisdom** toward them that are without, redeeming the time. ⁶ Let your speech be always with grace, seasoned with salt, that you may know how you ought to answer each one.*

Paul again is advocating. Wisdom or discernment should be used regarding our actions – to 'walk' – toward unbelievers. What we do and what we say must be consistent, over time, and with each other, in order to clearly present the message of Jesus.

We are to make effective use of our time; 'making the most of every opportunity' is how some translations interpret this phrase. Paul believed that every moment of life is important and should be maximized in service to Christ, something that Paul was acutely aware of having been beaten, imprisoned, and shipwrecked over the course of his ministry. This perspective inspired Paul to boldly share faith in Jesus with unbelievers.

Time is short is a fundamental part of the gospel message. Whether by nature, accident, or the return of Christ, at any moment, everyone will one day come face-to-face with God. Paul emphasized that believers should be motivated by the knowledge that the people around us, those who are outside (without), will die apart from Christ unless they hear and receive the gospel.

Women

These two passages from Acts tell us something about the zealous nature of Saul.

Acts 8:1 *"Saul was in hearty agreement with putting him [Stephen] to death."* And Acts 8:3 tells us that, *"Saul began ravaging the church entering house after house, dragging off men and **women**, and he would put them in prison."*

Acts 9:1 *"Saul, still breathing threats and murder against the disciples of the Lord, went to the High Priest, and asked for letters from him (the High Priest) to the synagogues at Damascus, so that if he found any belonging to The Way, both men and **women**, he might bring them bound to Jerusalem."*

Timothy is mentioned as being the son of a Jewish woman was a believer. This was (as far as we know) the first time Paul and Timothy had met.

Acts 16:1
*Paul came also to Derbe and to Lystra. A <u>disciple</u> was there, named Timothy, the son of a Jewish **woman** who was a <u>believer</u>, but his <u>father</u> was a Greek.*

Lydia, a woman *'from the city of Thyatira, a seller of purple goods, who was a worshiper of God'* was one among a group of women who heard Paul speak at a prayer gathering outside the city walls at Philippi. Luke writes, *'The Lord opened her heart to respond to Paul's message. ¹⁵ When she and the members of her household were baptized, she invited us to her home. "If you consider me a believer in the Lord," she said, "come and stay at my house." And she persuaded us.'*

The Compiled Teachings of The Apostle Paul

Acts 16:13
*And on the Sabbath day we went outside the gate to the riverside, where we supposed there was a place of prayer, and we sat down and spoke to the **women who had come** together. [14] One who heard us was **a woman named Lydia**, from the city of Thyatira, a seller of purple goods, who was a worshiper of God.*

In Thessalonica, '*As was his custom, Paul went into the synagogue, and on three Sabbath days he reasoned with them from the Scriptures,* [3] *explaining and proving that the Messiah had to suffer and rise from the dead. (Acts 17:2-3)*

Acts 17:3b
*"This Jesus, whom I proclaim to you, is the Christ." [4] And some of them were persuaded and joined Paul and Silas, as did a great many of the devout Greeks and **not a few of the leading women**. [5] But the Jews were jealous*

Paul and Silas left Thessalonica and went to Berea where Paul's teaching was well received by the Berean Jews.

Acts 17:11b
*...they received the word with all eagerness, examining the Scriptures daily to see if these things were so. [12] Many of them therefore believed, with not a few Greek **women** of high standing as well as men.*

From Berea, Paul travelled to Athens in Greece where Paul preached the resurrection of Christ; Acts 17: 24-32.

Acts 17:33
*So Paul went out from their midst. [34] But some men joined him and believed, among whom also were Dionysius the Areopagite and **a woman named Damaris** and others with them.*

Paul returned from his third missionary trip to Jerusalem where he was seized in the temple by Jews from Asia who were there visiting from the cities that he had preached the Gospel to, but the Commander of the Roman cohort rescued Paul from the crowd who were beating him and preparing to stone him, and then put Paul on 'public trial'; Acts 21: 34-40.

Acts 22:4
*I persecuted this Way to the death, binding and delivering to prison **both men and women**, [5] as the high priest and the whole council of elders can bear me witness.*

Gal. 4:4
*But when the set time had fully come, God sent his Son, **born of a woman**, born under the law, [5] to redeem those under the law, that we might receive adoption to sonship (adoption as sons).*

These two verses summarize the gospel of Jesus Christ. This was the good news Paul preached to the Galatians, and which they had believed; that God's Son Jesus was born to a human woman, Mary, who was a virgin (Matthew 1:18) and so her pregnancy was a mysterious miracle. But Mary carried the child of God and he was born, as the scriptures and the prophets foretold, into the family line of Abraham, Isaac, Israel (Jacob), and King David. [Matt. 1; Luke 3:23-38]

Paul is aware that the Galatians are being pressured by false teachers (Judaizers) are arguing from the Old Testament Scriptures that the Galatian Christians must follow the law in order to be saved (Galatians 2:4) and he is endeavoring to explain why that is not the truth. Paul analogizes Ishmael and Isaac as one being born a slave and the other being born free. They both live in the same home and are equals except that Ishmael is destined to inherit nothing and Isaac is destined to inherit everything. However, after Christ was crucified, was buried (entombed), and was resurrected by God to whom he cried, "Abba Father," pleading for all who would believe in him, all who were slaves have been given equal standing as explained by Paul in Gal. 4:1-7.

Gal. 4:22
*For it is written that Abraham had two sons, one by the slave woman and the other by **the free woman**. [23] His son by **the slave woman** was born according to the flesh, but his son by **the free woman** was born as the result of a divine promise.*

Quoting Isaiah 54:1, Paul again references Sarah and Hagar. Genesis 21:9 tells us that Ishmael mocked Isaac and this caused Sarah to turn against Hagar which leads to the next passage.

Gal. 4:27
*For it is written: "Be glad, **barren woman**, you who never bore a child; shout for joy and cry aloud, you who were never in labor; because more are the children of **the desolate woman** than of her who has a husband."*

Because Sarah was angered she wanted Hagar sent away [Gen, 9-13]. God told Abraham to do as Sarah wished and so giving Ishmael to her, he sent Hagar away. However, God promised that Ishmael would become the father of a great nation as would Isaac.

Gal. 4:30
*But what does Scripture say? "Get rid of **the slave woman** and her son, for **the slave woman's son** will never share in the inheritance with the free woman's son." [31] Therefore, brothers and sisters, we are not children of **the slave woman**, but of **the free woman**.*

The Compiled Teachings of The Apostle Paul

In this passage and the following verse (1 Cor. 7:2) Paul is stipulating monogamy, and this chapter continues teaching about and giving guidance for marriages.

1 Cor. 7:1
*It is good for a man not to touch a **woman**. [2]But, because of fornications, let each man have his own wife, and let each woman have her own husband.*

Paul leads into this next passage with the words, "*I want you to be free from concern*." As explained elsewhere 1 Cor. 7:32 is pointing out that it is difficult to serve two masters, a theme that Jesus addressed. You cannot be focused entirely on God if you have a wife and a family. There are clearly times when a man with a family has to spend time with his family or else he is leaving them abandoned. Paul is basically saying that only the unmarried, including the virgin, are able to give themselves 100 per cent to the Lord.

1 Cor. 7:32[b]
*He that is unmarried is careful for the things of the Lord, how he may please the Lord: [33]but he that is married is careful for the things of the world, how he may please his **wife**, [34] and is divided. So also **the woman that is unmarried** and the virgin is careful for the things of the Lord, that she may be holy both in body and in spirit: but **she that is married** is careful for the things of the world, how she may please her husband.*

---

1 Cor. 11:3-16, is a lengthy passage which includes the word 'woman' being used no less than 16 times, but it is not just women that Paul is talking to.

First Paul talks about '*the head of every man is Christ*', meaning '*every man and every woman*'. Then Paul teaches on head coverings advising that women should either be veiled or have their hair shorn. Next Paul teaches that '*(the man) is the image and glory of God: but the woman is the glory of the man. [8] For the man is not of the woman; but the woman of the man: [9] for neither was the man created for the woman; but the woman for the man*'. Paul then states that '*the woman (ought) to have a sign of authority on her head,*'. Paul's next teaching 1 Cor. 11:11-12 appears to take a different direction: '*neither is the woman without the man, nor the man without the woman, in the Lord. [12] For as the woman is of the man, so is the man also by the woman; but all things are of God.*' It is important to understand that Paul does not teach that women are inferior to men. Throughout his teaching Paul extols the value and spiritual equality of women (1 Cor. 7:4; Gal. 3:28). Many women in Corinth came into the church on their own without their husbands (1 Cor. 7:13), and Christianity drew in many women because of the clear teaching that God welcomes everyone without regard to gender to receive His grace by faith in Jesus. Paul emphasize that women and men are dependent on each other in the Lord; neither gender is self-existent. Christianity rejects the independence of both men and women from each other, insisting that both need the other and both need the Lord, and neither gender is inferior, and neither is dispensable. [Credit: www.bibleref.com]

Finally in this passage, Paul returns to discussing hair and presents guidelines that today, and in the past, are not popular to accept or follow. First he poses the question '*is it seemly that a woman pray to God unveiled?*' and rhetorically points out that '*even nature itself teach you, that, if a man has long hair, it is a dishonor to him*'. Today many Christian churches teach that women should, or even must, wear a head covering, and some insist on the head being veiled, while many churches leave the decision to the individual, and many men in churches today wear their hair long. For women that have long hair and would prefer not to wear a head coving or veil, Paul, at least partially, redeems himself in the penultimate verse of this passage by stating that '*if a woman has long hair, it is a glory to her: for her hair is given her for a covering.*' In the final verse Paul states uncompromisingly that man should not, even cannot be allowed to wear their hair long.

In verse 16, Paul throws out a defense against any criticism by anyone who might not want to agree with his teaching by stating, '*we have no such custom, neither (have) the churches of God.*' By '*we have no such custom*', I take that to mean, 'my ministry has no such custom' which might be the first 'mic drop' line ever written.

1 Cor. 11:3-16
*But I would have you know, that the head of every man is Christ; and the head of **the woman** is the man; and the head of Christ is God. [4] Every man praying or prophesying, having his head covered, dishonors his head. [5] But **every woman praying or prophesying** with her head unveiled dishonors her head; for it is one and the same thing as if she were shaven. [6] For if a **woman is not veiled**, let her also be shorn: but if **it is a shame to a woman to be shorn or shaven**, let her be veiled. [7] For a man indeed ought not to have his head veiled, forasmuch as he is the image and glory of God: but **the woman is the glory of the man**. [8] For **the man is not of the woman; but the woman of the man**: [9] for neither was the man created for **the woman; but the woman for the man**: [10] for this cause ought the **woman to have a sign of authority** on her head because of the angels. [11] Nevertheless, neither is the **woman without the man, nor the man without the woman**, in the Lord. [12] For as **the woman is of the man, so is the man also by the woman**; but all things are of God. [13] Judge yourselves: is it seemly that a **woman pray to God unveiled**? [14] Does not even nature itself teach you, that, if a man has long hair, it is a dishonor to him? [15] But **if a woman has long hair, it is a glory to her**: for her hair is given her for a covering. [16] But if any man seems to be contentious, we have no such custom, neither the churches of God.*

The Compiled Teachings of The Apostle Paul

The next guidance that Paul gives for women is that they should keep silent. Quite surprisingly, Paul here refers to the Law (the Torah): '*it is not permitted to them to speak; but let them be in subjection, as also says the law.*' Giving the reason that '*it is shameful for a woman to speak in the church*', Paul suggests that they '*ask their own husbands at home*'.

Yes, in many of today's churches this would not be easily accepted. After all, one needs to learn from '*a preacher, a teacher, or a prophet*' if one is to learn and be guided correctly.

Now let the discussion and debates begin on the issues of how to handle the teachings of Paul on the topics of hair length, head covering, veils, and, now, the role and latitude of women in church meetings.

1 Cor. 14:34
*As in all the churches of the saints, ³⁴ let the **women keep silent** in the churches: for it is not permitted to them to speak; but let them be in subjection, as also says the law. ³⁵ And if they would learn anything, let them ask their own husbands at home: for **it is shameful for a woman** to speak in the church.*

Rom. 1:26
*For this reason God gave them up to dishonorable passions. For their **women** exchanged natural relations for those that are contrary to nature; ²⁷ and the men likewise gave up natural relations with **women** and were consumed with passion for one another, men committing shameless acts with men and receiving in themselves the due penalty for their error.*

This passage written to the church in Rome – a city that Paul has not yet visited – in the culture of the western world and the 21ˢᵗ Century goes hard against the grain of those that believe that 'being gay' – homosexual, lesbian, transgender or in any other way than being straight – is not ungodly. Paul's words in this passage speak clearly against all except for natural man-woman intimacy and celibacy.

Rom. 7:2
*For the **woman** that has a husband is bound by law to the husband while he lives; but if the husband dies, she is discharged from the law of the husband. ³ So then if, while the husband lives and she is joined to another man, she shall be called an adulteress: but if the husband dies, she is free from the law, so that she is not an adulteress and [even though] she may be joined to another man.*

From the notes for 1 Corinthians 7 in Section 3, Paul uses the direct analogy of a man being joined to a woman who becomes his wife which is to the glory of God for procreation by a man and his wife is blessed. When a wife loses her husband by cause of death, Paul explains, the wife is free to remarry. However, if the woman while married has sexual relations with a man other than her husband she is deemed guilty of adultery.

Philipp. 4:3
*...**help these women**, for they labored with me in the gospel*

Philipp. 4: ² I exhort Euodia, and I exhort Syntyche, to be of the same mind in the Lord. ³ Yes, I ask you also, true yokefellow, help these women, for they labored with me in the gospel, with Clement also, and the rest of my fellow-workers, whose names are in the book of life.

Paul rarely named names when referring to disagreements in the churches. To mention these two women so specifically may have indicated they were well known in the congregation. It might also mean that their dispute was very public, particularly bitter, or even both. However, their dispute did not mean these women were ungodly, and Paul mentions that they had worked together with him and with Clement and other godly leaders. Paul also said their names were in the "book of life," noting his confidence that they were believers. *[Credit: www.bibleref.com]*

---

1 Thess. 5:2
For yourselves know perfectly that the day of the Lord will come as a thief in the night. ³ When they are saying, Peace and safety, then sudden destruction comes upon them, as travail upon a woman with child; and they shall in no wise escape.

Paul is quoting what Jesus taught Matt. 24:⁴² '*Watch therefore: for you do not know on what day your Lord comes. ⁴³ But know this, that if the master of the house had known in what watch the thief was coming, he would have watched,*' (also Luke 12:35-48.)

Matt. 24:42 is part of Jesus' teaching to the disciples on the Mount of Olives:

Matt. 24:⁷ *For nation shall rise against nation, and kingdom against kingdom; and there shall be famines and earthquakes in diverse places. ⁸ But all these things are the beginning of travail. ⁹ Then shall they deliver you up to tribulation, and shall kill you: and you shall be hated of all the nations for my name's sake. ¹⁰ And then shall many stumble, and shall deliver up one another, and shall hate one another. ¹¹ And many false prophets shall arise, and shall lead many astray.*

(Paul will have most likely have learned Jesus' teachings from the other apostles.)

Matt. 24:¹⁴ *And this gospel of the kingdom shall be preached in the whole world for a testimony to all the nations; and then shall the end come.*

The Compiled Teachings of The Apostle Paul

In Paul's letter to Timothy Paul echoes parts of what he wrote in his letter to the church in Corinth *(1 Cor. 11: 3-16)*, guidance that many current day (Western culture, 21st century) churches do not fully subscribe to; such as how women should wear their hair and that women should *'learn in quietness'*, and not be permitted to teach; echoing 1 Cor. 14:34, which is teaching that is based on the Torah. Paul adds that, *'the woman being beguiled has fallen into transgression'* referring to the fall of mankind. which is charged to Adam and the sin is considered his even though the first to actually disobey was Eve (Genesis 3:17; Romans 5:12). Paul specifies here that "Adam was not deceived." This clarifies that even though Adam ate the forbidden fruit, he did not do so due to the serpent's influence; he did so by taking the fruit from Eve. Instead, "the woman was deceived." In Gen, 3:13, Eve said, "The serpent deceived me, and I ate."

1 Tim. 2:8
I desire therefore that the men pray in every place, lifting up holy hands, without wrath and disputing. [9] *In like manner, that **women adorn themselves in modest apparel**, with decency and sobriety; not with braided hair, and gold or pearls or costly raiment;* [10] *but (which becomes **women professing godliness**) through good works.* [11] ***Let a woman learn** in quietness with all subjection.* [12] *But I **permit not a woman to teach**, nor to have dominion over a man, but to be in quietness.* [13] *For Adam was first formed, then Eve;* [14] *and Adam was not beguiled, but the woman being beguiled has fallen into transgression.*

In 1 Timothy 3, Paul is giving Timothy guidance on selecting leaders in the church initially referring to overseers but in verse 8 targeting Deacons specifically and in 1 Tim. 5:1 and 1 Tim. 5:17 Paul refers specifically to Elders, both of which are terms/position titles used in many Christian churches. *(I have capitalized these titles so as to make the distinguishable from 'elders' who are qualified solely by their age.)* In verse 11, Paul references women and lists qualities that they should subscribe to. Is Paul suggesting here that women are candidates to be Deacons or other positions of leadership? Verse 12 in some translations (ESV, CSB, NLT, KJV) suggest that Paul is referring only to the wives of Deacons and not to all women. Verse 12 in some translations (NASB, CSB) state that Deacons must be married, while others state, 'may be married' or 'Let the deacons be the husbands of one wife' (ESV, KJV) which would seem to allow a single male to be appointed a Deacon.

1 Tim. 3:10-12
And let these also first be proved; then let them serve as deacons, if they be blameless. [11] ***Women** in like manner must be grave, not slanderers, temperate, faithful in all things.*

This passage uses the term 'elder' for a person, man or woman, who qualifies to be referred to as an elder solely because of their age. In his guidance regarding widows in 1 Tim. 5:9, Paul stipulates the age of 60, *'Let none be enrolled as a widow under threescore years old*, an age which, one even today, might consider a reasonable guideline for considering one to be an elder, and those younger as brothers and sisters.

1 Tim. 5:1
Rebuke not an elder, but exhort him as a father; the younger men as brethren: [2] ***the elder women as mothers**; the younger as sisters, in all purity.*

---

1 Tim. 5:16
If any woman that believes has widows *(in her care), let her relieve (continue to help) them, and let not the church be burdened; that it may relieve (help) them that are widows indeed meaning widows without any family to provide them with support.*

This passage is also addressed in the notes concerning widows. Here the emphasis is on a woman in whose family there is a widow that needs to be cared for. Paul writes that she should care for that widow and not let the church be burdened as the church has enough of a challenge providing care for widows who are desolate.

In this passage Paul makes a reference to prostitution and human trafficking. "Silly women laden with sins" are those who allow themselves to get drunk and who have given up all dignity and have become vulnerable to being persuaded or even taken by scam artists and others who physically seduced women. *(The idea of a false teacher taking advantage of women in their own homes would have been repulsive to Timothy and other believers.* [Credit: www.bibleref.com]*)* Because of whatever their lifestyle becomes, Paul writes that they are *'never able to come to the knowledge of the truth'*.

2 Tim. 3:6
*For of these are they that creep into houses, and take captive **silly women laden with sins**, led away by divers lusts,* [7] *ever learning, and never able to come to the knowledge of the truth.*

In Titus 2:2, the verse prior to this verse, Paul references older men, that they are to *'be temperate, grave, sober-minded, sound in faith, in love, patient:'* and now Paul addresses the older women:

Titus 2:3
*...that **aged women** likewise be reverent in demeanor, not slanderers nor enslaved to much wine, teachers of that which is good;* [4] *that they may **train the young women** to love their husbands, to love their children,* [5] *to be sober-minded, chaste, workers at home, kind, being in subjection to their own husbands, that the word of God be not blasphemed.*

The Compiled Teachings of The Apostle Paul

ADDENDA:

Study On Paul's Teaching On Circumcision
Topic Words List
Table of Contents – Complete Listing

Study On Paul's Teaching On Circumcision

On circumcision, Paul preaches first that Abraham was not circumcised when God established a covenant with him; the promise that he would be the father of a great nation. Abraham agreed to be circumcised in order that the covenant be established *[Gen. 17:11]*

1 Chronicles 16:16 / Psalm 105:9 [ASV]
the **covenant** He made with **Abraham**, the oath He swore to Isaac.
¹³ O ye seed of Israel his servant, Ye children of Jacob, his chosen ones.
¹⁴ He is Jehovah our God; His judgments are in all the earth.
¹⁵ Remember His covenant forever, The word which He commanded to a thousand generations,
¹⁶ The covenant which He made with Abraham, and His oath to Isaac,
¹⁷ And confirmed the same to Jacob for a statute to Israel for an everlasting covenant,
¹⁸ Saying, To you will I give the land of Canaan, the lot of your inheritance.

Genesis 17
Now when Abram was ninety-nine years old, the Lord appeared to Abram and said to him, "I am God Almighty; walk before Me, and be blameless. ² I will make My covenant between Me and you, and I will multiply you exceedingly."

¹⁰ This is My covenant, which you shall keep, between Me and you and your descendants after you: every male among you shall be circumcised. **¹¹ And you shall be circumcised in the flesh of your foreskin, and it shall be the sign of the covenant between Me and you.** *¹² And every male among you who is eight days old shall be circumcised throughout your generations, including a slave who is born in the house or who is bought with money from any foreigner, who is not of your descendants. ¹³ A slave who is born in your house or who is bought with your money shall certainly be circumcised; so My covenant shall be in your flesh as an everlasting covenant. ¹⁴ But as for an uncircumcised male, one who is not circumcised in the flesh of his foreskin, that person shall be cut off from his people; he has broken My covenant."*

*¹⁸ And Abraham said to God, "Oh that Ishmael might live before You!" ¹⁹ But God said, "No, but your wife Sarah will bear you a son, and you shall name him Isaac; and I will establish My covenant with him as an everlasting covenant for his descendants after him. ²⁰ As for Ishmael, I have heard you; behold, I will bless him, and make him fruitful and multiply him exceedingly. He shall father twelve princes, and I will make him into a great nation. ²¹ **But I will establish My covenant with Isaac, whom Sarah will bear to you at this season next year.***

Genesis 22
*¹⁵ Then the angel of the LORD called to Abraham a second time from heaven, ¹⁶ and said, "By Myself I have sworn, declares the LORD, because you have done this thing and have not withheld your son, your only son, ¹⁷ indeed I will greatly bless you, and I will greatly multiply your seed as the stars of the heavens and as the sand, which is on the seashore; and your seed shall possess the gate of their enemies. ¹⁸ **And in your seed all the nations of the earth shall be blessed**, because you have obeyed My voice." ¹⁹ So Abraham returned to his young men, and they got up and went together to Beersheba; and Abraham lived in Beersheba.*

In The Gospels...

John 7:22-23
(Jesus said) Moses gave you **circumcision** (not that it was of Moses, but it was of the fathers); and on the sabbath you circumcise a man. If a man receives **circumcision** on the sabbath, that the law of Moses may not be broken *(because it must be performed on the eighth day);* are you angry with me, because I made a man every part whole on the sabbath?

In Acts...

Peter Preaches In The Temple
And you are heirs of the prophets and of the **covenant** God made with your fathers. He said to **Abraham**, 'Through your offspring all peoples on earth will be blessed.' [Acts 3:25 / Gen. 22:18]

Stephen Preaches To The High Priest
...And he gave him the covenant of **circumcision**: and so *Abraham* begat Isaac, and **circumcised** him the eighth day; and Isaac *begat* Jacob, and Jacob the twelve patriarchs. Then he gave **Abraham** the **covenant** of **circumcision**, and **Abraham** became the father of Isaac and **circumcised** him eight days after his birth. Later Isaac became the father of Jacob, and Jacob became the father of the twelve patriarchs. *[Acts 7:8 NASB]*

The Compiled Teachings of The Apostle Paul

In Paul's Epistles (Letters)...

Paul Writes To The Church In Galatia

*Gal. 2:7 when they saw that I had been entrusted with the gospel of the **uncircumcision**, even as Peter with the gospel of the **circumcision** [8] (for he that wrought for Peter to the apostleship of the **circumcision** wrought for me also to the Gentiles); [9] and when they perceived the grace that was given to me, James and Cephas and John, they who were reputed to be pillars, gave to me and Barnabas the right hands of fellowship, that we should go to the Gentiles, and they to the **circumcision**;* [Gal. 2:7-9]

As we see here, the term 'the circumcision' means the Jews, and the term 'the uncircumcision' means the Gentiles.

Galatians 2:12
*For before that certain came from James, he ate with the Gentiles; but when they came, he drew back and separated himself, fearing them that were of the **circumcision**.*

Here Paul is explaining that there was a fear of being shunned or rejected by the Jews if a Jew, such as the one referred to as 'certain', was to be known to have been eating with Gentiles.

Galatians 5:2
*Behold, I Paul say to you, that, if you receive **circumcision**, Christ will profit you nothing.*

Here Paul is explaining to Gentiles that choosing to be circumcised brings no advantage as it is only the descendants of Abraham, Isaac and Jacob that can benefit from being circumcised. A Gentile cannot become covered by or be committed to the Law and to the covenant that God made with Abraham.

Galatians 5:3
*Yea, I testify again to every man that receives **circumcision**, that he is a debtor to do the whole law.*

Here Paul is explaining to Gentiles that choosing to be circumcised causes you to become 'a debtor' committed to observing and keeping all of the Law.

Galatians 5:6
*For in Christ Jesus neither **circumcision** avails anything, nor **uncircumcision**; but faith working through love.*

Here Paul is explaining that being circumcised is not a requirement of being saved through confession of believing in Jesus Christ, but having faith is.

Galatians 5:11
*But I, brethren, if I still preach **circumcision**, why am I still persecuted? then has the stumbling-block of the cross been done away.*

Here Paul is offering a reminder that although he regards himself to be the Apostle to the Gentiles, he is a Jew and still has the right to preach circumcision to Jews.

Galatians 5:12
*I would that they that unsettle you would even go beyond **circumcision**.*

Paul is suggesting emasculation* be justified and is appropriate in certain circumstances. Here, Paul is specifically referring to agitators and troublemakers who are (still) preaching that circumcision is a requirement for all.

  __NASB__: 'would even emasculate themselves: __NLT__: I just wish that those troublemakers who want to mutilate you by circumcision would mutilate themselves.

Galatians 6:13
*For not even they who receive **circumcision** do themselves keep the law; but they desire to have you **circumcised**, that they may glory in your flesh.*

Here Paul is suggesting that those who wish and attempt to persuade Gentiles to be circumcised have an ulterior motive, that of claiming some kind of recognition as if the Gentiles were a sport that they can brag about, even claiming you as their disciples [NLT].

Galatians 6:15
*For neither is **circumcision** anything, nor **uncircumcision**, but a new creature.*

In Gal. 6:14 Paul references Christ's sacrifice on the cross, explaining that the only thing that one (he or anyone) should brag about is the opportunity for each of us to become saved by acknowledging who Jesus Christ is (was, is and forever will be): '[14] *But far be it from me to boast, except in the cross of our Lord Jesus Christ, through which the world has been crucified to me, and I to the world.*' In 6:15 Paul writes to the Galatians stating that circumcision is not important (other than to the Jews who wish to keep the covenant) that whether circumcised or not, being born again, becoming '*a new creature*' - a reference to the conversation that Jesus had with Nicodemus [John 3:1-21] in which Jesus told Nicodemus that we all have the opportunity to be born again and through Him - can gain eternal life: *For every one that does evil hates the light, and comes not to the light, lest his works should be reproved.* [21] *But he that does the truth comes to the light, that his works may be made manifest, that they have been wrought in God.* [John 3:20-21]

1 Corinthians 7:18-19
*[18] Was any man called being **circumcised**? let him not become **uncircumcised**. Has any been called in **uncircumcision**? let him not be **circumcised**. [19] **Circumcision** is nothing, and **uncircumcision** is nothing; but the keeping of the commandments of God.*

In contrast to what Paul had written regarding circumcision and uncircumcision to the church in Galatia, in his first letter to the church in Corinth, Paul again writes that '***Circumcision** is nothing, and **uncircumcision** is nothing*', but instead of writing '*but a new creature*' he writes, '*but the keeping of the commandments of God.*' Here Paul is writing specifically to the Jews and is explaining that if a person is criticized because they are circumcised, they should not change their ways or they will become uncircumcised. This is not a reference to have a surgery reversal to change them physically (if such was possible in those days), but Paul is telling those who are Jews and are circumcised that they must keep the Commandments or else they will break the covenant and so become as if uncircumcised.

What Paul wrote to the Corinthians about keeping the Commandments is repeated in his letter to the Romans:

Romans 2:25
*[25] For **circumcision** indeed profits, if you are a doer (keeper) of the law: but if you are a transgressor of the law, your **circumcision** is become **uncircumcision**.*

Paul has advised the Church in Rome – just as he did the church in Galatia – that a person who breaks any of the Commandments (Laws of Moses) is in effect nullifying the legitimacy of their circumcision, and knowing that there are practices within the church in Rome that are violating the Commandments, he continues to explain:

Romans 2:26-29
*[26] If therefore the **uncircumcision** (meaning the Gentiles, should be required to) keep the ordinances of the law, shall not his uncircumcision be reckoned for **circumcision**? [27] and shall not the **uncircumcision** which is by nature, if it fulfil the law, judge you, who by the letter (of the law) and **circumcision** are (yourself) a transgressor of the law? [28] For he is not a Jew who is one outwardly; neither is that **circumcision** which is outward in the flesh: [29] but he is a Jew who is one inwardly; and **circumcision** is that of the heart, in the spirit not in the letter; whose praise is not of men, but of God.*

Paul then continues in Romans:

Romans 3:1
*What advantage then has the Jew? or what is the profit of **circumcision**?*

Having presented this question, Paul provides a response (Rom. 3:2-29), and he concludes in verse 30:

Romans 3:30
*if so be that God is one, and he shall justify the **circumcision** by faith, and the **uncircumcision** through faith.*

This concluding statement of Rom. 3 is telling the Jews who comprise the leadership in the church in Rome that it is by faith, and by faith alone, that man is justified, and not just because he is circumcised, and, in fact, faith also justifies those who are not circumcised.

Romans 4:9-12
*Is this blessing then pronounced upon the **circumcision**, or upon the **uncircumcision** also? for we say, To Abraham his faith was reckoned for righteousness. [10] How then was it reckoned? when he was in **circumcision**, or in **uncircumcision**? (It was) Not in **circumcision**, but in uncircumcision: [11] and he received the sign of **circumcision**, a seal of the righteousness of the faith which he had while he was in **uncircumcision**: that he might be the father of all them that believe, though they be in **uncircumcision**, that righteousness might be reckoned unto them; [12] and the father of **circumcision** to them who not only are of the **circumcision**, but who also walk in the steps of that faith of our father Abraham which he had in **uncircumcision**.*

Again Paul poses a question; 'If we say that Abraham was reckoned for his righteousness, and he was not at that time circumcised, then shouldn't the uncircumcised (Gentiles) also be reckoned for their righteousness?' and Paul writes, '*that he might be the father of all them that believe*' and if all are to be reckoned (judged) according to their righteousness, doesn't 'all' include those who are not circumcised?

Paul reaches a conclusion regarding circumcision that Jesus had to be born a jew *(of the circumcision)* in order for God to show that the people of Israel were (still) His chosen people. Implicitly Paul is also saying, 'and to fulfill the teachings of the prophets'.

Romans 15:8
*For I say that Christ was made a minister of the **circumcision** for the truth of God, that he might confirm the promises given to the fathers,*

The next writing of Paul that references circumcision is found in Paul's letter to Titus, a letter reflecting what Paul recalls from his visit to the island of Crete.

The Compiled Teachings of The Apostle Paul

Titus 1:10
*For there are many unruly men, vain talkers and deceivers, specially they of the **circumcision**,*
In this passage Paul is addressing the traits and qualities that church leaders, specifically bishops, should have:
*⁷ For the bishop must be blameless, as God's steward; not self-willed, not soon angry, no brawler, no striker, not greedy of filthy lucre; ⁸ but given to hospitality, a lover of good, sober-minded, just, holy, self-controlled; ⁹ holding to the faithful word which is according to the teaching, that he may be able both to exhort in the sound doctrine, and to convict the gainsayers. ¹⁰ For there are many unruly men, vain talkers and deceivers, **specially they of the circumcision**, ¹¹ whose mouths must be stopped; men who overthrow whole houses, teaching things which they ought not, for filthy lucre's sake. ¹² One of themselves, a prophet of their own, said, 'Cretans are always liars, evil beasts, idle gluttons'.*

There are two possible ways of interpreting 'they of the circumcision'. Paul could be talking about Cretans, who are Gentiles, criticizing Jews and their culture including being circumcised, or it could be taken to mean that some of the *'unruly men, vain talkers and deceivers'* that Paul is referencing are in fact 'of the circumcision' meaning that they are Jews. In the latter case that would mean there are others beside himself who have taken the Gospel to Crete, but they are teaching a false Gospel. In my view, this is what Paul is referring to.

Ephesians 2:11
*Wherefore remember, that once you, the Gentiles in the flesh, who are called **Uncircumcision** by that which is called **Circumcision**, in the flesh, made by hands; (meaning you Gentiles are called uncircumcised by the Jews) ¹² that you were at that time separate from Christ, alienated from the commonwealth of Israel, and strangers from the covenants of the promise, having no hope and without God in the world. ¹³ But now in Christ Jesus you that once were far off are made close in the blood of Christ.*
In his letter to the church in Ephesus, Paul explains that the Jews refer to themselves as the Circumcision and to all others as the Uncircumcision, and that before Christ the Gentiles were without hope because they were separated from and unable to be reconciled to God. That, at least, was what the Jews were teaching. But now Jesus Christ, the Messiah whom the Jews had long been waiting for has come, and through His sacrifice on the cross has fulfilled God's promise to Abraham that all nations, all people *(see Romans 4:9-12)*, have now been given the opportunity of being reconciled to God.

Philippians 3:3
*for we are the (true) **circumcision**, who worship by the Spirit of God, and glory in Christ Jesus, and have no confidence in the flesh:*
To the church in Philippi, Paul writes: *² Beware of the dogs, beware of the evil workers, beware of the false circumcision; ³ for we are the true circumcision, who worship in the Spirit of God and take pride in Christ Jesus, and put no confidence in the flesh, ⁴ although I myself could boast as having confidence even in the flesh. If anyone else thinks he is confident in the flesh, I have more reason: ⁵ circumcised (on) the eighth day, of the nation of Israel, of the tribe of Benjamin, a Hebrew of Hebrews; as to the Law, a Pharisee; ⁶ as to zeal, a persecutor of the church; as to the righteousness which is in the Law, found blameless.*
He is listing his credentials as one of the Circumcision, adding *'a persecutor of the church; as to the righteousness which is in the Law, found blameless.'* But now Paul is preaching the Gospel to the Gentiles.

Finally, to the church in Colossae, on the topic of circumcision Paul writes about the circumcision of Christ, 'a circumcision made without hands' which has forgiven us all our transgressions. So in Colossians Paul is not addressing the need to become circumcised or not but rather teaching about the spiritual aspect of Christ's sacrifice for us.

Colossians 2:9-11
*⁹ For in Him all the fullness of Deity dwells in bodily form, ¹⁰ and in Him you have been made complete, and He is the head over all rule and authority; ¹¹ and in Him you were also **circumcised** with a **circumcision** made without hands, in the removal of the body of the flesh by the **circumcision** of Christ; ¹² having been buried with Him in baptism, in which you were also raised up with Him through faith in the working of God, who raised Him from the dead. ¹³ When you were dead in your transgressions and the **uncircumcision** of your flesh, He made you alive together with Him, having forgiven us all our transgressions, ¹⁴ having canceled out the certificate of debt consisting of decrees against us, which was hostile to us; and He has taken it out of the way, having nailed it to the cross.*

Colossians 3:9-11
⁹ Do not lie to one another, since you laid aside the old self with its evil practices, ¹⁰ and have put on the new self who is being renewed to a true knowledge according to the image of the One who created him – where there cannot be Greek and Jew, circumcision and uncircumcision, barbarian, Scythian, bondman, freeman; but Christ is all, and in all.

In this final passage in which circumcision is recorded, Paul is using the term as in 'the circumcision' referring to the community of the Jews.

Colossians 4:10-11
*¹⁰ Aristarchus, my fellow prisoner, sends you his greetings; and also Barnabas's cousin Mark (about whom you received instructions; if he comes to you, welcome him); ¹¹ and also Jesus who is called Justus; these are the only fellow workers for the kingdom of God who are from the **circumcision**, and they have proved to be an encouragement to me.*

The Compiled Teachings of The Apostle Paul

Topic Words List

Abuse	Faith	Kind	Prophecy
Abuser(s)	Faithful(ness)	Kindness	Prophetic
Anger	Forgiving	Knowledge	Prophet(s)
Alert	Forgiveness	Longsuffering	Redeem(ed)
Appeared	Gentle	Love(d)	Righteous
Appoint(ed)	Glory	Marriage	Shame
Appointment	Good	Mother	Shameful
Ashamed	Goodness	Mystery	Shameless
Bad	Gossip(s)	Necessity	Strong
Belief	Hatred	Need	Temptation
Believer(s)	Healing	Perdition	Transgression
Brother	Hope	Perfect	Unrighteous
Care	Husbands	Persecute(d)	Want
Concern	God	Persuade(d)	Weak(ness)
Danger	Government	Please(d)	Wed, Wedding
Demon	Governor	Pray	Widowed
		Prayer	

The Seven Congregations in Relation to Colossae

Full Table of Contents

The Compiled Teachings of The Apostle Paul

Introduction 1

Section 1 3

A Summarization of The Teachings of Paul The Apostle 3

The Apostles Preaching of the Gospel in Jerusalem   3

Paul In Pisidian Antioch 3
Paul In Jerusalem 4
Paul In Caesarea 4

Section 2 6

Saul and His Conversion to Paul 6
Paul's Teaching in the Book of Acts 9
Paul's First Missionary Trip 11

How old was Saul, the Saul that became Paul? 11
Peter Preaches 12
Paul Preaches In Antioch of Pisidia 14
Paul and Barnabas preach again at Antioch in Pisidia 14
Paul and Barnabas at Iconium 15
Paul and Barnabas at Lystra 15
Paul Stoned at Lystra 15
Paul and Barnabas Return to Antioch in Syria 15
The Jerusalem Council 16
The Council's Letter to Gentile Believers 17
Paul and Barnabas Separate 17

Paul's Second Missionary Trip 17

Timothy Joins Paul and Silas 17
The Macedonian Call 17
The Conversion of Lydia at Phillipi 18
Paul and Silas in Prison 18
The Philippian Jailer Converted 18
Paul Reports That He Is A Roman Citizen 18
Paul and Silas in Thessalonica 19
Paul and Silas in Berea 19
Paul in Athens 20
Paul in Corinth 20

Paul's Third Missionary Trip 21

Paul Returns to Antioch 21
Paul Returns to Ephesus 22
Paul in Macedonia and Greece 23
Luke rejoins Paul on His Mission 23
Eutychus is Raised from the Dead 23
Paul Speaks to the Ephesian Elders 23
Paul Goes to Jerusalem 24
Paul Visits James 24
Paul Arrested in the Temple in Jerusalem 24
Paul Speaks to the People 25
Paul Shares His Testimony 25
Paul and the Roman Tribune 25
Paul Before the Council 25
A Plot to Kill Paul 26
Paul Sent to Felix the Governor at Ceasarea 26
Paul Before Felix 26
Paul Kept in Custody 26
Paul Appeals to Caesar 27
Paul's Defense Before Agrippa 27
Paul Tells of His Conversion 28
Paul Sails for Rome 28
The Shipwreck 29

The Cities and Regions Visited on Paul's Missionary Trips....30

Section 3

The Letters of The Apostle Paul

Standing of Each of the Pauline Letters (Epistles) 32
The Greetings of each of the 'Letters Books' 32
The Chronological Order of Paul's Letters 33

The Teachings In The Letters 35
Transition Passages 38
Galatians 42

The Council At Jerusalem 44
Paul Opposes Cephas (Peter) 45
Faith Brings Righteousness 45
Intent Of The Law 46
Sonship In Christ 46

The Compiled Teachings of The Apostle Paul

Paul's Concern for the Galatians 47
Hagar and Sarah 47
Walk by the Spirit 48
Life by the Spirit 48
Bear One Another's Burdens 49
Not Circumcision but the New Creation 49

1 Corinthians 50
Proclaiming Christ Crucified 50
Wisdom from the Spirit 50
Divisions in the Church 51
The Ministry of Apostles 51
Sexual Immorality Defiles the Church 52
Lawsuits Against Believers 52
Flee Sexual Immorality 53
Principles for Marriage 53
Live as You Are Called 54
The Unmarried and the Widowed 54
Food Offered to Idols 55
Paul Surrenders His Rights 55
Living Off The Gospel 56
Warning Against Idolatry 56
Flee From Idolatry 57
Do All to the Glory of God 57
Be Imitators of Me, As I Am of Christ 57
The Lord's Supper 58
Spiritual Gifts 58
One Body with Many Members 59
The Way of Love 59
Speaking In Tongues 60
Orderly Worship 60
The Resurrection of Christ 61
The Resurrection of the Dead 61
The Resurrection Body 62
Mystery and Victory 63
The Collection for the Saints 63
Plans for Travel 63
Final Instructions 63
Salutations 64

2 Corinthians 65
Paul's Change of Plans 65
Reaffirm Your Love 65
Ministers of a New Covenant 66
Paul's Apostolic Ministry 67
The Temporal and Eternal 67
Paul Commends Their Ministry 68
Paul Reveals His Heart 69
Great Generosity 70
God Gives Most 71
Paul Describes Himself 71
Paul Defends His Apostleship 72
Paul's Vision 73

All Things Beloved Are For Your Edifying 74
Examine Yourselves 74

Romans 75
The Righteous Shall Live by FaithRomans 1:16-32 76
God's Wrath on Unrighteousness 76
The Righteous Judgment of God 76
Judgment and the Law 77
Righteousness 77
Righteousness Through Faith 78
Justification Through Faith 78
God's Promise To Abraham 79
Faith and Grace 79
Promise Realized Through Faith 79
Faith Brings Peace 79
Through The Gift of Righteousness Comes Justification 80
Being Dead to Sin is to be Alive to God 80
Slaves to Righteousness and Sanctification 80
Released from the Law 80
The Law and Sin 81
Life in the Spirit 82
Heirs with Christ 82
Our Victory In Christ: Redemption 82
All Things Work Together For Good 83
God's Everlasting Love 83
God's Sovereign Choice; Solicitude For Israel 83
Israel's Unbelief 84
The Message of Salvation to All 84
Denial By Israel 85
The Remnant of Israel: Israel Is Not Cast Away 85
Salvation Comes To The Gentiles (Who Are Grafted In) 85
The Mystery of Israel's Salvation 86
Dedicated Service: A Living Sacrifice 86
Gifts of Grace: Abhor What Is Evil 87
Marks of the True Christian 87
Submission to Government Authorities 87
Fulfilling the Law Through Love 88
Put On The Armor Of Light 88
Do Not Pass Judgment on One Another 88
Do Not Cause Another to Stumble 89
Self-denial: The Example of Christ 89
Christ is the God of Hope of Jews and Gentiles 89
Paul the Minister to the Gentiles 90
Paul's Plan to Visit Rome 90
Personal Greetings 90
Final Instructions and Greetings 91
Doxology 91
Observations: 91

1 Thessalonians 92
Thanksgiving For These Believers 92
Paul's Ministry 92
Encouragement of Timothy's Visit 93

Sanctification and Love	93
Those Who Died in Christ	94
The Day of The Lord	94

2 Thessalonians 95
Thanksgiving For These Believers	95
Man of Sin	95
Exhortation	96

1 Timothy 97
Misleading Teaching In Doctrine and Living	97
A Call To Prayer	98
Overseers and Deacons	98
Apostasy and A Good Minister's Discipline	99
Treat Others With Respect	99
Concerning Elders	100
Instructions to Those Who Minister	100

Titus 102
Qualifications of Elders	102
Duties of the Older and the Younger	102
Godly Living	103
Personal Concerns	103

Ephesians 104
The Blessings of Redemption	104
Gratitude and Prayers	104
Made Alive In Christ	105
Paul's Stewardship	106
Unity of the Spirit	106
The Christian's Walk	107
Be Imitators of God	107
Marriage Like Christ and the Church	108
Children and Parents	108
Slaves and Masters	109
The Armor of God	109

Philippians 110
Thanksgiving	110
The Gospel is preached	110
To Live Is Christ	111
Be Like Christ	111
Timothy and Epaphroditus	112
Warnings and Reminders	112
The Goal of Life	113
Stand Fast In The Lord	113
God's Provisions	113

Colossians 114
Thankfulness for Spiritual Attainments	114
You Are Built Up in Christ	115
Put On the New Self	116
Family Relations	117
Speak With Grace	117

2 Timothy 118
Timothy Charged to Guard His Trust	118
Be Strong	118
Difficult Times Will Come	119
Preach the Word	120

Philemon 121
Philemon's Love and Faith	121
Plea for Onesimus, a Free Man	121

Section 4 122

Quick Reference Listing of The Teachings of Paul 122

An Expanded Summarization of The Teachings of Paul 124

ADDENDA: 181

Study On Paul's Teaching On Circumcision	181
Topic Words List	185

Full Table of Contents 186

An Expanded Summarization of The Teachings of Paul The Apostle

... of The Lord *124*
Admonish *133*
Adulterer, Adulteress *133*
Adultery *133*
Anointing *133*
Apostle(s) *133*
Believe, Believed, Believer(s) *134*
Bishop(s) *136*
Circumcise(d) / Circumcision *136*
Daughter(s) *136*
Deacons *137*
Elders *137*
Emasculation (Castration) *139*
Encourage(d), E'ment, Exhort *139*

Faith *140*
Faithful(ness) *143*
False Gospel / False Teaching *144*
Father(s) *145*
Father Abraham *147*
Forgave, Forgive, Forgiving *147*
Forgiveness *148*
Fornication, Fornicator(s) *148*
God (of our Fathers) *149*
Grace of God *149*
Husband(s) *151*
Marriage, (Married, Unmarried) *153*
Prophecy, Prophetic, Prophet(s) *155*
Redeem(ed), Redemption *158*
Salvation *156*

Son(s), Son of God *160*
Son of God *163*
Sons of God *165*
Son of Perdition, Son of The Devil *166*
Steward(s), Stewardship *167*
Tattler(s) / Gossip *168*
Teacher(s) *168*
Temptation *169*
Tongues *169*
Transgression *170*
Virgin(s) *171*
Widow(s), Widowed *172*
Wife, Wives *172*
Wisdom *174*
Women *176*

Printed in Great Britain
by Amazon